'David Childs, Pro... int... ction ... [His] ... e... taken away to be read and used!...' — M... J. **Field**, *Talking Politics*

...ds ... clearly presents a wide range of information, in a ...which will be of help to students.' — **Gerard Evans**, ...*ional Affairs*

...ere is a wealth of factual information ... Two particular fe... s stand out. Firstly, and unusually, the book incorporates ou... material on Ireland for the whole period covered. Sec- on... comprehensive use of political biographies and memoirs and ...he author's interviews with political leaders provides a colo...ful and convincing narrative.' — **Steve Ludlam**, *Political Studies*

'... this book certainly provides a useful guide to what hap- pened over the past half century.' — *Labour Research*

'... the book covers most of the post-war developments which hav... fected Britain, and attempts to balance obvious symptoms of ...ine with more positive trends ... The main purpose of bo... like this ... is to stimulate readers to carry their inquiries fur... *Britain since 1939* certainly fulfils this aim.' — **Mark Garn...** *The Times Literary Supplement*

'For i... scope and popular appeal, this book deserves to be- come... standard study of modern British history. Students of politic... and history will find this a useful study because it is easy to ...se and is enriched by Childs' wide knowledge of the period.' — **William Gibson**, *Archives*

'... provides the undergraduate reader with a clear and con- cise account of political, social, economic and diplomatic history since the Second World War (indeed since the First World War, as the first two introductory chapters focus on inter-war Brit- ain).' — **Kevin Jeffreys**, *History*

C151

D0528048

British Studies Series

General Editor JEREMY BLACK

Published

Alan Booth **The British Economy in the Twentieth Century**
John Charmley **A History of Conservative Politics, 1900–1996**
David Childs **Britain since 1939** (2nd edn)
John Davis **A History of Britain, 1885–1939**
David Eastwood **Government and Community in the English Provinces, 1700–1870**
Philip Edwards **The Making of the Modern English State, 1460–1660**
W. H. Fraser **A History of British Trade Unionism, 1700–1998**
John Garrard **Democratisation in Britain: Elites, Civil Society and Reform since 1800**
Brian Hill **The Early Parties and Politics in Britain, 1688–1832**
Katrina Honeyman **Women, Gender and Industrialisation in England, 1700–1870**
Kevin Jefferys **Retreat from New Jerusalem: British Politics, 1951–1964**
T. A. Jenkins **The Liberal Ascendancy, 1830–1886**
David Loades **Power in Tudor England**
Ian Machin **The Rise of Democracy in Britain, 1830–1918**
Alexander Murdoch **British History, 1660–1832: National Identity and Local Culture**
Anthony Musson and W. M. Ormrod **The Evolution of English Justice: Law, Politics and Society in the Fourteenth Century**
Murray G. H. Pittock **Inventing and Resisting Britain: Cultural Identities in Britain and Ireland, 1685–1789**
Nick Smart **The National Government, 1931–40**
Andrew Thorpe **A History of the British Labour Party** (2nd edn)

British Studies Series
Series Standing Order
ISBN 0–333–71691–4 hardcover
ISBN 0–333–69332–9 paperback
(*outside North America only*)

You can receive future titles in this series as they are published by placing a standing order. Please contact your bookseller or, in case of difficulty, write to us at the address below with your name and address, the title of the series and the ISBN quoted above.

Customer Services Department, Macmillan Distribution Ltd, Houndmills, Basingstoke, Hampshire RG21 6XS, England

Britain since 1939: Progress and Decline

Second Edition

David Childs

First edition 1995
Second edition 2002

Published by
PALGRAVE
Houndmills, Basingstoke, Hampshire RG21 6XS
Companies and representatives throughout the world

PALGRAVE is the new global academic imprint of
St. Martin's Press LLC Scholarly and Reference Division and
Palgrave Publishers Ltd (formerly Macmillan Press Ltd).

ISBN 0–333–97165–5

This book is printed on paper suitable for recycling and made from fully managed and sustained forest sources.

A catalogue record for this book is available from the British Library.

10   9   8   7   6   5   4   3   2   1
11   10   09   08   07   06   05   04   03   2

Printed in China

Contents

Acknowledgements to the Second Edition

I am grateful to the following MPs who took the trouble to write to me about their early life experiences especially in the 1939–45 war: Sir Richard Body, Michael Colvin, Tam Dalyell, Mrs Llin Golding, Dennis Skinner, David Winnick and Sir Raymond Witney. I wish to thank Martin Bell, MP, for sharing with me his views on the House of Commons and life as an independent MP. My thanks are due to the Rt Hon. Stephen Dorrell, MP, for a lengthy and interesting interview. I am grateful to my former students Kelvin Hopkins, MP, and John Hayes, MP, for giving me their impressions of the Commons as newly elected Members and for their hospitality. I wish to thank Piara Khabra, MP, for describing his life in India and as an immigrant in Britain. I am grateful to the late Lord Rothermere for telling me about his family and his experiences leading to his conversion to Blair's New Labour. Mrs Gisela Stuart, MP, Parliamentary Under-Secretary of State, Department of Health, gave me an interesting perspective on her life and times for which I am grateful. I thank Andrew Stunell, MP, for answering questions about his life and for giving me a Liberal Democratic view on contemporary politics. I wish to thank Dr Julian Lewis, MP, for sharing with me his thoughts on security matters and for his hospitality. My thanks are due to the Howard League for Penal Reform, the Police Complaints Authority and to the Ministry of Defence for material provided. Finally, the Rt Hon. Sir Paddy Ashdown, MP, answered my request for information for which I am grateful. Once again I must emphasise that I alone am responsible for the views expressed and for any errors of fact or judgement in this second edition.

Nottingham   DAVID CHILDS

Acknowledgements to the First Edition

In a way, I started interviewing for this book when I had a long conversation with Lord (Clement) Attlee in 1963. Since then, I have been privileged to meet many other public figures who, to a greater or lesser degree, have helped to shape Britain since 1918. Apart from the Rt Hon. Kenneth Clarke, PC, MP, I have not attempted to re-interview those I met in connection with my other contributions on recent British history. I remain indebted to them and to those who, more recently, agreed to be interviewed, or to answer my written enquiries: Rt Hon. Lord Callaghan, KG; Rt Hon. Tony Benn, MP; Field-Marshal Lord Carver, MC; Mrs Edwina Currie, MP; Stefan Lorant, founder of *Picture Post*; Bill Newton Dunn, MEP for Lincolnshire; Martin Groves, Office of the Houses the Oireachtais, Dublin; Rt Hon. Neil Kinnock, MP; Rt Hon. Lord Longford, KG; Rt Hon. Lord Parkinson; Professor Alan Watson, CBE, former President of the Liberal Party. I am once again in debt to my old friend Dr Robert L. Frazier, formerly of the History Department of Nottingham University, who read an earlier version of the manuscript and made many valuable suggestions for improvements. Finally, I would like to thank Kate Craine, MA, for her help in preparing the final draft of the manuscript. I must, of course, emphasise that I alone am responsible for the views expressed in the book, as well as for any errors of fact or judgement.

Nottingham   DAVID CHILDS

Introduction

The title of the book is *Britain since 1939: Progress and Decline*, but I felt I would have produced an incomprehensible account if I had started in the year war broke out, decisive though the Second World War was for Britain's subsequent political, social and economic development. I decided, therefore, to write two introductory chapters covering the interwar period.

This book is about the general developments in British politics and society, but there is an underlying theme which is difficult to ignore – that is, the decline of Britain since the 'Great War' of 1914–18. And although the book attempts to tell the story in chronological order, using the different political administrations as convenient, recognisable signposts, this underlying theme is discussed, implicitly or explicitly, throughout. Some will argue that, although Britain has declined in economic terms, it has not done so in other respects; in particular, its institutions have adapted and survived better than those of most European states. To a degree, they are right. In addition, great progress can be seen, in the arts and sciences, standards of living and people's opportunities. Yet the decline in the economy means that Britain is less able to support the things its citizens want and need – better education and training, better health care, better transport systems, better law enforcement, and defence forces adequate to our commitments. In one or all of these areas, many European, and some non-European, states have caught up with, or overtaken Britain. It is baffling that a nation with so much talent at its disposal declined so much, at least in relative terms, right down to the 1990s. I have done my best to provide some clues to that puzzle, but I do not claim to have a definitive answer. As another recent writer admitted, at the end of his study of Britain's decline, 'Our understanding of Britain's relative failure . . . remains incomplete and unsatisfactory.'[1]

Britain had also made great progress during the same period,

1

and this cannot be ignored if one wishes to understand the political development of the country. However, in attempting to document both our progress and decline, I have invited the student and the general reader alike to pause and think about particular incidents and general themes – education, colonialism, immigration and racism, crime, the media, the monarchy, popular opinion, the changing role of women, etc. – in the history of the period. These are often neglected in a general book of this relatively modest size. I hope I have covered the main events in a fairly objective way so that readers who do not agree with some of my assessments nevertheless find the book useful.

Originally I had no intention of writing about Ireland, except to cover, briefly, events leading up to the treaty of 1921, and some more recent events in Northern Ireland. However, I found it difficult to discuss these without, at least, glancing in the direction of Dublin. The more I looked, the more I got involved. I do not regret this. Considering that our histories and populations are so intertwined, Ireland is all too often seen as a far-away country of which we know little. I hope my references to the 'south' will be seen merely as an aid to British readers who do not normally consider Ireland as part of their studies or interest. My hope is that they will then move on to more substantial accounts. It has not been my ambition to compete with the excellent Irish and British writers who cover Irish history in greater depth. Nor is it my intention to imply that Ireland is in any sense part of the United Kingdom – on the contrary, I believe Irish independence was a positive development.

1 Interwar Britain, 1919–39

Impact of the Great War

Virtually anyone who was alive in the interwar period was marked in some way by the Great War of 1914–18. Those who were too young to have been in it, or even remember it, had relatives who had served. One heard of them; one also heard the survivors' tales – not always sad or horrific. For many, it was clearly their greatest experience of life. There were also many limbless ex-servicemen to be seen. Some 745,000 men from Britain had been killed – that is, 9 per cent of all men aged twenty to 45 (many victims were younger than twenty). About 1.7 million were wounded and 1.2 million of them received disablement pensions; though some of these did find employment.[1] The war was remembered too in countless films – *The Great Parade* and *All Quiet on the Western Front*, for example – books, plays and the haunting pictures of Paul Nash, Stanley Spencer and Percy Wyndham Lewis. Once a year there was also 'the Great Silence' which engulfed the land at 11 a.m. on 11th November. This remembrance ceremony for the war dead brought the whole country to a halt and was at once both impressive and frightening. Whether it was intentional or not, it became a medium of inspiring patriotism, reinforcing subservience and enforcing control.

Most people, especially younger ones, wanted to get away from the war and enjoy life a little. To them, the war seemed to be something that happened very long ago. This was particularly so for those growing up in the 1930s. Life appeared to be changing rapidly, the more so for those enjoying modest prosperity.

The interwar period lasted only twenty years but it seems longer. Why should this be? Probably because, unlike earlier periods, many visual images of it survive and these images reveal great changes. Take women's dress, for instance. Women in 1919 still had a nineteenth-century look about them. Yet women in the early 1930s look closer to us now than they did to their sisters at the end of the First World War. By comparison, the change in men's clothing was less dramatic. The appearance of cars and planes also greatly changed during these years. Even in the 1920s, cars still looked like 'horseless carriages'. At the end of the 1930s, they looked much more smooth and streamlined. The same is true of planes. Compare the rickety converted Vimy bomber in which John Alcock and Arthur Brown made the first non-stop trans-Atlantic flight in June 1919 with the American Douglas DC-3 of 1935 or the British sleek DH91 of 1937. By 1939, the Germans had developed the first jet-propelled aeroplane, the Heinkel HE 178, and Igor Sikorsky, a former Czarist officer living in America, made the first successful flight in his single-rotor helicopter. Strangely, the furniture and architecture of the German *Bauhaus* school still appears 'modern' today.

Media Changes

Another aspect of the impression of great change between 1919 and 1939 was the development of electronic media and the change in newspapers. In 1919 there was silence across the land once industry had stopped. By 1939, in addition to the increased noise from trams, buses, cars and planes, most people sat listening to radio (the 'wireless') or went to the cinema (the 'pictures') in the evening. The British Broadcasting Company was established in 1922 as a monopoly and became a public corporation in 1926. It brought news, information, religion, sport, entertainment, the concert hall, the variety theatre, the dance hall, great books and much else into the majority of homes by 1939. In Britain, as in France, Germany, the Soviet Union and America, regular television broadcasts started in the 1930s, though very few people could receive them.

In 1919 the cinema was silent. The film was poor and jerky. Sex was often the theme in such Hollywood romps as *Why Change Your Wife?* (1920). By 1939, millions were thrilled by the colour spectaculars, Hollywood's *Gone with the Wind* and *The Four Feathers* by the Hungarian Anglophile Alexander Korda. In 1919, the cinemas were likely to be converted theatres. By the later 1930s, the new, purpose-built cinemas were attracting large audiences. The writer on films, Leslie Halliwell, recalls his first visit to the Bolton Odeon as an eight-year-old boy, in 1937: 'My first impression, when I got my breath back, was . . . the immensity of the red velour curtains; the cunningly concealed lighting; the great golden honeycomb grills on each side of the screen; the green octagonal clocks in which the letters THE ODEON took the place of numerals; all these played their part in the magnificence of that massive decorated space.'[2] It is difficult to know just how the films seen influenced their audiences. The British Board of Film Censors sought to maintain *status quo* values on sex, social relations and politics by its decisions.[3] Nevertheless, many working-class people came to feel that their way of life was very poor, dull and dreary compared with that of the many Americans they saw on their screens. And one often hears that cinema-goers gained at least some vague perception of a world beyond their neighbourhood. Perhaps all this helped, in a vague sort of way, to aid those who sought change in society.

In Germany, the firm Ernst Leitz marketed the Leica camera in 1925, making it easier to take candid shots. It was the first precision 35mm camera – the most popular modern format. Captain Macfarlane of the New York *Daily News* and Harry Guy Bartholomew, editor of the London *Daily Mirror*, invented a system of sending photographs by radio. These two developments did much to transform the press and make possible the founding of weekly pictorials such as *Everybody*, *Illustrated* and *Picture Post* in England and similar publications elsewhere in the late 1930s. The above three magazines were all founded by the remarkable Hungarian–Jewish journalist Stefan Lorant, who lived in Britain for several years before going to America in 1940. He had been a highly successful editor in Germany but had to leave after the Nazis took over in 1933.[4]

During this period, the 'Press Lords' continued to dominate much of the national press and sought political power. On the available evidence, this appears to have been more a case of considerable influence than power.[5] Lord Beaverbrook (*Daily Express*) and Lord Rothermere (*Daily Mail* and *Daily Mirror* to 1935), two of the most typical, ran campaigns which were largely unsuccessful. Both put their weight behind Empire Free Trade and Rothermere supported domestic and foreign Fascism and opposed any measure of Indian self-government. Generally, they gave their support to the Conservative Party. However, when they tried to interfere too much, Stanley Baldwin, the Conservative leader, accused them in March 1931 of seeking to exercise 'power without responsibility'.[6] Surprisingly, the Labour-supporting *Daily Herald* was one of the most successful papers of the time. This was partly because it turned, after 1929, from being a narrowly focused Labour paper to becoming a more commercially orientated daily. The weekly journal *New Statesman & Nation* had considerable influence among the middle-class radicals and usually supported Labour. On the whole, however, Labour was greatly disadvantaged in the national, regional and local press. The *Manchester Guardian* and the *News Chronicle* supported the Liberals. The numbers of newspapers fell over the period due to concentration and the rising costs of production. On the other hand, total circulation rose as interest in sport, job vacancies, films and radio – all covered by the papers – increased.

In 1914, the people of Britain read of the outbreak of war in their newspapers. In 1939, most of them heard the Prime Minister, Neville Chamberlain, announce it on the wireless. The radio had replaced the newspaper as the key source of news.

Monarchy

One thing the media did was to assist in popularising the monarchy. The BBC inaugurated the monarch's Christmas broadcast in 1932. George V read a speech written for him by Rudyard Kipling. It was a fantastic experience for the listeners to hear their king's voice for the first time, and in their own homes at that. Increasingly, the BBC broadcast royal occasions and the cinema newsreels showed them. Among the most awe-inspiring were the Silver Jubilee of 1935, the funeral of George V in 1936, the Coronation of George VI in 1937 and the visit of George VI and Queen Elizabeth to the USA and Canada in 1939. They were seen increasingly at lesser events, such as sports meetings, launching ships, opening housing estates, hospital wards and new town halls. This is not to imply that the media alone created the 'myth' of the monarchy. This had started in the nineteenth century. After being unpopular, the monarchy gained ground in the closing years of the long reign of Queen Victoria (1837–1901). The growth of Empire and the inculcation of respect for the monarchy in the new school system after 1870 helped in this process. The popular press fostered this spirit and interest in the monarchy. The press gave the royal family complete privacy, especially shielding them from potential scandals. Edward VII (1901–10) could hardly have survived without such discretion. Edward VIII (1936) also got such protection until his private affairs had been so widely discussed abroad that it was virtually impossible to hold the line any longer. Anti-German feeling in the 1914–18 war threatened the monarchy as George V's family was of German descent (House of Saxe-Coburg). However, George wisely changed the family name to Windsor in 1917. The newsreels depicted George V and the Prince of Wales (later Edward VIII) as soldier figures in uniforms with the troops. The successive monarchs undoubtedly added their weight to the conservative forces in the state and lived, for the most part, as country squires.[7]

Lloyd George, Baldwin and MacDonald

Given the problems Britain faced and the changes in the franchise, it is surprising, in some ways, that there was not more radical political change between 1919 and 1939. In 1919, David Lloyd George, the flamboyant wartime Prime Minister, had led a mainly Conservative coalition, which secured a massive majority based on a 58.9 per cent turnout. Many soldiers could not vote and many newly enfranchised voters were not on the register. It is difficult to sum up this election victory but it cannot be seen as a straight win for Conservatism. Lloyd George had been a radical Liberal reformer as Chancellor of the Exchequer (1908–15) and those seeking election under his banner included Liberals and a few Labour candidates. Some who were Conservative did not label themselves as such. Lloyd George had promised sweeping reforms but was brought down by his Conservative coalition partners in 1922. Britain then had two years of Conservative government, led first by Andrew Bonar Law and then by Stanley Baldwin. It was the first purely Conservative government for nearly seventeen years. The

Conservatives had been in crisis after so long in the wilderness. Some of their leaders had hoped for a new centre party, led by Lloyd George, to halt the growth of socialism. Many Conservative backbencher MPs and activists in the country had not forgiven Lloyd George for his pre-war radicalism, which included his Insurance Act (1912), often seen as the most important piece of social legislation before 1945, and the way that he had 'given away' Ireland by agreeing to the seting up of the Irish Free State in 1921 (see Chapter 2). They wanted their party to re-establish its independence. Others were tired of the dynamism of Lloyd George and wanted peace and quiet. Bonar Law, who had to resign in May 1923 because he was dying of cancer, and Baldwin, both offered that.

Baldwin (1867–1947) had little experience of office before becoming Prime Minister, having reached the Cabinet in 1921. He served as President of the Board of Trade, 1921–2, and Chancellor of the Exchequer, 1922–3. Educated at Harrow and Cambridge, he came from a family that belonged to the business class rather than the gentry. He was regarded as safe, a man who would not lead the country into foreign adventures, and a conciliator who would give the country hope. He was more willing than some of his colleagues to use the state, if this should prove necessary, to get the economy going again. He was also sympathetic to the introduction of welfare reforms. This was evident later on when he was returned to office after the brief Labour interlude of 1924. His government modified the nineteenth-century Poor Law under the Local Government Act of 1929; under an Act of 1925 a widows' pension scheme was introduced.[8]

Labour had increased its vote in the elections of 1918, 1922 and 1923, overtaking the Liberals to become the official Opposition. On a turnout of 70.8 per cent in 1923 the three parties were fairly close in their shares of the votes (Conservative 38.1 per cent, Liberal 29.6 and Labour 30.5). After Baldwin's government was defeated in the Commons, George V invited James Ramsay MacDonald to form the first Labour government. Labour survived in office for a few short months with qualified Liberal support.

MacDonald's first government could achieve little.[9] In domestic policy its Minister of Health, John Wheatley, steered a Housing

Act through Parliament which provided government aid for council house building. Subsequent governments used it to stimulate the economy and assist re-housing. The government also gave unconditional recognition to the Soviet Union. The first Labour government fell after only nine months. Conservatives and Liberals accused it of bowing to left-wing pressure not to prosecute a Communist editor, J. R. Campbell, for sedition. They combined to defeat it in the Commons. In the election that followed, Labour actually increased its vote. The main loser was the Liberal Party, which lost heavily to the Conservatives on a high turnout of 76.6 per cent.

The Labour government appears to have struck fear in the hearts of many middle- and upper-class voters. The first British Fascist movement came into existence at this time, in response to this government.[10] The Labour Party had adopted a socialist constitution in 1918, committing it to 'the common ownership of the means of production, distribution and exchange and the best obtainable system of popular administration and control of each industry or service'. It sang 'The Red Flag' and had a leader who had opposed the 1914–18 war. On the other hand, its leaders had shown consistently that they opposed Soviet-type communism. Their socialism was based on ethical principles, not Marxism. Many Conservative voters, however, could not understand the difference. In addition, MacDonald's establishment of diplomatic relations with the Soviet Union was interpreted by many as proving that he was soft on Bolshevism. The use against Labour, in the 1924 election, of the Zinoviev letter, allegedly sent by the Secretary of the Communist International to the British Communists urging them to prepare for violent revolution, was a sign of this great fear.[11] Of course, the Russian Revolution of 1917 was fresh in the minds of the voters. Other revolutions had taken place in Germany, Austria, Hungary, Bulgaria and Ireland. Mussolini, with his Fascists, had 'saved' Italy from revolution in 1922. Britain itself had experienced considerable unrest, strikes by the police and military mutinies. It was to experience the General Strike of 1926, which threw many middle-class voters into a panic.

The General Strike

Baldwin's Chancellor of the Exchequer, Churchill, against his better judgement, had succumbed to the pressure of the Treasury and the Bank of England to return to the Gold Standard in 1925. This meant fixing the value of the pound against other currencies on the basis of its value in gold. Moreover, the pound was returned its pre-war parity giving it an official value of $4.86. Thus it was greatly overvalued and this damaged the prospects of industries like cotton, shipbuilding, steel and coal, heavily dependent on exports. It helped to make a bad situation worse leading to a miners' strike which in turn led to the General Strike of 1926.

The miners had struck in 1921 and been defeated, but won in 1925. Employing more than a million men, the mining industry was the major provider of basic energy for both industrial and domestic consumption in the interwar period. Baldwin had granted it a subsidy in 1925, to be ended in 1926. The owners then demanded severe cuts in pay. Meanwhile, the government had made preparations for an emergency. When an official enquiry recommended pay cuts, the miners went on strike (26th April), at the same time asking for assistance from the Trades Union Congress (TUC). The TUC then called a selective sympathy strike, carefully avoiding a full general strike. It was mainly in iron and steel, transport, building, electricity and printing. The strike was largely peaceful, although violence erupted in a few places. The strike lasted for nine days (4th–12th May). Then the TUC, realising the situation was hopeless and dangerous, called upon its members to return to work. The miners continued the strike for another six months before they were forced to capitulate. Their families had suffered, union funds were depleted and union membership fell. The Trade Disputes and Trade Union Act (1927), making all sympathetic strikes illegal and imposing the 'contracting-in' system on union members who wished to pay the political levy to the Labour Party, was passed by the Baldwin government. The failure of the General Strike, and the slump, which was to come, resulted in trade unions turning away from industrial action in favour of reform through Parliament.[12] One novel aspect of the General Strike was the use by the government of the radio to get its message across. Remarkably, it refused to allow the Archbishop of Canterbury or MacDonald to broadcast because they were regarded as too conciliatory to the strikers.

MacDonald's Second Administration

After five years of Conservative rule under Baldwin, the election of 1929 represented a loss to the Conservatives, their share of the vote falling from 48.3 to 38.2 per cent. They appear to have lost to the Liberals, whose share increased from 17.6 to 23.4 per cent. Labour also increased its share from 33 to 37.1 per cent. Women over 30, and men over 21, had first gained the vote in 1918. In 1928 women had been granted the vote on equal terms with men.[13] It is not clear how their votes affected the election, though they were generally more pro-Conservative than men in the interwar period and beyond.

In 1929 the British electoral system gave Labour more seats, for the first time, than the Conservatives, even though the Conservatives were a little ahead on votes. Labour did not, however, have an overall majority and once again secured office with the help of the Liberals.

MacDonald formed his second government with Arthur Henderson as Foreign Minister and Philip Snowden as Chancellor of the Exchequer. Henderson had served in the wartime coalition and had been Home Secretary in the first Labour government. Snowden had served as Chancellor in that government; from Yorkshire, he was a former Inland Revenue civil servant, teetotaller and permanent invalid. J. R. Clynes became Home Secretary and A. V. Alexander took on the then important job of First Lord of the Admiralty. The Colonial Office, also a key ministry, went to the Fabian Lord Passfield, who had previously served as President of the Board of Trade. J. H. Thomas, the railwaymen's leader, who had held this post in 1924, became Lord Privy Seal; his brief was to tackle unemployment. Like MacDonald's first administration, in social terms the Labour government represented a shift from the few to the many. MacDonald, Snowden, Henderson, Clynes, Alexander and many of their colleagues were all 'working men', the products of elementary schools rather than ancient universities. For the first time, a woman was given a cabinet appointment – Margaret Bondfield as Minister of Labour. Bonfield had left school at thirteen and was a full-time trade union official for most of her working life. In 1918, she was the first woman member of the TUC Council. MacDonald's government also included the more traditional type of minister. Lord Parmoor (Winchester and Oxford), a former Conservative MP, was appointed Lord President; Lord Sankey (Lancing and Oxford) was Lord Chancellor, and Sir Charles Trevelyan (Harrow and Cambridge) took on Education. Among the younger members were Dr Hugh Dalton, an old Etonian, Cambridge graduate and ex-officer, and Sir Oswald Mosley (Winchester and Sandhurst).

In a way, Dalton and Mosley illustrate the success and the weakness of Labour during this period. Dalton was junior to Henderson at the Foreign Office. They succeeded in exchanging ambassadors with the Soviet Union. Through the League of Nations (forerunner of the United Nations) they negotiated for the Allies to withdraw from the Rhineland in 1930, five years before they were required to do so under the Versailles Treaty. They also negotiated the Young Plan for German Reparations. In London, MacDonald chaired the Naval Conference (1930). This achieved a measure of international agreement on naval armaments. Britain, Japan and the United States, the major naval powers, agreed to end competition in warship construction for five years.

Mosley was the most senior minister outside the Cabinet. Before joining Labour, he had been a Conservative MP who had worked for Anglo–Irish understanding as secretary of the Peace with Ireland Council. MacDonald appointed him Chancellor of the Duchy of Lancaster, with special responsibility (under Thomas) for unemployment. In January 1930, he submitted a memorandum to the Cabinet advocating a major public works programme, to be financed by a £200 million loan. Snowden followed the orthodox deflationary policy of those with whom he had a 'true marriage of minds', his Treasury officials and Norman Montagu, Governor of the Bank of England, and rejected it.[14] An impatient man, Mosley resigned. When his proposals were narrowly defeated at Labour's annual conference in 1930, he set up his own party, the New Party. Mosley's memorandum linked up with what the Lloyd George Liberals were advocating and could have been a further bridge of co-operation between the two. One weakness of the Liberal position was, however, that many of them were still wedded to free trade (as were many in the Labour Party). Mosley's policy, on the other hand, involved import controls to protect domestic industries and large-scale public works. This was a fundamental flaw in the thinking of many British politicians at a time when the major world economies were increasingly protectionist.

In February 1931, the Conservatives tabled a motion of censure against the government on the grounds of its 'extravagance'. The Liberals demanded a committee of enquiry. The government responded favourably to this by setting up a Committee on National Expenditure, chaired by Sir George May of the Prudential Insurance Company.

1931: 'National' v. 'Bolshevism run mad'

The government, which called itself the 'National Government', came into existence on 24th August 1931, when George V asked the outgoing Labour Prime Minister to head such a government. The Labour government had decided to resign because of lack of unity over cuts in unemployment benefit proposed by May's Committee on National Expenditure. This followed an ultimatum from Wall Street via the Bank of England. In addition to MacDonald, the 'National Government' included Baldwin and Sir Herbert Samuel of the Liberals. It was supported by the Conservative Party and by most of the Liberals. Labour opposed it. Of MacDonald's old colleagues only Snowden, Thomas and Sankey followed him. To begin with, the Cabinet consisted of four Labour members, four Conservatives and two Liberals. The new government pledged itself to maintain the parity of the pound and then dissolve itself. Snowden, still Chancellor, proposed a Budget which involved substantial tax increases and cuts in public expenditure including pay cuts for the police, armed forces and teachers. These measures were not enough to appease Britain's creditors and their confidence remained shaky.

The *coup de grâce* for Snowden came on 15th September with the 'mutiny' of the sailors of the Atlantic fleet, at Invergordon in Scotland, against proposed pay cuts. The fifteen ships included the biggest battleships afloat worldwide. Many of the men stood to lose 25 per cent of their pay, as well as facing higher taxes on a whole range of goods. The Admiralty called the strike a mutiny and the government considered using force to break it. Ministers and admirals remembered the naval mutinies in Russia and Germany, which had been crucial in the revolutions of 1917 and 1918 respectively. Earlier in 1931 a naval mutiny in Chile was crushed by military force. The British did not emulate their Chilean colleagues, with whom they had close ties. Instead, promises and threats were used to get the men back in line. Despite an undertaking that there would be no discrimination, some 120 sailors and marines were disciplined and then dismissed.[15] But the damage was already done to Britain's financial credibility and a second wave of heavy withdrawals of funds from London followed. Within four days, on 21st September 1931, the Gold Standard [Amendment] Bill was passed through all its stages. A devaluation of the pound by 20 per cent resulted. With the end of the gold standard went free trade as well. This happened, initially, because a number of states, which stayed on the gold standard, raised their tariffs on imports, hitting the trade of Britain and other non-gold standard states. Britain's new tariff policy helped its balance of trade and its economic recovery.

Despite assurances that there would be no immediate election, the National Government sought a mandate from the electorate in October 1931. It won convincingly after what Thomas described as 'the cruellest and most brutal election I have ever known'.[16] One notorious aspect of the election was Snowden's radio broadcast on 17th October in which he likened Labour's programme to 'Bolshevism run mad'. Apparently this was 'devastatingly successful'.[17] On a 76.3 per cent poll, the National Government candidates gained 67 per cent (of which the Conservatives won 56 per cent), Labour 30.6 per cent and independent Liberals 0.5 per cent. The Communists gained 0.3 per cent and Mosley's New Party 0.2 per cent. Although Labour's vote declined only by 7 per cent, its parliamentary representation fell from 288 MPs to 52. Labour must have felt sorry that it had turned down Liberal proposals to bring in proportional representation in 1917. The Liberals lost heavily in votes to the Conservatives.[18]

Law and Order

The government had been totally taken aback when the Metropolitan Police went on strike in 1918 because of the dismissal of Constable Tommy Thiel. He had been attempting to recruit members for the banned National Union of Police and Prison Officers. The strikers demanded a pay increase, the reinstatement of Thiel and recognition of the union. Almost the whole of London's police had struck. The authorities had no alternative but to concede to these demands.[19] They deferred the question of the police union until the war was over. The government was better organised when the union called out its members again in 1919. In London the strike was ineffective but substantial numbers came out in Liverpool and the army was sent in to restore order. The strikers were dismissed from the service and the union was destroyed. The Police Act of 1919 provided for the standardisation of pay and conditions throughout the country. The Police Federation was established to represent the lower ranks of the police service. It was not allowed to affiliate to the TUC and its members were forbidden to strike.

Today, the interwar years appear as a relatively crime-free period and certainly there was less visible and violent crime, compared with the last decades of the twentieth century. The number of murders in the interwar period was actually lower than it was before 1914. Organised crime, on the American model, was virtually unknown. Guns were not the weapon of the 'criminal classes' as they were in the USA. Bank clerks could walk or take a leisurely bus from suburban branches to headquarters carrying briefcases full of the day's transactions. Offences related to alcohol fell compared with the pre-1914 period, probably reflecting changing life-styles. For one thing, the cinema was becoming a cheap alternative to the pub. Nevertheless, recorded crime, especially robbery, was slowly increasing. Juvenile crime, for instance, was increasing and concern about this, led to the passing of the Children and Young Persons Act (1933). Overall, there is the impression that there was far more unrecorded crime, especially 'white collar', and many more incidents that would be regarded as criminal today than is normally supposed. Among these were child abuse, homosexual assaults on minors, physical assaults by teachers on their pupils, assaults by police on prisoners, sexual harassment of women and physical attacks on women by their partners, including rape, which the police often regarded as 'domestic', and therefore, private matters. The moral climate of the day was such that women could end up in mental asylums for giving birth to 'illegitimate' children. Nevertheless, the trend in penal policy was towards a more humane approach. The Infanticide Acts (1922 and 1938) were designed to reduce the chances of women being convicted of murder for killing their babies. Sentences involving imprisonment or corporal punishment were falling. The death penalty was used less frequently. Attempts were made to improve prison conditions, with the first 'open prison' being established at Wakefield, but such attempts were often the victim of financial restraint. Poor prison conditions led to one of the worst prison disturbances in the twentieth century. This was at Dartmoor, in January 1932, and troops had to be called in to deal with the situation.

High Street Changes

During this period, the high street started to change. There were the new picture palaces, some capable of seating several thousand patrons. There were the new dance halls, new pubs with Art Deco furnishings, and there were restaurant chains like Lyons Corner Houses. There were the new food, cosmetics and clothing stores pioneered by the entrepreneurs John Sainsbury, Jack Cohen (Tesco), Jessie Boot, Montague Burton and Israel M. Sieff of Marks and Spencer, and the department stores like those of John Lewis. The role of the co-ops during this period should not be forgotten, the best introducing relatively cheap products, sold in pleasant surroundings. Gradually, hire purchase became normal as a means of financing purchases of furniture, electrical goods and much else.

In most cases, the products of the high street revolution – clothing, including that made from new artificial fibres, vacuum cleaners, radios, cameras, cheap furniture and processed food – arrived from modern factories, among them the Hoover factory in London, the Imperial Typewriter Company factory at Leicester and the Boots factory at Nottingham. There were other modern factories as well, like that of de Havilland Propellers outside Bolton and some of the vehicle factories around Coventry. These had little in common with the 'dark satanic mills' of the past.

'This blot on our national life'

By careful selection, it should have been possible to produce a picture of Britain based on the above facts which would have given it an image as a very modern, prosperous state during the 1930s. Certain books published at the time produced a very different picture. Walter Greenwood's *Love on the Dole* (1933) and George Orwell's *The Road to Wigan Pier* (1938) emphasise the squalid side of the North West during the 1930s. Something of this comes through in the less well-known book by J. B. Priestley, *English Journey* (1934), based on his travels through England in 1933. At the end of the journey, Priestley concluded he had visited at least three Englands. One was that described above. The second was 'Old England, the country of the cathedrals and minsters and manor houses and inns, of Parson and Squire, guide-book and quaint highways and byways England'. This was tourist England and he warned: 'There are people who believe that in some mysterious way we can all return to this Old England; though nothing is said about killing off nine-tenths of our present population, which would have to be the first step'. Priestley's third England was that of the majority – nineteenth-century industrial England with its 'cynically devastated countryside, sooty dismal little towns, and still sootier grim fortress-like cities. This England makes up the larger part of the Midlands and the North and exists everywhere.'[20]

Priestley was, of course, right – much of Britain was a grim place between the wars. The grinding poverty of many, the horrific housing conditions and the worry and fear are difficult to describe. In 1933, the then Prince of Wales declared, in a reference to housing conditions, that he was appalled that such conditions existed and called for 'this blot that disgraces our national life' to be swept away.[21] Most working-class homes at that time had no bathroom, many still used gas for lighting, and less than one home in five was owner-occupied. Housing conditions did, however, greatly improve during these years, as a result of slum clearance and the development of private housing projects. Private house building took off in 1930 reaching a peak in 1937 when 273,516 houses were built (the total figure, including council houses, was 346,053). One sign of improvement was the growth in electric lighting: by 1930 one dwelling in three had electricity, and by 1939, two out of three.[22]

For most families, life was a constant battle in the interwar period. The pawnshop, second-hand clothing shops and repossession of goods bought on the 'never, never' were a normal part of life. So was the dread of having children who could not be maintained. This led to anxiety about having sexual relations and must have caused tensions between married partners. Knowledge of birth control, and willingness to practise it, was limited, despite the efforts of Marie Stopes and others like her. There was fear of becoming unemployed, which must have reduced trust among people at work.[23] These problems afflicted much of the middle class, as well as the numerically greater working class. The new owner-occupiers moved into their mock-Tudor homes on streets with names like Eton, Harrow, Haileybury and Repton, full of hope, dread and fear. Many thought they had to be mean to survive – mean to their relatives lower down, mean to their neighbours and mean to themselves. The *Daily Mail* sought to win readers as the champion of the 'New Poor', the struggling middle class, trying to keep up appearances by scraping and saving to make ends meet and dreading any unforeseen expense.

Unemployment and Industrial Activity

Unemployment was another blot, which disgraced national life. There had always been unemployment, but it became less and less acceptable, especially after the sacrifices in the 1914–18 war and the promises of better times to come. It reached a peak of around 3 million registered unemployed in 1932 and only dropped below 2 million in 1937, to rise again to just over 2 million in January 1939. It exceeded 20 per cent in the depression years of 1931 and 1932. In the 'good' year of 1937 it was still 10.8 per cent, with between 1,373,000 (September) and 1,739,000 (December) registered as out of work. Even in January

1940, unemployment still stood at 1,471,000[24] despite conscription and the mobilisation of the economy for the war effort. It virtually disappeared in the second year of the war.

Unemployment was present throughout the land, although certain regions were designated 'depressed areas' by the government because of the high level there. North East and North West England, Yorkshire, Northern Ireland, South Wales and Clydeside in Scotland were among the worst affected areas. They were the homes of the traditional industries – cotton, coal, iron and steel and shipbuilding – which were experiencing severe difficulties due to foreign competition and lack of demand. All these industries, and others, had greatly expanded during the First World War. After it there was not as much demand for their products. Cotton products had represented 25 per cent of British exports by value in 1910–13. The industry exported 70 per cent of its output. This had been impossible during the war and production overseas had developed, production based on cheaper labour but also often on better-equipped factories. Britain had been responsible for the bulk of shipbuilding before the war, but it was slow to adopt newer types of ship. The world slump devastated it. In 1933, launches fell to 7 per cent of the pre-war figure. The mining industry suffered from foreign competition in its overseas markets and was generally dependent on the health of the British economy as a whole. Employment in mining fell from 1,226,000 in 1920 to 702,000 in 1938.[25] The iron and steel industry suffered from cheap imports in the 1920s and steel works were antiquated (though some improvements did take place).[26] In general, British industry also suffered from a lack of skilled workers, technicians and trained managers. This was something that had been discussed countless times going back at least to the Samuelson Royal Commission on Technical Instruction in the early 1880s. But little had been done to remedy the situation.

Agriculture had greatly profited from the war when German submarines had threatened the nation's food supply. The government encouraged wheat production by guaranteeing the price, but when peace came the government withdrew the guarantee. Prices fell and competition from imports increased. Some relieve came from the Import Duties Act (1932). Yet Britain faced a dilemma in that it could not help its own farmers and simultaneously support empire producers, as it was pledged to do under the Ottawa Agreement of 1932. Suffering traditionally from high rents and small fields, many farmers went back to producing fruit, dairy products and meat. Under Acts of 1931 and 1933, marketing boards were established for milk, potatoes and other produce to fix prices, encourage consumption and set standards. However, because of the costs of slaughtering infected cattle, TB-infected milk was often sold to the public. The numbers engaged in agriculture fell from 860,000 in 1930 to 697,000 in 1938.

Transport was in poor shape. The railways were suffering from increased competition from buses, private cars and trucks, but road development was lagging. Britain had neither roads nor railways to compare with France or Germany. Today the 'Mallard' steam record holder in the National Railway Museum at York, gives an entirely wrong impression of interwar railways. Most passengers travelled in old, dirty rolling stock and the station facilities were poor. Between the wars, 240 miles of track and 350 stations were closed. One major improvement was the electrification of the Southern Railway.

The economic revival in the mid-1930s did not help these traditional industries all that much. The recovery was based on improving world trade, a domestic building boom, demand generated by new technology and, not least, re-armament. Much of British industry appeared antiquated, failed to modernise and sought refuge in restrictive and monopolistic schemes.[27] In the interwar period, Britain 'turned from one of the least into one of the most trustified or controlled economies, and largely through direct government action'. The railway companies were amalgamated (1921), the electricity supply was concentrated and partially nationalised (1926), the government sponsored a monopoly in iron and steel (1932), a national coal cartel was established (1936) and the main airways were nationalised (1939).[28] All this and more under right-wing governments! The Balfour Committee on Industry and Trade had, in 1927, pointed out that in Britain progress was slow in respect of scientific research compared with German and American industry. However, by 1939 much progress had been made.[29] Owing to the changing pattern of industry, the development of chemicals, electronics, motor vehicles, aircraft and the service sectors of the economy, 'Britain looked a great deal more like a twentieth century economy than she had done – in comparison with other industrial states – in 1913.'[30] Despite the progress, the gap with Germany and the USA had not been closed.

Right and Left: 'from death to birth'

Given the world economic crisis and the British crisis, it was only to be expected that there would be interest in the more unorthodox solutions to the problems of modern society. True, most voters opted for Conservative or Labour and most members of those parties wanted to have nothing to do with either Fascism or Communism. Yet there is an impression that more people than was apparent had some sympathy for such 'modern movements'. There were those who were impatient with the slowness of the parliamentary process and the complacency of its advocates. This seemed to contrast with the decisiveness of the dictators, whose propaganda machines never stopped. Churchill, then Chancellor of the Exchequer, had publicly recorded his great admiration for Mussolini in 1927.[31] More cautiously, Dalton, later Labour Chancellor, recorded in his diary that there was no other living man whom it would have thrilled him to meet than Mussolini. He pondered whether, in England, 'where now there is so much impotence in the face of the economic crisis', they could not catch something of the spirit of Italy under Mussolini's Fascism. He greatly admired the *energia* that he found in Italy in December 1932.[32] Mosley went the whole way, and, after visiting Mussolini, set up the British Union of Fascists (BUF) in October 1932. The BUF gained little support among the general public. One wonders what they thought when Mussolini developed the use of poison gas (delivered from aircraft) against tribesmen during his invasion of Abyssinia in 1935. Later, Mosley and others turned their admiration to Hitler.[33] David Lloyd George and King Edward VIII (later Duke of Windsor) were among those who believed Hitler was responsible for the welfare and prosperity they saw in Germany after 1933.[34] Other establishment figures went much further, individuals like Lord Rothermere, owner of the *Daily Mail*, and Sir Barry Domville, Director of Naval Intelligence (1927–30) and later founder of the Link (an Anglo–German friendship association). General Franco, who led the rebel armies against the Spanish Republic in 1936, also had his fans among whom was the Earl of Home, whose son and heir, Lord Dunglass, MP, was Parliamentary Private Secretary to Prime Minister Neville Chamberlain and a future Prime Minister.

Among the writers of the day Noel Coward was a symbol of sorts for the moderate mass of theatre-goers, as was, slightly farther to the left, J. B. Priestley. However, many significant writers were leaning towards the political extremes. On the Left were W. H. Auden, Stephen Spender, C. Day Lewis, the Scottish poet Hugh MacDiarmid and the Irish playwright Sean O'Casey. George Orwell, as an anti-Stalinist, occupied a special place on the left. Roy Campbell 'produced the most purely fascist verse in the English language'.[35] Some thought D. H. Lawrence, who died in 1930, T. S. Eliot and Evelyn Waugh were not far behind. The messages of the nominally Fabian socialists H. G. Wells and G. B. Shaw veered erratically between Communism and Fascism.

John Strachey,[36] Labour MP 1929–31, became well known as a Marxist theorist. With *The Coming Struggle for Power* (1932), he expressed the feelings of other political travellers looking for utopia when he wrote, 'To travel from the capitalist world into Soviet territory is to pass from death to birth'. The book found its way into many households through Victor Gollancz's Left Book Club; it even entered the Thatcher home in Grantham![37] Oxford and Cambridge universities were the targets of Soviet infiltration, both open and secret. Bright students like Denis Healey got involved in Communist politics at this time and Kim Philby, Anthony Blunt and others got embroiled in the more sinister world of Soviet espionage.[38] Some dons, like Maurice Dobb, preached the virtues of the Soviet economic system, while, off campus, Sidney (Lord Passfield) and Beatrice Webb claimed, in their book entitled accordingly, that the Soviet Union was a 'new civilisation'.

In electoral terms, Fascism and Communism were not very successful. Two Communists, J. T. W. Newbold (Motherwell) and S. Saklatvala (North Battersea), were elected in 1922 but both stood under the Labour banner. Saklatvala, a remarkable Indian, was the second Indian to be elected to Parliament. He followed another remarkable Indian, Dadabhai Naoroji (1825–1917),

Liberal MP for Finsbury Central, 1892–5, professor at University College London and sometime President of the Indian National Congress. Saklatvala was defeated in 1923 and then re-elected in 1924. In that year the Labour Party ruled that no member of the Communist Party could be a member of the Labour Party. The BUF boycotted the 1935 election and the Communists put up only two candidates, one of whom, William Gallacher, was returned as Member for West Fife in Scotland.[39]

Election 1935

The election of 14th November 1935 was a fairly quiet one. This helps to explain the relatively low turnout of 71.2 per cent, compared with those in 1924, 1929 and 1931. The economy was recovering, unemployment was falling and the clouds of war had not yet darkened the sky, although Hitler had been in power in Germany since January 1933 and, as we saw, Italy invaded Abyssinia in 1935. The November weather would also have put off some voters. Rumours about the introduction of compulsory military service were an issue of some significance, used by Labour to assault the government. Labour also harried the government on re-armament, which it opposed. Pipe-smoking Baldwin, who had taken over from MacDonald in June, projected himself as a mild-mannered man and used the radio to good effect.[40] The equally mild-mannered Clement Attlee[41] had just been elected leader of the Labour Party, replacing the pacifist George Lansbury.

Perhaps the electors of 1935 had been helped to optimism by the films of Gracie Fields, a genuine working-class 'lass' – *Sally in our Alley* (1931), *Looking on the Bright Side* (1932), *Love, Life and Laughter* (1933) and *Sing as we Go* (1934). All were in keeping with the optimism of the government and its view that the nation was one big family, which needed to think positively and pull together to get out of the slump. Many American films, which were very popular, broadcast the same message. The British Board of Film Censors saw to it that nothing controversial, from the Establishment's point of view, got on to the screen.

In the election, Labour gained a higher percentage vote than ever before – 37.9 per cent (plus 0.7 per cent for the Independent

Labour Party), as against 53.7 per cent for the Conservatives and their allies and 6.4 per cent for the Liberals. However, under the first-past-the-post-system, Labour's score was not reflected in seats, its total going up to 154 (plus four ILP).

George V enjoyed his silver jubilee in 1935, and this too had contributed to the mood of optimism and stability which was likely to have helped the government in the 1935 election. George V died on 20th January 1936 and was succeeded by his son Edward VIII. Previously, as Prince of Wales, Edward had given some glamour to the monarchy and was often the subject of newspaper and newsreel stories. His father, however, had harboured doubts about the Prince of Wales's fitness to reign. Similar worries haunted Baldwin because of Edward's attitude 'of irresponsibility, selfishness, and dislike for any of the functions of kingship other than easy popularity and personal privilege'.[42] He was thought to be sympathetic to Hitler's régime, but this could have been simply an admiration of German social welfare and a desire to avoid another war, rather than sympathy with Nazism's sinister side. Edward gave the Establishment its opportunity to dethrone him through his relationship with Mrs Wallis Simpson, an American already parted from her second husband, who was regarded as sympathetic to Nazism.[43] Determined to marry Wallis Simpson, Edward VIII avoided a constitutional crisis by abdicating after only 325 days as king, giving way to his younger brother George VI on 10th December 1936.

A More Secular Society

Britain was becoming a more secular society: if some gained faith, as a result of the Great War, many more lost it. In any case, the churches were losing some of their social welfare and entertainment functions. People were mainly looking to the state for their welfare, and there were more leisure alternatives than there had been in the past. The Catholic Church maintained its position, even improved it, but this was partly through the continuing flow of Irish migrants into Britain. It was also helped by its network of schools and clubs and the fact that Catholics were concentrated in a few areas. For those who wanted certainty

in their belief the Catholic Church offered much, as did totalitarian movements. This certainty attracted a small number of
well-known Catholic converts like the writer Graham Greene.
Except for Catholics and some pockets of Nonconformism in
Wales, Northern England and parts of Scotland, church-going
was largely a middle-class affair. Some working-class youngsters
were brought into the orbit of the Church of England through
the Boys' Brigade and the Church Lads' Brigade. All denominations had their Boy Scouts and Girl Guides.

Catholics and Jews continued to suffer discrimination in the
interwar period. In the 1930s 'No Catholics need apply' signs
appeared on factory gates.[44] Especially in places like Glasgow
and Liverpool, there were still interdenominational 'punch-ups'.

On the whole, the Church of England remained politically
conservative, though the 'Red Dean', Hewlett Johnson of Canterbury, supported Soviet Communism, and the Archbishop of
York (1929–42), and later Canterbury (1942–5), William Temple,
supported Labour. Leading Labourites Attlee, Cripps, Dalton
and Lansbury were 'C of E'; but many of their colleagues were
Methodists. The majority of Methodists remained supporters of
the Liberal Party. The majority of Catholics and Jews, partly as
outsiders, partly because they were working class, voted Labour.
The churches mostly supported the appeasement policy of the
government. In Catholic circles there was sympathy for General
Franco.

A Moderate Conservative Consensus

Britain was ruled by a moderate Conservative consensus from
1931 until a truly national consensus government was formed
in 1940. Unlike Germany, there was no real crisis in the politics
of the country. The government's massive majority made debate
possible but ensured there was no room for the extremes of
Right or Left. Despite the newsreel footage of unemployed
marchers, demonstrations for the Spanish Republic, and brawls
between blackshirts and 'anti-Fascists' at home, and riots, violence and wars abroad, the 1930s were far less political than
many later believed them to have been. Then, as now, many
voters were interested in sport, hearing about the private lives

of stars and celebrities, reading about crime, having a flutter on the football pools, planning holidays and worrying about finance, than they were about political antics. The popular press and the radio fed these interests.

The great developments of technology – radio and television, cinemas, aviation, the automobile industry and consumer goods – in which Britain played a major role, helped to cloud people's perception of the declining position of Britain in the world. Because Britain was still a major scientific and technological power, and ruled over an enormous Empire, people still saw Britain as the world's greatest power.

In economic terms, although Britain's economy improved in the 1930s it was still in a precarious state. Britain was not paying its way. It was running a huge deficit on its manufacturing (or *visible*) overseas trade, and this was not covered by its exports of services like banking, shipping, insurance and foreign investments (*invisible* trade). According to the official *Board of Trade Journal*, it had a trade surplus in 1935, but deficits in 1936, 1937 and 1938. Thus Britain was in poor shape to embark upon the great and hazardous adventure of the Second World War.

2 Britain and the World, 1919–39

Palestine, India and the Empire

Anyone who had suggested in 1931 that by 1961 the most important parts of the British Empire would be independent and that by 1991 Britain would be merely a medium-weight European state, would have been regarded as, at best, a fool and, at worst, a traitor. The monarch, politicians, churches, the education system and mass media, all contributed to the myth of the Empire. Under the terms of the peace settlement in 1919 more areas of the globe were painted red, the colour traditionally used to indicate British territory. Officially, this was done on the authority of the League of Nations, and these areas were not colonies but mandated territories. In Africa, Britain took over German East Africa, calling it Tanganyika (now part of Tanzania), and Togo. Britain created Iraq and Transjordan (Jordan) from the Arab lands which had been part of the Turkish Empire. Both were indirectly under British control. Britain virtually controlled the strategically important Egypt and oil-rich Iran. Palestine became a British mandate.

In the hope of winning the support of Jewish opinion in the USA and Russia, Britain made the Balfour Declaration of 1917. It promised that the British government would use its best endeavours to create a Jewish national home in Palestine. It went on to state that 'nothing shall be done which may prejudice the civil and religious rights of existing non-Jewish communities in Palestine'. The people of Palestine were not consulted on the issue. Indeed, Britain had given certain wartime undertakings to the Arabs, to encourage them to revolt against their Turkish overlords. In 1914, there were approximately 500,000 Arabs living in Palestine and 90,000 Jews.[1] Most of the Jews were recent arrivals, seeking to escape persecution in Russia and eastern Europe. The Turks had allowed them in and many had set up agricultural communities. In 1920, the Arab population of Palestine made the first of many revolts, under British rule, to prevent further Jewish immigration. Other Arab resistance followed in 1921. The result was that Sir Herbert Samuel, the High Commissioner (who was, in fact, Jewish himself), temporarily suspended all immigration. Open Arab attacks on Jews and Jewish property broke out again in 1929. By that time, there were 590,000 Arabs and 150,000 Jews in Palestine. Over half the Jews had entered the country since 1918. Economic depression led to a slowing down of Jewish immigration. Nazi persecution of the Jews after 1933 caused a new influx, which the Nazis encouraged. This produced the Arab revolt of 1936–9, which the British put down by the internment of suspects and the bombing and burning of Arab villages. In 1938, 5,700 major acts of terrorism were recorded. Some 100 Arabs were convicted by military courts and hanged. In addition, the death toll included 69 Britons, 92 Jews, 486 Arab civilians and 1,138 Arab rebels.

As war approached, however, the British felt they had to appease Arab opinion. They restricted Jewish immigration further and called for the partition of Palestine into a Jewish state, an Arab state and an area remaining under British control (Peel Commission 1937, Woodhead Commission 1938). The White Paper of 1939, the work of Malcolm MacDonald, announced restrictions on Jewish land purchases, a final quota of 75,000 more Jewish immigrants over a five-year period and the setting up of self-governing institutions at the end of the five-year period. British policy satisfied few Arabs and fewer Zionists (as those wanting a Jewish State were known). In Britain, the pro-Zionist Labour Party and Churchill roundly condemned MacDonald's proposals.

Parliament probably spent more time discussing India than any other single issue between 1919 and 1939. Ireland and Palestine also took up much time. The India Act, which became law in 1935, was the culmination of years of bitter debate in Parliament. The main architects of the National Government, MacDonald and Baldwin, favoured a federal system for India with a wide measure of self-government on internal matters in the individual states. Baldwin set constitutional reform in motion in 1927 by establishing a commission to investigate the matter. Churchill led a furious onslaught against any change in the direction of Indian self-rule. He resigned from the Conservative shadow cabinet in January 1931 in protest against Baldwin's line on India. Basically, Churchill felt India was not ripe for democracy. On 26th April 1932, in the Commons, he attacked those who foolishly believed 'that the ideas and processes of democracy, to which Western nations are attaching less and less faith year after year, are the sole means by which the welfare of the Indian people can be secured'. Thus Churchill put himself beyond the pale, making it more difficult for both Conservative and Labour anti-appeasers to line up with him later in the 1930s. The pity was that the India Act was too little and too late for the great majority of articulate Indian opinion, which supported Gandhi's Congress Party in its demands for Indian independence. Disappointed, Congress mounted a campaign of civil disobedience, glimpses of which were occasionally shown in the cinema newsreels. Many probably thought the disturbances showed the Indians to be both unwise and ungrateful. Others, like Churchill, believed that: 'The clashes which take place are only in the political classes which stand between us and the great masses of the people.' Churchill predicted that, if the British left, 'something like the dark ages would descend on India'.

A few more thoughtful and knowledgeable Britons, Attlee, the Labour leader, among them, realised that India wanted to take the road first taken in 1867 by Canada when it gained self-government; a road later taken by Australia, Newfoundland, New Zealand, South Africa and Ireland. By the Statute of Westminster (1931) these states had become, in practical terms, fully independent, in no way subordinate to the United Kingdom. This was a natural development but one speeded up by the 1914–18 war. In future these states would not be bound by a British declaration of war.

Anglo–Irish Relations

Developments in Ireland were a severe shock to the British and difficult for them to understand. There had been the Easter (nationalist) Rebellion in Dublin in 1916, which was suppressed by the British, after which the leaders were executed. Fighting broke out again in January 1919 and continued to July 1921. The insurgents were encouraged by the British government's procrastination over the question of home rule – internal self-government – for Ireland, and by its determination to introduce military conscription there in 1918. After winning most of the Irish seats in the election to the Westminster Parliament in 1918, the Irish nationalist party, Sinn Féin, set up a separate parliament in Dublin and proclaimed independence from Britain. The British government attempted to solve the problem, and placate domestic and foreign opinion, by passing the Government of Ireland Act (1920), under which two parliaments were to be established in Ireland, one in Dublin, and one covering the six counties in the North. The two parliaments were to have limited jurisdiction, and the whole of Ireland was to continue to be represented in the Westminster 'imperial' Parliament. A Council of Ireland with representatives from North and South would consider matters of mutual interest. This solution was rejected by the Irish Republicans and the struggle continued.

The Irish Republican Army (IRA) commanded by Michael Collins,[2] and the British armed forces were locked in a ruthless struggle, which involved Irish attacks on the police and military units followed by British reprisals. These meant the burning of homes and other buildings where the attack had occurred, and the summary execution of known Irish nationalists. On the British side, the Auxiliary Cadets (all ex-officers), the 'Black and Tans' and the Royal Irish Constabulary (RIC) gained notoriety. British reprisals and the intractability of the conflict appalled wide sections of British opinion, and this helped to force the government to seek a negotiated settlement. The 'war', as Lloyd George called it, ended with the signing of 'Articles of agreement for a Treaty between Great Britain and Ireland' on 6th December 1921. The Irish Free State was set up in Southern Ireland, its relation to Britain being similar to that of what was then the 'dominion of Canada'. The parliament of Southern Ireland voted for this by 64 to 57 on 7th January 1922. Most of those who voted against wanted independence. Collins headed the new government, only to be gunned down by anti-Treaty nationalists a short time later. He was only 31. In the civil war that followed in the South, the Irish imprisoned and killed each other on a far larger scale than had happened before 1922, in their war with the British.[3]

Britain's relations with the Irish Free State were under strain after Eamon de Valera's Fianna Fáil (Warriors of Destiny) party gained office in 1932, replacing Premier William Cosgrave, a 1916 survivor. Cosgrave's government had been backed by conservative farmers and many in the business community. De Valera too had taken part in the 1916 rebellion but had opposed the 1921 Treaty. He remained in office until 1948. The new government sought to abolish the Oath of Allegiance to the British Crown (which Free State MPs were obliged to take) and suspend the payment of land annuities to the British Treasury. Essentially, these represented inherited debt for loans from the British government to enable Irish peasants to buy the land which they worked. An economic war then broke out, with Britain imposing a 20 per cent duty on Irish agricultural products. This lasted until 1938 and probably hurt Ireland more than it did Britain. Ireland then agreed to pay a lump sum of £10 million in final settlement of the claims, which were many times that figure. In an increasingly crisis-ridden world, the British government was ready to compromise: the British withdrew from the so-called Treaty ports – these were Southern Irish ports still occupied by the Royal Navy after 1922. In 1937, de Valera also introduced a new constitution, which abolished the Oath of Allegiance but stopped short of proclaiming the Free State a republic. Ireland was now known as Eire, which meant the South. In 1938 the Gaelic scholar, writer and Protestant, Douglas Hyde, was unanimously elected first 'President', a post he held until 1945.

Perhaps one thing, for which de Valera is not given enough credit, was his defence of democracy in the Free State. It was a new state, torn by intense internal rivalries in an unstable world. Extremists of Right and Left increasingly threatened parliamentary democracy. In Ireland the threat came from the so-called Blueshirts, initially an ex-servicemen's anti-Communist association.[4] This uniformed movement, led by General Eoin O'Duffy, former Commissioner of Police, was part of the Fine Gael, the newly created party of former Premier Cosgrave. It adopted Fascist symbols and organisation, including the Fascist salute. It came to prominence in 1933 and 1934 when it attempted to exploit rural discontent. By 1936, when it was virtually dead, some of its members, commanded by O'Duffy, went off to fight for Franco in the Spanish Civil War. De Valera resisted pressure from the Catholic Church to support Franco, declaring the Free State neutral. On the Left, de Valera banned the IRA, the armed, guerrilla wing of extreme Republicanism with which he had been originally identified. A few IRA volunteers fought on the Republican side in Spain. De Valera loyally supported the League of Nations' policy of imposing sanctions on Italy, following its invasion of Abyssinia.

In Northern Ireland, the Ulster Unionists, led by Sir James Craig (later Viscount Craigavon), and backed by the Protestant majority, ruled unchallenged throughout the interwar period, enjoying internal self-government through their Stormont Parliament and, in addition, sending MPs to Westminster. Usually about 38 to 40 Unionists faced a variety of opposition Labour, nationalist and Republican Labour members numbering twelve to fourteen in the 52-seat House of Commons (at Stormont). Catholic representation, at all levels, was reduced by gerrymandering constituencies. Internal security was secured by building up the Royal Ulster Constabulary as a Protestant force,[5] and by giving that force wide powers under the Special Powers Act. Nevertheless, in 1935, British troops had to be called in to restore order after a new round of 'the troubles'. The Boundary Agreement, signed by North and South, under which the South recognised the existing boundary between the two parts of Ireland, gave the Northern majority some comfort. But later, they felt under threat from de Valera, especially as the new constitution of 1937 laid claim to the North. The Ulster Protestants also noticed that Eire's constitution enshrined Catholic principles, thus making it even more difficult for them to contemplate any union with the South. De Valera's attempt to force the revival of the Irish language, making it compulsory in the schools, and knowledge of it a necessary qualification for civil service entry, further alienated the Ulster Unionist Protestants. The Irish nationalists in the North did compete in the elections, gaining several seats each time. Their division, however, mirrored those in the South and they remained ineffective. A small Northern Ireland Labour Party, which did not question the frontier, attempted to represent working-class interests.

Chamberlain and Appeasement

Baldwin remained in office until 1937, when Neville Chamberlain replaced him. Chamberlain was 68 when he took over and looked rather out of date with his winged collar and umbrella. His voice had a slightly pleading air about it. A former Lord Mayor of Birmingham, Chamberlain had done two stints as Chancellor of the Exchequer (1923–4 and 1931–37) and three as Minister of Health.[6] The scion of a political and business dynasty, his half-brother, Austen, had also served as Chancellor and Foreign Secretary, and briefly as leader of the Conservative Party. Neville Chamberlain's weakness was that he had no experience of foreign affairs. However, it should be stressed that, although he is most closely associated with 'appeasement' of Nazi Germany, MacDonald and Baldwin were in charge for most of the period after 1933 and Anthony Eden served as Foreign Secretary from 1935 to 1938. The fact is, no British politician wanted war and they only differed on how best to avoid it. Attlee, Dalton, Eden, Harold Macmillan, Mosley and many other MPs had served in the trenches and did not want others to suffer this experience. Apart from Mosley, none of them was for appeasement of Nazi Germany but they too wanted negotiated settlements rather than a new conflagration. Hitler and Mussolini had survived the First World War as ordinary soldiers. Both were wounded, both were decorated. It was difficult to believe that they were indifferent to the threat of war, let alone deliberately planning one. Their claims to be peace-seekers and their war service must have done much to mislead British politicians.

Many British politicians also suffered from a sense of guilt regarding Germany. The Treaty of Versailles, which ended the 1914–18 war, was widely discredited as being too harsh on Germany. It *was* harsh, depriving Germany of all its colonies, as well as much of eastern Germany and Alsace-Lorraine. Germany was not allowed an air force or heavy weapons of any kind. It lost most of its navy and merchant fleet. Its army was reduced to a volunteer force of 100,000, well below that of neighbouring Poland or France. Finally, it had to pay massive reparations and acknowledge its sole responsibility for the war.[7]

Two other factors, which helped to build a mood of appeasement, were fear of aerial bombardment and fear of the consequences of re-armament upon Britain's finances.[8] Bombardment from the air had taken place in Britain in the Great War. Contrary to popular myth, planes rather than airships had carried out most of the attacks, in which several thousand people had been killed. Since then, there had been press, radio and newsreel reports of bombing in the Spanish Civil War and of the Japanese bombing of China from 1937 onwards. A number of feature films – *Things to Come* (1936) and *The Dawn Patrol* (1930 and 1938) – also contributed to the rising fear of aerial assault, as did expert opinion. The strength of the new German air force, developed by Hitler and Göring after 1933, was exaggerated. As Chancellor of the Exchequer until 1937, Chamberlain took the Treasury view that Britain did not have the financial resources for more than very modest re-armament and this should be concentrated on key projects. Even the modest level of re-armament was hampered by shortages of skilled workers, especially in aircraft production.

Traditionally British policy had been to consider its Empire first and Europe second. This was also a factor in the appeasement of the dictators, discussed separately below.

Finally, there was also fear of Communism, which should be neither exaggerated, nor dismissed, as one of the roots of appeasement policy. Writing in his diary on 6th June 1938, Harold Nicolson, a government MP, commented: 'People of the governing classes think only of their own fortunes, which means hatred of the Reds. This creates a perfectly artificial but at present most effective bond between ourselves and Hitler.' Chamberlain hated Communism and Baldwin feared the spread of Bolshevism if war should break out in Europe. There were others who took a less doctrinaire line but it must not be forgotten that Stalin was busy killing off his rivals at this time. There were also doubts about the effectiveness of the Red Army as a potential ally, as Stalin liquidated most of the top Soviet officers in 1937.

For all the above reasons, the British did little when Hitler re-introduced conscription in 1935, took over the Saar in the same year and remilitarised the Rhineland in 1936. Nor was there anything more than a formal note of disapproval when he seized Austria in 1938. During the Sudeten crisis of September 1938, war looked a distinct possibility. It ended with Hitler achieving his objectives. In all these cases, it was argued, 'The Germans have a case', as indeed they had. Germany was the only state in continental Europe not imposing conscription. The Saar was returned to Germany by League of Nations plebiscite. The Rhineland was a recognised part of Germany. The majority of Austrians had favoured union with Germany (forbidden under the peace settlement) but they were given no real chance by Hitler to decide whether they wanted union with *Nazi Germany*. In the case of the Sudetenland, the people there had not lived as German citizens before 1918, but 3 million of them, the great majority in many areas, were German-speakers. They seemed to prefer to join the German Reich than remain under Czech rule. In Britain and France, there were those who detested Hitlerism but believed Germany was right on these issues. They did not really appreciate the threat that Hitler posed. Chamberlain belonged to this category. He thought he had solved the problem with Germany by the Munich Agreement.[9]

Fear of Communism and fear of war kept Britain out of the Spanish Civil War of 1936–9. Britain, in agreement with France, pursued a policy of non-intervention, refusing to sell arms to either side. This, in fact, aided the Nationalists rather than the legitimate government of the Spanish Republic. Germany and Italy assisted Franco's Nationalists and the Soviet Union helped the Republic, to a lesser extent. Because of Gibraltar, Britain sought to keep its options open.

Britain and Japan

At the beginning of the twentieth century, Britain saw Japan as a potential counterweight to Russia in the Far East. There was no opposition to Japan's annexation of Korea in 1910, or to her earlier seizure of Taiwan (Formosa) in 1895. Japan was regarded as a progressive and orderly country and a good market for British products as it strove to modernise. Britain helped to build up the Japanese navy and in 1904 the two states became official allies. Britain was sympathetic to Japan in the Russo–Japanese War of 1904–5. In the 1914–18 war, Japan was allied to the Western powers, using the opportunity presented to seize German colonies in China. In the interwar period, as Japanese aggression mounted, invading Manchuria in 1931 and then China proper in 1937, opinion changed somewhat. There was unease about the growing influence of the armed forces within Japan. However, many in the Establishment still saw Japan as a force for order in Asia, needed to halt Communist Russia and chaotic China with its competing Nationalists and Communists, both of whom were seen as dangerous to Western interests. Finance again played a role in British considerations and it seemed easier to appease Japan than to oppose it. Nevertheless, at Singapore Britain spent heavily to build up a kind of Asian Maginot Line, an impregnable fortress.

Britain and the USA

About 4.25 million Britons emigrated to the United States between 1820 and 1914. In the 1920s the boom in America attracted many more. Thus the two states continued to be linked by blood ties. The cinema played the most important role in forming the British perception of America and the American perception of Britain in this period. American films in Britain were far more important than British films in America. In fact, the American view of Britain was mainly the Hollywood view. British as well as American audiences were subjected to it. Images of historical Britain were presented in *Mutiny on the Bounty* (1935), *David Copperfield* (1935), *The Charge of the Light Brigade* (1936), *The Adventures of Robin Hood* (1938) and *Wuthering Heights* (1939). As the Americans wanted to penetrate the markets of the British Empire, they had to present an essentially positive picture of that Empire, as in Paramount's last silent film, *The Four Feathers* (1929), and in *Lives of a Bengal Lancer* (1935) and *Wee Willie Winkie* (1937). For the British, the USA appeared a wild and exciting place, but many Hollywood films presented a negative, even frightening, image of America. The British Board of Film Censors regarded many of them as decadent and subversive. The Quota Act of 1927 was an attempt to stem the flow of foreign, especially American, films and encourage British cinema. The Act failed because American films were popular and because US companies simply bought production and distribution facilities in Britain. Thus, even such well-known 'British' films as *Sixty Glorious Years* (1938), about Queen Victoria, *The Citadel* (1938) about a doctor in a Welsh mining community, and *Goodbye, Mr Chips* (1939), extolling the public school spirit, had their origins in American resources.

The American way of life impinged upon Britain in other respects too. American popular music, literature and fashions gained increasing influence in Britain. Ford, having established itself in Britain before 1914, became an increasingly important part of the British motor vehicle industry. Corn Flakes, Heinz beans and other American food products entered many homes and Woolworth became a normal part of the high streets of most towns.

At the political level, Britain and the USA had much in common. Both wanted, as far as possible, to keep out of European quarrels and to concentrate on their respective empires and spheres of influence. They were rivals and allies in the Pacific: the Americans were more sympathetic to Nationalist China than were the British. Many Americans were less enthusiastic about the British Empire. President Harding's Washington Conference (1921–3) was an attempt to reduce naval armaments and solve problems in the Pacific area. It limited navies, binding the USA, Britain, France and Japan to respect each other's rights in the Pacific and to confer in the event that any question threatened to disrupt harmonious relations. A nine-power treaty, in 1922, guaranteed China's political and territorial integrity and the 'open door' for trade. In 1931, Japanese armies occupied Manchuria and in 1935 they invaded the five northern provinces of China in direct violation of the pact. Neither Britain nor the USA did anything. In 1937, the Japanese broadened their invasion of China, becoming notorious for their attrocities against civilians. In the course of the invasion, they sank the US gunboat *Panay* and the Royal Navy's *Ladybird*, but the US State Department rejected proposals from the British Foreign Office for joint action.[10] Despite the attack, a Gallup poll reported that 70 per cent of Americans opposed any intervention and more than a two-third majority in Congress voted against imposing sanctions upon the Japanese.[11]

This isolationist mood among the American people was a restraining influence on the White House. Although some British politicians visited the USA as private citizens (Churchill for instance), there were no official top-level meetings. President

Roosevelt attended the Inter-American conference in Buenos Aires, Argentina, in 1936.[12] He did not visit Europe. On 5th October 1937, Roosevelt called for the quarantining of aggressor nations by the international community. Chamberlain believed that it was 'always best and safest to count on nothing from the Americans but words'.[13]

The Neutrality Acts of 1935 and 1937 reflected American fear of European involvement and the suspicion that they had been conned into joining the First World War by their arms manufacturers. Britain and the USA suffered tension in their relations over war debts. Finally, there were powerful Irish interests in the USA who did not like Britain's treatment of Ireland, and increasingly influential Jewish interests who thought Britain was not fully implementing its promise of a Jewish national home in Palestine. After its setback in the Great War, German influence was regaining ground in the USA.

Munich and Beyond

The establishment of Czechoslovakia after the First World War was not the wisest act of the victors. It was carved out of the Austro–Hungarian Empire and within its frontiers were territories claimed by Hungary and by the newly created Polish state. There was also territory where German-speakers formed the great majority, and they did not wish to be part of a Czech state. The two main groups, Czechs and Slovaks, did not feel happy together. The Slovaks were Catholic and rural, the Czechs more urban and less pious Catholics and Protestants. By the standards of its neighbours, Czechoslovakia in 1938 was thoroughly democratic and modern, with a wide range of industries, including armaments. Its minorities did, however, have cause for complaint. Led by Konrad Henlein, a bank official and gymnastic instructor, the Sudeten German Party polled 1,249,530 in 1935, becoming the biggest political party. Even so, only 63 per cent of the Germans had voted for this party. The majority of the German-speakers took hope from Hitler's annexation of Austria and pressed their demands.

On 24th April, Henlein made his so-called Carlsbad Demands which included, in effect, the right to repudiate the principles of the Czechoslovak state by claiming 'full freedom to profess German nationality and the German Weltanschauung'. Hitler's denunciation of Czechoslovakia at the Nazi party rally at Nuremberg in September 1938 looked close to a declaration of war. Shocked by this, Chamberlain made his first flight (15th September) to Germany, in an attempt to save the peace. He made two more flights, on 22nd and 28th September, in order to conclude an agreement which gave in to Hitler's demands. Even then, the British had mobilised the Royal Navy and taken air-raid precautions, the French had taken defensive measures and the Czechs had mobilised. The Munich Agreement was signed by Hitler, Chamberlain, Mussolini and Daladier, the French Prime Minister. It meant that the Czechs, who were excluded from the conference, were to evacuate all territories where 50 per cent or more of the population were German-speakers. The evacuation was immediate and the Czechs had to leave every-thing intact.

The Munich Agreement was a disastrous mistake. The Soviet Union was bound by a friendship treaty with Czechoslovakia, but this only became active if the French went to the aid of the Czechs. Likewise, the French were only prepared to move if the British did so. Britain had no contractual obligations to Czecho-slovakia. Czechoslovakia had built up modern armed forces and if these states, combined, had threatened Hitler it is likely he would have seen that he could not win. Not known at the time were the plans within sections of the German army to depose Hitler if war seemed imminent. Both the French and the British governments had been warned by their military advisors of the superiority of the German air force.

The unhappy Czechs ceded their territory, as agreed. The Poles and Hungarians then forced them to agree to their re-spective claims. Finally, on 15th March 1939, Hitler marched into Prague after blackmailing the Czech President. A German protectorate was established, except for Slovakia, which was given nominal independence. Hitler got control of the powerful Czech arms industry. The only thing which can be said for the Munich Agreement is that it gave Britain more time to re-arm. This time was used constructively, to the extent that the RAF was further expanded and limited conscription was introduced, the latter despite opposition from the Labour and Liberal parties. In April,

Britain concluded an alliance with Poland, which, it was hoped, would never be put to the test. Hitler then denounced the 1935 Anglo–German Naval Agreement and the German–Polish Non-Aggression Pact of 1934. The British guarantee to Poland could only really be fully effective in conjunction with a Soviet–British–Polish understanding. Under the pressure from his critics, Chamberlain agreed to explore such an alliance. He proceeded slowly because of his fear of Communism, lack of confidence in the Red Army, and because the Polish military régime would not agree to Soviet forces entering their territory even to defend Poland. On 23rd August the political bombshell of the Soviet–German Non-Aggression Pact was announced. The secret clauses of this, by which the two dictators divided up Poland and agreed spheres of influence, made war inevitable.

Public Opinion

The Gallup poll came to Britain from the USA in 1937. From that time on it was possible to measure public opinion, on specific issues, with some degree of accuracy. The first polls in 1937 revealed the fear of war and the support for international agreements to avoid war. In June 1937, 71 per cent of those interviewed wanted Britain to continue to support the Geneva-based League of Nations in its efforts to keep the peace. The League, set up in 1919 mainly by Britain and France and their allies, had failed to stop the aggression of the Japanese in Manchuria (1931), the Italians in Abyssinia (1935) or the Nazis. The three aggressor states were no longer members, nor was the USA. The League looked increasingly irrelevant. But, in December 1937, 72 per cent of the public still wanted Britain to remain a member. The month before, when asked which they would prefer if they had to choose between Fascism and Communism, 26 per cent opted for Fascism and 28 per cent for Communism; the rest could not decide. After the Munich Agreement, 51 per cent said they were satisfied with Chamberlain, 39 per cent were not. Yet, in September 1938, 57 per cent of those polled sympathised with the Spanish Republic and only 7 per cent with Franco. After the Nazi pogrom against the Jews in November 1938, 73 per cent of those interviewed expressed the opinion that Nazi ill-treatment of the Jews was an obstacle to Anglo-German understanding; only 15 per cent disagreed.[14] Although about half the population still gave their support to Chamberlain as Prime Minister up to the spring of 1939, opinion had moved strongly against Germany and towards better relations with the Soviet Union. The fact that public opinion was changing was also revealed by the results of by-elections. Between March 1936 and August 1939 the Conservatives lost thirteen seats to Labour and three to independents.

After this time the three main political parties did not oppose each other until after 5th July 1945 because Britain was at war.

3　Britain at War, 1939–41

'wicked and unprovoked attack' on Poland

Richard Body, MP, remembered 'a trace of a tear appeared in my eye'.[1] It was 3rd September 1939, Richard was twelve and had just heard Prime Minister Chamberlain tell the nation in a radio address that Britain was at war with Germany because of its 'wicked and unprovoked attack' on Poland two days earlier. Hitler had not responded to Britain's call to withdraw. Many others had tears in their eyes on that Sunday morning listening to the sad, weary, yet dignified voice of the Prime Minister. To some, Chamberlain sounded in agony.[2] Mrs Llin Golding, MP, then six, who lived in a Welsh village, remembered 'rushing out and looking down the hill to see if the soldiers or the aeroplanes were about to attack. I had a real sense of fear.'[3] Many who heard Chamberlain felt a mixture of fear and relief. The fear was born of the widespread expectation that massive aerial bombardment would shortly follow a declaration of war. In fact, air-raid sirens went in what turned out to be a false alarm.[4] The relief stemmed from the end of uncertainty, which had prevailed from at least March 1939. Aneurin Bevan, a left-wing Labour MP and future minister, responded to the news of war by playing Spanish Republican marching songs on his gramophone.[5] It appeared to him that at last Britain was resisting Nazi/Fascist aggression. Clement Attlee, the Labour leader, recovering from an operation, was playing a leisurely game of golf in North Wales when he heard the news.[6] There is no record of whether he continued. Meanwhile, up and down the country, thousands of Labour supporters were already united with their Conservative and Liberal neighbours on the practical task of filling sandbags. It was to require near disaster to unite their leaders. Many, on both sides of the Commons, doubted Chamberlain's ability to lead the nation through the war. Harold Nicolson, a government MP, heard the broadcast with some other government supporters, and concluded Chamberlain could not possibly lead the country into a great fight.[7]

War of 'the Money Power'

Though there were few in Britain who were enthusiastic about going to war, there were fewer still who were against it. Among Labour MPs there was little opposition in principle to supporting the war effort, apart from George Lansbury and one or two pacifists. However, some still objected to conscription. Labour rejected an offer to join the government but agreed to a political truce, under which the three main parties did not oppose each other at by-elections.

Further left, the 18,000-strong Communist Party (CPGB) supported the war – at least initially. The Hitler–Stalin Pact did not at first make any difference. Even the Soviet invasion of eastern Poland on 17th September was seen as a defensive move by many Communists and even a few pro-Churchill Conservatives.[8] It was believed the Soviets were attempting to save as much of the crumbling Polish state as possible from being overrun by Hitler. By 7th October, the CPGB was urging opposition to the war. They now saw it as an imperialist war and condemned Chamberlain's government and the Labour and Liberal opposition. In this they were merely echoing the line of the Soviet-run Communist International (Comintern).[9] Harry Pollitt, Secretary of the CPGB, and Willie Gallacher, MP, had both argued against the new line but then fell in behind it. Dave Springhall, the CPGB's representative in Comintern, returned from Moscow to explain the new line – Pollitt and *Daily Worker* editor, Campbell, were dismissed from their posts and made to sign humiliating admissions of error.[10] When the Soviet Union opened hostilities against Finland, in November 1939, the CPGB presented it as a defensive measure. The attack did not do anything for the Soviets' moral or military standing but ended in March 1940 with the Finns being forced to sue for peace. Finland was obliged to cede territory to the Soviet Union.

The small Independent Labour Party (ILP), which had broken from Labour in 1931, resisted the call to arms from the start, denouncing the war as imperialist. It called for non-violent resistance in all the belligerent states.[11] Though its membership was smaller than that of the CPGB, it had three MPs, due to working-class loyalty in three Glasgow constituencies. When Hitler proposed peace negotiations after his victory in Poland, these elements urged serious investigation of his offer. Former Liberal Prime Minister David Lloyd George, Bernard Shaw and some other prominent personalities also took this view. The Communists claimed that Nazi aggression had been checked by Soviet action in Poland and that *Der Führer* was suing for peace!

What did Mosley think of the war? He sent a message to his British Union of Fascists and National Socialists denouncing it:

> The dope machine of Jewish finance deceived the people until Britain was involved in a war in the interest of the Money Power which rules Britain through its Press and Parties. Now British Union will continue our work of awakening the people until peace is won, and until the People's State of British Union is born by the declared will of the British People.

He went on, 'Our country is involved in war. Therefore I ask you to do nothing to injure our country, or to help the other Power.'[12]

In February 1940, the voters were given the chance to show what they thought about the war in the West Ham Silvertown by-election. Labour defended the seat against Communist and Fascist challengers. The Labour vote was 14,343, Pollitt gained only 966 votes and his right-wing rival only 151. This result was typical. Between September 1939 and June 1941 there were nineteen contested by-elections, six in Labour seats and thirteen in Conservative. They were held in the main areas of England and Scotland. Turnout was low partly due to men being away on war service and evacuations. Only in two cases did seats change hands. These were Cambridge University and Newcastle North, both of which rejected Conservatives for independent Conservatives.

Domestic Problems

There were, of course, issues to exploit by anti-government candidates. At the beginning of 1939 there were 1,841,372 registered unemployed – a 10 per cent increase on 1938 – and many more were not registered. Only as the demand of re-armament and conscription mopped up all available labour would this figure gradually fall.[13] About 1,300,000 people were employed as domestic servants.[14] Many of them would later seek the higher pay and greater freedom of factory work making armaments. The cost of living rose rapidly – 14 per cent between 1939 and 1940. There were problems associated with evacuation, conscription, rationing and shortages. The families of ordinary servicemen lived poorly in most cases. There was the beginning of the bitterness that was felt towards those in reserved occupations whose civilian jobs were considered too important for them to be conscripted for military service. There was anger about those receiving black-market goods, and those who simply remained privileged, whatever the state or fate of the nation. Life in high society in London and the great country houses went on almost as usual.[15] Many on the left were worried that Britain was becoming a Fascist state, with identity cards, direction of labour, internment without trial, and censorship. In the Labour Party, Bevan expressed these fears. Outside it the ILP, CPGB and some Liberals made similar claims. Right-wing critics believed Britain had gone socialist, with rationing, control of business activities, increasing taxation, forced billeting of evacuees, exit permits for those wishing to leave the country and the threat that property could be commandeered.[16] An IRA campaign in Britain, which began in 1938, continued. The Prevention of Violence Bill was rushed through the Commons on 24th July. By then there had been 127 terrorist attacks.[17] On 25th August five people were killed and twelve were badly injured by a bomb in Coventry.[18] In addition, explosions occurred in London, Birmingham and Liverpool and at sorting offices in Manchester, Birmingham, Lincoln and Leicester.

Britain: 'untrained and unfitted'

There was surprise that Poland had been overrun so rapidly.[19] The Poles were shocked that there was little military activity involving the British and the French in the first seven months of the war. It is difficult to evaluate the claim made by historians

like A. J. P. Taylor and backed by German General Halder that
if the French, with limited British support, had attacked western
Germany when Hitler's forces were still tied up in Poland, the
war would have been a very short one.[20] The fact is that the
French and British armies were poorly prepared for the conflict.
The famous Spitfire and the less famous Hurricane fighters
masked the fact that British aviation was, in many respects, behind
the aero-industries of Germany, the USA and France. On the
eve of major re-armament, in 1936, 'the British aircraft industry
remained a cottage industry with obsolescent products'.[21] Aircrew lacked proper training. On 4th September, the RAF went
into action against German naval installations at Wilhelmshaven
with poor results. On 6th September a radar fault caused a false
alarm and the RAF shot down three of its own planes! Berlin
was hit on 1st October with leaflets not bombs. There was a fear
of bombing civilians and possible retaliation. The Army was fairly
amateur. The units which had seen recent service had done so
mainly against lightly armed tribesmen in India or Arabs in
Palestine. Britain, unlike its European neighbours, did not maintain a large army based on conscription. Relatively speaking, it
was an army of amateurs. The case of Quintin Hogg (Lord
Hailsham), then a pro-Chamberlain MP, illustrates the point.
Because of his support for the Munich Agreement he felt compelled to seek military service. 'The trouble was I was too old
to be wanted as a junior officer, useless as a private soldier, and
too young honourably to avoid armed service. . . . I had positively no qualifications except an infantry Certificate "A" obtained
at Eton in 1925.' Through a friend he was able to get a place as
a second lieutenant.[22] Writer Evelyn Waugh was another who
was too old. At 36 he was commissioned to lieutenant without
completing an officer-training course due to an influential friend.
W. F. Deedes, in 1999, recalled the June of 1939, when he was
a 26-year-old reporter on the *Daily Telegraph*: 'they asked me in
the casual way all good regiments then went about their business
whether I would accept a commission. Wholly untrained and
unfitted for the rank . . . I became 2nd Lieutenant.'[23]

Although in better shape than the Army, the Royal Navy called
back older reservists suffering from Parkinson's disease.[24] It was
better equipped in capital ships than the German Navy but weak
in submarines. The loss of the new, pride of the navy, subma-

rine *Thetis* at Liverpool Bay on 1st June 1939, with the death of 99 men, seemed to symbolise this. What German submarines could do was revealed on 3rd September, when the U-30 sank the unarmed passenger liner *Athenia*, on its way from Liverpool to Montreal, killing 112 passengers including 28 Americans. On 17th September the U-29 sank the British aircraft carrier *Courageous* with the loss of 518 sailors. Worse still, on 13th October the U-47 penetrated the British naval defences at Scapa Flow and sank the battleship *Royal Oak* as she lay at anchor. A total of 833 British sailors lost their lives. Meanwhile, the pocket battleship *Admiral Graf Spee* seemed to be sinking British merchant shipping at will. Churchill, in charge of the Admiralty, appeared to have been outmanoeuvred. Better news was on the way. In December, the Royal Navy gave him an early Christmas present. The *Admiral Graf Spee* was badly damaged by three lighter armed British cruisers. Forced to seek sanctuary in neutral Uruguay, its commander, Hans Langsdorff, decided to scuttle it. Pictures of the burning Nazi ship went round the world and became one of the photographic highlights of the war. Another German naval weapon was also neutralised. This was the magnetic mine, which had proved a menace to shipping.[25]

Norway Overrun

Norway had remained neutral in the 1914–18 war and intended to do so again. Life went on as normal in Oslo.[26] Northern Norway had become important as a route through which Swedish iron ore, vital to the Nazi war economy, reached Germany. Churchill mined Norwegian waters and was planning to seize the port of Narvik but Hitler struck first. On 9th April 1940, his forces invaded both Norway and Denmark on the pretext of saving them from British invasion. Denmark surrendered immediately; Norway was overrun only after fierce fighting. In encounters with both the British and the Norwegians the German navy paid a heavy price. The British and French troops, originally intended to aid the Finns, were the victims of faulty planning and hesitation. The British were certainly not trained nor equipped for action on this snow-bound terrain. Their evacuation followed.

Hitler's military victory was lessened by what followed in politics. First, the invasion of Denmark and Norway helped to weaken isolationist opinion in the USA, especially among Americans of Scandinavian descent. King Haakon of Norway and his socialist government declared war on Germany and carried on the fight from Britain. Second, Iceland declared itself independent of Denmark and asked for British protection. It was to serve the Allies well as an air base for the remainder of the war. Third, these events helped Hitler's great rival in Britain, Winston Churchill, to gain power. In a sense, this is remarkable, as the failed Norwegian campaign had been the brain-child of Churchill and his responsibility, as First Lord of the Admiralty.

Churchill's Government

The rapidly deteriorating situation in Norway in May 1940 led to a crisis of confidence in the government. In the Commons, on the second day of the debate on Norway (8th May 1940), Herbert Morrison (Labour) delivered a powerful attack on the government. Chamberlain regarded this as a matter of confidence and so a formal vote was taken. Although Chamberlain got his majority by 281 to 200, 60 of his normal supporters abstained and 41 voted against his government. He then attempted to draw Labour into a coalition. Their refusal sealed his fate and he resigned the day he got word from Labour's National Executive Committee meeting at Bournemouth, where the party was holding its annual conference. Lord Halifax was favoured as Prime Minister by many Conservatives and by the King, but he did not want the job.[27] Churchill then became the most credible candidate, and on 10th May a National Government was established, headed by Churchill, with members from all three parties. The inner War Cabinet comprised three Conservatives – Churchill, Chamberlain and Halifax – and Labour's Clement Attlee and Arthur Greenwood. Greenwood was removed in February 1942, at which time Attlee was appointed Deputy Prime Minister. He was the only member, apart from Churchill, to serve from the beginning to the end. Halifax was Foreign Secretary until December 1940, when Anthony Eden was appointed. Chamberlain served briefly, as he was terminally ill with cancer. His death gave Churchill the chance to take over as leader of the Conservative Party. The War Cabinet was later increased to eight. Of the non-Cabinet posts, fifteen were held by Conservatives, four by Labour and one went to the Liberals. In addition, a few non-party figures also held office. Churchill secured his role as war lord by styling himself Minister of Defence as well as Prime Minister. The three service ministers – A. V. Alexander (Labour) at the Admiralty, Archibald Sinclair (Liberal) at the Air Ministry and Eden (Conservative), succeeded in December 1940 by David Margesson and in turn by Sir John Grigg, at the War Office (Army) – were mere administrators, deprived of any say over policy. The Defence Committee met less and less. Two other Labour members served in the War Cabinet: Ernest Bevin, the leader of Britain's biggest trade union, joined in October 1940 as Minister of Labour and National Service; Herbert Morrison served as Home Secretary and Minister for Home Security from the beginning but was only promoted to the War Cabinet on 22 November 1942. Churchill also included the popular left-wing maverick Sir Stafford Cripps, thinking he was less dangerous in the government than outside it. Among the others in the War Cabinet was Churchill's friend Lord Beaverbrook, the proprietor of the *Daily Express*. He served from August 1940 to February 1942.

Dunkirk: 'Operation Dynamo'

As Britain was in the middle of its political crisis, Hitler's armies struck in the west, attacking Holland, Belgium and Luxembourg. Under General Guderian, German armoured columns made their way through the Ardennes, a thickly wooded area thought to be too difficult for tanks to negotiate, then swept towards the Channel ports. Anglo–French forces, which had gone forward from their defensive positions in France to help the Belgians and the Dutch, were in danger of being cut off. Their situation was made worse by the capitulation of the Dutch (14th May) and the Belgians (28th May). Poor co-ordination between the British and the French increased the difficulties, causing friction between the two allies. Some looting and summary executions of suspected 'fifth columnists' by the British gave the Nazis propaganda opportunities.[28] One other shameful aspect of the retreat was the treatment of Indian troops serving with the British Expeditionary Force (BEF). Their British officers were ordered to save themselves and abandon their Indian subordinates.[29] The British and other Allied forces fell back towards the coast and the British decided to use Dunkirk as a suitable evacuation point. Then, remarkably, the German armoured columns halted on 24th May, ten miles from the port. The Allies strengthened the defences. The British, however, started the evacuation of their troops, codenamed 'Operation Dynamo', on 26th May, apparently without informing their French ally.[30] Between then and 4th June, 338,226 servicemen, including 120,000 French and Belgians, reached safety. Every conceivable type of boat was used to get the troops out, but most were taken from the harbour by the Royal Navy and the French navy, not from the beaches by small boats. Good weather favoured the evacuation, as did the absence of the German navy. The *Luftwaffe*, the German air force, did strike with increasing ferocity, being held in check by RAF planes from bases in southern England.

Hitler's decision to halt his armoured forces facing the BEF saved it from being forced to surrender. Why he did this no one knows for certain. Perhaps he was influenced by his respect for Britain, expressed in his book *Mein Kampf* and elsewhere. A military consideration was that the armour could be cut off from the infantry by its rapid advance. Another was the need to refit the tanks for the campaign southwards into France.[31] Hitler was apparently suspicious that his success had been too easy. It is also argued that he wanted to give *Luftwaffe* chief, Hermann Göring, the chance to demonstrate what his men could do. The *Luftwaffe* was more influenced by the Nazis than the more traditional army.[32]

Churchill reluctantly agreed to the evacuation of 156,000 British and Polish troops from Cherbourg on 14th June. He had hoped they would help the French to continue resisting but was persuaded their safety required it after the crack 51st Division had been forced to surrender to General Rommel.[33]

Pétain: 'it is necessary to stop fighting'

The French fought on with their still considerable forces and with British troops still in France. French tanks were often superior to German *Panzerwagen* but they were badly deployed. The French had planes to match anything the Germans had, but not in sufficient numbers. French communications equipment was obsolete. Above all, as the British military theorist of that time, Basil Liddell Hart, explained, the French generals were the prisoners of out-of-date military doctrine. With each setback, their resolve weakened further.[34] General Weygand, military commander of the French, urged his government to seek an armistice. On 11th June, Churchill made the hazardous journey by air to Tours to confer with his French colleagues, in an effort to keep them in the war. The day before, Italy had declared war on France ignoring British and French attempts to bribe it into remaining neutral.

One thing Churchill did not do was to respond to French requests for more RAF squadrons to stem the German advance. Sir Hugh Dowding, Commander-in-Chief of RAF Fighter Command, persuaded him that they could not save France but would be needed to defend Britain. It was also argued that extra RAF squadrons could not have been accommodated and maintained at short notice in France. It is uncertain whether the decision not to send more British planes was right, though most historians believe it was. What is certain is that it embittered Anglo–French relations. It also played a part in tipping the scales in favour of the French seeking an armistice with Germany.

In an effort to keep the French in the war, Churchill made an imaginative proposal, put to him by General Charles de Gaulle, then a junior minister in the French government. This was for a Franco–British Federal Union. It was rejected by the French and a new government, under Marshal Pétain, hero of the 1914–18 war, took over on 16th June. Many in France thought this meant they would fight on. Instead, the Marshal told the French people, in a radio address on the following day, that 'it is necessary to stop fighting'. Many of his audience shed tears.[35] He sought an armistice and, on 22nd June, accepted the German terms, which included occupation of northern France and its Atlantic coast, as well as Paris. The mighty French fleet was to be disarmed and most of the army either ended up in captivity or was demobilised. France retained its vast overseas empire. The Marshal, who despised the republican France of the Third Republic, set up his new régime in the spa town of Vichy and began his collaboration with Hitler's Reich.

Churchill, obsessed with the possibility of the French fleet falling into German hands, ordered action to prevent this happening. Accordingly, a British force attacked the French fleet at anchor at Mer-el-Kebir, in Algeria, on 3rd July 1940. The attack caused heavy loss of life. The French had refused the options of making for a British port, heading for North America or scuttling themselves within six hours.[36] The British naval commanders in London believed the French assurances that they would not allow their fleet to be taken over by the Nazis. Churchill felt he could not take the risk. His action led to France breaking off diplomatic relations and soured Anglo–French relations down the decades after the war. On the other hand, Churchill's recognition of de Gaulle's Free French movement helped in the postwar rebirth of French democracy.

Channel Islands: 'bombs . . . on defenceless town'

The three small Channel Islands – Guernsey, Jersey and Alderney – were occupied by the Germans on 30th June, 1st and 2nd July respectively. There had been indecision and confusion about evacuating the inhabitants and panic spread among them. In the end, 17,000 of the 42,000 on Guernsey and 6,600 of the 50,000 from Jersey left.[37] Only 200 of the 1,100 on Alderney were left.[38] Although the British announced that the islands had been demilitarised, they suffered several air attacks before the invasion. In one raid, 44 islanders were killed, with another 30 injured.[39] Apparently the Germans had difficulty believing that the islands had been left undefended. Yet they had mounted several reconnaissance flights previously. On 28th June they bombed indiscriminately, dropping 180 bombs on the two main islands in less than an hour. Eye-witness Douglas Ord saw six planes 'with guns blazing and bombs falling on the defenceless town and harbour' of St Peter Port.[40]

Most of the inhabitants left behind tried to carry on as before, but, as elsewhere, there were informers and collaborators. The German military behaved in a relatively civilised way towards the inhabitants. However, the Gestapo deported a few to prisons or concentration camps for breaking German regulations or for resistance activity. About 2,000 residents who were British subjects not born on the islands were deported to internment camps in Germany.[41] The islanders had to wait to the very end of the war for their peaceful liberation. For obvious reasons, the capture of the islands was not given much publicity in Britain.

On the British mainland, fear of invasion mounted. Even before the fall of the Channel Islands, Eden, the Minister of War, broadcast an appeal for Local Defence Volunteers, between the ages of sixteen and 65. Six days later, 250,000 had been enrolled – a remarkable response. They were later known as the Home Guard. Lacking, at first, uniforms, arms and equipment, they were supposed to relieve the front-line troops. Few believed they could have made much difference had the Germans landed in 1940.

Hitler's Call 'to reason' Rejected

According to Liddell Hart, Hitler had no plans to invade Britain because he was counting on the British government's agreement to a compromise peace, on the favourable terms he was disposed to grant.[42] On 22nd June, he ordered the demobilisation of 35 divisions. In secret messages to both sides, the Pope offered to act as mediator in peace negotiations and the King of Sweden urged Britain to seek a settlement. Americans, such as Ambassador Kennedy, worked in the same direction. On the evening of 19th July, Hitler made his final peace offer to Britain in a public address. William Shirer, then an American correspondent in Germany, felt it was 'moderate in tone, considering the glittering circumstances'. Hitler made no specific proposals, he simply appealed 'to reason and common sense in Great Britain as much as elsewhere'.[43] Churchill later responded (3rd August) with deliberately unacceptable conditions. The War Cabinet had already discussed the question of possible negotiations on 27th May, even before the Dunkirk evacuation. Halifax and Chamberlain favoured such a move, using Mussolini as intermediary. Even Churchill considered that, if Hitler were prepared to agree peace in exchange for the return of German colonies and overlordship in central Europe, 'That was one thing'. He thought Hitler was unlikely to make any such offer. Attlee and Greenwood opposed any compromise. The following day, Churchill swung firmly against negotiations. He was backed by the whole government.[44] However, the appeasers in the government (Halifax and R. A. Butler) kept open communications with the enemy through Sweden, in case Churchill changed his mind.[45] In the Commons the ILP tabled a motion in December 1940 calling for a compromise peace. It was defeated by 341 votes to four.

The decision to soldier on against Nazi Germany was perhaps Britain's greatest contribution to the satisfactory outcome of the Second World War. Britain was virtually alone and was rapidly using up its resources. Had Britain decided otherwise, the isolationist forces in the USA would have won. Europe would have remained under Nazi domination for many years to come.

Eire's 'Emergency'

On the day Britain declared war on Germany, two British seaplanes landed separately in Southern Ireland's waters. Their pilots claimed bad weather had forced them off course and they were allowed to head for home. The Irish took the outbreak of the war in a leisurely fashion. Partly because de Valera had announced that his state would remain neutral in any conflict, his Fianna Fáil government had secured a renewed mandate in 1937. He was not sympathetic to Nazism or Fascism. He had condemned Italian aggression in Ethiopia in 1935, and had supported the League of Nations' non-intervention policy in Spain when many of his countrymen had sympathised with Franco. He believed a pro-British stance would damage the fragile political stability in Eire. A further complication was that Eire claimed the whole of the island of Ireland, not just the south, which made it difficult to be allied with the 'occupiers' of part of the national territory. Nevertheless, de Valera let the Germans know that Eire's neutrality incorporated a 'certain consideration' for Britain. At first, most Irish people opposed Germany, if only because it had a pact with the Soviet Union and had attacked Catholic Poland. Later, with Italy and Vichy France siding with Germany against Stalin, there was less opposition to Germany. In Fine Gael, the descendant of the pro-1921 Treaty party, there was more sympathy for the Allies. De Valera condemned the invasion of the neutral Low Countries and declared a state of emergency on 7th June 1940. The parties formed

a common front on defence issues but a national unity government was not formed.

There were some in Britain who regarded the Irish as 'traitors',
and many who thought they were profiting from the war. However, Eire did not have an easy war. It had to spend its limited
funds on building up its defence forces. And it suffered severely from lack of industrial raw materials, which had to be
imported. Coal, electricity, gas and petrol were among many items
rationed. The rail system was reduced to a skeleton service. By
1943 only 16 per cent of normal gas and coal requirements
were available and 20 per cent of petrol.

The Germans planned to invade Ireland, helped by an IRA-
led rising. Aware of this possibility, de Valera moved against the
IRA. Firing squads dispatched six of its agents, three were allowed
to die on hunger strike and around 600 were interned. German
planes were met by anti-aircraft fire when, by accident, they bombed
the South, killing some civilians. De Valera pursued a pro-British
policy (which also helped Eire) by exporting labour and goods
to Britain. In August 1944, there were 165,000 next-of-kin Irish
addresses in the British forces.[46] Crucial weather forecasting was
sent to London daily. De Valera's military advisor, General Dan
McKenna, consulted with General Sir Harold E. Franklyn,
Commander-in-Chief Northern Ireland. Franklyn met de Valera
in the summer of 1941.

In the 1943 election, because of discontent over wartime shortages, Fianna Fáil lost ground to Labour and the new farmers'
party. De Valera carried on until May 1944, when he held a
'snap' election. Aided by American demands that Axis diplomats be removed from Dublin, which he rejected, de Valera
improved his position. Perhaps his only mistake was calling on
the German Minister to express his condolences, on the death
of Hitler, in 1945.

Detained

The collapse of Britain's allies in 1940 was believed to be, in
part, due to enemy agents disguised as local police or military,
who ordered surrenders. These included traitors sympathetic
to Germany. The press fuelled the fears and the government

felt forced to act. In May 1940, Mosley, his wife, Captain A. Ramsay, MP, and some other right-wingers, were interned. Mosley was released by Herbert Morrison, amid widespread opposition, on health grounds, in November 1943. Ramsay was detained until September 1944. Some others remained in custody until the end of the war. Morrison was also responsible for the controversial decision, in 1940, to ban the Communist *Daily Worker* and *The Week*. They had consistently followed the Moscow anti-war line.[47] Other Communist publications, such as the so-called *Labour Monthly*, were not banned. The ban on the *Daily Worker* was lifted after the German attack on the Soviet Union. Prominent British Nazi William Joyce, nicknamed 'Lord Haw-Haw', could not be apprehended. Millions listened to his propaganda broadcasts from Berlin.[48]

At the urging of the War Office, MI5, and such newspapers as the *Daily Mail*, the government decided on the mass internment of 'enemy aliens' in May and June 1940. This eventually involved all males aged between 16 and 70 and many females. Many internees were sent to the Isle of Man. Largely because of the speed of the operation, conditions to begin with were very poor. Hauled in were a few Nazi sympathisers, more non-political aliens and thousands of anti-Nazi refugees, many of them Jewish. Several thousand Italians were also interned. There was a good deal of criticism of these measures and in July 1940 it was announced that many categories were to be released. Thousands subsequently helped the Allied cause, either in uniform or on scientific or other work. Some were not so lucky. Churchill wanted enemy aliens removed from Britain to other parts of the British Empire. More than 700 died when a German submarine sank the *Arandora Star* on 2nd July 1940, on the way to Canada. Others, on the overcrowded troopship *Dunera*, were treated very badly by their guards on the crossing to Australia. This was later condemned in Parliament and punishment followed action by military courts.[49]

The *Dunera* incident revealed the prejudice against Jews, Italians and 'Central Europeans' in Britain. The POWs on board were treated with consideration. The arrival of Irish, black workers and troops, and other foreigners in Britain also caused tensions. Thousands of citizens of Eire volunteered for the British armed forces and thousands more worked in civilian jobs. The government was glad to have them, despite a small number of IRA bomb attacks. A number of West Indians were recruited as munitions workers or by the RAF, and a few British Hondurans went to Scotland as forestry workers. They suffered from various kinds of prejudice. The West Indian cricketer, Learie (later Sir Learie) Constantine, was employed as a welfare officer for West Indians in the North West. On official business, he was forced to leave the Imperial Hotel, Russell Square, London, because of the alleged sensitivities of white Americans staying there.[50] The American servicemen who fought for freedom did so in segregated units!

Among the women from the Empire who fought for Britain was Noor Inayat Khan, who served as a secret agent in France until she fell into the hands of the Gestapo. She was killed in the concentration camp at Dachau.

Battle of Britain

Hitler reluctantly ordered his commanders to plan 'Operation Sealion', a plan to invade Britain, should 'reason' fail. The attempt was flawed because Germany lacked naval supremacy and, in any case, needed to gain air supremacy. Göring was ordered to achieve this. He launched his machines against Britain, the main thrust – the Battle of Britain – being between 15th August and 15th September. Despite its apparent successes so far, the *Luftwaffe* was weaker than generally supposed. Its bombers could only operate with fighter escorts and carried a relatively light load. Fighters and bombers could remain over enemy territory for very limited periods. British radar and air-to-ground communications were ahead of those of the Germans. The British had inside information as to German intentions through use of a stolen German Ultra coding machine. The Observer Corps took up where radar left off, in that its members, waiting in forward positions, tried to count the enemy formations and types of planes (something radar was unable to do) and telephoned the information to HQ. At the heart of the British effort was Dowding's Operations Room at Bentley Priory. From there, he directed the squadrons of Fighter Command. This enabled Dowding to make the best use of his limited resources of men and materials.

At the start of the battle, he had 1,456 pilots, of whom 1,259 were usually available for service. Of the pilots, a small number of volunteers came from others branches of the armed services, from Australia, Canada, New Zealand, South Africa, France, Belgium, Holland, the USA and, above all, from Poland and Czechoslovakia. Despite these factors working in favour of the defence, the German attacks were taking a heavy toll, grinding down the capacities of the RAF. Then, on 7th September, the German onslaught was switched from attacking airfields to bombing London. Some sources say this was an accident; the German planes were off course.[51] The incident caused Churchill to order an attack on Berlin. That, in turn, led Hitler to launch full-scale attacks on British towns and cities.

By 17th September, Hitler had stood down the invasion fleet which had been built up to attack Britain and was turning his attention to the Soviet Union. The air attacks continued, however, on both sides. The 'Blitz' (lightning), as the heavy bombing raids became known, started properly on 14th November 1940, with a murderous attack on Coventry. They continued until the invasion of the Soviet Union in June the following year. Most big cities – Belfast, Birmingham, Bristol, Glasgow, Leeds, Liverpool, Manchester, Nottingham, Portsmouth, Sheffield, Southampton – as well as London and smaller towns were hit.

No official figures of casualties taken by the RAF and the German air force can be given; both sides suffered heavily. The German General Werner Kneipe summed up the significance of the Battle of Britain for the *Luftwaffe*; it was 'bled almost to death and suffered losses which could never again be made good throughout the course of the war'.[52] Some 30,000 civilians were killed by German air raids on Britain during the Blitz, millions lost their homes.[53] Far more casualties had been expected.

Defeats in Greece and North Africa

As the months slipped by and Hitler's invasion did not take place, British morale lifted a little and 1940 ended with notable British victories over larger Italian forces in Cyrenaica (Libya). If British cinema audiences did not know quite where that was, they were at least pleased with the pictures of 130,000

Italian prisoners. They were to be disappointed by other news. A pro-British coup in Yugoslavia (March 1941) scaled that country's fate and it fell to German invaders within a week in April. At the same time, German troops were swarming into Greece, which capitulated on 24th April. The British Empire forces, who had gone to the aid of the Greeks, faced another forced evacuation, losing all their equipment. Also in April came major reverses for Britain in the North African desert. General Erwin Rommel's bold armoured stroke reversed the earlier British gains against the Italians. In a daring airborne assault, the Germans captured the Greek island of Crete in May. Once again British Empire troops had to be hastily evacuated with heavy losses. The British commander, General Sir Bernard Freyberg, had failed to take effective measures to defend the airfields. This omission and the lack of air power lost Britain this strategically important island.

Against the Italians, Vichy French and Iraqis, the British were more successful. They rolled up Mussolini's short-lived empire in Abyssina and Somaliland in March and, with Free French units, forced the Vichy French to surrender in Syria in July. A pro-Axis regime in Iraq was overthrown in early June. By this time, Hitler was losing his interest in the Middle East and unleashing the dogs of war on Stalin's empire.

4 From European War to World War and Victory, 1941–45

'A marvellous morning'

'A marvellous morning, with the smell of roses and hay and spring in the air . . . the 7 o'clock news announced that Germany had invaded Russia . . . Most people in England will be delighted.' That was from Harold Nicolson's diary entry for 22nd June 1941. Nicolson was not very happy at the prospects: '80 per cent of the War Office experts think that Russia will be knocked out in ten days.' He feared Hitler would get Russian oil and be free to 'fling his whole force against us'.[1]

Most ordinary people shared the experts' scepticism about the Red Army. However, their mood changed as the Russians went on fighting and proved to be more resilient than the French and other British allies, up to that date. In a memorable broadcast, on the day of the attack, Churchill, who had warned Stalin to no avail, offered the Russians an alliance and thus set the pace in transforming public sentiment towards the Soviet Union. The British Communists lost no time in making one of their greatest political somersaults, turning from revolutionary defeatists to thorough-going patriots, the scourge of strikers, and fanatical enemies of anything which threatened to hold up the war effort.

With the USA still not in the war, the British were desperate for any ally and any news of resistance to the Nazis. Most people had no idea of the geography of the Soviet Union and, therefore, no idea of the vast area soon overrun by Hitler's *Wehrmacht*. Nazi claims, largely true, of Soviet losses sounded fantastic and could be dismissed as propaganda. Some people tried to bolster morale by claiming that Soviet retreats were simply part of a clever plan to draw the Germans deep into the country, where they could be more easily destroyed. In fact, the lack of roads in the Soviet Union and the severe weather probably played a significant role in saving Stalin from defeat, as did Nazi racist treatment of the Soviet peoples and their atrocities against them. *Picture Post*, the popular weekly, and other publications, reminded their readers of the fate of Napoleon's armies in Russia in 1812. By December, the Germans stood before Moscow. They got no farther. A Soviet counter-offensive pushed the invaders back, causing the *Wehrmacht* its first major reverse.

In 1942, the Germans renewed their offensive in Russia, making headway in the south. The world held its breath as the Russians held on in Stalingrad, an important industrial and communications centre, but psychologically far more important because of its name. The siege went on for months, ending in the surrender of what was left of the German Sixth Army, with its commander Field Marshal Paulus. Pictures of Paulus and his defeated men went around the world. After a heroic defence and martyrdom, Leningrad was saved. Interest in the Soviet Union soared. As Margaret Thatcher later wrote about life in provincial Grantham, 'Anglo–Soviet friendship groups sprouted. We attended, not without some unease, Anglo–Soviet evenings held in the town hall. It was the accounts of the suffering and bravery of the Russians at Stalingrad in 1942–3, which had most impact on us.'[2] Communist Party membership in Britain reached an all-time peak. People began to ask why it was that experts had been wrong in their estimates of Poland, France and other British allies. They were servants of a system, the British system, which was not doing too well against the Nazis or their Japanese allies. Could it be that we had something to learn from the Soviets?

Waiting for Uncle Sam

From the moment he became Prime Minister in May 1940, Churchill was looking for ways of winning the Americans over for the fight against Nazi Germany. It is often not appreciated that without US assistance, Britain could not have remained at war with Germany. The deficit on the balance of payments leapt from £70 million in 1938 to £250 million in 1939, £804 million in 1940 and £816 million in 1941. The US Ambassador in London, Joseph Kennedy, father of the future president, was no help. He had no belief in Britain's ability to survive. Within the USA, there were many, like Kennedy, of Irish descent, who were not keen to aid the oppressor (as they still saw England) of their old homeland. There were also significant numbers in America who saw Britain as an imperial power and therefore not worthy of help. Others felt the USA had been hoodwinked into joining the 1914–18 war by arms manufacturers and other dark forces, who benefited from war. American Communists (until June 1941) and pro-Nazis wanted to keep America out of the war, as did some Italian–Americans. However, Roosevelt did not believe it could be in America's interest to allow Britain to be overpowered by Nazi Germany. At the same time, he was aware of the need to get re-elected. In September 1940, he authorised the transfer of 50 First World War destroyers to Britain in exchange for 99-year leases on eight British bases in the Western Hemisphere. Roosevelt faced election on 5th November 1940, when, by convention, after two terms, he should have stepped down. Roosevelt's opponent, Wendell Wilkie, agreed with him on all aid to Britain 'short of war', but both also promised to keep the USA out of the European conflict.

After his re-election, Roosevelt got Congress to agree, early in 1941, to Lend-Lease. This authorised the sale, loan, lease, transfer or exchange of war materials to any country whose defence the President considered vital to the defence of the USA. Britain was the first recipient. From June 1941 the Soviet Union too received aid, along with 30 other states. Such aid was vital to British survival and later Soviet successes. In April and July respectively, the USA occupied Greenland and Iceland to increase control of the Atlantic. In June, German and Italian assets in the USA were frozen. Japanese assets were frozen in July. After a German submarine sank the US destroyer *Reuben James* (30th October 1941), Roosevelt issued his 'shoot on sight' order to naval commanders, concerning Axis submarines in American defence waters, which he extended across the Atlantic. This measure halved the distance the Royal Navy had to convoy merchant ships.

At the first of their nine meetings, Roosevelt and Churchill agreed the eight-point Atlantic Charter on 14th August 1941. It was controversial in a number of respects. First, it appeared to many to be an alliance, at a time when the USA was not at war. Second, it committed the two powers to ensuring that there would be no territorial transfers without the consent of the people involved. Third, all peoples had the right to choose their own form of government. Fourth, they would endeavour to ensure that all states, 'victor and vanquished', had access, on equal terms, to the trade and raw materials of the world. They also mentioned, as an object, 'improved labour standards, economic advancement, and social security'. Freedom of the seas was another objective, as were the abandonment of the use of force, and freedom from want and fear. Churchill later argued (9th September 1941) that he had in mind only the peoples of Europe when he agreed the Charter, not those of the British Empire and the other colonies. Roosevelt and Attlee (who was not there) took it to mean all peoples everywhere.[3] It helped to open the way to de-colonisation.

'beastly little monkeys'

On 15th February 1942 the British surrendered Singapore to the Japanese. The British defeat shattered forever the myth of European superiority. A great deal of parliamentary time and public money had been lavished on the base at Singapore in the interwar period. Its heavy naval guns were useless against the Japanese, who attacked from the rear, cutting off the water supply. Lack of air power was another key factor in the British defeat. Undoubtedly, complacency was another. Many British and Americans saw the Japanese as racially inferior beings who could scarcely be regarded as a match for European forces. Sir Alexander Cadogan, Permanent Under Secretary at the Foreign Office, referred to the Japanese in his diary as 'beastly little monkeys', and in January 1942 *Punch*, the weekly satirical magazine, depicted the Japanese troops as monkeys, swinging from tree to tree in the jungles of Malaya.[4] What is difficult to understand, even allowing for a different military code, was the shabby way the Japanese treated their prisoners, even denying them Red Cross parcels and medical aid, and clothing from the masses of material they had captured. Thousands of prisoners died.

The Japanese achieved notable successes at sea as well. Two of the Royal Navy's big ships, *Prince of Wales* and *Repulse*, sent to reinforce Singapore and operating without air power, were sunk, for the loss of only three Japanese planes. Escorting destroyers managed to save over 2,000 out of their crews of 2,800. The Japanese fleet also scored an impressive victory over a combined British–US–Dutch squadron in the Battle of the Java Sea.

Having taken over French Indo-China in July 1941, the Japanese launched attacks on Hong Kong, Burma, Malaya – all British – and the Philippines in December 1941. The Dutch East Indies (Indonesia) fell shortly afterwards. Their first attack, however, was on the US naval base at Pearl Harbor on 7th December 1941. Their aim was to neutralise American sea power, and thus enable them to seize the colonies, rich in natural and human resources, of the European powers already brought to their knees by Hitler. In military terms, their victories were as cleverly staged as anything done by the Germans. The Japanese moves followed the imposition of an oil embargo by the USA, which was backed by Britain and the Dutch. Lacking raw materials, the Japanese feared their economy would soon crumble. Roosevelt had banned exports of oil to Japan in an effort to halt Japanese aggression against China and to force them to withdraw from French Indo-China (Vietnam, Cambodia and Laos).

Roosevelt's response to the Japanese attack was to declare war on Japan. In a supremely foolish move, Hitler declared war on the USA, thus allying them both to Britain and the Soviet Union.

'Quit India'

The India Act of 1935 had done little to assuage the demands of politically orientated Indians for independence. Unlike Gandhi, most of the Indian Congress leaders were not pacifists. They would have been ready to urge their followers to support Britain in the war effort if they could have secured agreement with Churchill over independence. He remained resolutely opposed to it. He maintained this position until he was forced, by Japanese advances, the Americans, Chinese leader Chiang Kai-shek and his Labour colleagues, to think again.

In March 1942 Churchill sent Sir Stafford Cripps, a socialist with many contacts among the Congress leadership, to make an offer. This amounted to 'dominion status' for India – *after* the defeat of Japan. The Indians were divided. On the one hand, the considerable Communist Party supported the British war effort after the German attack on the Soviet Union. The Muslim League, led by Mohammed Ali Jinnah, was suspicious of Congress and inclined to assist the British. On the other hand, abroad, the powerful figure of Subhas Bose was enlisting German and Japanese support for a rebellion in India against the British. No one could be certain how much support this charismatic leader had.

Gandhi rejected Cripps' offer with the jibe that it was a post-dated cheque drawn on a failing bank! Jawaharlal Nehru – next to Gandhi, one of the most important figures in India at that time – was far more sympathetic. The negotiations appeared to be succeeding after Cripps offered the Indians a quasi-government under the Viceroy, in which the Indians would hold all portfolios, except foreign affairs and defence. London repudiated this under pressure from the Viceroy, Lord Linlithgow. In any case, on the Conservative benches in the Commons many were worried. Major-General Sir Alfred Knox, on 30th July 1942, asked Leo Amery, Secretary of State for India and Burma, to remember that 'we have hundreds of millions of British capital invested in India'. On 8th August 1942 Congress accepted Gandhi's 'Quit India' resolution, calling on the British to leave India immediately. The British then swooped, arresting Gandhi, Nehru and thousands of other Congress leaders throughout the land. Thousands of Indians took to the streets, hundreds of police stations and post offices were burnt down, and trains were derailed. The Viceroy wrote to Churchill calling it the worst rebellion since 1857.[5] The British responded with their traditional weapons – internment, the cane, the gun and the gallows. Answering questions in the Commons, on 8th October 1942, Amery reported, 'Mobs were machine-gunned from the air on 15th, 16th, 21st an 22nd August and 6th September'. Casualties were 'believed to be light'. On 23rd September 1943, Amery told the Commons that between August 1942 and June 1943 73 death sentences had been passed in connection with the disturbances, of which 39 had been confirmed. In the same period, 2,401 caning sentences had been passed. Emmanuel Shinwell, 8th October 1942, questioned the machine-gunning, 'Is that not something which is not in accordance with our practice?' A few Labour MPs continued to press the government on India.[6] Both Roosevelt and his Republican opponent in the 1940 election, Wendell Wilkie, were strongly critical of British rule in India.[7]

'Token Payment' Needed

It was just after the fall of Singapore that the British government lost its first by-election, at Grantham on 25th March 1942. The Conservative candidate, unopposed by Labour, Liberal and Communist parties, in line with the wartime political truce, was defeated by an independent, Denis Kendall, an industrial manager, who fought a populist campaign. As Grantham native Margaret Thatcher later recalled, the complacent Conservatives did not expect it.[8] Other Conservative defeats followed at Rugby and Wallasey on 29th April. Both successful independents had connections with the local Labour and trade union movements. On 25th June another Conservative seat fell to an independent, this time at Maldon. The successful candidate was the left-wing journalist, Tom Driberg. His victory came five days after the defeat of British forces at Tobruk, at the hands of Rommel. Over 35,000 British and South African troops had been forced to surrender.[9] The news broke while Churchill was in Washington, and was another blow to his prestige.

On his return, Churchill faced a vote of no confidence on 2nd July 1942 in the Commons, something which had not happened to the Prime Minister in the First World War. He survived by 476 to 25, with some 30 deliberate abstentions. Among the 25 were the ILPs, the ex-War Minister, Leslie Hore-Belisha, the newly elected independent, W. J. Brown (Rugby), the future Liberal leader Clement Davies, Admiral of the Fleet Sir R. Keyes and Nye Bevan. The Communist William Gallacher voted for Churchill. MPs from all parts of the House voiced criticism but voted for the government.

Churchill had survived and he had also outmanoeuvred Cripps, Leader of the House, who was seen by some as a possible successor. A brilliant lawyer and former ambassador to Moscow, Cripps had been expelled from the Labour Party in 1939 for his continued advocacy of a popular front with the Communists. He resigned from the government, being replaced by Eden, who remained Foreign Secretary.

After the Rugby and Wallasey by-elections, Professor Harold Laski wrote a confidential memorandum (3rd May 1942) to Labour's National Executive Committee (NEC), of which he was a member, warning that independent victories could undermine the party system and therefore democracy. He called for Labour to appeal to Churchill for a 'token payment', some immediate social gains, to help stop the rot.

In 1943, opposition to the government took on a more organised form with the appearance of Sir Richard Acland's Common Wealth Party. It only campaigned against 'reactionary' candidates. With its openly socialist, but non-Marxist, programme it fought nine by-elections, winning three of them – in April 1943, January 1944 and April 1945 – and got decent votes at other by-elections. The Conservatives lost two other seats to independents, in 1944 and 1945, and their ally, the Ulster Unionist Party, lost West Belfast to the Eire Labour candidate on 9th February 1943. Labour only lost one by-election during the war and that was to the left-leaning Scottish National candidate at Motherwell, on 12th April 1945. Clearly, Britain was swinging to the left. The Parliamentary Labour Party read the writing on the wall and tried to put itself at the head of this movement heading left.

Beveridge's Report

Sir William Beveridge's *Report on Social Insurance and Allied Services*, in November 1942, recommended comprehensive public protection for all individuals and families, 'from the cradle to the grave', against the 'giants': sickness, poverty, unemployment, squalor and ignorance. Given the experience of the 1930s, it appeared a utopian scheme, but a necessary one. Churchill was not prepared to implement any legislation incorporating any of the Report's proposals during the war. He wanted any action to be left to a newly elected postwar government. Public opinion polls indicated that the majority of people in the country were disappointed with the government on this issue, feeling that vested interests had won once again.

In December 1941, 42 Labour MPs voted for an amendment recommending the nationalisation of coal and transport. In July 1942, Labour rebels gained a vote of 63 in a debate on old age pensions. On 16th February 1943, all but two Labour backbenchers voted against the government, and therefore their own leaders, and in favour of the immediate implementation of the Beveridge Report. They were defeated by 338 to 121: the latter included 97 Labour, three ILP, one Communist, eleven independents and nine Liberals.

The ordinary voters were disappointed on other counts too. The rations had to be cut and coal, used in most homes for fuel, was scarce. Inside the Labour camp, many in the rank and file began to feel their leaders were achieving nothing in the coalition. The Labour ministers had vigorously promoted reform within the government. Greenwood pressed for education reform, which later bore fruit in the shape of the Butler Education Act, and it was pressure from the TUC that secured the setting up of the Beveridge Committee in July 1941.[10]

Women at War

The only occasion when Churchill's government was defeated on a major issue was an amendment to the Education Bill in March 1944, which proposed equal pay for women teachers. This was carried by 117 votes to 116, but was overturned the following day on Churchill's orders.[11]

As in the First World War, women increasingly replaced men in a wide variety of trades and professions, in factories, on farms and in the services. The schools were denuded of male teachers and in agriculture the Women's Land Army played a major role. In industry, women took on many engineering jobs; one in three engineering workers was a woman at the height of the war.[12] If the work was hard, it was often regarded as liberating, giving women incomes of their own, new experiences and friendships. Many women entered the civil service and other white-collar occupations. Women made their appearance in the postal services and on the railways. They were recruited as 'auxiliaries' in the three armed services, performing mainly domestic, administrative and maintenance work, and staffed the medical services. A minority were key workers in radar units, air traffic control and in cypher work; others acted as spies in occupied Europe, or served in anti-aircraft batteries. Women of the Air Transport Auxiliary (ATA) flew unarmed military aircraft across the Atlantic, as well as within Britain. Amy Johnson, the pre-war record breaker, was the most famous casualty of the ATA. Other uniforms worn by women were those of the fire service, the police and the Women's Voluntary Service. Women were not sent directly to fight, as in the Soviet Union, nor down the mines.

At first there was no conscription of women, as there was of men. It was hoped more women would respond to calls to take up essential work. However, they did not volunteer in the numbers required. Some would have done so, had they been able to combine their domestic commitments with work outside the home. Many men objected to women going to work outside the home, a fact that also helped to stem the flow. Some women felt that taking up factory work or joining the services was stepping down in social terms.[13] By January 1942, conscription of single women aged 20 to 21 began. By contrast, men, single or married, aged between 18 and 51, could be called up.

By September 1943 there were 470,000 women in the armed forces.[14] In Germany, with a somewhat larger population, 470,500 women were employed by the armed services (they were not officially members).[15] The part played by women in the RAF can be estimated from the fact that, by 1945, the air force had a total strength of 1,076,758, of whom some 141,529 were women.[16] In 1931 women made up 29.8 per cent of the total civilian occupied labour force. In 1943 the percentage was 38.8.[17] Clearly, many women still did not work outside the home. In Germany, in 1943, women made up 48.9 per cent of the total German civilian labour force, and in the USA 34.1 per cent.[18]

At the last pre-war election, of 1935, only nine women were elected to Parliament – six Conservative, one Labour, one Liberal and one independent. Two of them, Ellen Wilkinson (Labour) and Florence Horsbrugh (Conservative) found their way into government. Wilkinson served as Parliamentary Secretary at Home Security, and Horsbrugh as Parliamentary Secretary to the Minister of Health. Despite the small numbers of women politicians, women must have contributed to the changing political climate. With so many men being away in the forces they must have been important as voters and activists, defeating Conservatives in by-elections.

Though one or two films, such as *Millions Like Us* (1943), depicted women in new and unglamorous roles, much emphasis was still placed on them as pin-ups, 'sex goddesses', and dutiful wives and helpmates for men. Two of the best-known women on radio were the singer Vera Lynn and the comic character 'Mrs Mop'. In 1943 MGM's *Cry Havoc* was a novelty among war stories having an all-female cast. It was a poorly executed drama about US nurses captured by the Japanese. The many Hollywood films often projected forceful female characters, played by Bette Davis, Joan Crawford, Gladys Cooper and Barbara Stanwyck, which, no doubt, helped to change ideas about the role of women. However, Ingrid Bergman, Greer Garson and very many others presented the traditional image. Whatever the merits of realistic films depicting contemporary problems, escapist films tended to be more popular.

'An absolutely, devastating, exterminating attack'

In May 1940 the War Cabinet, on the advice of the RAF, took the decision, apparently unanimously, to initiate a strategic air offensive against Germany. This had indeed been the policy of the RAF from the early 1920s. First, the decision was partly due to the fascination, of politicians and servicemen alike, with the most recent and technological of the three services.[19] Second, it was partly the result of drawing the wrong conclusions about the Spanish Civil War (1936–9), where there had been appalling bombing of major cities, but such bombing had had no *military* results. In that war, air forces had got the best results working closely with the land armies. Third, it resulted from the wish to avoid the crippling casualties of the 1914–18 war. It was based on the belief that the sinews of war, such as oil dumps and marshalling yards, could be easily identified and then easily destroyed, thus bringing the advancing armies to a halt. Later, it helped to relieve the frustration felt because British land forces had hardly any contact with the German land forces. At that time, Britain could not bomb Germany very effectively. It had not yet got the heavy bombers, the trained aircrews and other necessary equipment and it was always at the mercy of the weather. In that month, May 1940, a start was made with twin-engined Wellingtons, Whitleys and Hampdens, though it had to be interrupted because of other pressing needs, including the training of more aircrew to replace those shot down.

Just before the Battle of Britain began, Churchill wrote to Beaverbrook that the Nazis would be defeated by 'an absolutely, devastating, exterminating attack by very heavy bombers from this country on the Nazi homeland'.[20] Later, Churchill had certain doubts; his air chiefs did not. Air Chief Marshal Sir Charles Portal, Chief of the Air Staff, 1940–5, on 25th October 1940, prescribed two primary targets for Bomber Command: oil and morale. Behind this directive was the idea that the enemy civilian population would crack under the strain of massive bombing. The British population had not cracked in 1940, nor the Spanish before them. The attitude of the British air chiefs towards the Germans can only be described as one of racial superiority.[21] Even as early as November and December 1940, Berlin, Hamburg and other German towns were being hit; 'oil and morale' were the targets. Little damage was done, losses were heavy. It was later established that a bombing raid on Berlin in November 1941, which cost 120 aircrew, caused nine German deaths, 32 injuries and the destruction of 398 homes.[22]

In February 1942, the man who became most closely associated in the popular imagination with Bomber Command took over as its Commander-in-Chief, Air Chief Marshal Sir Arthur Harris. Harris got to work immediately with 'concentrated incendiarism'. The medieval towns of Lübeck and Rostock, which contained many wooden buildings, went up in flames. Harris was encouraged by these raids and pressed on, but was hampered by lack of aircraft, given the needs of the Battle of the Atlantic, the Middle East and the war with Japan.

The massed raids, which ultimately failed, met with some scepticism in the Commons. A considerable number of military MPs, like Major S. Furness, believed that if more attention had been given to RAF co-operation with the Army, the disasters of 1942

could have been avoided. To feed the air offensive, massive resources were being used which could have gone to the other
services. Another regular critic of the government, Labour's R.
R. Stokes, argued (19th May 1942), 'I have been through practically every raid on London . . . and I do not believe for a single
moment that you are going to destroy the morale of the people
by bombing from the air.' Such assessments did not deter
Churchill.

The raids continued, with targets both in Germany and in
occupied Europe. The US Eighth Air Force was also increasingly visible over the skies of Europe. At the Casablanca
Conference, 21st January 1943, Churchill and Roosevelt agreed
that the US Air Force should attack enemy targets by day and
the RAF would operate by night. Among the most spectacular
raids were those against Hamburg in July and August 1943. This
important port and industrial centre had been hit many times
before, but not on this scale. After several raids, approximately
44,600 civilians and about 800 German military personnel had
been killed. Over 37,000 were injured.[23] Most are believed to
have died in a firestorm caused by the second RAF raid. This
figure certainly includes some of the thousands of foreign workers
compelled to work in the city. A total of 552 British and Allied
airmen – mainly Canadians, Australians and New Zealanders –
were killed, 65 were taken prisoner and seven were interned in
Sweden. The Americans lost 46 servicemen, with 106 taken prisoner.[24] Though the civilian casualties and damage to buildings
were horrendous, the city was quickly operational again. Berlin
was subjected to massive attack from November 1943 to March
1944. Other German cities were also attacked repeatedly.

The raids on Germany were a race between attackers and
defenders to think out ever more sophisticated devices and tactics to beat each other. The British and Americans constantly
improved the range and quality of their planes. The Americans
introduced the P-51 Mustang, which could accompany the bombers as far as Berlin and back. The Germans improved their
defences and went over to the attack against Britain with their
'revenge' weapons, the V1 ('flying bombs') and V2 rockets. These
came into operation in July 1944 and briefly looked like a serious
threat to London. However, most of the launching sites were
soon overrun by the Allies, as were German fighter bases.

El Alamein and Operation Torch

The unfolding drama of the Russian front led to increasing calls for a 'Second Front' to ease the burdens of the Soviets. Stalin asked for one and Churchill promised one but it did not materialise. Partly to help the Russians and partly to secure the British-owned assets of the Anglo–Iranian Oil Company (against possible German attack), British and Soviet troops invaded neutral Iran in August 1941. They achieved their objectives within three days, with light casualties on both sides. The Soviets established a zone in the North, and the British likewise in the South. The centre around Tehran, the capital, remained unoccupied. The British, and later also the Americans, used the trans-Iranian railway to send supplies to the Soviet Union. Although little commented on then and since, the invasion strengthened Iranian suspicions of Britain and the Soviet Union/Russia, two states which had long records of interference in Iran.

As mentioned above, the British had done well against the Italians in North Africa, but had been outwitted by the dynamic General Rommel. He had achieved much with limited resources, but he fatally overstretched his forces. He was held at El Alamein, only 60 miles from the strategically important port of Alexandria, in May 1942. The British had superiority in tanks, guns, manpower and supplies. Under its new commander, General Bernard Montgomery, the British 8th Army built up its strength and launched its offensive on 23rd October. British Empire forces of 230,000 took on 80,000 Germans and Italians. Rommel had gambled and lost. His depleted forces were pressed back to Tunisia to await their final defeat. Churchill made much of the victory in the mass media and a widely shown, and dramatic, documentary film made it appear far more important than it was.

As a try-out of a possible cross-channel invasion, an Anglo–Canadian raid was made on Dieppe on 19th August 1942. It failed, with the majority of those taking part being either killed or captured. The next major assault on French territory was on 7th November, but this time it was a full-blown invasion of French North Africa, Morocco and Algeria. Unlike the British, the Americans still had relations with the pro-German, Vichy French régime and it was hoped they would not oppose the landings by the mainly US forces. Operation Torch, as the North African landings were known, was British inspired but American controlled. General Dwight D. Eisenhower had overall command and his appointment was symbolic of the relegation of Britain in the alliance. The Americans would have gone for establishing a bridgehead in France itself, but Churchill regarded this as impossible at that stage. He wanted a softer target, which would be certain of success; thus bringing political dividends to his hard-pressed government. It would also have the advantage of strengthening Britain's position in the Middle East at a time when that region was still important to the UK. For Roosevelt, it was meant to placate the voters in the Congressional elections but it came too late for that. Critics saw it as an unnecessary diversion, which ran the risk of bringing Anglo–American forces into serious conflict with the French.

Although the Americans had made every effort, by secret diplomacy, to achieve a peaceful landing, with the French forces having the option of joining the Allies, there was some fighting. But the landings were an excellent rehearsal for the later landings in France. One negative aspect of Operation Torch was the fact that Free French leader General de Gaulle had not been consulted about it. This helped to sow the seeds of future mistrust between him and the Anglo–Americans. Torch paved the way for the total expulsion of the Germans and Italians from North Africa, with the Americans linking up with Montgomery's drive from the west.

The next move by Anglo–American forces was the invasion of Sicily on 10th July 1943. Remarkably, they landed more troops there than they did in France eleven months later. There was little opposition, but the landing helped to convince the Italian king and ruling circles that Mussolini must be removed. This happened on 25th July, and after much delay and confusion on both sides, the British 8th Army, under Montgomery, was put ashore on the Italian mainland. Italy formally changed sides but Anglo–American progress was slow, with the Germans taking control of most of the country.

Battle of the Atlantic

German submarine activity proved to be a deadly weapon in the two world wars. In both wars it boomeranged, in that it helped to get the USA involved. In the two wars it very nearly proved disastrous for Britain. In the 1939–45 war, the situation was worse because Germany controlled continental Europe, which meant it could attack British (and other) shipping from many more bases. Yet the service which bore a major responsibility for overcoming this threat, coastal command, suffered from a paucity of aircraft and of trained crews.[25] It was another victim of the strategic bombing of Germany. Luckily, to begin with, the Germans did not have too many submarines. The advantage the Germans did have was that they had penetrated British naval codes. They also had an effective reconnaissance bomber, the Focke-Wulf Condor. The situation for the British got steadily worse until 1942–3. The Germans were building submarines faster than the Allies could sink them and they were better able to protect their own codes. Then, in 1943, British code breakers mastered the German codes again. In addition, the British introduced two new weapons, a high-frequency direction finding device which located submarines, and centrimetric radar, which was small enough to be used on planes and small naval vessels. The Americans contributed an air-launched torpedo with an acoustic homing head. This became operational in May 1943; in the same month Grand Admiral Dönitz, the German naval commander, called off the North Atlantic battle. The technological seesaw continued to the end of the war. The turn around in the Atlantic was of vital importance to keep Britain from starving and, indeed, keep it in the war. It enabled it to serve as an effective base for the massive US forces needed for D-Day, the start of the liberation of France.

D-Day

The experience gained by the Allies in Operation Torch and by the invasion of Italy was put to good use on 6th June 1944, D-Day, when 175,000 American, British, Canadian and Polish forces disembarked along the Normandy coast of France. The landing – Operation Overlord – was under the command of Eisenhower, with Britain's Bernard Montgomery in command of the ground forces. Montgomery did not exploit the initial success and the original targets were not reached. This was partly because of the traffic jam on the beaches, the obstacles the Allies created by their own bombing and their gross overestimate of the enemy forces opposing them.[26] The Germans were at first able to exploit the caution of the Allied commander, rush their available forces to the danger spots and thus hold up the Allied advance. Nevertheless, the inadequate German forces were overcome and the Allies reached Paris on 25th August. They took the Belgian capital, Brussels, on 3rd September. The Allied advance then stalled through lack of fuel, at a time when there was a 100-mile-wide gap in the German defences. Liddel Hart wrote: 'Rarely in any war has there been such an opportunity.' Although the Allies had an effective superiority of 20 to 1 in tanks and 25 to 1 in aircraft, the British push was further reduced at the crucial time because 1,400 British-built three-ton trucks, and all the replacements for this model, were found to have faulty pistons. Rivalry between Montgomery and his US colleagues was a constant problem.

In an effort to shorten the war by seizing the bridges over the rivers Maas, Waal and Rhine at Grave, Nijmegen and Arnhem, airdrops were made behind the German lines. The bridges were to be held until Allied troops, advancing overland, arrived. The drops – Operation Market Garden – were made on 17th September, but the British were dropped too far from their target at Arnhem, the Rhine bridge. Bad weather then hampered the flying in of reinforcements and supplies. Disregard of intelligence reports meant that the British 1st Airborne Brigade faced much greater resistance than anticipated. After bitter fighting the survivors attempted to reach Allied lines, with only 2,400 out of the original 10,000 managing to do so. This was Montgomery's plan and reckoned to be his only campaign failure.

That the Americans were not immune from making false assessments was exposed in December 1944, when Hitler made his last effort to turn the tide against the Allies. Using surprise, he attempted to repeat his 1940 success by, once again, attacking through the wooden Ardennes area, in the hope of throwing the Americans off balance and forcing a second Dunkirk-style withdrawal on the Allies. After initial success, aided by bad weather, which reduced Allied air activity, his offensive ran out of steam. The Allies then regained the initiative and advanced into Germany.

The Nazis Defeated

On 5th July 1943, five days before the Anglo–American landings in Sicily, the Battle of Kursk began. It was the biggest tank battle of the war and marked the final turning point in the east. Never again were the Germans able to challenge the Red Army. For the *Wehrmacht*, the long retreat began. By January 1944, Leningrad was freed from its 890-day siege. By the summer of 1944, the Soviets had forced Germany's allies Bulgaria, Finland and Romania to seek terms and then to join in the fight against their erstwhile ally. The Soviets took the Yugoslav capital, Belgrade, in October 1944. In January 1945 they took Warsaw and Budapest.

The Red Army's final offensive, to take Berlin, was planned for 20th January 1945, but it was brought forward by eight days to relieve the pressure caused by the Ardennes offensive in the west. The Soviets moved forward on a 755-mile route from the Baltic to the Carpathians. By 31st January, they had advanced almost 300 miles to the River Oder, the last natural barrier to Berlin. In the west, the US and British forces had recovered from the shock of the Ardennes offensive and launched their own thrusts. To the east and the west, the Germans were overwhelmed by the firepower and manpower of the anti-Hitler coalition.

In the air, the Allies gained total superiority. In the final stage of the war, their aim was to knock out enemy communications centres and fuel dumps. Operation Thunderclap was not part of this. It was part of the old 'area bombing' policy, designed to undermine enemy morale. In this case, Dresden, the Elbe metropolis, was the target. It was hit by British and US bombers in February 1945 in the most destructive raids of the war in Europe. Dresden's normal population of over 600,000 was swollen with refugees. Even Churchill had his doubts about the bombing of this fine old town, so late in the war. The defenders of the decision argued that Germany still appeared to have a lot of military and civilian reserves left. It is well to remember that at the time of the Dresden raid V2 rockets were falling on the London area. They killed few people.[27]

Knowing the end was near, Hitler killed himself on 30th April in his underground command centre in Berlin. Berlin was formally surrendered to the Red Army on 2nd May. The war in Germany finally came to an end on 7th–8th May, with the unconditional surrender of all German forces.

Yalta and Potsdam

The 'Big Three' Allied leaders – Churchill, Roosevelt and Stalin – met on a number of occasions during the war. This was quite remarkable, given the security, medical and other problems involved. Their foreign ministers also met. At Casablanca, in January 1943, Roosevelt and Churchill agreed that the war would continue until the 'unconditional surrender' of their enemies. Roosevelt and Churchill met again, this time with the Chinese leader Chiang Kai-shek, at Cairo in November 1943. There they agreed that any territory taken from China by Japan with 'violence and greed' would be restored to China and that Korea should regain its independence from Japan. Roosevelt dealt directly with Chiang, largely ignoring the British, bringing home to them the weakness of their position.[28] Roosevelt, Churchill and Stalin met together for the first time at Tehran, later in the same month. They agreed on what was to become Operation Overlord and discussed the future of Poland. Poland was to lose territory to the Soviet Union on the line proposed by British Foreign Secretary, Lord Curzon, in 1918 – roughly what Stalin had taken in 1939 – but was to gain compensation at German expense. Meeting in Moscow in October 1944, Churchill and Stalin agreed their respective degrees of influence in Bulgaria, Hungary, Romania, Greece and Yugoslavia. On 4th February 1945, the three leaders met again at Yalta in the Soviet Union. On the face of it, they committed themselves once again to the democratic proposal of the Atlantic Charter. They sealed the fate of Poland and agreed the division of Germany. Among the secret agreements was the commitment of the Soviet Union to attack Japan, in exchange for getting the Kurile Islands, a controlling position in Manchuria and certain other advantages. The final wartime meeting of the leaders of the USA, the Soviet Union and the UK was at Potsdam, outside Berlin, in July 1945. There the leaders confirmed their arrangements for dealing with Germany and agreed the prosecution of the war against Japan. The Soviet Union confirmed that it would join in this venture. Harry S. Truman had replaced Roosevelt, who had died suddenly on 12th April, and Churchill gave way to Attlee, after losing the election to Labour.

Labour's Victory

Attlee, Bevin and Dalton, and the Liberal leader Sir A. Sinclair, had wanted to continue the Churchill-led coalition but the Labour Party conference meeting at Blackpool rejected this.[29] The use of British troops to crush left-wing partisans in Greece (December/January 1944–5) was seen by many Labour activists as further evidence that the party leaders were duped by Churchill. In any case, most Conservative ministers favoured an immediate election, believing they would win.[30] On 21st May, Attlee offered to continue the coalition until October.[31] This was rejected by Churchill, who, after resigning as National Prime Minister on 23rd May, re-emerged as head of a largely Conservative caretaker government, which continued until 26th July. To some it looked like 'the "old gang" back with a vengeance'.[32]

On 5th July 1945 – a hot, summer day – most of Britain went to the polls in the first general election since 1935. Because of Wakes (holiday) weeks, some constituencies in northern England and parts of Scotland voted a week later. The Conservatives and Labour fought almost all constituencies, 618 and 603 respectively, the Liberals 306, the Communists 21, Common Wealth 23 and the ILP four. Labour won 48 per cent (38.1 in 1935), Conservatives 39.6 per cent (53.3), and Liberals 9 per cent (6.8). Labour returned 393 MPs, the Conservatives 213 and the Liberals twelve. In addition, on the left there were two Communists, one Labour independent (D. N. Pritt, who had sided with the Communists), one Common Wealth, three ILP and one Labour independent from Belfast. There were fourteen independents, at least some of whom, like C. V. O. Bartlett, were left of centre.

In Scotland and Wales, Nationalist candidates were defeated, but in Northern Ireland, two were elected.

The Labour victory came as a great surprise, particularly its scale.[33] Despite wartime by-elections and opinion polls, few thought Churchill could be defeated, and the Conservatives had placed much emphasis on him during the campaign. A myth grew up that Labour owed its great victory to the armed forces vote. Logically, many servicemen were the natural clientele of Labour, in that they were young and working class. In fact, a considerable number of them not being aged 21 or over, were not entitled to vote. Of the rest, less than 40 per cent voted. Some did not bother, many did not get the opportunity through the failure to get ballot papers to far-away garrisons.[34] Among the civilians, a fairly large number found they were not on any resister. This was due to the movement of population since 1935 and the inadequate organisation for drawing up new registers. Even though Churchill found he was one of those missed off the register, Labour and the other non-Conservatives were probably hurt more than the Conservatives by these factors. Thus, it seems likely that the actual vote underestimated the shift of opinion from right to left. Women and middle-class voters must have contributed more than some realised to the leftward swing. Many of the London suburbs – Barnet, Bexley, Chislehurst, Dulwich among them – swung left. The same happened in suburban constituencies outside other big towns. Some rural constituencies went Labour for the first time.

Why were the Conservatives defeated? First, it should be recalled that the drift to the left started before the war, as by-election results indicated. There was widespread feeling that the Conservatives had failed on the economy and believed in an unfair, inefficient and complacent society; that their party was the party of the stuffy, the smug and the well heeled. Second, less widespread, there was the belief that they had failed to prepare the country to meet the challenge of Nazi Germany and militarist Japan. Wartime reverses, such as Dunkirk and Singapore, strengthened this feeling. During the war years the media had discussed social issues more widely. To mobilise the masses, they had, in many cases, been encouraged to do so. British films such as *Love on the Dole, The Life and Death of Colonel Blimp, Millions Like Us* and many others, attacked the indifference, inefficiency, privilege, prejudice and even treachery of Britain's rulers. A series of often more impressive American films pointed in the same direction. The Conservative election campaign was not very effective, concentrating too much on Churchill and not enough on policy. Labour, by contrast, presented a team of well-known and respected leaders: Morrison, Bevin, Cripps, Dalton and Attlee, and seemed to have a well-thought-out strategy. Churchill was illiberal with his utterances, claiming in a broadcast that Labour would have to fall back on some sort of Gestapo to impose its policies.[35] This sounded incredible, because the public had got to know the Labour leaders. Attlee could not have looked more like the English gentleman that he was.

Japan Surrenders

Although the Americans had agreed to put the war against Nazi Germany first, they had gradually gained the upper hand in the war against Japan. They stormed one island after another across the Pacific towards the Japanese home islands. The capture of the Marianas, in the summer of 1944, gave the Americans the possibility of bombing Japan using the giant B29 Super-fortresses. They had bombed Tokyo before, in 1942, with great difficulty. Now they could do so with ease. It was soon decided that area bombing with incendiaries would be more effective than using high explosives. On 9th March 1945, 270 B29s destroyed roughly one quarter of Tokyo, with massive loss of life. Only fourteen US planes were lost. This then became the pattern in one Japanese city after another.

A government seeking peace had replaced the Japanese pro-war government. It sought the help of the Soviet Union, then still at peace with Japan, but the Soviets, for Stalin's own reasons, withheld this request from his allies for some time. In the meantime the atomic bomb had been perfected and President Truman decided to use it. He was persuaded by those who argued that its use would save the lives of millions on both sides. Japanese atrocities and fanaticism, including the use of Kamikaze suicide pilots, human torpedoes and suicide divers,[36] had convinced many Americans that the Japanese needed to be crushed. Truman did not accept the advice of atomic scientist

James Franck, who warned of a possible arms race if the bombs were used.

On 6th August, a B29 dropped a 20-kioton atomic bomb on Hiroshima. Of the 300,000 population, it is believed that, in an instant, 80,000 were killed and more than 35,000 injured. Many others died later. Of the 200 doctors in the city, 180 were killed or badly injured.[37] Three days afterwards, Nagasaki was hit. Of its 230,000 population nearly 40,000 died and about 25,000 were injured.[38] The surrender of Japan was announced the following day. By that time, with US and British agreement, Soviet units were deep into Japanese-held territory.

The war was over, but the new world of peace, co-operation and prosperity for all peoples, based on the United Nations, set up in 1945, and the nuclear deterrent, which would make large armed forces redundant, was not to be.

5 Britain under Attlee, 1945–51

In some respects, most British people seem to have had a fairly realistic view of Britain's postwar position in the summer of 1945. According to a Gallup poll, the USA was seen as the most influential country in world affairs by 38 per cent, followed by the Soviet Union (31 per cent) and Britain (14 per cent). In the same survey, 52 per cent thought that the atomic bomb would make war less likely in the future. A remarkable 51 per cent were prepared to see the abolition of national armies in favour of an international force.[1]

Attlee's Colleagues

The key figures in Attlee's Cabinet were Ernest Bevin (Foreign Secretary), Herbert Morrison (Lord President), Hugh Dalton (Chancellor of the Exchequer), Sir Stafford Cripps (Board of Trade), Lord Pethick-Lawrence (India and Burma) and Arthur Greenwood (Privy Seal). Ellen Wilkinson (Education) was the first woman Cabinet minister since Margaret Bondfield, in the Labour government of 1929.[2] All but two had experience of government. In terms of their education, for ten members, formal education had ended with elementary school only. This meant they had left school to start work at eleven or twelve years of age. From the age of eleven, Aneurin 'Nye' Bevan had worked long hours after school as a butcher's boy. He started full time in the Ty-Tryst colliery when he was thirteen. Of the others, four had gone from secondary schools to non-Oxbridge universities; one had gone from grammar school to Oxbridge; one went to London after public school and four were the products of public schools and Oxbridge. It was a Cabinet of great social contrasts and life experiences, as well as great personal rivalries. Yet it is doubtful whether any other peacetime Cabinet was made up of members with greater moral purpose.

American Loan

On VJ Day (Victory over Japan), 15th August 1945, Dalton recorded in his diary: 'I am conscious of having some mountainous problems in front of me, especially with "overseas financial liabilities"; Lend-Lease may be stopping any time now and the resulting gap will be terrific.' It did and it was! The blow came within a few days of the Japanese surrender. From the opposition benches, Churchill (29th August 1945) called it a 'rough and hard' decision. The British government found that it could not get a gift, which some expected, or even an interest-free loan. What John Maynard Keynes, the economist and leader of the British delegation which went to Washington, eventually negotiated was a smaller than expected ($3.75 billion) loan, repayable over 50 years. Britain had to agree to the convertibility of its currency within a specified period, a year after the loan agreement became operative, and to commit itself once again to freedom of trade and payments. This was opposed by some in the Labour Party, because they saw it as limiting the government's ability to plan the economy, and by some Conservatives as a further step to dismantling the British Empire. The truth was that the government had little choice. The Commons accepted the terms on 13th December 1945, by 345 in favour to 98, from both sides of the House, against, with many abstentions.

Britain had paid a heavy economic price for the war. By 1944, her exports only amounted to one-third of those of 1938. Export markets had been disrupted and, in some cases, native industries had replaced imports. Many British industries had been trailing behind the world leaders before the war, and in some cases had deteriorated further. Moreover, Britain had taken on costly new overseas responsibilities and had to maintain large armed forces. The gold and dollar reserves had been run down from $4,190 million to $1,409 million. By contrast, the loan amounted to $3,750 million at 2 per cent (which although low by today's standards, was then considered a fairly high rate). Canada agreed to lend another $1,250 million. The only bright spot was that the formidable economies of Germany and Japan were temporarily not competitors. British exporters had a golden opportunity, if they could find anyone who could afford their goods.

To many Americans the termination of Lend-Lease seemed appropriate, as the war was over. However, the difficulties in negotiating a loan were in part the result of hostility to Britain as an imperial power, or Britain as a 'socialist' state, or to Britain as the oppressor of Ireland. By all accounts, Attlee and his colleagues grossly overestimated the goodwill they, or Britain, enjoyed in America.[3]

Taking the Commanding Heights

A great deal of time, and more emotional energy, was expended on both sides of the political divide over the nationalisation of certain key industries. For socialists, inside and outside the Labour Party, this was one of the fundamental tests for Attlee's government. For them, it represented a step on the road to the abolition of capitalism. For the empiricists in the Labour ranks, as well as for most Liberals and even some Conservatives, nationalisation was a necessary measure to rescue ailing industries.[4] Churchill, as a Liberal, had acquired for the British government the controlling interest in the great Anglo–Iranian Oil Company in 1914. The Conservatives had nationalised the BBC in 1926 and the main airways in 1939. They set up the Central Electricity Board to regulate the central distribution of electricity in 1926. MacDonald's National Government had established the London Passenger Authority in 1933. In both world wars, the railways and mines had been taken over by the government for the duration. Labour now took over the Bank of England (1946), the mines (1946), the railways, road haulage, docks and inland waterways (1947), electricity (1947), gas (1948) and iron and steel (1949). With the possible exception of road haulage and steel, it seemed to most people a sensible and moderate programme. Most of the gas and electricity undertakings had been owned by local authorities and their nationalisation was seen as a rationalisation measure. The mines and the railways were vital to the economy and were in a bad way. It was unlikely that private investors would have been found to modernise them. The mines were, in any case, in a separate category because of the bitter conflicts, which had gone on for a hundred years. By 1945, manpower in the mines was lower than at any previous time in the twentieth century, but it was still over 700,000. The mining communities had a way of life all of their own and they had great significance for the Labour Party.

Although Labour had advocated economic planning before 1945, little was attempted in office. For six weeks in 1947, Cripps headed a Ministry of Economic Affairs with its own planning staff, which disappeared when he became Chancellor later in the same year.

British Raj Ends

Once the war with Germany had ended the Viceroy of India, Lord Wavell, who had replaced Lord Linlithgow in October 1943, made another attempt to come to terms with the Indian leaders. At the Simla conference in June 1945, he offered a constituent assembly and an interim government in which the Indians would hold all portfolios. Only the Commander-in-Chief would remain British and he would also be in the government. Neither the Congress nor the Muslim League agreed to these terms. Congress wanted the British out first; the League wanted partition of India and the creation of a separate Muslim state.

The incoming Labour government, pledged to Indian independence, was faced with a deteriorating situation. There were anti-British riots in many Indian cities in the autumn of 1945. The Indian army and navy started to weaken as their members realised that the British Raj was coming to an end. The government wisely decided to be lenient with returning members of the armed forces who had collaborated with the Japanese under the influence of Subbas Chandra Bose (or of Japanese torture). A strike by members of the RAF at Dumm Dumm airfield was followed by similar occurrences in the Royal Indian Air Force and the Royal Indian Navy. Mutinies took place on warships in Bombay and Karachi. Early in 1946, elections were held for the central and regional assemblies (the last ones having been in 1937 and 1939 respectively), with Congress and the Muslim

League emerging as the major political forces. Attlee then sent Cripps, Lord Pethick-Lawrence and A. V. Alexander to seek the agreement of the Indians to the 'principles and procedures' whereby the Indians could frame their own constitution. The three envoys rejected partition and suggested a three-tier federal system, in which the Muslims would have their own states. Provisional agreement was reached but the Congress later repudiated it. The Muslim League then decided on 'direct action' to secure the setting up of Pakistan, starting on 16th August 1946. On that day, bloody intercommunal rioting broke out in Calcutta. Thousands died over the days that followed, as it spread across the land. Gandhi, then 77, helped to calm matters by going on foot from village to village in high-tension areas.[5]

In this situation, Attlee decided drastic action was called for. He decided to replace Wavell with Admiral Viscount Mountbatten of Burma, the successful Supreme Allied Commander Southeast Asia in the last war years, and a member of the royal family known for his liberal views. Mountbatten asked for, and got, full plenipotentiary powers. He was also given a date for British withdrawal. It was announced as 'not later than July 1948'. The idea was to force the Indians of all communities to realise that they must reach a settlement by that date. Mountbatten arrived in India in March 1947. By 3rd June, he announced the British government's agreement to partition as the only practical solution. The people of each province would decide, through their elected assemblies, to which state they wished to belong: India or Pakistan. Mountbatten also announced that the transfer of power would be 'immediate'; which became a few days later, 15th August 1947 – ten weeks ahead. This actually happened, with both states becoming independent members of the Commonwealth on that date. Mountbatten remained in India as Governor-General until May 1948. Mohammed Jinnah became Governor-General of Pakistan. Independence Day was marred by violence in the Punjab, which had been divided between the two states. Hundreds of thousands died, millions fled in both directions. In Calcutta, Gandhi declared 'a fast until death' until the violence stopped. 'It did: one man achieved more in Bengal than 55,000 troops could do in the Punjab.'[6]

Britain's actions in these countries contrasted favourably with those of the French in Indo-China and North Africa, and the

Dutch in Indonesia, where the colonial powers fought hard to retain hegemony.

Guerrilla Warfare in Palestine

In opposition, Labour had been pro-Zionist, favouring unlimited Jewish settlement in Palestine. This was, in part, a reflection of the strong support the Jewish community in Britain gave to Labour. It was also because many in the Labour Party saw Zionism as Democratic Socialism in action. The Arabs were seen as reactionary, living under a feudal order. The Grand Mufti of Jerusalem had foolishly sought German assistance during the war and this did the Arab cause no good. However, in government, Labour was confronted with the realities of power politics and the realisation that the Arabs too had a case. The Labour leaders were forced to consider Britain's dependence on Arab oil and its precarious position in the Suez Canal Zone of Egypt. There was also the reality of the Arab majority in Palestine, who remained completely opposed to further large-scale Jewish immigration into their country. Palestine was not 'a land without people for a people without a land' as the Zionists had proclaimed. The horrors of the Nazi persecution of the Jews led to increased sympathy for the Zionist cause in Europe and the USA. Correspondingly, there was increased pressure on Britain to admit the Jewish survivors of this persecution. In the autumn of 1945, US President Truman requested Attlee to admit 100,000 Jewish refugees immediately into Palestine, which was under British mandate.[7] Attlee turned this down. He was prepared to admit 1,500 a month as Palestine's contribution to solving the refugee problem. Living in camps in Germany, many of the refugees would have preferred to go to America, but Zionist relief workers held out promises of an early transformation of their situation, if they would opt for Palestine. The British were forced to intercept and turn back Jewish refugees arriving on overcrowded, leaky boats. It was easy to portray the British troops, marching the Jews to internment camps on Cyprus, as the successors to the Nazi SS.

   In Palestine itself, Jewish underground organisations waged a guerrilla war against the British. This started in February 1944, with the extremist Irgun group led by Menachem Begin, later Israeli Prime Minister. A smaller group, which had broken away from the Irgun, the Stern Gang, had been fighting the British for some time by then. The majority of the Jewish leaders, who controlled the secret Jewish defence forces, Hagana, wanted to hold their fire and review the situation once Nazism had been defeated. Most of the campaign was against communications with neighbouring states and against government buildings. However, there were also attacks on British personnel. In November 1944, the Stern Gang murdered Lord Moyne, the British Minister Resident in Cairo. Once the European war was over, all the Zionist groups decided to promote their aims by military, as well as political, action. The Zionist revolt commenced on 31st October 1945, with attacks on the railways, police patrol boats and the Haifa oil refinery. In November, there were riots in Jerusalem and Tel Aviv. Other attacks followed, on police, army and RAF installations. Just when an Anglo–American committee of investigation was about to report, there was further escalation. On 25th April 1946, the Stern Gang murdered seven unarmed British soldiers of the 2nd Parachute Brigade in Tel Aviv.

In the House of Commons, there were many, especially on the Labour side, who sympathised with the Zionists, but only a few of them – Richard Crossman[8] and Sydney Silverman were the most prominent – were prepared to embarrass the government over the issue. They also had to consider their constituents, whose sons were being conscripted and risked being sent to Palestine.

The Anglo–American Committee reported on 1st May 1946 and recommended admitting 100,000 Jews, but did not pronounce in favour of a Jewish state. Bevin demanded two preconditions in return: that both Jews and Arabs be disarmed, and that there should be agreement about the future constitutional structure of the Palestine government. A joint British–US group of experts was then set up to examine the practical problems of implementing the Anglo–American Committee's recommendations, but the violence continued. In an effort to stem this, the British swooped, arresting most of the Zionist leaders in Palestine. The response of those who evaded arrest was to step up the violence. In July 1946, the Irgun blew up the King David Hotel in Jerusalem, which housed the government secretariat and the GHQ, with the loss of 91 lives (41 Arabs, 28 Britons, seventeen Jews and five others). Bevin convened a conference in London to seek a settlement. This conference, and the negotiations around it, went on through the autumn and winter of 1946–7. The Arabs held out for a unitary state based on a majority vote. The Jews negotiating outside the conference wanted partition and their own state. Britain would still have preferred a federal state with equal Arab and Jewish cantons. When the conference failed, the British referred the problem to the United Nations.

On 30th July 1947, two British sergeants were abducted from the beach at Natanya and later hanged in a citrus grove. Their bodies were booby-trapped. This was the work of Irgun, in reprisal for the execution of two Jewish terrorists by the British. In Britain, there followed a sudden outbreak of anti-Semitic demonstrations in Gateshead, London, Liverpool, Leeds, Manchester, Newcastle and other towns. The editor of a local newspaper, *Morecambe & Heysham Visitor*, was prosecuted for writing and publishing a seditious libel concerning people of the Jewish faith and race resident in Great Britain. He claimed the Jews were hypocrites, were the worst black-market offenders and were 'a plague on Britain'. After only thirteen minutes' deliberation, the jury came to a unanimous verdict of 'not guilty'.[9]

Faced with a seemingly impossible situation, Bevin announced in the Commons, on 18th February 1947, the UK's intention of giving up the mandate in Palestine. After much further debate and intense lobbying in the UN, its General Assembly (a much smaller body then) agreed the partition of Palestine on 29th November 1947, by 33 votes to thirteen, with ten abstentions. Britain was among the abstainers, with Argentina and China. Newly independent India and Pakistan joined Cuba, Greece and the Islamic states in voting against. Those in favour included the West European states, the Soviet Union and its clients, the USA and many of its clients, together with Australia, Canada, New Zealand and South Africa. The Arab and Jewish states were to come into being two months after the termination of the British mandate, which had been scheduled for 15th May 1948. The Representative of Pakistan, Sir Zufrallah Khan, was among those warning of the consequences of partition. He also attacked the sincerity of the Western powers. 'They who paid lip service to humanitarian principles', he said, 'closed their own doors to the "homeless Jews", but voted Arab Palestine to be not only a shelter, a refuge, but also a state so that he (the homeless Jew) should rule over the Arab.'[10] Under this plan, there would have been virtually as many Arabs as Jews, even in the Jewish state, which would comprise 56 per cent of Palestine. Jerusalem and its suburbs were to become an international zone.

The day after the UN vote (30th November), Arab attacks on Jews and Jewish property in Palestine and beyond started rapidly escalating into a war. The British gradually withdrew, the last of their troops leaving the port of Haifa on 30th June 1948.

Bevan and the National Health Service

Although Bevan's name is irrevocably linked, and rightly so, with the National Health Service (NHS), it was Henry Willink, then Minister of Health, who first presented Parliament, in 1944, with a White Paper, entitled *A National Health Service*. Willink, a Conservative, served as minister from November 1943 until July 1945. His White Paper followed the Beveridge Report and Labour backbench pressure to adopt its proposals. Willink's background (Eton and Cambridge) could not have been more different from that of Bevan, the ex-miner charged by Attlee with introducing a suitable scheme.[11] It took him three years of hard bargaining before the NHS was inaugurated in 1948. The NHS, as introduced by Bevan, produced free care for all, as of right. Those in employment were required to contribute towards its upkeep through National Insurance contributions. This was no different from the pre-NHS heath service, except that, before 1948, health insurance was not administered by the state but by private companies or 'approved societies'. They provided a standard benefit and a capitation fee for the doctor. The insured person became a 'panel patient' as opposed to a private patient. Under this system, only those who were in paid employment, and pregnant women, were entitled to health care. This meant that married women, who were 'only' housewives, were not normally covered, nor were children under fourteen (the normal school-leaving age). Many retired people were not covered under this scheme. Even those who were insured had to pay for dentistry and glasses.

Most people simply went to somewhere like Woolworth and tested themselves for glasses. The nation's teeth were in a poor state. Unnecessary removal of teeth was widespread partly to avoid future costs. The Poor Law hospitals had been municipalised in 1930 but there were still voluntary hospitals, whose governing boards sought to raise funds by flag days. For most people, the whole of health care was still under the stigma of the old Poor Law of the nineteenth century.

At a stroke, the NHS swept this aside, giving everyone the right, as a citizen (or resident or visitor), to free health care. To achieve success, Bevan had to fight a long battle with the British Medical Association (BMA), representing general practitioners, and ably led by Dr Charles Hill. Many BMA members feared Bevan was attempting to turn them into salaried civil servants who would have to do the government's bidding. He also faced the anger of some of his more doctrinaire colleagues, who wanted the NHS to be based on local authority control, with doctors responsible to the local authority. Instead, he left general practitioners with most of their freedom intact. He nationalised the hospitals, giving specialists the right to work either full-time or part-time for the new service (or remain completely outside it). He also accepted private 'pay beds' in the NHS hospitals and gave the specialists substantial representation on the committees of management. For the specialists, this was a very satisfactory outcome and they led the way in integrating their colleagues into the NHS.

Republic of Ireland

By 1946, there were rumblings of discontent against the old order in Eire politics. This was not surprising as living standards got a good deal worse after the war than during it. Food and fuel were scarce. However, by 1948 considerable improvement was clear. Yet in the election of that year, Fianna Fáil lost its overall majority and was replaced by an 'Inter-party government' of five parties and some independents. Fine Gael was the most important component yet it held only 31 seats out of 144 in the Dáil. Its leader, John A. Costello, a distinguished lawyer, was elected Taoiseach (Premier). The two Labour parties were included, as were the farmers and a new force, Clann na Poblachta. Fianna Fáil had lost support because it had gradually shifted from being a party of the disadvantaged and the Republicans, to being a party of the better off, the moderates and even of a kind of establishment, through its long years in office. Fine Gael had remained a moderate middle-class party, ready to seek good relations with Britain. Labour was mainly a party of the working class of Dublin. Clann na Poblachta was Republican but was trying to cut across the old divisions, caused by the Treaty of 1921, and promote social and economic reform. It stopped short of calling itself socialist and tried to appeal to all social groups.

The new government pursued policies in many respects similar to those of Labour in Britain. The state was given a major role in economic development. An Industrial Development Authority was set up and the Land Rehabilitation Project introduced. Agriculture Minister, James Dillon, negotiated the Anglo–Irish Trade Agreement of 1948, which linked payments for Irish produce to those being paid to British farmers. The economy benefited, too, from the previous government's policy of joining the European Recovery Programme. Despite these advantages, Eire was isolated and as dependent on Britain as it had ever been. When Britain devalued the pound in 1949, Ireland had to devalue its currency. Much of what went on in the world came to the Republic via the filter of the British media. Its application to join the UN was vetoed by the Soviet Union until 1955. It decided not to join NATO because of the partition of Ireland. Its neutrality was held against it by some in England and by many more in the Protestant community in Northern Ireland.

The 1937 constitution was also condemned in the North. It contained many clauses which showed Catholic influence. It banned divorce and, in Article 44, recognised the special role of the Holy Catholic Apostolic and Roman Church 'as guardian of the Faith professed by the great majority of its citizens'. This constitution, which replaced the earlier one, was designed to remove all the signs and symbols of the British Commonwealth from Irish political life. Article 2 laid claim to Northern Ireland as well as the southern counties. The constitution was Republican in content but did not describe Eire as a republic. The Republic of Ireland Act, under which Southern Ireland formally became a republic, on Easter Day 1949, changed this. Thus, the last formal ties with the British Crown and Commonwealth were severed. However, the British Parliament enacted the Ireland Act (1949), which, whilst it recognised Eire as a republic, did not regard it as a foreign country and ensured full rights for all Irish migrants to Britain, as if they were UK citizens. The British Act also stated that the status of Northern Ireland would not be changed without the consent of its parliament. There were widespread protests in the Republic against the British legislation. Five junior ministers in Attlee's government were sacked or resigned because of their opposition to it. These developments hardened the position of Ulster Protestants, and in the Ulster election of 1949 the Unionists increased their majority. The remarkable thing about the Republic of Ireland Act is that it was introduced by a Fine Gael-led coalition. Fine Gael had been traditionally the pro-British Commonwealth party. Labour and Clann na Poblachta, whose leader, Sean MacBride, was External Affairs Minister, were strongly in favour of the change.

The biggest controversy surrounding the coalition was the mother-and-child scheme, which Health Minister, Dr Noel Browne, sought to introduce. Browne fell foul of the Irish Medical Association (IMA) and, worse still, the Roman Catholic hierarchy. The IMA used the same kind of arguments as the BMA had done in Britain against the NHS. In a letter to the Taoiseach of 10th October 1950, the bishops set out their objections. They claimed it would undermine the family and give too much power to the state. They strongly opposed the proposal that local medical officers should give sex education to Catholic girls and women, which could lead to 'provision for birth limitation and abortion'. MacBride, his party leader, forced Browne to resign. Browne, it should be mentioned, did much to irradicate TB in Ireland. The Browne controversy helped to destroy their party. It also helped to convince Northern Protestants that the Republic of Ireland was a state dominated by Roman Catholicism.

Like the British economy, the Irish was hit by inflation caused by the Korean War, and this also made the electorate restless. Yet Fine Gael gained seats in 1951 – perhaps because of its championing of the Republic of Ireland Act – at the expense of the small parties. Fianna Fáil remained, however, the biggest single party and this time, de Valera was elected Taoiseach of a minority government, with the help of Browne, who stood as an independent. His government lasted to 1954, during which time a Social Welfare Act (1952) was passed, and a Health Act (1953), which increased to 85 per cent those entitled to receive hospital treatment either free or at a reduced rate.

Cold War: 'challenge and peril'

After being swept from office, Churchill went travelling. He was in demand as a speaker. On 5th March 1946, he made a small American town, Fulton, Missouri, famous when, in a speech, he introduced the term 'iron curtain' into the English language. He warned against 'the two gaunt marauders – war and tyranny'. Developing the theme of tyranny, he cautioned: 'The Dark Ages may return . . . From Stettin in the Baltic to Trieste in the Adriatic, an iron curtain has descended across the continent. Behind that line lie all the capitals of the ancient states of central and eastern Europe.' Beyond that line, 'far from the Russian frontiers and throughout the world, Communist fifth columns are established to work in complete unity and absolute obedience to the directions they receive from the Communist center'. They represented a growing challenge and peril to Christian civilization.[13] Many saw Churchill's call to arms as the beginning of the Cold War between the Soviet Union and its former wartime allies. However, relations between the four states had been deteriorating for some time. The West was being forced to face the reality of Soviet power in Eastern Europe.

Stalin was not content to have governments that moderated their foreign policies to suit what he perceived to be Soviet interests. Increasingly, the states beyond the iron curtain were becoming mere satellites of Moscow. By setting up the Cominform, in September 1947, which formally linked the Soviet Communist Party with those of Eastern Europe, France and Italy, Stalin appeared to be confirming Churchill's analysis.

The West also had difficulties with the Soviet Union in Iran, Turkey and Greece. Increasingly, the USA was being forced into a leadership role. Britain had given aid to Greece and Turkey, but its weak economy forced it to review the situation early in 1947. On 12th March, President Truman announced what became known as the Truman Doctrine. He called for American aid to 'free peoples who are resisting attempted subjugation by armed minorities or by outside pressures'. Congress was persuaded to vote large financial aid to Greece and Turkey. Named after American Secretary of State, George Marshall, the Marshall Plan was announced in June. It involved dollar aid to the war-shattered countries of Europe, including the Western zones of Germany. The Soviet Union rejected the Plan as an infringement of sovereignty. The Poles and the Czechs were soon afterwards forced by Moscow, against their inclinations, to reject the Plan as well.[14] The Communist coup in Czechoslovakia, in February 1948, led to a further escalation of the Cold War. In the same year, Stalin fell out with his erstwhile comrade President Tito of Yugoslavia, expelling the Yugoslav party from the Cominform. Throughout the world Communist parties had turned to militancy in an attempt to exploit the postwar difficulties of their respective countries. The threat of a Soviet invasion of Yugoslavia, and events in Berlin, led many to think the world was again on the very edge of a world war.

On 23rd June 1948 the new West German mark, or D-Mark, was introduced into West Berlin. The following day, the Soviets imposed a blockade on the three Western sectors of Berlin. They cut the road, rail and water links between West Berlin, situated 100 miles inside the Soviet Zone, and West Germany. The Social Democratic mayor of Berlin, Ernst Reuter, believed the Soviets wanted to drive the Western powers from the city. In London, Bevan, previously a strong advocate of co-operation with the Soviets, supported in Cabinet an armoured thrust from the West to relieve Berlin.[15] The blockade was to last 322 days and was defeated not by tanks but by supply planes, which somehow took in enough food and fuel to feed the 2 million West Berliners. Ernest Bevin played a considerable part in persuading the Americans to aid the West Berliners. While the US Air Force received most of the credit for the airlift, the RAF contributed almost half of the resources and operations. The blockade was a defeat for Stalin, not only in Berlin, but also on a wider front. It was an important factor in convincing Democratic Socialists, as well as Conservatives, throughout Europe, that they would have to side with the USA in their attempts to prevent any further expansion of Stalin's empire.

Stalin's manoeuvres led the democratic states to look to their military defences. The Dunkirk Treaty of 1947 had united France and Britain in a defensive alliance against a possible future German threat. By March 1948, when Belgium, the Netherlands and Luxembourg joined Britain and France in the Brussels Treaty, it was much clearer that the danger was the Soviet Union, not Germany. There were, however, increasing doubts about the abilities of these five states to repel any Soviet invasion and, under Bevin's leadership, they sought to involve the USA as well. This happened in April 1949, when a treaty setting up the North Atlantic Treaty Organisation (NATO) was signed by the USA, Canada, Denmark, Iceland, Italy, Norway and Portugal together with the five Brussels Treaty states. In 1951 Greece and Turkey were admitted. It is in some ways remarkable that Attlee did not pursue greater economic co-operation, at least with the Brussels Treaty states, given his earlier enthusiasm for European unity and the chance for leadership Britain would have had at that time.

Britain's Bomb

One of the myths about Attlee's government is that it developed the nuclear bomb in secret. In fact, it made a quiet, unnoticed, public announcement about it on 12th May 1948. George Jeger, Labour MP for Winchester, asked the Minister of Defence, A. V. Alexander, whether he was satisfied that adequate progress was being made in the development of the most modern types of weapons. Alexander answered, 'Yes, Sir. As was made clear in the Statement Relating to Defence, 1948 (command 7327), research and development continue to receive the highest priority in the defence field, and all types of modern weapons, including atomic weapons, are being developed.' Jeger went on to ask whether Alexander could give any further information on the development of atomic weapons. Alexander did not think it would be in the public interest to do so. No great debate in Parliament or the media took place on the issue. Had there been such a debate the same outcome appears likely. Whatever the thoughts of individuals about this development, few, if any, expressed any misgivings in Cabinet or in the Parliamentary Labour Party. Perhaps there was a feeling that such weapons would be safe in the hands of men like Attlee. Perhaps the full implications were not yet known. Attlee himself, and his senior colleagues, who took the decision, were not pacifists and no doubt thought Britain could not afford to be without it. It prevented anyone blackmailing Britain and it ensured Britain's place at the top table. Undoubtedly, they were deeply impressed by the misdeeds of the Nazis and by what would have happened had *they* had the bomb and Britain had not. The French obviously felt the same and lost no time in getting to work on it. It was a very costly venture and of doubtful logic once Britain became dependent on the USA for its security. When the original formal decision was taken, on 8th January 1947, the position of America was unclear and the Americans were not prepared to share their nuclear secrets with Britain, even though British scientists and secrets had been used during the war to get their project under way. The Americans believed that nuclear proliferation increased the dangers. They also feared that British security arrangements were faulty. On the day of Churchill's Fulton speech (5th March 1946), Alan Nunn May, a British physicist involved in the original nuclear bomb project, was arrested as a Soviet spy. Under the McMahon Act (1946) it became a criminal offence to pass on US nuclear secrets. Britain felt the USA was reneging on wartime agreements giving it the right to such knowledge; so did US Secretary of State Dean Acheson.[16] Bruised but not browbeaten, Britain pushed on. Its first atomic bomb was exploded in the Monte Bellow Islands, off North West Australia, on 3rd October 1952. A month later, the USA exploded their first hydrogen bomb. The Soviets exploded their first bomb in 1949, and their first hydrogen bomb in August 1953.

Counter-insurgency in Malaya

One place where Communist militancy moved from strikes and demonstrations to murder and armed insurrection was Malaya. The British had backed the Communist underground, against the Japanese, providing them with training and arms. Probably on Moscow's orders, they turned to armed struggle in 1948, under the slogan of independence. Undoubtedly, they were encouraged by British withdrawals from the Indian Empire, from

Greece and from Palestine, and by Mao's successes in China. Their strength was the experience they had gained fighting the Japanese. Their weakness was the fact that their party cadre were mainly Chinese, not Malay. Excluding Singapore, only 38 per cent of the population were Chinese and Muslim Malays often resented them. The British dealt with the strikes by deporting suspected Chinese Communists who were not Malay citizens. The Communists attacked the 3,000 rubber estates and the tin mines, killing managers, 'collaborators' and members of the police and administration. The British government was compelled to commit British troops, many of whom were young national servicemen. As well as military operations, the British implemented forced resettlement of villages. At the political level, the Federation of Malaya was set up in February 1948 as a step towards independence. The emergency outlasted the Attlee government, ending in the mid-1950s, after the Soviet and Chinese leaderships decided to embark on more conciliatory relations with the non-Communist world.

Economic Progress

Labour faced an appalling situation when it took office in 1945. The economy was, in many fundamental respects, outdated and run down *before* the war. During the war, it had been fully stretched producing war material. A large proportion of the vast overseas investments had been sold and large debts incurred. Yet, in the elation of victory, the people were looking to a better standard of living. The American and Canadian loans provided a vital breathing space, but nothing more. At the same time, Britain had more responsibilities than ever before, in Germany, Austria, Italy, Greece, the former Italian colonies and the old British Empire. The government had to persuade the people to continue the strict discipline of the war years. The trade unions behaved responsibly and accepted this situation. The only advantage Britain had was that Germany and Japan, key pre-war rivals, were temporarily 'out of commission'. Britain was also able to exploit German inventions as war booty. Almost anything which could be produced, could be sold. But could it be delivered? About half of the British merchant fleet had been sunk during the war.[17] Of the workforce, only 2 per cent were producing exports and less than 8 per cent were engaged in maintaining the nation's capital equipment. It was estimated that the income from exports at the end of the war was only enough to finance a quarter of the pre-war volume of imports. Among these imports were foodstuffs which, during the war, had been just sufficient to keep the people fit to carry on normal activities. Over the six years of war, less than four years' normal supply of clothing, and less than four years' supply of household goods, had been provided for the population and most were expecting higher standards than before 1939.[18] Housing standards, for very many, had been poor before the war. Little maintenance was done during the war and some 470,000 homes were either completely destroyed or made uninhabitable by bomb damage. The only consolation was than many of those destroyed were among the worst slums.

One early achievement of the government was the planned demobilisation of large numbers of servicemen and women and war workers. In the eighteen months after the end of the war, over 7 million were released from the armed forces or from work supplying the forces.[19] Remarkably, however, for much of the period, Britain had more manpower in its armed services than the Americans had in their forces. This strained the economy but reduced the possibility of unemployment.

Apart from the problems it inherited, the government suffered from bad luck. The winter of 1946–7 brought severe freezing conditions, followed by widespread flooding. In February 1947, the economy was brought to a standstill when Shinwell cut off electricity to industry. Unemployment rose rapidly and production plummeted. The crisis lasted only a few weeks.

Production grew, reaching the highest level ever by 1950. Exports grew too. They increased in volume by 77 per cent between 1945 and 1950, reaching the pre-war level by the end of 1946. Imports were held down to an increase of only 14.5 per cent. Consumption rose by no more than 6 per cent. 'For a country which had been at war for six years and emerged exhausted but victorious this was no mean achievement.'[20] However, Britain had its old problem of a deficit on its visible exports – industrial products – over visible imports, which had to be balanced by a surplus on invisible exports, such as insurance, banking and shipping. One advantage it had on the 'invisibles' was the Sterling Area. All the dominions, except Canada, and all the colonies and some other states, where British influence predominated, were part of this Area. The Sterling Area was responsible for approximately one quarter of the world's international trade. Although they had their local currencies, they did their trade with each other in sterling. They held sterling balances in London, under the control of the Bank of England. These were not convertible into dollars. Debts which Britain incurred with these states were held in special accounts in London. This gave Britain a great deal of leeway.

Built up during the war through subsidies, agricultural production had gone on rising, so that in 1949–50 it was 40 per cent higher than in 1936–8.[21] By 1951, total milk consumption was almost twice as high as before the war.[22] Higher agricultural production meant a reduction of food imports that had to be paid for in dollars.

Like the other war-torn states in Western Europe, Britain received Marshall Aid (the European Recovery Programme) under the terms of the Economic Co-operation Act, finally agreed by the US Congress in spring 1948. This commenced just after the US loan had been used up. Britain had suffered from American inflation. After the Republicans won the congressional elections in the USA in 1946, price controls were either revoked by presidential decree or allowed to lapse. Prices rose rapidly as consumers attempted to buy goods in short supply. In addition, Britain had agreed, when it negotiated the original loan, to make sterling convertible within one year of the Loan Agreement. It did so on 15th July 1947 and this soon led to a run on the pound, forcing suspension of convertibility, with American agreement, on 19th August.

In the meantime, considerable damage had been done to the economy and the balance of payments, and an austerity programme had to be implemented. This included an extension of food rationing (potatoes were covered for the first time.)[23] Helped by Marshall Aid, Britain enjoyed a boom in 1948, yet by the summer of 1949 was suffering its second economic crisis since the war. This was, in part, a result of the American recession, which meant fewer export opportunities for Britain. It led to the devaluation of the pound from $4.02 to $2.80. It was a body blow to British self-esteem. Despite the difficulties, sufficient progress had been made in Britain, by 1950, for Hugh Gaitskell, who had just succeeded the ailing Cripps as Chancellor, to agree to the suspension of Marshall Aid by 1st January 1951. However, the economy was upset once again by the inflation caused by the rise of world commodity prices during the Korean War and by the re-armament drive.

British Society

One of the surprising things about postwar Britain was the extent to which the old pre-war class and social order remained intact. One important aspect of this was how women went back, in the main, to their pre-1939 roles. Their main role in life was supposed to be as wives and mothers. Those who did go out to work – virtually all before marriage – were expected to be unskilled workers, tracers, secretaries, shop assistants and nurses, rather than tool-makers and fitters, draughtsmen, managers, lawyers and doctors. Of course, in a few industries, like the Lancashire cotton industry, women had always done highly skilled work and continued to do so. One change was that the women's branches of the armed services were retained, unlike after the First World War. In theory, since the Sex Disqualification (Removal) Act (1919), women could do most things, but in practice great determination was required to gain entry into the professions. In education, separate boys' and girls' grammar and public schools were normal, though many local authorities maintained co-educational grammar schools. The 'ordinary' schools, which most children attended, had always been co-educational.

According to the census of 1951, the main occupations of women were: clerks, typists, secretaries – 1,416,000 (61 per cent of the total in these jobs); domestic servants – 783,000 (93 per cent); shop assistants – 614,000 (68 per cent); textile workers – 419,000 (65 per cent); garment workers – 394,000 (93 per cent); nurses – 237,000 (89 per cent); charwomen and office cleaners – 233,000 (94 per cent); metal manufacture and engineering workers – 225,000 (8 per cent); teachers – 217,000 (61 per cent); shopkeepers and managers – 180,000 (29 per cent); hotel, restaurant, etc. proprietors and managers – 111,000 (47 per cent);

laundry workers – 109,000 (88 per cent); waiting staff – 87,000 (77 per cent); telephone operators – 66,000 (76 per cent); social welfare workers – 12,000 (54 per cent); librarians – 11,000 (73 per cent).[24]

Given the part they played in the war, it is surprising that more women were not elected to Parliament. Since 1918, Labour had fielded more women candidates than the Conservatives. It did so again in 1945 (45 Labour; fourteen Conservative; twenty Liberal). Only one Conservative and one Liberal were returned compared with 21 Labour women. This was the highest number of women in Parliament since women first stood in 1918.

Women were not expected to go into pubs and bars by themselves and were expected to wait for men to make the first advance in any relationship, although this particular custom was breaking down. Women's magazines, radio programmes, the schools and the cinema all reinforced such 'proper' attitudes. British films such as *Wicked Lady* (1945) with Margaret Lockwood, *Good-time Girls* (1948) with Jean Kent, and the costume drama *Blanche Fury* (1948) with Valeries Hobson, entertained men and warned women. In *The Seventh Veil* (1945), Ann Todd, with the help of a psychiatrist, chooses her stern, disciplinarian guardian (James Mason), rather than the jazz musician or the artist who also seek her favours. Such films thrilled audiences and were more popular than David Lean's *Brief Encounter* (1945), a chaste romance between Trevor Howard and Celia Johnson, set on a dreary railway station. Alida Valli, in Carol Reed's *The Third Man* (1949), possibly Britain's best postwar film, portrayed a far more interesting (foreign) woman.[25]

The film industry continued to flourish as a medium of popular entertainment. The Labour government took an interest in it, not as a means of propaganda, but as a hard-currency saver and earner and as a vehicle for projecting Britain. In 1947, Dalton imposed a 75 per cent *ad valorem* tax on foreign films. The Americans then imposed a boycott on the British market. This gave a short-term boost to the British film industry. Within a year, both sides were ready to compromise and Harold Wilson (Board of Trade) worked out a deal. J. Arthur Rank – a flour miller and a Methodist, who had gone into the film business in the 1930s – dominated the film industry. He owned not only many production facilities, but the Odeon cinema chain as well.

His empire was so complex, however (including links with American studios), that he could not control all that was produced. Wilson set up the National Film Finance Corporation, in an effort to help independent producers by channelling modest sums of public money to them, but by the end of the decade, studios were closing and the film industry was in crisis. American films remained popular and they, having more than covered their costs in their huge domestic market, could be sold cheaply in Britain.

Looking back at them today, many British films depicted Britain as a grim place (*Gas Light*, 1940), or as just plain silly (*The Chiltern Hundreds*, 1949). The 'Ealing comedies' (*Lavender Hill Mob*, 1951) gave some welcome relief from the austerity of the time. There were many other comedies, crime films, costume dramas, war films and adaptations from the classics, especially Dickens. One or two films helped their audiences understand Ireland. *Captain Boycott* (1947) was set in the nineteenth century; *Odd Man Out* (an Irish film, 1947) presented James Mason as a doomed, but likeable, IRA gunman in contemporary Belfast. About the only film to deal with the Labour movement, *Fame Is The Spur* (1947), taken from the book of the same name, presented Michael Redgrave as the Labour MP who had lost his roots and sought only fame. It must have convinced many who saw it that their representatives were self-seeking and not worth all the effort needed to get them elected.

Law and order was a problem in postwar Britain, with chronic shortages encouraging a growing black market, stocked by robbery and corruption. Thousands of deserters from the armed forces swelled the ranks of the 'villains'. The 'spiv' was a detested character who seemed to have everything, except a regular job, yet cleverly avoided the attention of the police. *It Always Rains on Sunday* (1947) featured John Slater and Sydney Tafter as Jewish spivs in London, with the popular Jack Warner as a detective. The men in blue were strongly supported in *The Blue Lamp* (1948), with Warner as a London constable who is shot dead. It was the top box-office film of the year. In 1948, the Criminal Justice Act abolished hard labour, penal servitude and flogging; hanging was retained, however, by popular request. In the films of the day, murderers often met a sticky end before they could be sentenced to the gallows.

Sex remained a taboo subject, which was thought to be of greater importance to men than to women. The average person, educated or not, learnt little about it from school or parents. Those bold enough, sent off for books, which promised enlightenment and were dispatched under plain covers. Such books were only advertised in relatively obscure publications, like the weekly *New Statesman and Nation*. Condoms were usually only on sale in barbers' shops or, again, by mail order. Homosexuality was illegal and little talked about. Although Acts of 1923, 1927 and 1950 extended the grounds for divorce, it was still difficult to obtain, unfair to women, and burdened by the need to expose the guilty party. Divorce was, however, on the increase. In 1939, only 9,970 petitions were filed. By 1945 the figure was 24,857. In 1947 petitions reached 47,041, their highest level until then, falling in the following year.[26] The Family Allowances Act (1945) marked a new departure in that the money was paid to the mother – not the father – of the children claimed for.

The monarchy helped to reinforce the message of order, hierarchy and 'proper' attitudes. King Edward VIII, later Duke of Windsor, had been a grave embarrassment to the pre-war Establishment, having an affair with a married woman and then abdicating to marry her. He and his lady were virtually banned from Britain. His brother and successor, the shy, stammering George VI, and Queen Elizabeth, had gained popularity by remaining in Britain with their two daughters throughout the war. But was George VI the right head of state for the reduced, postwar Britain? His main passions were shooting, clothes, medals, orders and decorations.[27] New glamour was added to the monarchy when Princess Elizabeth married Philip Mountbatten, later Duke of Edinburgh, in 1947.

The education system, too, worked hard to inculcate attitudes of loyalty, respect and obedience to those in authority. The much-praised 'Butler' Education Act (1944) did little to change this. After decades of discussion, the school-leaving age was finally raised from fourteen (which it had been since 1918) to fifteen. It must be admitted that some saw this as a bold move, in view of the manpower shortages. At eleven, children were selected for places at either grammar schools or, for the great majority, secondary modern schools. The grammar schools were élitist, academic, and pupils wore uniforms. Given the greater prosperity, probably more working-class children who passed the eleven-plus exam actually took up their places. The secondary modern schools often instilled a sense of failure in their pupils, with most of them having no chance of gaining any leaving qualifications. In 1951 the General Certificate of Education (GCE) replaced the School Certificate, and, because it was not so rigid in requiring passes in several academic subjects at one time, did make it possible for secondary moderns to develop academic streams. Only the best did so. A very small number of secondary technical schools were established during this period, with good results. Outside the 'state' sector – that is, local authority maintained schools – the public and other private schools continued as before, often providing better opportunities to those whose parents could afford to pay.

The war had revealed, once again, Britain's backwardness in education and technical training compared with its main foe, Germany; but not enough was done to remedy the situation.[28] Germany appeared to be no more, money was short and there was also a feeling that too much education for too many would only cause social discontent. Nevertheless, three university colleges became full universities – Nottingham (1948), Southampton (1952) and Hull (1954). Founded partly because of German competition, it had been a long wait for Nottingham – 67 years! The numbers of those in higher education expanded considerably (see Table A 7). The growth in numbers probably reflects the increase in available public finance and also better private family resources. Remarkably, the number of women as a percentage of the total remained constant at around 22 per cent.

In general the media, schools, the advertising industry, churches and the armed forces all worked to give people a sense of insecurity, inferiority and self-doubt. This was all the more so if you were working class and/or female and/or Irish, Jewish, born 'illegitimate', 'queer' or even left-handed. This is by no means an exclusive list.

London Olympics

On a postal vote of the International Olympic committee in 1946, the XIV (summer) Olympic Games were awarded to London.

They were held between 29th July and 14th August 1948. Representatives of 59 states participated, comprising 4,099 competitors, of whom 385 were women. At the previous games, held in Berlin in 1936, there were 4,066 competitors (328 women) from 49 states. Although Germany and Japan were not invited and the Soviet Union did not compete, the numbers of states, competitors and women taking part represented record numbers. The male competitors were housed in armed forces camps and the women in colleges. Wembley Stadium was used for most events, with rowing competitions on the Thames and yachting at Torbay. Britain had never been an Olympic giant. There had never been much investment of public money to finance potential team members and most of them were giving up their own time and resources to compete. Amateur sports bodies were poorly endowed with facilities. On this occasion, Britain came twelfth in the unofficial league table, with three gold, fourteen silver and six bronze medals, which can be compared with its tenth place four gold, seven silver and three bronze in 1936. Britain was top in 1908, the last time the Olympics had been held in London, when only 22 states were represented by 2,056 competitors, of whom 36 were women. In 1948, most of Britain's medals were in rowing and yachting. British women did, however, pick up four silver medals in track and field events. Among them was Dorothy Tyler (née Odam), who came second in the high jump, as she had done in 1936. On both occasions she cleared the same height as the winner. Tom Richards was regarded as something of a hero when he took the silver in the marathon. But the 'stars' of 1948 were Francina 'Fanny' Blankers-Koen, the Dutch runner who won four golds, and Emil Zatopek of Czechoslovakia, who won the 10,000 metres and came second in the 5,000 metres.

Some of the competitors from the more affluent countries were surprised by the austerity they experienced in London and the ruins of bombed buildings. However, for the British it was a coup to stage the games so soon after the war and it was something of a morale booster, even if most of the medals went elsewhere, particularly to the Americans. Remarkably, the British recorded a profit on the games.

The Festival of Britain, in 1951, was also regarded as a morale booster, and an event which would show the world that Britain had many and varied modern manufactures for export. The Royal Festival Hall, on the south bank of the Thames, in London, was built for the event. Designed by Robert Mathew, it was a London County Council project. The whole architectural side of the Festival came under the direction of Hugh Casson. The Festival was, apparently, the idea of Gerald Barry, of the liberal daily *News Chronicle*, and was meant to be in the tradition of the Great Exhibition of 1851. Special stamps were printed to celebrate the event. Given the expense of travel and the even greater difficulty of accommodation, the Festival made greater impact in and around London than in the rest of the country.

'migrants of good human stock . . .'

In 1949, the Royal Commission on Population stated that immigration to Britain could be welcomed if 'the migrants were of good human stock and not prevented by their religion or race from intermarrying with the host population and becoming merged into it'. There was pressure to recruit suitable candidates because of the shortage of labour. Some 15,700 German, and 1,000 Italian former POWs remained to work in agriculture. Polish ex-servicemen, who did not wish to return to a Communist-dominated Poland, were allowed to remain in Britain. In 1951, there were 162, 339 Polish-born residents in Britain compared with 44,462 in 1931. Thousands of Ukrainians, Estonians, Latvians and Lithuanians chose Britain for the same reason. Other Italians, Germans and East Europeans were recruited to work in specific areas of shortage in the economy. They met with some hostility as 'Nazis' or 'Fascists'. In 1939, there were 239,000 aliens over the age of sixteen resident in Britain. In 1950 the figure was 429,329,[29] by which time many of the earlier aliens had become British citizens.

In a different category, not classified as aliens, were the British Empire immigrants who arrived on the SS *Empire Windrush* from Kingston, Jamaica, on 8th June 1948. There were 492 of them seeking a new life. They joined the existing black communities in London and elsewhere. They met with some hostility and more discrimination. The government worried about them but did little, either to help them or to dissuade others from coming.

During these years tens of thousands of British citizens sought a new life in Canada, New Zealand, South Africa, Rhodesia and, above all, Australia. Little known at the time, children were still being sent, with no say in the matter, from institutions run by various religious charities. They were often exploited and abused.[30]

Election 1950

By 1950, the few people who could go abroad were often astonished by what they found. Belgium, France and Switzerland, three popular destinations, gave the impression of being more prosperous than Britain. So did Germany, despite the ruins, and Denmark. In Southern Ireland and Spain there was a rich display in the midst of great poverty. Rationing had been abolished in Western Europe but it was still enforced in Britain. Clothes rationing ended in March 1949, petrol in May 1950 and soap in September of that year. Most basic foods remained rationed. A decade of full employment was beginning to make people less servile, more complacent, more demanding than before. There was a strong feeling that Britain had won the war, Britain was a top power, British products were the best; yet Britain was a very austere place to be. The better off, who were more likely to have travelled, felt this more keenly than the less well off. They also felt that they were taxed too much and that the blue-collar workers had benefited too much, at the expense of the white-collar employees. This must have caused Labour some loss of support among middle-class voters. The Cold War also influenced attitudes. There was a feeling that, in some vague sort of a way, Labour's socialism was a milder form of the Soviet totalitarian version. George Orwell's *Nineteen Eighty-Four*, and less popular works like F. A. Hayek's *The Road To Serfdom*, contributed to this feeling. J. B. Priestley distanced himself from Statism though not from socialism, and pacifist Bertrand Russell advocated using the atomic bomb against the Soviets. Labour had faced a strong campaign by the business community against further nationalisation in 1949. For example, a proposal to take sugar and cement into public ownership (on the grounds that they were private monopolies) met with 'Mr Cube', a cartoon figure arguing against nationalisation, carried on all packets of sugar.

One pressing problem the Conservatives successfully raised was housing, which was given considerable space in their manifesto. Labour virtually ignored housing in its own manifesto.

Labour also suffered a disadvantage in the media. The BBC still retained its monopoly of sound broadcasting and was generally impartial in terms of party politics. Yet Labour ministers were the butt of many jokes on popular radio programmes. 'Shiver with Shinwell, starve with Strachey' (ministers of fuel and food respectively) was one such jibe.[31] The press was largely sympathetic to the Conservatives and was of great importance before the age of mass television. The hate figure for the Conservative press was undoubtedly Bevan. He seemed to enjoy his notoriety but it did Labour no good, especially when, in a speech on 4th July 1948, he spoke of his 'deep burning hatred of the Tory Party . . . so far as I am concerned they are lower than vermin'.[32] The cinema newsreels probably did not have much direct influence on party politics, except in the sense of strengthening Cold War attitudes. Labour did little to help itself with the media; Attlee was notorious for his indifference to public relations.

The Conservative Party, which, after 1945, even thought of changing its name,[33] came bouncing back. Under the influence of R. A. Butler, it reformed its organisation, its ideas and to some degree, its image. It easily overtook Labour in building up a professionally manned grass roots organisation. This Labour weakness was not made good until the 1990s. Ideologically, the Conservatives accepted most of Labour's reforms, like the NHS, the commitment to full employment and most of the public ownership (except iron and steel, road haulage and further nationalisation). Later there was talk of 'consensus politics' but the rhetoric of politics was often bitter and angry. The Conservatives said they accepted many policies associated with Attlee's administration, yet would they have introduced them? Perhaps had they won in 1945, they would have seen their victory as a mandate *not* to introduce them. The Conservatives could claim that they were simply carrying on the tradition of Disraeli Toryism. They also adopted a *Workers' Charter* 'designed to give security, incentive and status'. As for the trade unions, 'We have held the view, from the days of Disraeli, that the trade union movement is essential to the proper working of our economy . . .' They wanted to humanise not nationalise.[34] There was also an

Agricultural Charter. The Conservatives attempted to improve their image by encouraging a new generation of parliamentary candidates, like Edward Heath, Reggie Bevins, L. R. Carr, Gerald Nabarro and the popular 'Radio Doctor', Dr Charles Hill, from less privileged backgrounds. Most, however, were not of this mould.

The changes in the franchise had brought more gains than losses for the Conservatives. The Representation of the People Acts (1948 and 1949) abolished university seats, which had been in existence since 1603.[35] In 1945, twelve members, none of them Labour, had represented seven university constituencies. The business vote was also abolished and election expenses curtailed. The average Conservative candidate spent more than the average Labour or Liberal. However, the Conservatives more than made up for any loss under this Act by their gains from other changes. Postal voting was introduced, which assisted the Conservatives (and continued to do so for the rest of the century). Boundary changes also cost Labour a considerable number of seats. Most of the large majorities were gained by Labour candidates, most of the small ones by Conservatives. Finally, on Election Day – 23rd February 1950 – the weather was generally fine,[36] which would have helped Labour, but the Conservatives had more cars to get their supporters, especially the old, to the polling stations.

Labour had not lost a single by-election since 1945, which augured well for them, despite poor showings in the opinion polls. They ended up with just over 46 per cent of the vote, to 44 per cent for the Conservatives and 9 per cent for the Liberals. Interest in the election was indicated by the second highest turnout (84 per cent) of the century (in 1910 turnout was 86.6 per cent). Labour won 315 seats, the Conservatives 298, Liberals nine and others three. One aspect of the election was the massive effort by the Communists, who put up 100 candidates.[37] All were heavily defeated and together they attracted fewer votes than the 21 Communists did in 1945. The five pro-Communist, expelled Labour MPs, standing as independents, met the same fate.

War in Korea

When they heard that North Korea had invaded South Korea,
most people in Britain and the USA had no idea where this
ancient country was. It had been turned into a colony by the
Japanese at the end of the nineteenth century and liberated in
1945, by the Soviets in the North, and the Americans in the
South. Like Germany, it had been divided but the intention was
to reunite it later after free elections. Well armed by the Soviets,
the armies of Kim Il Sung swept south in June 1950. It is not
clear whether Stalin had directly encouraged the move but
neither the Russians nor the North Koreans expected the USA
to intervene. In neighbouring China, completely independently
of Moscow, Mao's Communists had defeated America's ally,
Chiang Kai-shek, in the previous year. Chiang had been forced
to abandon mainland China for the island of Taiwan, where he
gained US protection. To the Americans, Korea, not then important in itself, looked to be part of a pattern of Communist
expansion, which had to be stopped. The USA moved quickly,
getting the UN to sanction intervention to protect South Korea.
The Soviets, who could have vetoed the move, were boycotting
the Security Council in protest at the UN's refusal to recognise
Mao's China.

Although the main burden of the war was shouldered by the
USA, Britain immediately agreed to support the UN action, and
organised the Commonwealth Division, of which one half was
British and the other half was made up of Canadian, Australian
and New Zealand troops. Contingents also went from Turkey,
France, Greece, Benelux, Ethiopia and some other states. The
UN forces fought a highly indoctrinated army on rugged terrain in appalling climatic conditions. In a complex amphibious
landing at Inchon (September 1950), the UN forces outflanked
the North Koreans, forcing a general retreat to the Chinese
frontier. On 25th November, China sent in volunteers to assist
North Korea. Overwhelmed, the UN forces fell back. The stand
made by the (British) Gloucester Regiment against massive Chinese forces enabled a large portion of the UN forces to gain
safety. The front was stabilised in March 1951. Eventually the
fighting ended, in July 1953, in a truce, roughly along the 38th
parallel, where it had started. Seventy-one British officers and

616 other ranks were killed, 187 officers and 2,311 other ranks were wounded, and 52 officers and 1,050 other ranks were 'missing', most of whom were taken prisoner and eventually repatriated. By comparison, 33,629 American lives were lost in action, 20,617 died off the battlefield and 103,284 were wounded.

The war became very controversial as press reports of atrocities by Britain's South Korean ally appeared. British officers intervened on a number of occasions to stop executions of suspects, including women and children. In a letter to *The Times* (20th December 1950), the Archbishop of York argued, 'if these barbarous executions continue, all sympathy with South Korea will vanish'. Another fear in Britain was an extension of the war against China. Attlee, pressed by his colleagues, made a celebrated trip to Washington to urge Truman not to use the A-bomb or extend the war. Many believe he did exercise a positive influence. The US/UN commander, General Douglas MacArthur, had asked to be allowed to bomb bridges in China over which the volunteers passed, and to carry out reconnaissance missions over China. Later, he upped his demands, each time being overruled by Truman. Finally, Truman dismissed him, in April 1951. In Britain, there had been an energetic campaign – through Labour-orientated 'Peace with China' committees – against any extension of the war. The Communist *Daily Worker* ran its own campaign against the war using reports about how well British prisoners were being treated. Once the prisoners were repatriated, the true barbarism of the North Korean régime was revealed. Though there were, rightly, many doubts about South Korea in the 1950s, it justified the support it got. North Korea remained a dark land terrorised by an obscurantist dictator.

Labour in Turmoil

Labour had readily endorsed the intervention in Korea, with Michael Foot, in the left-wing Labour weekly *Tribune*, contrasting the UN's resolution approvingly with Britain's pre-war appeasement policy. In the Cabinet, Bevan started to have doubts, once it became clear that the massive re-armament demanded by the USA of their ally would threaten NHS spending. He resigned, on 23rd April 1951, after much deliberation and more procrastination. Harold Wilson (Board of Trade) and John Freeman (junior minister at the War Office) joined him. There were, of course, personal animosities and rivalries, mainly between Bevan and Hugh Gaitskell (Chancellor of the Exchequer). Bevan and his two supporters were not against re-armament as such, nor were they 'soft' on Communism, but they thought the scale and pace of re-armament was unrealistic and damaging to the economy. On this they were right. They made the imposition of health service charges the symbol of their opposition. On this they made a mistake.

In its last eighteen months, the Labour government seemed to lose its way. It was a government of tired and bickering rivals. Ernest Bevin died of cancer in 1951, Cripps was ill and was to die in 1952. Greenwood had left the government in 1947. Attlee was sick and Dalton was tired. Gaitskell, as Chancellor, and Morrison at the Foreign Office, lacked experience in their respective spheres. Attlee, Dalton and Morrison had been in office, apart from the few weeks in 1945, since 1940. Worse still, having implemented their programme of 1945, they lacked a clear idea of where they wanted to lead the country next.

Although most of their supporters in the country, and in the Commons, backed them, there was a considerable minority who thought they were jeopardising their socialist credentials. At home, the government was prosecuting, under the wartime measure Order 1305, gas workers and dockers who had gone on strike. Under this Order, disputes were referred to compulsory arbitration, with a 21-day cooling off period during which industrial action was prohibited on pain of prison. Abroad, it was feared, Britain seemed to be in danger of becoming a tool of an increasingly reactionary USA. Yet Attlee's government had recognised Mao's China, the USA had not, and Labour continued to regard Red China as 'progressive'. There was fear of becoming embroiled in a war with this poor, yet 'pure', state. A smaller group in the parliamentary party still believed that the Soviet Union had much to recommend it, even though they disapproved of Stalin's methods.

Attlee went for an autumn election in 1951, presenting the electorate with a moderate programme in which socialism was not mentioned. Neither Labour nor the Conservatives had much new to offer the voters. The Conservatives did promise more houses and lower taxes. The rising cost of living was a key issue, to the disadvantage of Labour. Foreign policy played a considerable part in the campaign because of a dispute with Iran. Under Premier Mohammed Mossadegh, Iran had nationalised the Anglo–Iranian Oil Company. Labour warned the electorate of the dangers of a Conservative finger on the trigger. However, Morrison sent the fleet to evacuate British personnel from Abadan and paratroops were placed on standby in Cyprus. In the end, Mossadegh was overthrown in 1953 by the American CIA, with British approval. By that time, Labour was in opposition. Just about the last thing Morrison did, as Foreign Secretary, was to sign the peace treaty with Japan in September 1951.

When the votes came to be counted on 25th October, Labour still had a majority of votes behind it but not a majority of seats. On an 82.5 per cent turnout, Labour gained 48.8 per cent or 13,948,605 votes, to the Conservatives' 48 per cent, 13,717,538. The Liberal vote dropped dramatically to 730,556. Labour gained the highest popular vote recorded for one party up to that time. In terms of seats, it held only 295, with 321 going to the Conservatives, six to the Liberals and three to others. Labour had suffered from the rise in the postal vote, the drop in turnout on a rainy day and the lack of Liberal candidates (only 109), many Liberals voting Conservative in preference to Labour.

6 From Churchill to Macmillan, 1951–60

At 76 Churchill was eager to form a government after the Conservative victory of October 1951. Perhaps he was encouraged by the thought that Adenauer, West Germany's leader since 1949, was 75 and Stalin was 72. Churchill, however, was far from being a 'young' 76-year-old. When Adenauer visited him in December 1951 Churchill's speech was jerky, spluttering and hesitant.[1] It seemed unlikely that he would continue to 1955.

In the new government there were many old faces. Eden was given the Foreign Office, his rival R. A. Butler the Exchequer and David Maxwell Fyfe, the Home Office. Maxwell Fyfe (Lord Kilmuir) had served as Solicitor General, 1942–5, and then as Attorney-General in the caretaker government of May–July 1945. Lord Woolton was back as Lord President and the Marquis of Salisbury as Lord Privy Seal. Oliver Lyttelton, another veteran of the wartime coalition, got the Colonial Office, Harold Macmillan, the potentially risky job of Housing, and Sir Walter Monckton, the equally risky job of Minister of Labour. There were no women in the Cabinet until Miss Florence Horsbrugh (who was 62) was appointed Minister of Education in September 1953. She had been Parliamentary Secretary to the Minister of Health, 1939–45, and again at the Ministry of Food in May–July 1945. After representing Dundee for fourteen years, she was defeated in 1945, being returned in 1950 for Moss Side, Manchester. In 1938, she had created modest parliamentary history by being the first woman to move the Address in reply to the King's Speech. Her membership of the Cabinet was brief; in October 1954 Sir David Eccles replaced her. In some key ministries there were frequent changes of minister, which must raise questions about their effectiveness. Churchill served as his own Minister of Defence, until March 1952, when he handed over to Earl Alexander. Alexander made way for Macmillan in October 1954, who was replaced by

Selwyn Lloyd in April 1955. In December, Sir Walter Monckton took over, to be replaced by Anthony Head in October 1956. In less than four years (1951–55) Commonwealth Relations had four ministers. Churchill's health was deteriorating; he had a stroke in June 1953, but persisted in carrying on until April 1955. He played cat and mouse with his colleagues, especially with his crown prince, Eden, in an effort to remain in office. Eden also had health problems. He was out of action from April to October 1953 – a decisive time in world history. Stalin died on 6th March, leaving uncertainty and the potential for great changes in the Soviet Union and Eastern Europe. In June came the revolt in East Germany, when both Churchill and Eden were off the bridge. Butler ran the government during Churchill's incapacity. In addition to their increasing irritation with each other over the succession, Churchill and Eden often differed on foreign policy. Churchill was more pro-European, Eden more Empire-orientated; Churchill was more inclined towards the USA than Eden was.

Elizabeth II

On 6th February 1952, George VI died in his sleep after a happy day's shooting.[2] Aged 56, he had suffered a coronary thrombosis; a few months earlier, he had had his left lung removed because of cancer. His stammer and rather frail appearance had contributed to his popularity. Despite wartime visits to the East End and other bomb-damaged areas, he remained remote from his subjects. His daughters, Elizabeth (born in 1926) and Margaret (born in 1930) were equally remote, despite attempts to popularise them through the media. Both had been educated by private tutors. Elizabeth had, it is true, joined the ATS at eighteen, and had been photographed and filmed in uniform, driving a military vehicle. Her husband since 1947, Prince Philip, of German and Danish descent, was, nevertheless, a minor member of the Greek royal house. When she was proclaimed Queen, Elizabeth was already the mother of two. Her coronation took place on 2nd June 1953, amid nineteenth-century – if not feudal – splendour, with a hint of Hollywood thrown in. It was given lavish television coverage by the BBC, thus increasing its popularity.

Remarkably, many in the Establishment had at first opposed televising the ceremony – they understood little of this medium. In the end, it was watched by more than 20 million people, even though there were only 2 million television owners. Apparently, some people still stood up in their own homes, as the national anthem was played on television. The ceremony was relayed 'live' to France, West Germany and Holland, a considerable feat in those days. Canberra jet bombers flew films of it to Canada. There can be little doubt that the accession of Elizabeth II to the throne was seen by many in the Establishment as an opportunity for a fresh start. Simultaneously, they sought to re-assert declining British influence in the world and to cement the crumbling edifice of conservative values at home. There was talk of a new Elizabethan Age. Inevitably, the amount of time and space given to royal events over the years must have given many people a false sense of their importance, in relation to other events in both Britain and abroad. Their view of reality was distorted.

The royal family was soon in the news again, this time in a way it did not wish. Princess Margaret had fallen for Group Captain Peter Townsend. There was great controversy for several years in the media over the affair. Townsend's handicap was that he was divorced. The Church of England would not have married them. Margaret eventually decided to end her relationship and retain her official position, rather than becoming a private person, as she would have been forced to do, on marrying Townsend.

The Queen herself was also under fire because, it was said by Lord Altrincham and others, she was not giving the right lead to the nation. In an article he published in his own journal, *The National and English Review*, in 1957, he criticised the Queen for being surrounded by a highly unrepresentative circle, making her remote from her people and the Commonwealth and in danger of lagging behind the temper of the age. He felt her clothes, speech and interests – horses and dogs – were a manifestation of this. Such controversies reduced the credibility of Britain abroad. When the Queen gave her first Christmas broadcast in 1957, observers noticed an improvement. In the same year, Prince Charles was sent to school, albeit an exclusive, fee-paying establishment. An Australian was appointed to the Palace press office in 1960. The much-criticised practice of presenting debutantes to the monarch was discontinued. These were slight but welcome changes.

Election 1955

Although he could have waited until 1956, Eden decided to call an election within seven weeks of being appointed Prime Minister. He instructed Chancellor R. A. Butler to present a tax-cutting Budget. 'It was to be an early illustration of "stop-go" economic management,' which required an emergency budget in the autumn. Then, 'practically every one of his election-winning measures . . . was reversed'.[3] The Conservatives had no clear lead in the opinion polls, yet they had certain advantages. Attlee remained at the head of Labour but was clearly nearing the end of his tenure. Labour was divided over specifics like German re-armament and the British H-bomb, and over its future direction in general. Strikes and strike threats marginally helped the Conservatives. Eden appeared an experienced, moderate, handsome, gentlemanly leader, who avoided attacking the Labour leaders and who was not tainted by his party's domestic record before the war.[4] He made successful television appearances in the first election on which television had any impact (just over one-third of the public had TV sets in their homes). The Conservatives had introduced few controversial measures. They had revoked steel nationalisation and privatised road haulage. They had also achieved their target to build 300,000 new homes. All food rationing ended in July 1954, which perhaps won the Conservatives extra votes among the housewives. They were lucky too. The Korean War had ended, Stalin was dead and the new Soviet leaders were more willing to mend fences. During the election period Austria regained its freedom, with the Soviets agreeing to a treaty which led to the withdrawal of Soviet, US, British and French forces. With international tension eased and full employment, there was a mood of moderate optimism. A number of other events contributed, if only marginally so, to this. A New Zealand beekeeper, Edmund Hillary, and a Nepal Sherpa, Tenzing, were the first to climb Mount Everest, in May 1953, and return to tell the tale. They were part of a British team and therefore regarded as British heroes. In May 1954, a medical practitioner from Oxford University, Dr Roger Bannister, was the first to run a mile in four minutes. He seemed a fine example of British 'guts', determination and skill. In June 1953, the new queen had her fairy-tale coronation, watched by millions on television. In October 1953, Sir Winston Churchill was awarded the Nobel Prize for Literature. Britain was leading in the peaceful use of nuclear fuel with Calder Hall power station under construction (opened in May 1956). This optimism helped the government, and the electors gave the Conservatives their confidence. On a lower turnout than 1951, they gained 49.7 per cent of the vote. Labour polled 46.4 per cent and the Liberals only 2.7 per cent. Owing to financial difficulties, as in 1951, the Liberals had been unable to contest most seats. They stood in 110 constituencies, as against 109 in 1951. There were seventeen Communists and 39 other candidates. In most cases, the electors had a clear choice between the government and Labour. Over 50 government candidates called themselves National Liberal, National Liberal and Conservative, Conservative and Liberal, or similar. It is impossible to say just how much this helped Eden's cause. The Conservatives won 334 seats, Labour 277 and the Liberals six. There were only 89 women candidates, 24 of whom were elected. Of these, fourteen were Labour and ten were Conservative. The Conservative percentage vote was the best recorded at any election from 1945 to 1997.

Economic Progress and Decline

The Conservatives were lucky to have taken over when the worst of the Korean War was over. The US stockpiling of strategic goods, which had hit its NATO partners and other friends, was slowing. The terms of trade went in favour of Britain and the other industrialised Western states. The government of Winston Churchill could release the brakes and let the economy go into top gear. The arms programme could be brought under control.

The Conservatives seemed to be the bringers of good times. The standard of living, in terms of personal consumption, was, without doubt, rising. Unemployment remained negligible. Macmillan succeeded in building the 300,000 council houses that he had promised even if it was by reducing their size. However, the underlying trend for Britain, compared with other industrial nations, was one of relative decline. Germany, France and Italy were moving forward more rapidly and Japan was stirring. British industry was complacent. During the years when it had faced only the USA in world markets, its 'take it or leave it' attitude had got more ingrained than ever. Before Churchill left office in 1955, it was Italian design, rather than British, which was determining the shape of things. The textile industry was doomed by 1952, with resulting unemployment in Lancashire, as a result of competition from India and Japan.[5]

The British were burdened, too, by an awkward way of doing things. They still used their own peculiar system of measurement instead of the metric system. They still drove on the left-hand side of the road, rather than on the right, like most other people. Over the decades this must have cost them dearly. Often, British industry was divided into too many competing units with high unit costs. There were also too many unions, making industry-wide agreements more difficult to achieve. Interunion disputes were responsible for some damaging strikes in the docks and on the railways. The car industry, which was still Britain's pride and joy in the early 1950s, suffered from too many units and too many unions. Complacency was certainly an additional problem. Volkswagen, for example, was regarded as a non-starter in the British automobile industry. All these problems were also present in the aviation industry: the Bristol Brabazon, designed to carry 100 passengers, never saw service. De Havilland led the field with the world's first all-jet airliner in 1952 (the Comet), but eventually it had to be withdrawn after several had crashed. Shipbuilding was another industry, which went into steep decline. In 1953, the UK was responsible for 26 per cent of new tonnage launched; West Germany contributed 16 per cent and Japan 11 per cent. By 1961, the respective percentages were 15, 12 and 23. Aided by lavish amounts of public money, the defence industry abounded with projects that had to be abandoned. Indeed, overspending on defence must rank as one of the principle reasons for Britain's decline since 1945. In relation to what it earned, between 1945 and 1990, it consistently spent more money on defence than West Germany, Italy, Japan and virtually all other modern nations. Only the USA showed itself to be quite so profligate. This was known at the time of the Churchill, Eden, Macmillan and Home governments. Already, in the late 1950s, television programmes were asking how Germany had produced its economic miracle and Britain was falling behind. The fall in Britain's share of world trade is shown in Table A 8.

Conflict over Capital Punishment

Opinion polls revealed that a majority of the public remained in favour of the death penalty in the 1950s.[6] However, there was growing concern over the use of the death penalty because of three cases in the 1950s. One was that of two young men, Craig and Bentley, who were convicted of shooting a policeman. Bentley was executed, even though he did not fire the shot. This was attributed to Craig, who was under age at the time. Ruth Ellis was executed for murdering her lover, who had treated her badly. Timothy Evans was innocent of the crime for which he was hanged, and received a posthumous pardon many years later, as did Bentley. In retirement, their executioner, Albert Pierrepont, who had dispatched 450 men and women during his career, expressed doubts about the usefulness of the death penalty.[7] Sydney Silverman, a Labour MP, campaigned for the abolition of capital punishment under Attlee. In 1949, a majority of 23 was secured in the Commons to suspend the death penalty for five years as an experiment. The government and the Lords opposed this. Instead, a Royal Commission was established. It reported in September 1953, recommending that the age limit for suffering the death penalty be raised from eighteen to 21 and that juries be empowered to substitute a lesser sentence. The government rejected this. Conservative Party conferences consistently supported the death penalty and so did many grass roots activists. For itself, the government still regarded capital punishment as a deterrent. However, despite its majority, it was worried about putting the issue to the Commons because it feared another vote in favour of abolition. This actually happened in February 1956, when a Labour amendment, calling for abolition for an experimental period, was passed by 293 to 262 on a free vote. Later in the year, Silverman's Private Member's Bill was passed by the Commons but rejected by the Lords with the private approval of the government. Eventually, under Macmillan's premiership, the Homicide Act was passed in 1957. This curtailed but did not abolish the death penalty.

Suez

Eden, who succeeded Churchill in 1955, was influenced by his experiences in the First World War and of interwar diplomacy. This was also true of his Foreign Secretary, Harold Macmillan. Whereas the Americans, President Eisenhower and his Secretary of State John Foster Dulles, gave priority to the Cold War, Eden still saw the world in terms of spheres of influence and gave priority to the British Commonwealth. He saw the Middle East as the British sphere of influence. When Churchill was still Prime Minister and Eden Foreign Secretary, the two were at loggerheads over Iran, when in 1953 American influence replaced British there. They took differing views on Egypt in 1956.

Britain and France had long exercised great influence in Egypt. The French built the Suez Canal and had commercial and cultural influence in Cairo and Alexandria. British influence was more directly political and military. Both countries had financial interests in the Canal and elsewhere. As a result of Egypt's inability to pay its foreign debts, it had fallen under Anglo–French control, from 1876, and then British control, after 1882. This, in turn, caused resentment against the British. Egypt was nominally part of the Ottoman Empire but, as that empire broke up, after the First World War, Britain unilaterally declared Egypt independent in 1922. It continued to rule Egypt *de facto*. The rise of Mussolini and his desire to build a new empire in Africa caused the British to make concessions to Egyptian nationalism. In 1936, a new treaty was negotiated. Although this represented an advance for Egypt, its terms were such that they left the British in effective control. They had the right to station army, navy and air force units in the Canal Zone, their ambassador took precedence over all other foreign diplomats, they could declare martial law, and so on.[8] The 1939–45 war and the postwar decolonisation encouraged nationalism throughout the region. In 1952, the corrupt King Farouk was overthrown in a military coup and a republic declared. In 1954, the military government insisted on a new relationship with Britain, including the withdrawal of British troops from the Canal Zone by June 1956. Less than a month after the Anglo–Egyptian Agreement was signed, Colonel Gamal Nasser overthrew the more moderate General Neguib as head of the military régime. As the British and Americans were not prepared to arm the Egyptians, they concluded a deal with Communist Czechoslovakia, in 1955. Britain and the USA had hoped to placate Egypt with economic aid and offered to finance the Aswan Dam project, which was meant to lay the foundations of an economic revolution in Egypt. When Nasser made the mistake of recognising Communist China, the two Western powers withdrew their offer. In retaliation, Egypt nationalised the Suez Canal. The Americans were not as directly concerned about this as the British and the French. Two-thirds of Western Europe's oil imports passed through the Canal. British and French investors (including the British government) owned the Canal. Both seemed to think that they would lose all respect in the area if they allowed nationalisation to go ahead. France was angry with Egypt because of its support for the independence movement in Algeria. In fact, Egypt was unlikely to prevent British and French ships using the Canal, as they were an important source of revenue. Moreover, Nasser promised the shareholders compensation at the current rate.[9] But the British and French thought the Egyptians could not run the Canal, regarding them with great contempt. A further complication was that Eden, a sick man, increasingly saw Nasser as a Mussolini-Hitler figure, who needed to be stopped. There were superficial resemblances. Nasser's regime was a dictatorship. Nasser did see himself, and was seen, as the man to unite all the Arabs and give them a new sense of dignity and purpose.

In secret, Britain and France prepared Operation Musketeer, the seizure of the Canal and the overthrow of Nasser. Also in secret, the two states drew in the Israelis, who agreed to attack Egypt. Britain and France would then give an ultimatum to both sides to withdraw, knowing Egypt would not agree. It would then be attacked. Dulles attempted to seek non-violent ways out of the crisis and called for negotiations between Egypt and the Canal users. Eden formally supported this, as a means of gaining time to complete the preparations and put the Egyptians off guard. On 13th September, Dulles publicly rejected the use of force.[10] President Eisenhower, facing re-election in November, did not wish to appear bellicose. He also wanted to maintain good relations with the oil-rich Arab states. The attack by Israel commenced on 29th October 1956. The Anglo–French attack started with sorties against Egyptian airfields on 31st October. On 5th November, there were airborne landings at Port Said. On the following day, seaborne landings took place. By midnight, a cease-fire was in force. Eden miscalculated that, once the Americans were faced with armed conflict, they would support their allies. Instead, 'Eisenhower was upset at their use of nineteenth-century colonial tactics; he was livid at their failure to inform him of their intentions. The Americans introduced a resolution in the UN General Assembly urging peace, a truce and imposed an oil embargo on Britain and France.'[11] The Soviets threatened nuclear war. British oil links with Iraq were put out of commission. The British economy went into a nosedive. Faced with these pressures, and mounting domestic controversy as well, Eden was forced to agree to a withdrawal. By 22nd December, the withdrawal had been completed.

British and French casualties were slight, just a handful of dead and wounded in each case.[12] Egyptian casualties, many of them civilians, ran into several thousands [13] It had been a brutal assault. The economic consequences for Britain were severe. It lost a quarter of its meagre gold and dollar reserves in November alone.[14] It faced the collapse of its currency and with it the sterling system (the instrument that still financed half the world's trade and payments). Its oil supplies were in danger, thus further undermining its economy. The Canal was blocked, another blow to Britain's trade and communications. Britain's prestige was sinking. It was under attack in the UN and on the streets of normally friendly cities. There were many that thought that the Suez operation had played into the hands of the Soviets and made it easier for them to assault Hungary. Suez certainly enhanced Soviet credibility in the Arab, African and Asian states. Nasser gained in popularity as the Arab David against the imperialist Goliath. As for Eden, he was forced from office.

When the Suez crisis broke, Eden faced a united Conservative Party and could count on the support of most of the opposition in Parliament. Labour's Hugh Gaitskell commented: 'it is exactly the same that we encountered from Mussolini and Hitler in those years before the war . . . I believe we were right to react sharply to his move.'[15] Gaitskell, however, wanted any action agreed with the UN. The UN would have been unlikely to sanction action against Egypt. The Cabinet was not as united as at first appeared. On 4th November it voted, by twelve votes to six, in favour of limited military action; well below the level Eden had originally envisaged. Butler, Kilmuir, Salisbury, all senior figures, and Monckton were doves.[16] Home (Commonwealth), Selwyn Lloyd (Foreign Secretary) and Lennox-Boyd (Colonial Secretary) were among the 'war party'. Macmillan, a hawk at first, changed his stance when, as Chancellor of the Exchequer, he saw the economic ruin the 'adventure' was causing. He also saw his chance to replace Eden. Two junior ministers, Anthony Nutting and Edward Boyle, resigned. On 9th January 1957, Eden announced his resignation on health grounds.

Missing the Bus for Europe

Under Attlee's government, Britain had been eager to join with its European neighbours in defence matters but, in 1951, rejected participation in the Iron and Steel Community (Schumann Plan). Churchill and Eden continued Labour's policies. It is difficult to understand why Churchill, having supported European unity in opposition, turned his back on it in government. Probably, when they thought of the new constellation rising in Western Europe, Britain's leaders saw it as smaller and less significant than the British Commonwealth, which they still thought they controlled. The European Coal and Steel Community (ECSC), which later became the European Economic Community (EEC), comprised only West Germany, France, Italy, Belgium, Holland and Luxembourg – the six. Churchill and Eden, Attlee and Bevin, had seen Germany twice defeated and seen it shrink before their very eyes. The rump West Germany, with its tiny capital in Bonn, had no armed forces, no aviation industry and no nuclear capacity. By comparison with that of Britain, its banking system was puny, even its fishing fleet was, in 1960, still smaller than those of Britain and Norway. In the 1950s, West Germany was something of an unknown quantity. France was in a state of crisis, culminating with the overthrow of the Fourth Republic, in 1958, and fears that it could become like Franco's Spain. Italy was seriously underestimated owing to its wartime military incompetence, small cars, the Mafia and the Catholic Church. Britain was Protestant; in the six, Catholicism predominated. In Britain there was a tendency to think that the six needed to get together to add up to something. To the British, Australia, New Zealand, Canada and even South Africa and Rhodesia, seemed psychologically nearer. After all, they had stood by Britain in the two world wars and you could emigrate to such places – you could not emigrate to the six! It was a pity that more British people did not speak other European languages and that, of those who did, more did not understand economics and politics. Germany and France had fought each other three times in the space of a single lifespan. There seemed a likelihood that their mutual antagonism would resurface. At the more practical level, in 1955 the Treasury advised Eden that an EEC would damage the British economy. Britain, it was believed, having been protected since 1932, would have difficulty in competing with EEC industries. Britain still did much of its trade with the Commonwealth – though this was a declining percentage – and enjoyed the benefits of cheap commodities, especially food, from the Commonwealth. In the circumstances, it was decided Britain was to make every effort to stop the EEC being formed, though without appearing hostile.[17] Nevertheless, the European bandwagon was rolling. In June 1955, the ECSC ministers met at Messina to create an atomic community, for the peaceful development of nuclear energy, and to establish a customs union. The Treaty of Rome followed in 1957, which established the EEC on 1st January 1958. Euratom was also established. The British set up the European Free Trade Association (EFTA) with the smaller economies – Austria, Denmark, Norway, Portugal, Sweden, Switzerland – in 1959 (see Table A 9). Finland joined later. Although its members generated one-fifth of world trade, EFTA was too weak to succeed and Britain sought entry to the EEC in 1961. Britain got a sympathetic hearing in Bonn, but not in Paris. In January 1963, President de Gaulle of France vetoed Britain's application.

Independent Television

In 1950, about half a million television licences were issued. By the early 1960s, the number had risen to over 12 million. In 1950, there was just one BBC television channel. In 1964, BBC 2 was launched. But the big breakthrough was the launch of Independent Television (ITV), under the Television Act of 1954. The Act set up an Independent Television Authority (ITA), which owned the transmitters and awarded franchises to fourteen companies to provide programmes. These companies got their income from firms buying advertising time. They were responsible to the ITA for the quality of their programmes. The BBC continued to derive its income from licence fees. The Pilkington Report on Broadcasting (1962) criticised certain aspects of the operation of ITV, which led to the Television Act of 1963. This strengthened the ITA and placed more emphasis on the broadcasting of information and education, not just entertainment. It also taxed advertising receipts.

The original decision to set up ITV was hard fought. The Labour Party, trade unions, churches, university vice-chancellors and professional bodies of education and various other interests, including much of the press, had opposed the move. They thought Britain would inevitably go down the American road, with advertisers demanding, and getting, low grade, popular programmes. They feared the small screen would be dominated, like the press, by Conservative-inclined tycoons. They also argued that the Conservatives had not put this option to the electorate in 1951. The victory of the pro-ITV campaigners was the result of skilful lobbying by Selwyn Lloyd and Norman Collins. Because of the opposition, ITV was severely restricted at first in what it could discuss. Although the ITA cancelled a programme in which Malcolm Muggeridge was to have criticised the monarchy, ITV soon showed itself to be more adventurous than the BBC. Both Granada TV, operating in the North, and Associated Television (ATV), operating in the Midlands, chipped away at existing rules and conventions and broadened the discussion of current affairs. In the 1959 election, Granada announced an election *Marathon*, which broke new ground, offering candidates in its area the opportunity to make a televised address. The BBC soon followed. However, it was the BBC which led the field with its satirical programme *That Was The Week That Was* in November 1962. It launched the careers of David Frost and Willie Rushton (with his unflattering impersonations of Prime Minister Harold Macmillan). It was taken off before the 1964 election. At a more popular level, as well, television was contributing to the Cultural Revolution (see Chapter 7).

In December 1960, Granada started broadcasting *Coronation Street*. Against the expectations of some, this soap opera, set in the dingy, depressing, terraced houses of Salford, soon hit the top rating and continued to do so for decades. BBC's *Z-Cars*, which ran from 1962–78, attempted a more realistic portrayal of a police force, in this case on Merseyside. It challenged the cosy, unrealistic *Dixon of Dock Green*, which lasted for 21 years (1955–76). The competition for viewers meant that both BBC and ITV attempted to entice the maximum audiences for quiz programmes, chat shows, sport and pop music. But they were obliged to compete with serious drama, films and documentaries too. ITV's advertisements came under fire from women's organisations for their old-fashioned stereotyping of women.

Colonial Retreat

In 1953 the Queen became officially 'Head' of the Commonwealth. She remained Queen of the UK, Canada, Australia, New Zealand and South Africa. For the Commonwealth, the Crown had become entirely symbolic. Most of Britain's political élite thought the new Commonwealth, rather than the old Empire, would give Britain, British influence and British trade a new lease of life. In the best possible way, men like Churchill, Attlee, Eden and Gaitskell saw the Commonwealth as a unique institution of different nations, races, religions, political and economic systems, all coming together for their common good. The reality was rather different. These nations could agree on little. Britain's economy, even had it been more successful than it was, could not have provided all the trade and aid needed by one single large member such as India. The Second World War had revealed that these states could not look to Britain for their defence. Australia and New Zealand depended more and more on the USA for this. Canada was being drawn ever faster into its southern neighbour's orbit, causing anger and tension in French Canada. Ethnic and territorial conflicts brought wars between India and Pakistan (which was to leave the Commonwealth in 1971). Conflict, rather than concord, was often the legacy of the old Empire in Uganda, Kenya and elsewhere, as ethnic minorities were later thrust out. Instability often followed independence, partly because, in a number of cases, the states were the creation of colonialism, cutting across ethnic and tribal boundaries. Finally, South Africa left the Commonwealth in 1961, after continuing criticism of its Apartheid régime.

Under Churchill, the bandwagon of independence had stopped. Under Eden, the Sudan became independent outside the Commonwealth on 1st January 1956. Increasingly, there was pressure from within the UN for decolonisation; the General Assembly of the UN was soon dominated by the ex-colonial states. The Soviet Union and the NATO states competed with each other for the attention of these newly emerging states. In the British case, the big divesting gained momentum under Macmillan. The Gold Coast became the Republic of Ghana in March 1957, when the Union Jack was hauled down. Malaya followed in August 1957. British Somaliland, Cyprus and Nigeria gained their independence in 1960; Sierra Leone, North Cameroon (which joined Nigeria), South Cameroon and Tanganyika in 1961. In the following year, it was the turn of Western Samoa, Jamaica, Trinidad and Tobago, and Uganda. North Borneo, Sarawak, Singapore, Zanzibar (which joined Tanganyika to form Tanzania) and Kenya gained independence in 1963. Finally, under the Conservatives, Nyasaland, Malta and Northern Rhodesia (Republic of Zambia) became independent in 1964.

As with other empires, the road to independence was more complicated where sizable British minorities had settled, or where a state was considered of strategic importance. Kenya and Southern Rhodesia belonged to the first category, Cyprus and Malta to the second. In Kenya, the small, mainly British, white minority had settled the rich, fertile highlands, leaving the poorer land to the Africans. There was also a small Asian trading community. African advancement had been moderate. Missionary schools, as elsewhere in Africa, provided a road to upward mobility for Africans, who then increasingly filled the lower grades of the civil service. The army was also a kind of advancement.

However, there were still strict legal and more practical limits to black progress. Political development was hampered by tribalism. Frustration built up and Jomo Kenyatta attempted to mobilise this through the Kenya African Union. A graduate of missionary schools, Kenyatta had spent fifteen years in Britain and had good contacts there in left-wing circles. He returned in 1946. Members of the Kikuyu tribe, a considerable minority of whom was urbanised, formed an underground organisation, known as Mau Mau, to fight the whites. The British colonial administration was taken by surprise as Mau Mau unleashed a campaign of violence. In 1952, a state of emergency was declared and 183 Africans, including Kenyatta, were arrested. The result was that a younger, more militant cadre took over.[18] Violence escalated on both sides. Mau Mau sought to intimidate loyal Kikuyu by murder, and the security forces carried out resettlement policies, which had been tried elsewhere. In 1954, the RAF flew nearly 4,500 bombing sorties against Mau Mau gangs in the forests. This did not break the rebels but did harm the wildlife.[19] The weakness of Mau Mau was that it was confined to one tribe and had no outside source of weapons and supplies. When their leader, Dedan Kimathi, was wounded and captured in October 1956, the revolt came to an end. Some 10,500 Mau Mau had been killed. The security forces lost twelve British troops and 578 police and Kings African Rifles, of whom 63 were Europeans. The civilian death toll was 32 Europeans, 26 Asians and 1,817 loyal Africans. The Mau Mau campaign had an important impact on British political thought. It had taken 10,000 British and African troops, 21,000 police, 25,000 home guards and the unopposed RAF four years to defeat the badly equipped Mau Mau. The lesson learned by British politicians was that they had to speed up the attainment of independence by the colonies.[20] Kenyatta was not released from prison until 1961. He then led his country to independence in 1963.

The problems of the Central African Federation threatened to engulf the British armed forces as well. The Federation of Northern and Southern Rhodesia and Nyasaland was an ill-advised attempt, in 1953, to hold together three disparate states, one of which, Southern Rhodesia, had gained internal self-government by the white minority in 1923. After some disturbances in all three territories, including the arrest of Dr Hastings Banda of Nyasaland, Nyasaland (Malawi) and Northern Rhodesia (Zambia) were allowed to go their own way. In Southern Rhodesia, the whites, increasingly influenced by events in South Africa and the Belgian Congo (Zaire), voted in the Rhodesia Front, in December 1962, indicating their determination to resist black majority rule. In theory, Britain still had responsibility for Southern Rhodesia. It dissolved the Federation, in December 1963, and tried to bring together the different political groups in Southern Rhodesia.

Cyprus Emergency

Cyprus was regarded as of key importance by the British, who took it over from the Ottoman (Turkish) Empire in 1878. The majority of its people were Greek and Greece claimed it. Greece offered to leave the British bases intact. Unfortunately, this was not acceptable to the strong Turkish minority or to the Turkish state. In 1946, Attlee had offered a measure of internal self-government but this was turned down by Greeks of all political persuasions on the island. They demanded Enosis – union with Greece. Bombs, which went off on 1st April 1955, signalled the start of a campaign of violence to achieve this aim. Led by Colonel George Grivas, an officer in the pre-war Greek army, the EOKA units planted bombs and killed Cypriots, who worked for the British, as well as the British themselves. Violent demonstrations, by school children and students, were organised to embarrass the British. A few guerrillas were able to operate because of the passive support of a much larger community. Archbishop Makarios, the leader of the Greek Orthodox Church on Cyprus, was also, in effect, the political leader of the Greek Cypriots. He had at first opposed violence. Later he was carried along by the rising tide of sentiment. The British made the mistake of deporting him to the Seychelles. It only made him more popular at home and abroad. The Turkish minority backed the British and inter-communal fighting broke out. There was fear that violence could erupt between Greek and Turkish Cypriots living in London. Increasingly, NATO, to which both Greece and Turkey belonged, brought pressure to bear, to bring about a settlement. This was

achieved in February 1959. Cyprus became an independent republic within the Commonwealth; Makarios was elected president
and Britain kept its bases. By 1964, the situation was so bad
again between the two communities that the UN sent a peacekeeping force.

'bricks for Empire building'

After 1945, child migrant agencies sent off some 10,000 British
children to Australia. This practice, which had started in the
nineteenth century, carried on until 1967.[21] Other children were
sent to Canada, New Zealand, Rhodesia and South Africa. Although the numbers going to most areas fell after the Second
World War, the numbers going to Australia actually increased
between 1956 and 1966. The children were in charitable
children's homes because they were orphans, were from poor
homes or were dependent on single parents, who could not
maintain them. The charities collected subsidies for sending
the children. For the British government, the attraction was that
they were disposing of the unwanted poor and providing potential settlers, who would become 'bricks for Empire building'.[22]
They would ensure that the Commonwealth states remained closely
tied with Britain. They were thought to be a way of ensuring
British hegemony in areas of white settlement. No doubt many
of those sending the children thought that they were offering
them a better life, taking them from the slums of London,
Liverpool, Manchester, Glasgow or Belfast to the wide open spaces
of the dominions or southern Africa, giving them a chance to
better themselves. For some this was true, but many faced years
of harsh toil and loneliness, often denied proper schooling and
even knowledge of their origins. In many cases their hosts saw
them as cheap labour on the land or as domestic servants. Under
the Children Act (1948), the Home Secretary had the power to
make regulations that would control the way the voluntary
organisations – the Catholic Child Welfare Council, the Church
of England Council for Commonwealth and Empire Settlement,
the Fairbridge Society, Dr Barnardo's and other bodies – arranged
child migration. In fact, no regulations were made. Only in 1982
did it become a legal requirement for an organisation to get

the consent of the minister before sending a child abroad. As it was, 'The misjudgements of the child migration scheme destroyed the lives of thousands of children and cannot be spelt out too often.'[23]

Gaitskell and Bevan

After its disagreements over re-armament in 1951, Labour tore itself apart in the years which followed. To be sure, as in all parties, there was the clash of personalities. Bevin had said of his comrades, 'With friends like that who needs enemies?' Dalton had written scathingly about his colleagues. Bevan spoke with open contempt for his party opponents. He was a powerful figure who found it difficult to be just one of a team. He was also something of an intellectual, who was fired by a burning sense of grievance as a Welshman and as a former miner. He was in revolt against the overlordship of the southern English middle class; in Labour's case Attlee, Cripps, Dalton, Ede and Gaitskell. Even the working-class leaders of the period, Bevin and Morrison, were from the south. Labour was a 'broad church' as far as its make-up was concerned. All claimed to be socialists but there were many species if this peculiar animal. On the Left, there were former Communists who remained committed to Marxism and the Soviet Union. There were Trotskyists, there were democratic Marxists like Bevan, and there were pacifist-inclined, anti-imperialist radicals. In the middle, there were 'conservatives' who could not bear giving up party dogmas. On the right, there were those who saw Labour as the party best suited to introducing the democratic and socially just reforms needed in contemporary society. Some of these were former Liberals who regarded Labour as having taken over the progressive tradition of the Liberals. There were a few Christian Socialists and there were trade unionists that were suspicious of grand designs. There were those who supported Labour out of idealism and those who did so out of bitterness. There were those who, having been 'born' in the party, used it as a career ladder. There were middle-class 'traitors' who, as individualists, did not wish to be buried alive in the confines of their own class.

Broadly, Labour believed in a strategy to greatly reduce differences of wealth and status, gradually changing society so that class differences ceased to be important. This would be achieved via taxation, welfare policies and transferring ownership from the private to the public domain. Planning and public ownership would also achieve full employment and economic growth. Many in Labour's ranks rejected Stalin but thought there was something progressive about the Soviet Union. In most cases they failed to understand that the democratic Russian Revolution of 1917 had been destroyed by the Leninist coup of 1917. They failed to understand the nature of the Soviet industrial system and the spurious claims made about the welfare system. There was a syndicalist stream in the Labour Party which sought workers' co-operatives, co-ownership schemes, co-determination and the like, as the basis for a new industrial order. Professor G. D. H. Cole was its most important advocate. But this tendency was crushed by the crypto-Marxists and the believers in public corporations, such as Morrison. Bevan later gave his sympathies to Tito's régime in Yugoslavia, seeing it as an alternative to Stalinism and capitalism. Labour was essentially about collectivism and class, as opposed to individualism. Partly because of the Nonconformist background of many of its exponents, it tended to regard individual pleasures and achievements as sinful. Council housing was more progressive than private housing, public transport was more progressive than private cars, the Co-op than private shops, and so on. As some of its younger MPs, like Tony Crosland in his *The Future of Socialism* (1956), pointed out, Labour was failing to take into account the changes going on in society and the changing aspirations of millions of ordinary people. The industrial working class was in decline by the 1950s and the new white collar class was taking its place. The rhetoric of the 'working class' would not appeal to most teachers, nurses, office workers, shop assistants, technicians, local government officers and small businessmen. Yet so often when such individuals plucked up the courage to join Labour, they felt they had to apologise for the fact that they were not 'workers'. In his *In Place of Fear* (1952) Bevan stated the case for democratic, full-blooded socialism with public ownership at the heart of it. Morrison and Gaitskell were basically opposed to further nationalisation, except in special cases. Gaitskell wanted to amend the party constitution of 1918, which seemed to make 'common ownership' of the means of production, distribution and exchange, the only goal of democratic socialism. Bevan had a loose ginger group who became known as the Bevanites, including R. H. S. Crossman, Barbara Castle, Tom Driberg, Michael Foot, Ian Mikardo and Harold Wilson. After Labour lost the election of 1955, at which Bevan had been the bogeyman for the Conservatives, the Bevanites fell apart, with Castle, Crossman and Wilson moving nearer the centre.[24] The strength of these differing views was indicated by the election of a leader to succeed Attlee, in 1955. Elected by Labour MPs, Gaitskell received 157 votes, an absolute majority, Bevan 70 and Morrison 40. But Bevan was subsequently elected Labour's treasurer by the party conference. This was, to a degree, an indication of the strength of his support among constituency activists. By 1957, Gaitskell and Bevan were co-operating and Bevan made his famous reversal of view on Britain's H-bomb. At Labour's annual conference in Brighton, he opposed unilateral nuclear disarmament by Britain, claiming it would 'send a Foreign Secretary, whoever he may be, naked into the conference chamber'. With Bevan and Gaitskell united, Labour looked as if it had a good chance of winning, despite the increasing affluence. This was not to be, and Bevan died of cancer in July 1960. Gaitskell died unexpectedly in 1963.

Election 1959

In retrospect, the Conservative victory in October 1959 was not surprising. Britain, as a whole, had prospered since 1955, and indeed since 1951. Though still only a minority, a growing number of people who would never have thought it possible were buying cars and their own homes. Many more were buying washing machines, vacuum cleaners and other durable consumer goods. More still had television. There was a boom in holidays away from home. Aspirations were rising. Unemployment had risen since 1955 but was still very low – 1.9 per cent. Life seemed less drab and austere than it had done in the 1940s or before the war. Once again, unofficial strikes had furnished the Conservatives with ammunition. Macmillan (at 65) had proved to be a colourful Prime Minister. Influenced by the poverty in his

Stockton constituency in the 1930s, he was originally on the left of his party. Later, he became popular for the way he had hammered Labour when the Conservatives were in opposition. After his success at Housing (1951–4), he served briefly at Defence (1954–5), even more briefly as Foreign Secretary in 1955, and then at the Exchequer, until taking over as Premier in 1957. Like Eden, he was an old Etonian. He projected himself as slightly old-fashioned, determined to promote prosperity at home, and peace abroad. Notwithstanding all of this, Labour expected to win, or at least greatly improve their position. Gaitskell (53), educated at Winchester and Oxford, was a former economics lecturer and civil servant. His public image was rather stiff and too serious. But he and Bevan made a powerful duo. Labour had won four by-elections with considerable swings. Up to about ten days before polling, the tide had been running in Labour's favour. However, the cost of Labour's social programme became a major issue. Gaitskell made a serious error when he claimed that under Labour there would be no increase in the standard or other rates of income tax, so long as normal peacetime conditions continued.[25] The Conservatives ruthlessly exploited this opening. Labour could not repair the damage. The Conservatives made 28 gains, ten of them in the Midlands and nine in the London area. Defying the national trend, there was a swing against them in Clydeside and South East Lancashire. They won 365 seats, Labour 258 and the Liberals six. Their respective percentages were 49.4, 43.8 and 5.9. Turnout was up from 76.7 to 78.8 per cent. In what was the first full television election, Labour later concluded that they would have done better had ITV not screened a new Western serial, *Rawhide*, on polling day at 7 p.m. – the time when Labour traditionally got most of their voters out.[26]

7 Conservatives on the Run, 1961–64

The last years of Macmillan and his successor, Home, were years when there were increasing doubts about the Conservative agenda. Some, even among Conservatives, believed Britain had fallen prey to materialism and decadence. Many others were convinced urgent reforms were needed if the country was to keep up with its competitors.

Education

The replacement of the School Certificate by the General Certificate of Education (GCE) in 1951, a measure of the outgoing Labour administration, marked a step forward. Under the old system, the small numbers taking exams were required to pass in virtually all subjects at one sitting to gain their Certificate. The bulk of school leavers were not prepared for exams. Under the new system, a candidate could pass in one or any number of subjects at one or more attempts. It had the advantage of gradually introducing an increasing range of examination courses for pupils at secondary modern schools. It also made it easier for mature students to take courses leading to exams, at evening classes, and for those who had failed in vital subjects to make up the deficit in the same way. But progress was slow and most children who were condemned, by 'failure' in the eleven-plus, to go to secondary modern schools, left at fifteen with no qualifications. In the increasingly affluent and less deferential society of the late 1950s, more and more parents were dissatisfied with the system, including many Conservative voters who had aspirations for their children. Comprehensive schools, that is those taking all children from a given neighbourhood without external selection, were seen as an alternative to the tripartite system.

Labour and the Liberals favoured them. Increasingly, often under pressure from their own voters, Conservatives took up their cause, though they attempted to avoid abolishing grammar schools. By January 1963, there were still only 175 schools in England and Wales classified as comprehensives, out of a total of nearly 6,000 maintained secondary schools. In another move to quell dissatisfaction, a new Certificate of Secondary Education (CSE) was established. It was aimed at pupils who were considerably less able academically than those taking the GCE. This distinction however, soon became blurred, as the higher grades of the CSE were seen as representing a level of achievement equivalent to that of the GCE.

Apart from exams, the schools had other problems too. It was difficult to recruit and keep good teachers, especially in the inner urban areas. In 1961, only 19.8 per cent of the teachers in England and Wales held a university degree. In primary schools it was only 3.8 per cent, secondary moderns 17.3 per cent and grammar schools 78.2 per cent. In Scotland, 45.6 per cent of teachers were graduates.[1] In urban areas, London most of all, a significant number of teachers were temporary 'supply' teachers. Another recognised weakness of the system was oversized classes. Good progress was made in primary schools, with the percentage of children in oversized classes in England and Wales falling from 43.2 in 1953 to 18.9 in 1962. In secondary schools, progress was much more modest, falling from 58.2 in 1953 to 56.6 in 1962. In Scotland, the position was much better.[2] Once again, it was the inner urban areas, which were much less well served than the suburbs. It could be argued that they needed a much higher staff/pupil ratio if they were ever to motivate and equip their pupils to break out of the ghetto. This applied also to physical conditions. The government's White Paper on Public Investment (1961) admitted that 'About half our children are attending schools built before the 1914–18 war, many of which provide conditions well below modern standards.'

Other problems were identified in education: poor science and maths teaching; poor provision for technical education at all levels; too few graduates. As Britain declined industrially, observers noted that, in general, the more successful economies and more prosperous societies had higher educational standards than those prevailing in Britain. This had been identified in the nineteenth century as a problem. Crash programmes were put into operation but usually suffered setbacks, or were not implemented at all, as a result of financial stringency. The open secret was that Parliament never felt education to be an overriding priority because the great majority of MPs did not send their children to the maintained 'state' schools. Eden was concerned about technical education and Macmillan about higher education in general. He and others had been impressed by the West German economic miracle, France's successful, yet less spectacular, recovery and Soviet achievements in the nuclear field and into space. In October 1957, the world held its breath when it was announced that the Soviets had succeeded in placing the first artificial earth satellite in orbit. During Macmillan's premiership they put the first man into space, Yuri Gagarin (1961) and the first woman, Valentina Tereshkova (1963). Less real were Soviet claims about economic progress, which were, broadly speaking, accepted by Western experts and politicians.

As mentioned in Chapter 1, Britain's poor record on technical education had been identified by the Samuelson Commission in the 1880s. Yet little had been done. The 1944 Education Act had proposed the development of technical schools as part of a tripartite system of secondary education, but this had not happened. The White Paper *Technical Education* (1956) recommended a rapid expansion of this sector. Under this programme, ten technical colleges were transformed into colleges of advanced technology (CATs), with the emphasis on advanced work. In 1962, they were transferred from local authority control to independent governing bodies, receiving direct grants from the Ministry of Education.

In October 1963, the government accepted the Report of the Robbins Committee on Higher Education, that the CATs should be given university status. Among the new technological universities that came into existence under this scheme were Aston, Bradford, Brunel, Loughborough, Salford, Strathclyde and UMIST (Manchester). Robbins found that higher education in Britain was more economical because of the lower wastage rate and shorter, more concentrated, courses of study. Robbins recommended a massive expansion of higher education and this was accepted by the government. Under the Conservatives, seven other new universities were established: Sussex (Brighton), East

Anglia (Norwich), York, Canterbury, Essex (Colchester), Warwick and Lancaster. The university population expanded from 83,000 in 1951 to about 125,000 in 1964. The McKenna Report (1959) on business studies brought improvements in that field.

Cultural Revolution

In 1956, *Look Back in Anger* was produced at the Royal Court Theatre, Sloane Square, London. It was written by a very unhappy young man, John Osborne, and became a great success. It was one aspect of what became known, much later, as Britain's Cultural Revolution. This was, above all, a questioning of the old authority. It encompassed a questioning of class, conventional sexual morality, gender roles and the hegemony of middle-class culture. It started in the 1950s and continued throughout the 1960s. In part, this revolution was the result of a general coming of age of a generation who had only known relative prosperity and was not prepared to be quite so deferential as their parents had been. At the more conscious political level, it was a reaction to the perceived successes and failures of the Labour government and of Moscow Communism. It was influenced by the threat of nuclear war, with the certainty of the annihilation of Britain if it occurred. It was greatly influenced by developments in the USA, especially in Hollywood, and other forms of popular culture.

What struck critics about *Look Back in Anger* was the anger expressed by the main character of the play, Jimmy Porter, a self-pitying anarchist of sorts who persecuted his wife because of her superior social status. In the following year another angry young man, Joe Lampton, the 'hero' of John Braine's novel *Room at the Top* (1957), appeared. He found the innocent, upper class Susan and decided, 'I'll marry her if I have to put her in the family way to do it. I'll make her daddy give me a damned good job.' He achieved both goals, losing himself in the process. By comparison, Stan Barstow's *A Kind of Loving* (1960), set in Yorkshire, was relatively mild. Like Barstow and Braine, David Storey was born and brought up in working class Yorkshire. His *This Sporting Life* (1960) was based on his own experience in the tough world of rugby league. Also based on personal experience was Alan Sillitoe's *Saturday Night And Sunday Morning* (1958), about the life and loves of Arthur Seaton, a production worker at Raleigh's cycle factory in Nottingham. David Lodge's novel about life as a British Army conscript, *Ginger, You're Barmy* (1962), mingled horror with farce. Meanwhile, another young man was having success at the Royal Court. From a Jewish family in the East End of London came Arnold Wesker with *Chicken Soup with Barley*, *Roots* and *The Kitchen*. These interpreted a variety of working-class, Jewish and non-Jewish, experiences. What these writers had in common is that they were writing about working-class life and, with the exception of Wesker, the setting was the North or the Midlands. The authors also had in common that all of them, except Lodge, were non-graduates. They expressed the frustration and bitterness of outsiders. The media called them the angry young men and this suited the times. Under the Conservatives, Britain was becoming increasingly self-satisfied, and the anger was, indirectly, an expression of the political impotence of the left-wing intelligentsia. One book by an earlier angry young man was put on trial in 1959. This was D. H. Lawrence's *Lady Chatterley's Lover*, the publisher of which, the entirely respectable Penguin Books, was taken to court for publishing an obscene book. The prosecution failed. It did show, however, that there were powerful forces that opposed the new trend. The book was a love story about a gamekeeper's relationship with the wife of his impotent employer. Perhaps it was the fear of the potential challenge to the class system that frightened those bringing the prosecution.

The books of the angry young men became more significant when they were adapted for the cinema. These films formed part of what became known as the 'new wave' of the British cinema, but being made for the commercial cinema, any political messages were muted and their sexual themes were emphasised. Nevertheless, films like *Saturday Night And Sunday Morning* (1960) and *A Taste of Honey* (1961), shot respectively in Nottingham and Manchester, left vivid pictures of important segments of British life of that period. This was hardly less true of *Room at the Top* (1959), *The Loneliness of the Long Distance Runner* (1962), about life in a borstal, from another Sillitoe story, and the humorous *Billy Liar!* (1963). These films were influenced both by the neo-realist films of Italy and France and by Hollywood. The dramatic, yet depressing, *Rebel Without A Cause* (1955), with James Dean, and *The Wild One* (1953), with Marlon Brando, were just two of a number of American 'youth' movies which had a great deal of influence in Britain.

Behind the American movies was a new, mindless revolt of youth in the 'affluent society'. The expanding economies of the 1950s put easy money in the pockets of many young people and produced a new niche in the market, which was soon exploited by commercial interests. With few ideals or ideas and little education, many youngsters were frustrated and wanted to go their own way against the stuffy conformism of their parents. All the politicians could offer them was national service and nuclear death (or so it seemed). They expressed themselves through the music of Elvis Presley, and later the Beatles, the Rolling Stones and others. Elvis was given greater publicity through his films. The Beatles, from Liverpool, who were at first scorned by the record companies, gained currency on Radio Luxembourg at a time when the BBC still had a radio monopoly. Clothing too was part of the Cultural Revolution. Suits with narrow trousers and narrow jacket lapels started replacing the pleated wider trousers and wide lapels. The new styles gave an advantage to youthful figures. The strange Teddy Boy style was part of this trend. For women, the mini-skirt became more and more popular.

The Cultural Revolution focused mainly on men, but women's and gay issues were starting to be raised. In the cinema, *A Taste of Honey* dealt simultaneously with an unmarried, teenage mother to-be's friendship with a homosexual and with the black father of her child. *The L Shaped Room*, based on the novel by Lynne Reid Banks, was also about the problems of being pregnant and unmarried in 1950s Britain. Doris Lessing arrived in Britain from Southern Rhodesia in 1949 and published, throughout the 1950s, a series of novels and stories exposing the society she had left behind. Admired by men, she became a cult writer for feminists. At a time when homosexuality was still a criminal offence, the film *Victim* (1961), a thriller dealing with the black-mailing of a gay man, featuring Dirk Bogarde, was courageous.

Most of the writers mentioned were on the Left, some of them – Braine, Lessing, Storey and Wesker – were active in politics, as were many of the film directors. They joined the more politically minded young people, and often the better educated, in the Campaign for Nuclear Disarmament (CND) and/or the New Left. J. B. Priestley, (Lord) Bertrand Russell, John Braine, Michael Foot, Canon Collins, Peggy Duff and others founded CND in 1958. It was non-party and gave a cause to many (mainly middle-class) thinking individuals. It organised marches to nuclear weapons research establishments, such as Aldermaston, and nuclear bases, thus picking up the tradition of marches and demonstrations, and pacifism, of the 1930s. Most of the demonstrators were young people. In October 1960, Russell resigned the Presidency of CND to set up, with Rev. Michael Scott, the Committee of 100 to encourage civil disobedience against nuclear weapons. The New Left emerged in large measure from those who left the Communist Party in protest against the Soviet invasion of Hungary. Non-Communists and non-Marxists joined them at a series of successful events between 1957 and 1962. A string of New Left coffee bars were set up throughout the country and two journals were published, becoming the *New Left Review* in 1960. Ralph Samuel and Stuart Hall, the West Indian sociologist, were the prime movers, with others, like Raymond Williams and Ralph Miliband, joining in. Once Harold Wilson became leader of the Labour Party (see below), much of this activity was abandoned or lost its appeal. The broader Cultural Revolution continued.

It needs to be mentioned that most people were not directly influenced by these developments. The 'carry on' comedy films were far more popular than offerings like *Look Back in Anger*. The James Bond films, starting with *Dr No* (1962) and adapted from Ian Fleming's thrillers, were even more popular. They appeared as Britain grappled with its increasing self-doubt as it lost one colony after another and its European neighbours, and old enemies, overtook it economically. In spite of everything the suave, sexy, fictional British secret agent, Bond, could single-handedly outwit armies of foreign villains. Escapism was often more satisfying than reality.

Heart-searching over Immigration

In the summer of 1958, riots erupted in Nottingham and Notting Hill (London), which were the result of antagonism towards the newly arrived immigrants from the colonies. The three parties said little about this in the 1959 election. Sir Oswald Mosley, the pre-war Fascist leader, sought to use the issue of black immigration to propel himself back into Parliament. He was disappointed when he stood in the North Kensington constituency in 1959. In a four-cornered contest, he lost his deposit, attracting only 2,821 votes. A Jewish Liberal also lost his deposit but beat Mosley into fourth place. The Labour candidate scraped home with a majority of 877. The loss of votes by the Labour candidate appears to have had nothing to do with Mosley, who was advocating forcible repatriation of West Indians, combined with heavy British investment in the West Indies, to provide more employment there, and that Britain should purchase all its sugar from Jamaica. Mosley also advocated a United States of Europe and peace.[3] Like the Labour Cabinet before them, the Conservatives did discuss immigration on many occasions. There appears to have been a strong feeling that any legislation would adversely affect the future of the Commonwealth; any attempt to exclude West Indians only, even more so. The view was also expressed that the Irish could not be restricted, even though they were no longer in the Commonwealth, because the Irish were not a different race from the ordinary inhabitants of Great Britain.[4] It was estimated that, since 1945, 750,000 Irish had come to Britain. A civil service committee advised the Cabinet to legislate controls in September 1956, but, under threat of possible resignation by Alan Lennox-Boyd, the Colonial Secretary, they put off action.[5] When action was finally taken, Butler, the Home Secretary, was telling the truth when he said to the Commons (16th November 1961) that the decision to control immigration from the Commonwealth had been agreed, 'only after long and anxious consideration and a considerable reluctance'.

The problem escalated, with increasing numbers arriving from the West Indies, Pakistan, India, and Cyprus and to a lesser extent from Africa, Aden and Hong Kong. According to official figures, certainly an underestimate, in 1959 the net intake from these countries was 21,000, rising to 58,000 in 1960 and to about 136,000 in 1961. It was stated in the Commons (28th June 1962) that total net intake from these states since 1955 was about 450,000. Others too were arriving, from the old dominions and

Ireland. Under the 1962 Commonwealth Immigrants Act, which became effective on 1st July 1962, a quota scheme was introduced, under which vouchers were issued to would-be immigrants, with not more than 25 per cent of the vouchers going to any one country. All the Commonwealth states, old and new, were included. Those with special skills, training or education likely to be useful in Britain, and those with a definite job to come to, were to be issued with Ministry of Labour vouchers. Those who could support themselves without working could still come without restriction, unless they were unsuitable for reasons of health, on grounds of national security or because of their criminal records. The act did not apply to children of immigrants born in Britain or to those who held UK passports. The wives and children of *bona fide* immigrants could still come, and those who had served in the armed forces of the Crown, in the Second World War, or in the UK armed forces since then, would be given special priority. The Act was opposed by Labour and the Liberals as racist. Labour sought voluntary agreements with Commonwealth governments.

Labour's Revival

After their impressive victory in 1959, the Conservatives had 21 good months and then seemed to go into rapid decline. From August 1961 until the general election of October 1964 they trailed Labour in the opinion polls. After losing one by-election to the Conservatives in March 1960, Labour won three from them in 1962, two in 1963 and one in 1964.

Labour was badly shaken by the defeat of 1959 and inevitably there were widely differing theses accounting for that defeat. The Left felt the electorate had not been given a clear alternative, the moderates believed Labour's 'cloth-cap image' was losing them votes among the upwardly mobile. Others thought organisation was at fault. Commissioned by the National Executive Committee, Harold Wilson had investigated Labour's organisation in the early 1950s, and concluded that it was as out-of-date as a penny-farthing bike. Nothing much had changed since then. Gaitskell faced the full fury of the Left at Labour's annual conference, at Scarborough, in 1960. He was defeated on the issue of unilateral nuclear disarmament owing to the support that the biggest union, the Transport and General Workers Union, led by Frank Cousins, gave to the unilateralists. Bevan had died of cancer in the previous July. Gaitskell rejected the decision and issued an emotional warning that he would, 'fight and fight and fight again for the party' he loved. In the following year, the unilateralist vote was reversed, by which time Labour was in favour with the electorate. Gaitskell looked set to win as Labour's stock rose in 1962. But he too died, rather suddenly and, some believe, even mysteriously, in January 1963. Labour MPs elected Harold Wilson as leader in preference to George Brown (the moderates' candidate) and James Callaghan (the centre). Callaghan, in retirement, thought this was the best outcome for Labour.[6] Wilson was by no means left wing. He had voted for Gaitskell in the leadership contest of 1955 after which he became shadow Chancellor. He moved on, becoming the shadow Foreign Secretary in 1961. He represented the managerial-meritocratic class of the 'forgotten' provinces north of the Trent. He saw himself appealing to the graduates of the expanding universities and the growing army of white-collar employees in the new service sectors of the economy. Within the party, he was seen as the unity candidate, at one and the same time putting the emphasis on Labour's appeal to the emerging groups in society and yet not overturning Labour's traditional values.

'Not British, not independent and not a deterrent'

The Suez campaign had revealed deficiencies in Britain's armed forces and Britain's dependence on the USA. Increasingly, experts and politicians were coming to realise that Britain could not sustain its existing level of defence expenditure. Nuclear weapons started to look like a relatively cheap alternative to mass conventional armed forces. This was Macmillan's thinking and he appointed Duncan Sandys, Minister of Defence, to increase the significance of Britain's nuclear weapons and decrease defence expenditure. Sandy's White Paper of 1957, *Defence Outline of Future Policy*, incorporated these aims. It promised the phasing out of conscription by 1962, with service manpower falling from 690,000 to 375,000. As the Empire contracted, there appeared less need for soldiers to act 'in aid of the civil power'. National service was, in any case, increasingly unpopular. There were some who thought it endangered the morals and stability of young men; there were those who thought it was destroying the skills needed by industry. According to some evidence, a considerable minority of former conscripts found it difficult to settle back into civilian life and work.[7] It was also emphasised that modern armed forces needed highly trained specialists, rather than conscripts with basic training only. The Germans, it was noted, had no conscription and no armed forces between 1945 and 1955. Had this given them an unfair advantage over the British? The last registrations for call up were in 1961.

Having placed their faith in big bangs rather than big battalions successive governments had to develop the necessary technology. The so-called V-bombers were constructed to deliver Britain's deterrent. On 15th May 1957, a Valiant bomber dropped Britain's first H-bomb over the Christmas Island area in the Pacific. It soon became clear, however, that bombers were becoming obsolete as offensive nuclear weapon carriers. Intercontinental ballistic missiles were the next stage, given the improvements in defence against bombers. Accordingly, Britain set out to develop Blue Streak, its own ballistic missile. In addition, a stand-off airborne missile, Blue Steel, was being built to reduce the vulnerability of the V-bombers to Soviet counter-measures. Britain had proved she was capable of developing the bombs and the means to deliver them, which led the Americans to revise their attitude to Anglo–American nuclear co-operation. By 1958, the revision of the McMahon Act made it possible for the USA to exchange information with any suitable ally.[8] Britain then soon came to the conclusion that it could not continue to finance the development of its own delivery systems, and Macmillan cancelled Blue Streak in 1960. Britain was offered Skybolt by the Americans but they, in turn, cancelled this project. At their famous meeting at Nassau in December 1962, President Kennedy offered Macmillan, instead, the submarine-based Polaris missile system. Britain built these submarines under licence, with the steel for the hulls, as well as key components of the communications, navigation and guidance systems, coming from the USA.[9] This led Wilson and other critics to claim that Britain's deterrent was 'not British, not independent and not a deterrent', as it depended on US technology and was small in relation to the nuclear arsenals of the Soviets and the Americans. Moreover, British defence strategy was based on NATO; it seemed unlikely that Britain would ever contemplate using the bomb without American support. Despite reductions in manpower, Britain continued to spend a higher proportion of its wealth on defence than did its European allies or Japan.

'The cult of amateurishness'

What has never been satisfactorily explained is how France was able to retain a large army based on conscription, operate a significant navy and build up a nuclear force relying on its own forces, and yet spend a lower proportion of its wealth on defence than Britain. It had, in effect, lost the Second World War and later, colonial wars in Vietnam and Algeria. It had suffered the destruction of the Third Republic in 1940 and of the Fourth in 1958. Yet few were the critics of the strong armed forces in France. France, like its continental neighbours, retained conscription. The French did not seem to think these national servicemen were inadequate to the tasks of a modern, technologically based defence machine. Nor did they complain about the loss of manpower for the economy. The same was true in West Germany. Was their average conscript better educated than their British counterparts? Certainly, when reform of higher education was discussed, France was a model that attracted much attention. Its élite, it was said, were not divided between what C. P. Snow, himself a chemist as well as a writer, called 'the two cultures': the arts and the sciences. There was not the harmful early specialisation found in Britain. Those destined for the upper reaches of the public service were trained at the *grandes écoles*, something Britain lacked. The engineer, it was argued, had a much higher status in both France and Germany. Could it be that French projects were better thought out and controlled as a result? Gradually, this became the prevailing view in Britain. More professionalism was needed. Britain had too many classicists and not enough scientists, mathematicians and engineers in the administrative class of the civil service, and too many amateurs in the boardrooms. Arthur Koestler, writing more in sorrow than in anger, about his adopted British homeland, argued: 'The cult of amateurishness and the contempt in which proficiency and expertise are held, breed mediocrats by natural selection.'[10]

Ireland: De Valera Departs

In May 1954, the Irish were forced to go to the polls once again because the independents had withdrawn their support from the government. They had refused to support deflationary measures, which were producing economic stagnation. Fianna Fáil, identified with these measures, saw its popular vote fall from 46.3 to 43.4 per cent. Fine Gael gained from being on the opposition benches, its share rising from 25.7 to 32 per cent. It gained its highest number of seats – 50 – since 1932. With 65 seats (a loss of four), Fianna Fáil had its smallest number of seats since 1927. John Costello once again took over, with ministers from Fine Gael, Labour and Clann na Talmhan (a conservative small farmers' party). MacBride's Clann na Poblachta supported the government but was not represented in it. Costello's government fared no better than its predecessor with the economy. Falling agricultural exports, and a capital outflow combined with a consumer boom, resulted in a considerable balance-of-payments deficit in 1955. Higher taxes and special import duties followed in 1956. In March 1957, MacBride forced a new election by withdrawing support from Costello. In addition to the economic factor, he also opposed Costello's moves against a new IRA campaign in the North. Costello proposed a federal solution to Irish unity, but this made little impact in the South, and even less in the North.

In the election that followed, March 1957, MacBride paid the penalty by forfeiting his seat. His party, which had appeared as a new reforming force a decade earlier, was on the verge of extinction. Fianna Fáil gained an overall majority: 77 seats in a Dáil of 147. It was de Valera's greatest personal triumph. Fine Gael went down from 50 to 40 seats. Labour lost seven seats, retaining eleven. The other coalition parties also lost ground. Undoubtedly, the economic situation was the key determinant. Was the international situation another? The Suez and the

Hungarian crises were still in people's minds. De Valera had guided his country through the war. Perhaps some people wanted a trusted leader on the bridge once again. At 74, and nearly blind, he formed his last Cabinet. In 1959 he decided to give up as Taoiseach but to stand for the less exacting, more ceremonial, office of President. He also attempted to introduce electoral reform on British lines, to ensure stable governments in the future. He cunningly held the referendum on electoral reform on the same day as the presidential election. The electors revealed they were alert and independent. They gave him the presidency but denied him the British-style electoral system, with a vote of 52 per cent against the proposal. Seán Lemass (59), the long-serving Minister for Industry and Commerce, replaced him as head of government.

Like the Macmillan administration, Lemass was interested in economic expansion, indicative planning and promoting education. In 1960, the Economic Research Institute was established, followed by the National Industrial and Economic Council in 1963. It brought together the government, employers' organisations and trade unions. Ireland benefited from the favourable international climate. As a result of emigration and low birth rates, Ireland had become, by the 1950s, one of the most sparsely populated states in Europe. In the late 1950s, prosperity increased, emigration decreased, the decline in population was eventually halted. Housing for the less well off remained a problem. Sickness and insurance benefits continued to lag behind those of Western Europe and the health system still bore the stigma of nineteenth-century principles. Women made some progress during these years. Education minister, Jack Lynch, lifted the ban on married women continuing their careers in teaching. In 1959, the first women were enrolled in the police.

In 1960, Irish Television was established, partly because of the popularity of British television in the areas on the east coast that could receive it. It was a public body financed by licence fees and advertising revenue. One of the first major public events it covered was the visit of President Kennedy to Ireland in 1963.

In foreign affairs Ireland attempted to be more active and independent. Generally, however, it lined up with the NATO states. Nevertheless, being officially neutral, with an anti-imperialist past, it had some special credibility in the UN. Its soldiers served as

UN 'blue berets' in the Middle East, the Congo, Cyprus and Kashmir. Irish UN troops were killed in action in the Congo, Cyprus and the Middle East.[11]

One of the first things de Valera had done as Taoiseach was to reintroduce internment, in July 1957, and co-operate with the North to crush the IRA raiders. The energetic intervention of de Valera on this matter broke the IRA campaign in the South almost as soon as it started. In the North, it lasted a little longer but, lacking success, it was officially ended in 1962. The IRA then resolved to achieve its aim of a united socialist Ireland by political rather than military action. Northern Ireland had gained from progressive welfare legislation in Britain, since 1945, and from state aid. The standard of living was higher than in the South and welfare provision much better. There were, of course, economic problems. The traditional industries – shipbuilding and linen – which had boomed until about 1950, were hit by the recovery of Germany and Japan and then by other competitors. Unemployment remained higher than in the rest of the UK and Catholic unemployment remained higher than Protestant. Politically, the Unionists, the friends of the British Conservatives, remained firmly in control. Sir Basil Brooke (from 1952 Lord Brookeborough) served as Prime Minister from May 1943 to March 1963. His Unionists were opposed by the small Northern Ireland Labour Party (which supported the *status quo* on the border) and a variety of small Irish Nationalist bodies. Brookeborough's replacement by Captain Terence O'Neill (48) brought hope that the old sectarian divide would be broken down in Northern Ireland and between North and South. Ireland, like many other places, was influenced by the election of the first 'Irish' Catholic President of the USA, John F. Kennedy. Ireland was also influenced by the message of tolerance preached by Pope John XXIII. When Pope John died, in 1963, O'Neill, to the anger of Protestant extremists, sent a message of condolence. By making gestures of reconciliation and pursuing economic growth, O'Neill hoped he was inaugurating a new era. He was to be disappointed.

Enquiries and a Royal Commission

Early in 1961 there were signs that, once again, all was not well with the British economy. The boom of 1959 had spent itself, the balance of payments was in deficit for the second year in succession. Selwyn Lloyd, Chancellor of the Exchequer since 1960, went for deflation – higher taxes and cuts in public expenditure – in his April budget. More drastic action followed in July, including a 'pay pause'. As usual, public-sector employees bore the main burden. The government's popularity fell, with many voters believing it to be unfair as well as incompetent. To counter the criticism, Macmillan attempted to present his government as a modernising, reforming administration. In economic affairs, he swung round to indicative planning, something long denounced by the Conservatives. In July 1961, Selwyn Lloyd suggested the setting up of the National Economic Development Council (NEDC), to include representatives of the government and both sides of industry. It was to co-ordinate the plans of the public and private sectors; to set a target for growth and to tackle the obstacles to growth. A National Incomes Commission was established. In addition, the government set up committees to advise on many areas, among them: consumer protection (Molony), decimal currency (Halsbury), the railways (Beeching), education (Newson), higher education (Robbins), ITV (Pilkington) and the civil service (Trend). Although Macmillan had been a reformer in the 1930s, all these efforts appeared to many voters as a deathbed conversion.

One other area of reform was the police service. After falling in the early 1950s, the number of indictable offences known to the police increased over the late 1950s. Most of this crime was theft or various forms of dishonesty. Crimes of violence and sex crimes remained a relatively small proportion of the total. Yet there was a feeling that the police were unable to cope with the rising levels of crime. The 'Great Train Robbery' in 1963, yielding the greatest money haul in burglary to that date, seemed to confirm this and the amateurism of the police. Police pay and conditions had deteriorated during this period and the police service was undermanned. Training had been neglected. In 1960, a Royal Commission on the Police was set up under Sir Henry Willink. The reason for the Commission was not wastage and insufficient recruits but complaints about the police. Mal-administration of the Cardiganshire police was exposed. Corruption in the Brighton police led to two senior officers being sentenced to imprisonment. The Chief Constable of Worcester was convicted of fraud and sent to prison. There were other, less clear-cut cases.[12] Willink's final report was published in May 1962. It rejected the establishment of a national police force but recommended the Home Secretary should have the power to amalgamate smaller forces. It rejected an independent body to investigate complaints against the police, but introduced the system under which a chief constable could get assistance from another force to investigate complaints in his service. The Report set out more clearly the areas of responsibility of the Home Secretary for the police. The Commission also recommended large pay increases for the police. As a result, the highest annual intake since 1950 was recorded in 1962. The recommendations formed the basis for the Police Act (1964).

Home Replaces Macmillan

After a surprise Liberal win in the Orpington by-election (March 1962), considered a totally safe Conservative seat, Macmillan attempted another ploy. In the summer of 1962, he sacked one third of his Cabinet. To add to the government's woes, in 1962–3, the country suffered its worst winter since 1881. This led to a rise in unemployment. Abroad, his main initiative, to get Britain into the EEC, was vetoed by de Gaulle, in January 1963.

In the summer of 1963, the government was embarrassed by something entirely unexpected – the Profumo affair. John Profumo, Secretary of State for War, was a rising star in the Conservative Party. In June 1963, he was forced to resign after admitting he had lied to the Commons (in March) about his relationship with Christine Keeler. Contrary to an earlier statement, his relationship with her had been sexual. Keeler was also involved with the Soviet Naval Attaché, Captain Ivanov, and had also been a sexual partner of Peter Rachman, a criminal property rackeeter. Rumours had been flying around for some time about sex orgies in London's high society. Inside the House, Colonel George Wigg (Labour), had sniped continuously at the government; the *Daily Mirror* did so from outside. The Profumo scandal had more impact because it followed earlier accusations in connection with the Vassall case. In October 1962, John Vassall, an Admiralty civil servant, was jailed for eighteen years for passing secrets to the Soviets. A homosexual, he had been blackmailed while serving in the British Embassy in Moscow. The press implicated two ministers as having had connections with Vassall, but the Radcliffe Tribunal subsequently exonerated them. There had been several other spy cases which, taken together, cast doubt on the loyalty of civil servants and the efficiency of the security services. There had been the traitor diplomats, Burgess and Maclean, who successfully escaped to Moscow in 1951; the MI6 traitor George Blake, who had made a dramatic escape from prison; the Soviet spies Peter and Helen Kroger, Gordon Lonsdale and the Admiralty spy Harry Houghton in 1961. Finally, there was the blow of the defection of Kim Philby in 1963; a former high-ranking MI5 and MI6 official,[13] Philby had been given Macmillan's blessing in the Commons. Macmillan resigned on 10th October just before the Conservative annual conference. He had decided to fight on, but was struck down by an inflamed prostate gland requiring an urgent operation.

Macmillan's successor, recommended by him to the Queen,[14] was someone totally unexpected by most people – Lord Home (60), the Foreign Secretary. He 'emerged' from six possibles, which led to discontent within the Conservative Party about the way the leader was chosen. Home renounced his title and presently entered the Commons as plain Sir Alec Douglas-Home. On television the new leader looked 'gaunt and skull-like'.[15] As an old Etonian and rich landowner, who had served as Chamberlain's Parliamentary Private Secretary, 1937–40, he did not add to his party's efforts to portray itself as a thrusting, forward-looking party.

Wilson's Victory

The title of Michael Shanks's book, *The Stagnant Society* (1963), summed up what many had come to believe about Britain under Macmillan. A torrent of books, reports and articles attacked Britain's old ways and complacency; most of the intelligentsia did not believe the government would change things. Wilson corresponded much more to the mood of the decade than either Macmillan or Home. The Conservatives admitted that reforms were overdue and that the state had an important role to play in economic and social affairs. They also agreed that far more 'meritocrcacy' was necessary and desirable. Wilson looked much more convincing as a reformer than Home.

On 15th October 1964, Labour won an overall majority of only four seats: Labour 317, Conservative 304 (including the Speaker), Liberals nine. On a lower turnout than 1959, 77.1 per cent as against 78.7, Labour increased its percentage by only 0.3, the Conservative vote fell by 6 per cent and the Liberals gained an extra 5.3 per cent, their vote going up from 1.6 million to over 3 million. Labour's majority was surprisingly small, given the discontent recorded by the polls since 1962 and by-election results. Labour's relatively poor showing could have been in part a result of bad weather (especially in the Midlands) during the 'Labour' voting hours – from 6 p.m. onwards – and its traditional organisational weaknesses. Strikes and rumours of strikes probably cost it a few votes. The Conservatives aimed well when they targeted the likely cost of Labour's reform programme. They were on less strong ground when they attacked Labour on defence, simply because this was not an important issue for most voters. Unusually, there was no national swing, with Labour failing to make a number of expected gains in the West Midlands (Rugby, for instance) and even losing two seats there: Smethwick and Perry Barr (Birmingham). The factors in this area were, undoubtedly, the great increase in prosperity in the West Midlands and immigration. Smethwick, nearly everyone agreed, had been lost by Labour because of vigorous campaigning by the local Conservatives on the immigration issue. Opinion polls revealed that the Conservatives had a clear majority over Labour only among those over 65, with a slight lead among the 55–64 age group.[16] They also maintained their traditional lead among women. Labour had a clear lead among the younger age groups: 21–4, 25–34 and 35–44. These figures were not necessarily a guide to who actually went to vote. Labour had improved its position among the middle classes, but lost some support among the poorest in the land. The Liberal revival was a sign to Labour that many in the new and old middle classes preferred the

Liberals as an alternative to Conservatism. Jo Grimond, old Etonian Liberal leader, 1956–67, was well known from his television appearances and came across as a decent, intelligent 'David' who had to contend with the two Goliaths, the 'class warriors' of the two main parties. In 1964, Wilson could claim to have reversed Labour's decline; Home could claim that he had not done too badly in the circumstances.

8 Harold Wilson at the Helm, 1964–70

Sterling Crisis

The nerve-racking wait endured by Harold Wilson ended at 2.47 p.m. on 16th October, the day after polling, when he knew Labour had won Brecon and Radnor, Labour's 315th seat, and thus a majority in the Commons. The first sign of the transfer of power was the arrival of two detectives at Transport House (the Labour HQ) to act as personal bodyguards to the new Prime Minister.[1] Later, Wilson's family and assistants sat in a room at Buckingham Palace talking about horses to Palace officials, while he saw the Queen. Among those waiting was Marcia Williams, Wilson's private and political secretary, who wrote later: 'It struck me at the time as an ironic beginning to the white-hot technological revolution and the Government that was to mastermind it.'[2] Richard Crossman was no less negatively impressed when he and his fellow ministers had to spend their precious time being taught how to walk backwards, for when they were to be formally appointed by the Queen.[3] Meanwhile, sterling plummeted. James Callaghan, who had been appointed Chancellor of the Exchequer, felt it was the start of a great adventure as he sat with Wilson and George Brown, on 17th October. They decided there and then not to devalue the pound.[4] It was a difficult choice to make. They faced a financial crisis not of their own making. Devaluation would have stimulated exports but increased the cost of many imports. This should have brought the huge trade deficit, bequeathed by the outgoing government, into balance. However, it might have led speculators to conclude that another devaluation could follow. It would have pushed up the cost of living and would have been seen by some as surrender or financial mismanagement. The Americans would have been none too pleased by devaluation, nor would the many countries, often poor, who held their reserves in London. The value of these would have been drastically cut at a stroke.[5] Finally, Wilson was haunted by Attlee's devaluation of 1949. In an effort to turn the tide, Callaghan introduced a temporary 15 per cent surcharge on all imports except food and raw materials. There were also measures to boost exports.

On 11th November, he introduced an emergency Budget designed to satisfy both the international banking community and Labour's own supporters. Income tax, the duty on petrol, and National Insurance contributions were increased by significant amounts. On the other hand, pensions were raised and NHS prescription charges for drugs were dropped. The income tax increases were to take effect in the spring, as were changes in the taxing of companies. Both the surcharge and the Budget met with strong criticism from abroad and speculation against the pound increased; 'day after day the losses mounted'.[6] Callaghan later admitted that their failure to consult overseas trading partners had been a mistake.[7] Despite a 2 per cent increase in the bank rate later in the month, which made credit more difficult, the haemorrhage continued. A stormy meeting took place between Wilson, Callaghan and Lord Cromer, Governor of the Bank of England, at which the banker called for drastic financial measures, action on the trade unions and abandonment of Labour's plan to nationalise steel. Wilson kept his head and held his ground. However, international assistance was needed. The Americans perceived that if the pound fell, the dollar would be next to come under attack from speculators. They helped London, therefore, to find $3 billion, an enormous sum in those days, to be placed at the disposal of the Bank of England. The central banks of eleven separate countries had contributed to this amount. Major speculation then ended. Although Wilson's government had overcome its first hurdle, it was clear that its room for manoeuvre was severely limited.

Department of Economic Affairs

Apart from Home, Wilson was the first Prime Minister to be born in the twentieth century. Again Home excepted, he was the first postwar Prime Minister not to have taken part in the

1914–18 war, and he was the first postwar Prime Minister not to have been educated at a public school. At 48, he was the youngest twentieth-century Prime Minister. His image was that of a gifted economist who, nevertheless, had a popular, down-to-earth approach to the problems of ordinary people. His, and his party's, big weakness was that there had been no real planning for a Labour victory. Perhaps this was partly the result of group and individual rivalries during the Gaitskell period and of Labour's appalling lack of organisation. It was also due to Labour's lack of clarity about its aims. At any rate, George Brown was later to claim that the idea for a Department of Economic Affairs (DEA) had been drawn up by himself and Wilson in the back of a taxi. This was denied by Wilson and Callaghan and was probably not true.[8]

The DEA, headed by Brown, the ebullient Deputy Leader of the Labour Party, was, at best, an attempt to bring British government structures more in line with those of states like West Germany, and at worst, an attempt to satisfy one of Wilson's main rivals and critics. In the past, left-wing critics had often attacked the control of the Treasury over all aspects of government and wanted this control cut back. They thought the Treasury should be more like a continental ministry of finance, with a separate ministry of economics. Germany had this system from 1949 onwards. In theory, given the importance, in Labour Party terms, of the two ministers, both ministries should have been of equal importance, but the Treasury retained the upper hand. It had the advantage of being a powerful organisation, staffed by some of the best minds in the civil service, with a long tradition behind it. By the time he took over, Callaghan had some nodding acquaintance with economics, as a visiting fellow of Nuffield College, Oxford. Brown knew nothing about this field. There was also Douglas Jay at the Board of Trade. Jay was an economist with previous experience of government and he had opposed the setting up of the new ministry. His son, Peter, was married to Callaghan's daughter and worked at the Treasury.[9] The two ministers agreed that the DEA was responsible for the long-term aspects of economic affairs, for physical resources, incomes policy, economic growth, regional and industrial policy. The DEA minister would be chairman of the National Economic Development Council. It sounded grand, yet when Brown turned up at his new office, he found there were no chairs, desks, telephones, typewriters or stationery. To begin with, Brown had a staff of three who sat on the floor for their first meeting.[10] It is no wonder that Brown was suspicious.

The Treasury was in charge of the Budget, public expenditure, the balance of payments, exchange control and overseas financial relations, and short-term economic policy. The rivalries between the two increased month by month: 'The Treasury began to regard the DEA as unrealistic, and the DEA considered the Treasury obstructive. Both had some right on their side, but both erred because Ministers failed to come to a clear and uncluttered conclusion on what our first priority should be.'[11] The DEA published the first National Plan in September 1965. Brown had to fight hard to get the plan adopted by both sides of industry only to find that, as Peter Shore, also in the government, put it, it 'sank without trace within minutes of its being completed, to the detriment of the government's credibility'.[12] The DEA rapidly lost its initial glamour but it was not a bad idea as such; after all, much of Japan's success has been credited to a similar ministry – the Ministry of International Trade and Industry. There, they had indicative planning, with the government deciding the overall economic targets for the nation in a succession of five-year or six-year plans.[13]

Also new, and influenced by institutions of the successful Italian economy, was the Industrial Reorganisation Corporation, established in January 1966. Its purpose was to encourage concentration and nationalisation and promote greater efficiency and the international competitiveness of British industry. As promised in Labour's manifesto, the steel industry was renationalised. The main argument was that it was 'failing the nation'. Given the lukewarm attitude of a considerable minority of Labour MPs, and the unfavourable disposition towards the measure by investors at home and abroad, it is difficult to understand why Wilson persisted. The answer is probably that it showed his determination to stay the course and reassured the left.

Another area of potential friction for Brown was with his old party enemy, Frank Cousins, who was put in charge of the new Ministry of Technology. Before taking office, Cousins was still leader of the biggest union, the Transport and General Workers Union. It was a shrewd move of Wilson to get Cousins into the government, but not at Technology. He lacked credibility in the country, and in the scientific and academic community, as a leader to guide Britain towards a new golden age of fostering science and technology and applying them to its economy. He was given C. P. Snow, who became Lord Snow, as his Parliamentary Secretary. There was also a new Ministry of Land and Natural Resources, but its head, Fred Willey, was not in the Cabinet. One of its main tasks was to deal with the problem of building land. It was regarded as a failure and was wound up in February 1967.

Following what had been long regarded as crucial to the creation of the German economic miracle and the success of the Swedish economy, Brown attempted to bring employers and unions together to agree a prices and incomes policy. On 16th December 1964, the two sides signed the Declaration of Intent. This committed them to co-operate with the government on economic policy. A National Board of Prices and Incomes was created, headed by Aubrey Jones, a former Conservative MP. The implementation of this policy rested entirely on the goodwill of both sides; it was voluntary. In reality, it was doomed to failure from the start. Frank Cousins was opposed to it even though he was in the Cabinet, and took no action to get his union to agree to it. Had he attempted to make it work, it would have stood a better chance. However, it suffered from two other major defects. First, it was brought in against a background of relatively high inflation, making it more difficult to hold wage increases in modest proportions. Second, the structure and organisation of British trade unions were chaotic compared with those of Germany and Scandinavia. There were too many competing unions, with too many passive members. Small groups, totally out of line with the leadership and the silent majority, could wield enormous influence. The Wilson governments were dogged by damaging strikes, at least some of which were the result of poor union leadership and control.

Ice Cold Atmosphere

Wilson himself, together with Patrick Gordon Walker (Foreign Secretary) and James Griffiths (Welsh Secretary), had previous

Cabinet experience, but this was not true of their other col-
leagues. Brown, Callaghan, Jay, Herbert Bowden (Lord President),
Lord Longford (Privy Seal), Sir Frank Soskice (Home Secretary),
Michael Stewart (Education and Science), Fred Lee (Power)
and Tom Fraser (Transport) had served as junior ministers under
Attlee. This meant that twelve out of a total of 23 Cabinet members
had previous experience. Those without were: Barbara Castle
(Overseas Development), Lord Gardiner (Lord Chancellor), Fred
Peart (Agriculture and Fisheries), Anthony Greenwood (Colonial
Secretary), Arthur Bottomley (Commonwealth Relations), Denis
Healey (Defence), Richard Crossman (Housing and Local Govern-
ment), Ray Gunter (Labour), Douglas Houghton (Duchy of
Lancaster), William Ross (Scottish Office) and Frank Cousins.
The lack of experience must have been important in new ministries like Overseas Development and Technology. Marcia
Williams implies this was a factor in their subsequent difficulties;
she also found the leading civil servants, at best, cold and distant
and, at worst, hostile. 'The atmosphere at No. 10 was ice cold
and very restrained. We were treated as ships passing in the
night.'[14]

A 'parliamentary leper'

Another weakness of the Wilson administration was the way the
ministers were shunted about. Soskice was only at the Home
Office for just over thirteen months when Roy Jenkins replaced
him. At the same time, Greenwood made way for Lord Longford
at the Colonial Office. Greenwood moved to Overseas Development, and its minister, Castle, moved to Transport. There were
other changes outside the Cabinet. The biggest change had,
however, already taken place. This was the departure of Patrick
Gordon Walker from the Foreign Office in January 1965. He
was replaced by Michael Stewart, who, in turn, was replaced at
Education and Science by Anthony Crosland. Gordon Walker
was a tragic figure. After his defeat at Smethwick, Wilson had
stood by him on the understanding that he would return to the
Commons as soon as possible. Wilson had branded Alderman
Peter Griffiths, the local politician and headmaster, who had
defeated Walker, a 'parliamentary leper' because of the use of

the immigration issue by the Conservatives in Smethwick. It did his colleague no good. To everyone's astonishment, Walker was defeated at Leyton, normally a safe Labour seat, in January 1965. Once again immigration had been an issue, though some voters did not like the way the sitting member had been hustled off the stage to make way for the outsider. On the same day, Labour also lost votes at Nuneaton, where Cousins was elected, having been minister since October but not yet an MP.

Rhodesia: 'kith and kin'?

By the time Labour took over in 1964, most of the Empire had been 'given away'. The process continued with the Gambia and the Maldives gaining independence in 1965; British Guiana, Bechuanaland (Botswana), Basutoland (Lesotho) and Barbados in 1966; Aden (South Yemen) in 1967; Nauru, Mauritius and Swaziland in 1968. This process led to arguments about the role of the Commonwealth and whether there should be any more immigration into Britain from states that were now fully sovereign. As Smethwick and Leyton had shown, immigration was a touchy subject for many voters.

The problem of Southern Rhodesia put Wilson into a difficult situation. Some in Britain regarded the white minority there as their own 'kith and kin' and sympathised with them when, led by Prime Minister Ian Smith, they opposed black majority rule and moved towards a unilateral declaration of independence (UDI). The whites were strengthened in their resolve by contemporary events: independence in the former Belgian Congo (Zaire), where civil war conditions had prevailed; a military take-over in Ghana (1966); civil war in Nigeria (1967); the expulsions from Kenya (1967–8); and Idi Amin's Presidency in Uganda (1971). At best, Smith's government was prepared to see some African parliamentary representation, but in a permanent minority position. African tribal leaders, who were paid by the white government, were paraded in an effort to convince the world that the black majority supported Smith. The African politicians did not help matters by falling out among themselves. They suffered from personal and tribal rivalries. Labour, like the outgoing Conservative administration, was committed to unimpeded progress to majority rule, progress towards ending racial discrimination and so on. Smith decided to go to London, where he had sympathisers, in the hope that Wilson, hanging on by a thread with his small majority, would be ready to settle. No settlement was reached then, or subsequently, when Wilson visited Rhodesia in 1965. UDI was declared on 11th November 1965. In legal terms this was a rebellion, but Britain was not in a strong enough position to put it down by force. Wilson made a mistake by announcing at the start that force would not be used. At least one distinguished military authority has concluded that the loyalty of the Rhodesian security forces to Smith was questionable and that 'quick military intervention in December 1965 might have saved Rhodesia from the greater agony of a long guerrilla war'.[15] Smith's regime could get help from its political friends and neighbours in South Africa and the Portuguese colony of Mozambique. The two black African 'front-line' states, Botswana and Zambia, were weak. Zambia was economically dependent on Southern Rhodesia. If Britain had done nothing, it would have been fiercely attacked by the non-white Commonwealth states, by many in the USA, by the Soviet bloc and by China, as well as by left-wing opinion everywhere. Tanzania and Ghana actually broke off diplomatic relations over Britain's refusal to use force.[16] The official Conservative position was to abstain when Wilson introduced oil sanctions but some broke ranks, voting with the government, while others voted against. The UN and the Commonwealth backed the British decision. Sanctions were overestimated as a weapon, for although Rhodesia relied on oil imports and on its ability to export its tobacco crop, it was able to keep afloat without too much difficulty. Wilson made two more efforts to reach a settlement when he met Smith on HMS *Tiger*, in 1966, and again, in 1968, on HMS *Fearless*, on both occasions at Gibraltar. Progress towards a settlement eluded them. The issue led to passionate debate and a great deal of time and effort was spent on it. In the end, the white minority was forced to settle by others.

Aviation Crisis

Despite its commitment to technology and science, the Wilson government felt compelled to order early cuts in prestige projects, among which were the Anglo–French Concorde airliner and the TSR-2, destined for the RAF. Strong French opposition to cancellation probably saved Concorde. TSR-2 found no such powerful advocates and was scrapped. American planes were ordered as replacements and the government was faced with 10,000 demonstrating aviation workers in London on 14th January 1965. Wilson set up the Plowden Committee to investigate the prospects for the industry and it reported in January 1966. Its main thrust was that Britain should not again attempt, single-handed, to produce a major military aircraft, or missile, or a new long-range civil aircraft. Joint projects with other countries, which shared the cost and increased the market, could be economical and should be pursued. The problem was that military aviation was highly dependent on overseas sales, and they in turn depended on the political decisions of foreign governments. Clearly, US companies had a great advantage here with their large US domestic military market, thus reducing unit costs and enabling them to sell more cheaply abroad. The Americans also had far more influence than Britain around the globe. The same was true in civil aviation. The best designs were hardly ever likely to be the key factor in securing orders. In the case of the hugely successful West German and Japanese economies, they had not been allowed to continue in aviation after their defeat in 1945. Later, when the restrictions were lifted, they wisely decided to develop only modest projects. Japan did attempt to construct its own airliners in the 1960s, but these were not a success. Their military aircraft were American designs built under licence. A similar development took place in Germany. Much of their skill went into the automobile industry and in innovation in the consumer goods industries.

Defence: 'Over-commitment'

To a degree, Wilson's reaction to Rhodesia and other overseas problems was influenced by Britain's defence capacity, which in turn was under financial pressure. Denis Healey was appointed Defence Secretary by Wilson, in October 1964, and served until 1970, thus holding the office longer than any predecessor since the post was created in 1947. Traditionally, Labour had an ambivalent attitude to defence and few members were interested in it. This in no way detracts from Healey's ability, education, skill and professionalism. He had served with distinction in the Second World War. Given all of this, it is surprising that he was so behind the times in his assessment of Britain's situation. He too was a prisoner of the idea of Britain's world role, including east of Suez deployment of the armed forces, and its nuclear role. Healey's Cabinet colleagues let him get on with the job.[17] Most of them, it must be said, agreed with him in maintaining Britain's world role. A secondary reason for maintaining defence expenditure was employment. Thousands of jobs were at risk with every defence cut and they were mainly in Labour constituencies.

Richard Crossman was bitterly disappointed that little changed in defence with the change in government. On 3rd January 1965 he recorded his disappointment, feeling that Wilson and Healey were condemning Britain to 'over-commitment in overseas expenditure almost as burdensome – if not more burdensome – than that which Ernest Bevin committed us in 1945 and for the same reason: because of our attachment to the Anglo–American special relationship and because of our belief that it is only through the existence of this relationship that we can survive outside Europe'. It was a very perceptive comment. However, Healey immediately cancelled the fifth Polaris submarine and certain weapons, but Britain continued to spend more of its GDP on defence than any of the other industrial states, except the USA, until the end of the century (see Table A 22). Meanwhile, the Wilson government came under increasing pressure, from inside and outside Parliament, to abandon Britain's world role. Outside its own ranks, Liberal leader, Jo Grimond, attacked the east of Suez role at his party's conference in 1965. More surprisingly, so did Enoch Powell, Conservative shadow defence spokesman, at about the same time.[18]

From abroad came countervailing pressure from Singapore, Malaysia and Australia and above all from the USA. The Americans had stepped in, after the French withdrawal from Vietnam, and were attempting to stem that country's lurch into Communism. Wilson had promised President Johnson at their first meeting in Washington, in December 1964, that Britain would retain its global commitments. Johnson promised to back sterling and Britain's efforts in Rhodesia in return.[19] Fear that Britain would be dragged into the conflict persisted. When Wilson arrived in Washington, in December 1965, he received a telegram from 68 Labour MPs – 'not from the left only, right across the party'[20] – demanding that the USA stop bombing North Vietnam. Wilson presented himself in the role of mediator, which allowed him to avoid offending the Americans and went down well among many in the Labour Party. US bombing did not achieve the results hoped for and caused much hardship to civilians. As the Second World War experience had demonstrated, such bombing was questionable on military, as well as moral and diplomatic, grounds. However, those who opposed the Americans often had a naïve view of the nature of the North Vietnamese Communist régime. Some saw the Communists as nationalist revolutionaries fighting imperialism, others as David against Goliath, others simply did not like the Americans.

Wilson had less choice elsewhere. He inherited a shooting war with Indonesia, which had begun as a small rebellion in 1962. It grew out of competing claims for control of the oil-rich and feudalistic Sultanate of Brunei and other parts of North Borneo. Indonesia escalated what it termed 'confrontation' between 1963 and 1965. The Wilson government, like its predecessor, was committed to defending the new Commonwealth states from aggression. Wilson dispatched a naval and air task force of over 80 ships, which represented a force stronger than any other that had been there since the Korean War.[21] At the height of 'confrontation', in 1965, 17,000 Commonwealth servicemen were engaged in Borneo: 114 were killed and 181 wounded, a high proportion of them Gurkhas. It was estimated that the Indonesians lost 600 dead and 200 wounded.[22] The British held on until, in August 1966, the Indonesians called off their assault, a coup having brought down the previous régime, which was allied to Communist China.

Wilson also faced a serious situation in Aden, which had been a coaling stop on the way to India in the days of the Raj, and was seen for decades as a vital base. The tribal hinterland of the Yemen had been divided among a group of 'British protected' areas ruled by tribal chiefs. After Britain left Abadan in 1951, BP developed Aden as an oil depot. Yemeni workers were recruited and they soon became more numerous than the locals. In their desire to improve their conditions, they became the targets of various rival political forces – the agents of Nasser's Arab revolution and those seeking to organise the world on Soviet lines. By 1959, Britain had persuaded the chiefs to form the Federation of South Arabia, which included Aden. The (North) Yemen Arab Republic claimed sovereignty over the whole area. The first bomb went off in Aden at the end of 1963; it had been planted by the Yemeni National Liberation Front (NLF). At the same time, there was the People's Socialist Party (PSP) with its trade union affiliate, which sought to achieve its aims by democratic means. Violence and counter violence then continued until British withdrawal with Britain not getting such a good press much of the time.

In the end Britain was forced by economic circumstances to change course. On 16th January 1968 Wilson announced that all British forces were to be withdrawn from Malaysia and Singapore by 13th March 1971, and all Britain's aircraft carriers were to be scrapped by 1971. The order for 50 FB-111As planes from the USA was cancelled. Britain would, in future, maintain only small garrisons in Hong Kong, Gibraltar, Belize and the Falkland Islands. It was a case of better late than never, but the swingeing cuts were not the result of a defence review examining the needs of a European rather than a world power.

Heath: 'a replica'?

Sir Alec Douglas-Home retired on 22nd July 1965, after 21 months as Conservative leader. His poll ratings had been poor and there were rumblings in the party against him. There had also been the Conservative defeat in Sir Alec's backyard at the Roxburgh by-election in March, at the hands of the Liberal, David Steel. Finally, Sir Alec knew he had to give any successor time to establish himself before the next election, which, under the circumstances, could be at any time. Under a new constitution adopted in February 1965, the leader was to be elected by the Conservative MPs rather than 'emerging' after consultations. As the previous three leaders had been Old Etonians, it was thought that: 'To confront Wilson's image there had to be chosen not a contrast but, as far as was feasible, a replica.'[23] Three candidates stood: former Chancellor, Reginald Maudling; former Lord Privy Seal, Edward Heath, and former Health Minister, Enoch Powell. Powell had less experience than the other two and had already shown himself as a maverick. Maudling had greater popularity with the public but Heath was elected. Heath gained 150 votes, Maudling 133 and Powell only thirteen. Maudling immediately stood down and Heath thus became the new leader. Heath did not seem to do any better than his predecessor. In February 1966, his standing in the polls was lower than Home's had been. He was attacked within his own party for his 'coldness' and inability to communicate with the public at large. The fact that the party had fractured over Rhodesia was held against him. He also seemed to be veering to the Right politically.[24] Furthermore, in January 1966, Labour retained Hull North in a by-election they were expected to lose. Alarm bells started to sound.

Election 1966

After a number of false alarms, it was announced that the general election was to take place on 31st March 1966. Labour had strong cards to play, blaming its difficulties on the previous régime's incompetence and its own tiny majority. It had a great asset in Wilson, who to many, personified the 'treasured values of work-a-day provincial Britain'.[25] Wilson had been very active since taking office and had been seen on television in many parts of the world as well as in many parts of Britain. The main campaign themes were the state of the economy, the question of possible UK membership of the EEC, and the trade unions.[26] The Conservatives advocated strict immigration control and promised tax cuts. At one stage, Labour looked as if it could be derailed by a rash of trade union cases involving the victimisation or fining of workers, who had refused to join unofficial strikes. The Conservatives made much use of them. Some thought there was a deliberate attempt to harm Labour, by provoking irresponsible action at the factory-floor level. The Labour leaders condemned such victimisation. The Common Market divided both major parties, which made it more difficult to use it against the government. Basically, Labour's line was, 'We'd like to join, but not at any price.' Labour had a lead of 9 per cent in the Gallup poll, which was greater than any party had had at the start of a campaign since 1945. It seemed inevitable, therefore, that Labour would win. One problem for Labour was the possibility of apathy among its supporters. The turnout, at 75.8 per cent, was the lowest since 1945 and this was to Labour's disadvantage. Also to its disadvantage was the fact that in 24 seats the Conservative majority was less than the number of postal votes cast,[27] the great majority of which usually go to the Conservatives. Labour, nevertheless, swept back into office with an overall majority of 97 seats on a fairly even national swing. The victory represented Labour's greatest peacetime success. Labour won 363 seats (317 in 1964), Conservatives 253 (304) and Liberals twelve (nine). In terms of percentage vote, with 41.9 the Conservatives gained their lowest percentage since 1945. The Liberal percentage fell from 11.2, in 1964, to 8.5, but they had fielded fewer candidates. They gained one seat from Labour, Colne Valley, through tactical voting by normally Conservative voters. Labour was particularly pleased that it won back Smethwick and that Gordon Walker was returned in Leyton. Minor parties stressing immigration fell back from their 1964 results. The British National Party picked up 7.4 per cent (9.1 in 1964) in Southall, while Mosley scored only 4.6 per cent in Shoreditch and Finsbury (London). The small Communist vote declined slightly, the only 'success' being to deprive Labour of the Hornsey seat. In Wales, the Welsh National Party, Plaid Cymru (PC), put up twenty candidates (23 in 1964) without success. It attracted 4.3 per cent of the Welsh vote (4.8 in 1964). In Scotland, the Scottish National Party (SNP) increased its candidates from fifteen to 23, but it remained unsuccessful. Its percentage of the vote in Scotland increased from 2.4 to 5. Fewer women were elected (nineteen Labour and seven Conservative), than the record of 28 in 1964. As in previous elections, the Conservatives were only ahead of Labour in the polls among the over 65s. Finally, in their respective constituencies of Huyton and Bexley, Wilson saw his large majority increase still further, while Heath's majority fell from 4,589 to 2,333.

Wilson's Summer Cuts

July 1966 was not a good month for Wilson. On 3rd July, Frank Cousins resigned. He had been threatening to do so almost from the day he joined the government, and no doubt disagreed with the government on a wide range of issues. His immediate concern was the planned Prices and Incomes Bill, which gave the government power to require wage, price or dividend increases to be submitted to the Prices and Incomes Board. As we have seen, Cousins had never given Brown his support on this.[28] Anthony Wedgwood Benn replaced him. He was close to Wilson and had served as Postmaster General outside the Cabinet. Now he was in it. Benn recorded in his diary that he had a chance 'to create a new department that can really change the face of Britain and its prospects for survival'.[29]

Much worse was to come for Wilson. Within four months of his great electoral triumph, he faced a new speculative attack on sterling. A seamen's strike, poor balance-of-trade figures and rumours set the attack in motion. After deliberations between Wilson, Callaghan and Brown, Brown resigned and then withdrew his resignation, after appeals from colleagues. Wilson announced a massive £500 million package of cuts, on 20th July. They amounted to the harshest deflationary measures since 1949. They hit in all directions simultaneously: cuts in overseas expenditure; restrictions on hire purchase; a surcharge on alcohol and petrol; increased postal charges; and tighter building controls. Either by accident or design, the cuts came just before Parliament was due to go on holiday – as were many constituents – and this made opposition more difficult. Luck came Wilson's way, in that England defeated West Germany to win the World Cup, on 30th July. Somehow, some of this success became attached to Wilson, who used the narrow victory as a symbol of Britain's revival.

In August, Wilson gave his government a face-lift. Despite misgivings, he moved Brown to the Foreign Office, replacing him with his previous Foreign Secretary, Michael Stewart. Arthur Bottomley was moved to Overseas Development, and Herbert Bowden took his place at the Commonwealth Relations Office. Anthony Greenwood, son of Arthur Greenwood, became Minister of Housing, replacing Richard Crossman, who became Lord

President and Leader of the House. Greenwood had previously served at Overseas Development. Once again, doubts must be raised about what kind of grip these ministers had on their departments, given their brief tenure.

Wilson attempted new initiatives abroad but generally failed. He failed on Rhodesia, he failed as go-between on Vietnam and he failed to achieve British membership of the EEC. His Common Market policy was born of a growing conviction that Britain's world role was over. When India and Pakistan fought over Kashmir in 1965, they preferred the Soviet Premier Kosygin as mediator rather than a British personality. For many of the Commonwealth states, the USA had long ago assumed a greater importance as protector than Britain. Increasingly, they looked elsewhere for development aid. Other signs of change were the announcement, in June 1967, that China had exploded its first H-bomb, and the decision of Sweden, in September 1967, to drive on the right-hand side of the road. Britain, it was recognised, had not got the strength to go on alone. But there were still foolish illusions. As Willy Brandt, then West Germany's Foreign Minister, later recalled: 'The British were not especially adroit. When I met George Brown – as intelligent as he was mercurial – in the country, he told me, "Willy, you must get us in, [the EEC] so we can take the lead."'[30]

Devaluation: '. . . the pound . . . in your pocket'

When they got home from their summer holidays, the voters faced a wage freeze (July 1966 to January 1967), followed by a period of 'severe restraint' (February to July 1967). As was to be expected, belief in the government's ability fell sharply. Labour did badly in a series of by-elections, including one at Carmarthen (14th July 1966) in which Gwynfor Evans, President of Plaid Cymru (1945–81), snatched the seat from Labour, giving his party its first electoral win. At Rhondda West, a normally rock-solid Labour seat, Labour only narrowly avoided defeat, on 9th March 1967. On the same day, the Conservatives captured Glasgow Pollok. Worse was to come in the May local elections, including the loss of the Greater London Council, the first time Labour had lost control of London since 1934. More bad luck was to follow in June. The brief Arab–Israeli War resulted in the closure of the Suez Canal through which many of Britain's imports and exports passed. This undermined still further the fundamentally weak position of the economy. The government was then hit by strikes in the docks and on the railways. Once again, the balance of payments was in rapid decline. Drastic action was called for. It came on 18th November 1967, with the dramatic announcement of the devaluation of the pound from $2.80 to $2.40, a devaluation of 14 per cent. Wilson decided to defend the measure on television and radio and he broadcast the following day. His speech ensured that he would get into any book on modern political quotes,[31] but it was for the gaffe he made rather than for any wisdom. He claimed the devaluation, 'does not mean of course, that the pound here in Britain in your pocket . . . has been devalued'. Given Britain's dependence on international trade, on large-scale imports, this was a ridiculous comment, which is difficult to explain.

More, but not unexpected, bad news was about to break. On 27th November, President de Gaulle announced that France would vote against Britain's membership of the EEC. Wilson had made the effort, even though he knew the application was likely to fail. The attempt had created further uncertainty about the pound because it was believed that a condition of entry would be devaluation.

After devaluation, Roy Jenkins became the Chancellor of the Exchequer and James Callaghan took his place at the Home Office. They were both jumping out of the frying pan into the fire!

Swinging London

In its issue of 4th July 1966, the American publication *Time Magazine* published a feature on London, the 'swinging city'. Having had an international reputation for being prudish, stiff and reserved, Britain rapidly gained a reputation for being 'permissive'. In part, this was simply because Britain had elected a Labour government, something which many foreigners, on Right and Left, had thought impossible in normal times. The Attlee years were seen as an aberration caused by the war. Second, there was the new image of Britain given currency abroad by 'new wave' films, discussed above. Third, there was the rise of British pop music and fashion, above all, the Beatles; and fourth, there were the new laws, which replaced laws based on a more Victorian morality.

Following the efforts of Sydney Silverman, MP, capital punishment was abolished in 1965. Another Labour MP, Leo Abse, campaigned for a more tolerant attitude towards homosexuality, and this was embodied in a new law of 1967, which legalised homosexual acts in private between consenting adults. The armed services were excluded from this and it remained an offence to 'solicit' in public. The word 'gay' acquired a new meaning in the 1960s. The Liberal MP, David Steel, successfully proposed the Abortion Bill of 1967, which made abortion more widely available. Under the Act, it still required two doctors to agree that an abortion was necessary on medical or psychological grounds. Britain started to attract young women from abroad in search of abortions. The National Health Service (Family Planning) Act (1967) made it possible for local authorities to provide contraceptives and contraceptive advice. The Divorce Reform Act (1969) aimed to remove the notion of guilt from divorce, stating that the sole ground for divorce was that the marriage had broken down 'irretrievably'. This took much of the pain, and cost, out of this experience. In the following year, the Matrimonial Property Act established that a wife's work, whether within the home as a housewife, or as an earner outside it, should be recognised as an equal contribution to building the family home, and should be treated accordingly, in the event of the property's sale following divorce. The Equal Pay Act was also passed in the same year, though it did not become fully effective for another five years. It proved difficult to enforce. The arts too benefited from the new liberalism. Censorship of the theatre by the Lord Chamberlain was abolished in 1968, and a more liberal régime was introduced at the British Board of Film Censors. One other change, which was of more benefit to Labour than the Conservatives, was the lowering of the legal age of majority from 21 to eighteen.

Another libertarian move was the establishment of the Parliamentary Commissioner for Administration, in 1967. This was influenced by the Danish example.[32] The idea was to give the citizen redress against public bodies, when an individual considered maladministration had taken place. In comparison to the Ombudsman in Scandinavian states the Commissioner's jurisdiction was narrowly defined. But it was useful as the beginning of a process.

Many of these moves were non-party and were supported by most Liberals and some Conservatives, but they could only have been adopted when Labour had a majority, and were backed by Home Secretaries – Roy Jenkins (1965–7) and James Callaghan (1967–70) – who approved of them.

Britain was not at the forefront of the new liberalism to quite the extent that people make out. Most West European states no longer had capital punishment by 1965, and the Scandinavian states were more tolerant than Britain in all of the areas mentioned above. In some respects, Britain followed America. The association of certain aspects of pop culture with protest, starting with opposition to the Vietnam War, produced a powerful cocktail. From the campuses of America there spread to those of Europe an ever-increasing crescendo of protest in 1968.

As in America, Germany, France and elsewhere, campus revolts in Britain were confined to a minority of students at a minority of universities and other institutions. Richard Crossman, an ex-university lecturer, was deeply shocked. On 30th December 1968, he lamented that the student Left had 'shown itself imbecile in its anarchism and bogus leftism'. The students had been influenced by Che Guevara, the Cuban revolutionary killed in 1967, who claimed to be striving to build a society different from both Soviet Communism and Western Capitalism, and Mao Zedong, then instigating China's 'Cultural Revolution'. Feeling against the Vietnam War had become a more generalised revolt against the Establishment and its power structures everywhere. There was a feeling that ordinary people were being denied what was their due by those in power, under whatever label. In France, the students almost brought down de Gaulle, in May. At British universities, the grievances were limited to demanding student representation on university senates, establishing mixed halls of residence, ending irksome restrictions and so on. Such reforms were granted.

Education Reform and Welfare

Labour had always been strong on education. This was partly a result of having a relatively large number of former teachers among Labour MPs. It had won the debate on education before gaining office, with a majority of people rejecting the eleven-plus and calling for more educational opportunity. In 1965, Anthony Crosland, the Minister of Education (1965–7), required all local authorities to submit plans for reorganising education in a way that would eliminate the eleven-plus. Non-selective comprehensive schools were thought to be the answer. These schools combined within them different 'streams', some very similar to the old grammar-school range of subjects. Much still depended on the extent to which local authorities cared about education, how well off they were, and where schools were located within individual authorities. Inner-city schools, generally speaking, remained at a disadvantage. Most teachers did not wish to work in them. The private sector schools remained unaffected by these changes, although their syllabuses began to reflect more the mood of the time, with more emphasis being given to modern languages (in addition to French), technology, science and business studies. Gradually, they started to introduce a co-educational element.

For a long time, much expert opinion had felt that the school-leaving age, fifteen, was too low. In most modern countries it was sixteen. Accordingly, it was proposed to raise it to sixteen, but in January 1968 this was postponed by Patrick Gordon Walker (Minister of Education, 1967–8) from 1971 until 1973, as a cost-saving measure. Lord Longford, Lord Privy Seal, resigned in protest.

Labour continued the work, set in motion by the previous government, of extending the higher education sector. The Council for National Academic Awards was established in 1964, following the recommendations of the Robbins Report, to replace the National Council for Technological Awards. It was granted a Royal Charter empowering it to award degrees, diplomas and certificates comparable to university awards, to students completing courses at non-university institutions of higher education in Great Britain. Wilson's government supported the setting up of the Open University, which does not require its students to have formal entry qualifications and which pioneered part-time and distance learning.

Welfare, like education, was a victim of spending cuts between 1964 and 1970. There was a retreat from the principle of universality, which Labour, as well as Conservative experts, had come to believe was wasteful of resources, in that it spread inadequate benefits too thinly across the entire population. The major legislation of the period was the 1966 Ministry of Social Security Act, which attempted to remove the stigma that still deterred many individuals from applying for National Assistance, by replacing it with Supplementary Benefits. It was only partly successful. Pride and ignorance still prevented thousands of entitled individuals from applying. Prescription charges were abolished only to be reintroduced in 1968. The first successful heart transplant by Christian Barnard in Cape Town, on 3rd December 1967, sparked off a debate about the uses and abuses of medical science, the cost of complicated surgery to the NHS, and whether British medicine was still a world-class institution.

Trouble in Northern Ireland

Influenced by the civil rights movement in the USA and the changing atmosphere in Great Britain and in Ulster itself, the Campaign for Social Justice was founded in Dungannon, in January 1964. This, in turn, led to the setting up of the Northern Ireland Civil Rights Association (NICRA), in February 1967. It formulated a programme which included 'one man one vote', in local elections; no gerrymandering of constituency boundaries; fair distribution of council housing; the repeal of the Special Powers Act; disbandment of the B Specials; and a formal complaints procedure against local authorities.[33] Very many people in Great Britain were shocked and surprised when they first learned of the situation in Northern Ireland and of the position of the Catholic community there. Television pictures of violence by the (largely Protestant) Royal Ulster Constabulary (RUC) against a civil rights march in Derry, on 5th October 1968, brought this home to them. Partly under pressure from Wilson, O'Neill announced, on 22nd November, sweeping local government reforms designed to placate the Catholics. He also sacked his Home Affairs Minister responsible for the RUC, William Craig. By this time, a new element had stepped onto the political stage: People's Democracy, led by Bernadette Devlin, Michael Farrell and Eamonn McCann, whose ultimate aim was an all-Ireland workers' republic.[34] It organised its own march from Belfast to Londonderry, on 1st January 1969, only to be attacked by Protestant extremists. During the weekend that followed, there was more RUC violence in the Catholic Bogside area of Derry. Against a background of growing violence, an election to the Northern Ireland parliament was held on 24th February. Gains were made by civil rights leaders, such as John Hume, and anti-O'Neill Unionists. On 23rd April, the Unionist parliamentary party voted, by 28 to 22, to implement universal adult suffrage, at the next local government elections. Major James Chichester-Clark, Ulster Minister of Agriculture, resigned in opposition. O'Neill then resigned himself, and Clark was elected his successor with a single vote majority. O'Neill, it was said, was the wrong man with the right ideas. An old Etonian (yet enjoying a long Irish pedigree), his aloof manner alienated potential support.[35] His cousin, Chichester-Clark, was no more successful in dealing with the mounting tension. Extremists on both sides turned to rioting, in mid-August 1969, with violence in Derry, Belfast and elsewhere. It shocked viewers in Britain and Southern Ireland to see, on television, Catholic refugees heading for the Republic, to be treated at Irish Army field hospitals or being received into temporary accommodation in Dublin. Wilson reluctantly sent British troops to restore order. The Catholics initially welcomed them. Callaghan announced a reform programme in August 1969, together with an enquiry by Sir John Hunt into security matters. The Hunt Report (October 1969) recommended the disarming of the RUC, the disbandment of the B Specials and their replacement by the Ulster Defence Regiment (UDR), under British Army control. In Belfast, Protestant riots followed the publication of the Report. They were suppressed by British troops.

One other sinister development in Ireland was the split of the IRA into the 'Officials' and the 'Provisionals', on 10th April 1971. The Provisionals were dedicated to a military campaign; the Officials were prepared to look for political solutions, without, however, totally denying themselves the military option. Soon

the Provisionals were getting arms and money from the USA
and other sources.

Powell, 'We must be mad . . .'

On 20th April 1968, Enoch Powell, a member of Heath's shadow
cabinet, made a speech in Birmingham, which was 'a strange
mixture of populist assertion and anecdote, statistics and classi-
cal allusion'.[36] His subject was immigration. This had once again
flared up as an issue, following events in Kenya. Thousands of
Asians from Kenya were seeking asylum in Britain. Parts of the
press stirred up fears of chaos in Britain if the immigration
from Africa continued. Powell argued that a country and its
rulers who tolerated this, 'must be mad, literally mad. It is like
watching a nation busily engaged in heaping up its own funeral
pyre.' He predicted that Britain would face the kind of rioting
that was a feature of American life. It was not just what he said,
but the way he said it, which caused offence. He spoke about an
old lady who had complained to him that immigrants had pushed
excrement through her letterbox. Powell also attacked the Race
Relations Bill, then going through Parliament. Heath acted
immediately, expelling Powell from the shadow cabinet for a
speech that he considered racist in content and liable to exacerbate racial tension.[37]

Powell's speech must be seen against the background of what
was happening in America. The USA suffered from an unusual
number of riots in black areas of northern cities between 1964
and 1969, which led to President Johnson setting up a Commission on Civil Disorders.

The Kenya Asians had been born, in very many cases, in that
country and knew no other, though they had not taken out
Kenyan citizenship when Kenya became independent. They were
deprived of their livelihood (mainly in trade and the professions), and forced to leave the country. Mrs Gandhi, the Indian
Prime Minister, responded to British entreaties, and agreed
privately to accept them once they were deported, but did not
wish to say so publicly, as this would have made it easier for East
African governments to discriminate against the Asians.[38] Many,
however, decided to seek British passports. This option was open

to them under the Westminster Statute, framed by the Conservatives, granting Kenya and Uganda their independence. The provision had been designed to help British settlers and their descendants who wished to return.[39] Wilson wrote later, 'Few problems could have presented more difficult issues for the Cabinet or a greater issue of conscience for liberal-minded people throughout the country.'[40] After attempts to persuade the Kenyan leader, Jomo Kenyatta, to think again, the government decided to introduce legislation to bring the Kenyan Asians under immigration control, limiting the number of entry vouchers to be issued to them to 1,500 a year. In the three months ending in January 1968, 7,000 had arrived. In the first two months of 1968, 13,000 arrived.[41] The Bill passed through all its stages in both Houses of Parliament in seven days and became law on 1st March 1968. It restricted automatic entry in future to those citizens of the UK and Colonies, who had patrial ties with Britain. In practice, this meant, almost exclusively, white citizens whose forefathers were from Britain. The official Conservative position was to abstain, but thirteen Conservatives joined the Liberals and some Labour MPs, in voting against.

The government attempted to take positive action to improve the lives of the immigrants within Britain by the Race Relations Acts of 1965 and 1968. They were important historical steps. For the first time in British history, the government intervened, through legislation, to prevent racial discrimination.[42] By establishing the Race Relations Commission in the 1968 Act, it sought to promote the cause of racial harmony. Happily, immigration was not a major issue in the 1970 election.

1970 Surprise Defeat

One record which Wilson achieved – against his will – was his government's record in by-election losses. During the life of the outgoing Parliament, 1966–70, Labour lost fifteen seats, a record up to 1991. The last Conservative administration, 1959–64, had lost seven seats and won two. The Attlee governments, 1945–51, had not lost any seats in by-elections. It was surprising, therefore, that Labour looked like winning the election of 18th June 1970. Labour's strength was judged to be the popularity of Wilson and the weakness of Heath. The television channels concentrated most of their attention on the two leaders. After them, Powell was the most reported politician. On the day, turnout fell again, as it had done at every election since 1950; only 72 per cent of the electorate recorded their votes. The lower turnout was influenced by June being a holiday month.[43] Labour's percentage fell from 47.9 to 43, the Liberals' fell from 8.5 to 7.5 and that of the Conservatives increased from 41.9 to 46.4. This gave the Conservatives 330 seats (253 in 1966), Labour 287 (363) and the Liberals six (twelve). The Liberals lost votes to the SNP and PC. The most prominent Labour casualty was George Brown, who lost his seat partly due to the changing composition of the electorate in his Belper constituency. Some tried to explain the difference between the result and the predictions of the pollsters by a late swing. Equally, it is possible to argue that the Conservatives would have been denied a victory had Labour organisation more nearly equalled that of their main opponent.[44] Labour had fewer helpers and fewer cars on polling day and a less well-organised postal vote.[45] It possibly got fewer of its potential Y-voters – the new eighteen-plus category – registered than did the Conservatives. According to Jenkins, a poor set of trade figures, released three days before polling day, told against Labour. But he still thought Labour would win.[46]

Heath's success meant that little attention was paid to the relative success of the SNP and PC. Making a maximum effort, these two parties gained 11.4 per cent (5 in 1966) and 11.5 per cent (4.3 in 1966) respectively, in Scotland and Wales. PC overtook the Liberals in votes. It gained no seats. The SNP won one. The increase in the support for the SNP and the PC was the beginning of a trend rather than just an expression of temporary dissatisfaction. The SNP was founded in 1934, gaining its first success in a by-election against Labour at Motherwell in 1945. In the subsequent general election, the seat reverted to Labour. It did not score again until Mrs Winifred Ewing won a by-election at Hamilton, in 1967, defeating the Labour candidate. In Wales, Plaid Cymru was founded in 1925, with the aim of independence. It was unsuccessful until, as we saw, Evans won the by-election at Carmarthen, in 1966. In both countries the same factors were at work. Irish independence had helped to sow the seed of nationalism. In both cases, there were strong socialist, pacifist currents. In both cases, there were former Communists seeking a new political home. In addition, in some parts of Scotland and Wales, local Labour politicians ran local councils as their personal fiefdoms. Scotland and Wales, like Northern Ireland, had suffered more than southern England as Britain's traditional industries declined. Wilson had given temporary hope in the early 1960s, but his actual performance in office had dashed the hopes of many Labour supporters. The SNP and PC seemed respectable, if radical, alternatives to the three main parties.

During the election a coup was being organised in the Conservative Party to oust Heath if the party was defeated.[47] As it turned out, the election was a great, if unexpected, personal triumph for Heath, who had been rather badly treated by the media and underestimated by his opponents. He had gone into the election worrying about saving his own seat at Bexley, with the slender majority of 2,333. He too was somewhat surprised that he had not only saved his seat, but had gained entry into 10 Downing Street.[48]

9 Trouble and Strife, 1970–74

A meeting at Selsdon Park, near Croydon, of the shadow cabinet in January 1970 had given the impression that Heath's team had a clear strategy for government. However, except for Europe, 'Heath did not really have the slightest idea of what he wanted to do' in government.[1] He talked vaguely about modernisation but had no long-term plan. He was lucky that Labour was divided and busy allocating blame for its electoral defeat. But he was not lucky with his nineteen-member Cabinet. Ian Macleod, who was a popular figure in the Conservative Party, died suddenly after only a month in office. Anthony Barber replaced him as Chancellor. Reginald Maudling, the Home Secretary, was forced to resign in 1972 because of his involvement with the corrupt architect John Poulson. Poulson had spread his net widely and dragged down Labour and Conservative politicians, mainly at the local level. Maudling was replaced by Robert Carr. One unusual appointment was that of the former Prime Minister, Sir Alec Douglas-Home, serving as Foreign Secretary. This was the first time that a former leader had served under his successor since Chamberlain was a member of Churchill's 1940 government. Also unusual was the appointment of Maurice Macmillan, son of the former Prime Minister, as Chief Secretary to the Treasury. Lord Carrington took over at Defence and Peter Walker got Housing and Local Government, followed a few months later, by Environment. Geoffrey Rippon was put in charge of negotiations with the EEC, as Chancellor of the Duchy of Lancaster. Significant for the future were the appointments of Margaret Thatcher to Education, Keith Joseph to Social Security, Geoffrey Howe as Solicitor General, 1970–2, Minister of Trade and Consumer Affairs, 1972–4, and William Whitelaw, as Lord President and Leader of the Commons, Secretary of State for Northern Ireland, 1972–3, and Employment, 1973–4.

Barber (b. 1920) was educated at Retford Grammar School and Oxford. He was a Dunkirk veteran and pilot until his capture in 1942. A barrister, he was elected to the Commons in 1951. He was a member of Douglas-Home's Cabinet as Minister of Health, having served outside the Cabinet under Churchill, Eden and Macmillan. Carr (b. 1916) had served in a junior capacity under Churchill, Macmillan and Douglas-Home. He was educated at Westminster School and Cambridge. Carrington (b. 1919) the 6th Baron, was educated at Eton and Sandhurst and had served in the Second World War in the Grenadier Guards. He had served in junior posts under Churchill and Eden and as First Lord of the Admiralty, 1959–63. Under Douglas-Home, he was Leader in the Lords. Between 1956 and 1959 he was UK High Commissioner for Australia. Walker (b. 1932) was a self-made businessman, who was elected to the Commons in 1961. He was unusual in that he was not a graduate and had not served in the armed forces. Rippon (b. 1924) had served under Eden and Macmillan, reaching the Cabinet under Douglas-Home, in 1963, as Minister of Housing and Public Works. He was a barrister educated at King's College, Taunton, and Oxford. Joseph (b. 1918) was educated at Harrow and Oxford, and served as captain in the Royal Artillery. A barrister, he entered Parliament in 1956. He had held various junior posts under Macmillan and Douglas-Home. Howe (b. 1926) was elected to the Commons in 1966. Educated at Winchester and Cambridge, he was a barrister and company director. Whitelaw (b. 1918) was a farmer and a landowner who was educated at Winchester and Cambridge. A major in the Scots Guards during the Second World War, he was elected to the Commons in 1955.

It is worth noting, in view of future controversy, that under Thatcher a record number of grammar schools closed, and the proportion of children in comprehensive schools was almost doubled.[2] She also raised the school-leaving age, which had been postponed by Labour, and extended their policy of reducing free milk eligibility. The Labour government had scrapped free milk in all secondary schools. Thatcher abolished it for the over-sevens. It is also worth recalling that, although stern critics of Heath, neither Thatcher nor Joseph raised their voices in opposition to Heath's policies in government. This probably demonstrates that ministers are in far less control of their ministries than they claim during their terms of office, and that their ambitions ensure that they are unlikely to rock the boat. Heath, despite his presidential image, 'usually allowed others to lead the discussion . . . there were no serious disagreements in Cabinet'.[3] No Cabinet Minister resigned for political reasons, and none was sacked by Heath.

EEC Membership: one of 'decisive votes'

The death of Charles de Gaulle, the former President of France, on 9th November 1970, was another stroke of luck for Heath. The main obstacle to Britain's entry into the EEC had been removed. The man who had succeeded de Gaulle in the previous year, Georges Pompidou, needed to look over his shoulder no more. Wilson had been in the process of lodging a new application in 1969 and Heath lost no time in pressing forward on this front. Even so, it was to take until May 1971 before Pompidou pronounced himself satisfied with Britain's qualifications for membership. Heath was better able than most other leading politicians, Conservative or Labour, to put a convincing case. He had negotiated at the time of Macmillan and was known as a convinced European rather than an empiricist or, like many in both major parties, prepared to join in an attempt to shore up the lagging British economy and failing British prestige. Heath was prepared to commit Britain to accepting the Treaty of Rome, but he negotiated transitional arrangements to give the British economy time to adjust to the new situation. One of the big problems was, and was to remain, the Common Agricultural Policy (CAP), designed for states with much larger farming interests than Britain. The EEC Commission kept up farm incomes by imposing tariffs on food from outside the Common Market, and by buying agricultural products from within the EEC, at prices which gave farmers a reasonable standard of living. This often meant paying higher prices than those prevailing in world markets. It also resulted in agricultural surpluses being stored or sold at below cost with the help of subsidies. These subsidies were paid for out of taxation, so that a highly urban and industrial society like Britain would have to pay relatively large sums to help Italian and French farmers. The Republic of Ireland,

Denmark and Norway, with large agricultural sectors, applied at the same time. Membership of the EEC inevitably speeded up the weakening of Commonwealth ties, something, which was already under way. Geoffrey Rippon, who did much of the detailed work, negotiated an agreement to safeguard New Zealand dairy products and Commonwealth sugar. Membership, it was argued, took Britain into a vast market of prosperous states. If it remained outside, it would be less and less able to compete, because of the tariff barriers and because its EEC competitors would be benefiting from the economies of scale.

Most of the discussion about membership was about economics and not so much about politics. However, the Treaty of Rome looked forward to an ever-closer union of peoples living in democracies. It would remove the possibility of war between members and it would also gradually give members more of a voice in a world increasingly dominated by the superpowers. The fact that most members of Heath's Cabinet had served in the Second World War influenced its members, including Heath himself. Douglas-Home, who was not in the armed services, also saw the EEC as a vehicle for preventing renewed conflict in Europe.

The general principle of British entry into the EEC, was debated in Parliament, on 28th October 1971. Earlier in the month, the annual Labour conference had voted to reject entry. Some in the Labour Party opposed it as a rich man's club which would exploit the Third World, some opposed it because it was the Conservatives who secured entry, and a few opposed it because Moscow was against it. Wilson took a completely ambiguous and unprincipled position, seeming to oppose something he had been in favour of when in government. He could have used his still great influence to unite his party in favour of the move. Callaghan apparently announced that membership would threaten the 'language of Chaucer'.[4] EEC policy was a major item on the list of grievances that subsequently led to the split in the Labour Party. The Commons approved the application, by 356 votes to 244. Heath allowed a free vote, Wilson did not. On the government side, 39 Conservatives voted against, but 69 Labour MPs supported the proposal and twenty abstained. Among the pro-Marketeers was Roy Jenkins, deputy leader of the Labour Party. He believed 'it was one of the decisive votes of the century', and therefore ignored pleas from his colleagues to abstain. He saw it, 'in the context of the first Reform bill, the repeal of the Corn Laws, Gladstone's Home Rule Bills, the Lloyd George Budget and the Parliament Bill, the Munich Agreement and the May 1940 votes'.[5] Jenkins resigned later, when Labour decided to call for a referendum on British membership. Tony Benn had been largely responsible for Labour taking up the referendum demand. The Commons passed the third reading of the European Bill on 13th July 1972 by 301 votes to 284. Britain became a member of the EEC, on 1st January 1973. Ireland and Denmark joined too, after referenda endorsing membership. Norway voted against.

In the Republic of Ireland, both the Fianna Fáil government and the Fine Gael opposition supported EEC membership. The Irish farmers were very much in favour. Labour opposed entry. In the referendum, on 10th May 1973, 83 per cent voted in favour of membership. Ireland's economic dependence on Britain made membership imperative if Britain went in. On the other hand, membership gave Ireland greater independence in the future.

Industrial Relations

Labour had boasted before 1964 that its intimate relations with the TUC would ensure better industrial relations. Once in office, its record was not particularly good. It suffered from what Callaghan later called 'a plague of unofficial strikes'. It is worth pointing out that, with the exception of a few countries like West Germany, Austria and Sweden, Britain had fewer strikes and fewer days lost through industrial action, than most other industrial states. Nevertheless, in 1965, Wilson had asked Lord Donovan to head a Royal Commission to examine industrial relations.[6] Reform proposals were presented by Barbara Castle, Minister of Employment and Productivity (1968–70), in a policy document, *In Place of Strife*, in January 1969. These went beyond what Donovan had called for. Particularly controversial were proposals that there should be a ballot before an official strike, and that there should be power to impose fines, if unofficial strikers did not obey orders to return to work. The proposals failed because of the opposition from the TUC and from within the

Cabinet. James Callaghan, a former trade union official, led this within the Cabinet. He conceded that reform was needed but felt that legal sanctions would not stop unofficial strikes.[7] This attempt nearly led to a revolt to bring down Wilson and replace him with Callaghan.[8] Industrial relations were, then, a dangerous business even for a Labour government.

The experience of the Wilson administration in no way deterred Heath. The Industrial Relations Act was given the Royal Assent on 5th August 1971, thus becoming law. The previous December, Britain had been reduced to using candles because of electricity failures caused by industrial action by power engineers. There were many other disputes. In its first part, the Act recognised the rights of unions to organise and to conduct strikes. It established an Industrial Relations Commission to oversee their activities. The second part of the Act removed the immunity from legal suits by employers that unions had enjoyed since 1906. It also required unions to submit their rules to the registrar or forfeit their statutory rights. An Industrial Relations Court was to be established to hear cases of breach of contract and unfair labour practices, as defined by the Act. The Act provoked strong opposition from the TUC. The public, as a whole, were more favourably disposed towards it but felt uneasy when, in one or two cases, trade unionists were sent to prison for breaking the new law. The TUC threatened to expel any union that registered. There were strikes and demonstrations against it. Even without it, the number of strikes was rising. The number of days lost because of industrial disputes more than doubled in 1972, rising to 24 million. This was more than four times the average of the 1960s.[9]

In opposition, the Conservatives had attacked the policy of supporting 'lame ducks', assisting failing enterprises to stay in business in the hope that they could become profitable again. In government, they were less enthusiastic about letting market forces do their ruthless work. The failure of the highly prestigious Rolls-Royce (February 1971) could not be allowed to happen, as it was so closely associated with British quality and British technology. It was nationalised. Fear of social unrest was a factor in saving Upper Clyde Shipbuilders from closure, in February 1972. This 'U-turn' in government policy came in the middle of a miners' strike, which the government lost. Many other businesses were not so lucky and went to the wall. The Industry Act (1971) was another step in the direction of interventionism. It gave the Secretary of State for Trade and Industry more extensive powers of industrial and regional subsidy than had ever been envisaged by Labour.[10] It was conceived against a background of the highest unemployment since 1940. The computer firm ICL also received assistance. The aim was, according to Walker, who had been moved to Trade and Industry, 'to rationalise and modernise British industry'.[11]

Heath followed Wilson with intervention on prices and incomes. This was completely contrary to the Conservative election manifesto, but was deemed imperative. At first the Conservatives abolished the Prices and Incomes Board, but they soon did a U-turn. Tripartite talks between the Government, the TUC and employers' organisations failed to produce results. Heath resorted therefore to compulsion. A three-month standstill on pay and price increases was announced. Later, under phase two of this policy, a Pay Board and a Prices Commission were set up, in January 1973. A phase three was introduced, from 1st April 1973, which offered some mild relaxation.

Ireland: Embarrassment in the South

Some were surprised that the new troubles in Northern Ireland had not caused greater shock waves in the South. That they did not was a sign of just how far Southern Ireland had travelled since independence. There was still the 'Guinness Republicanism' of the pubs, but most voters were concerned about bread-and-butter issues. There was also the hope that if both Britain and the Republic became members of the EEC, the border would not matter as much. Jack Lynch, who replaced Lemass, in 1966, as leader of Fianna Fáil and Taoiseach, was a mild-mannered seasoned politician from Cork, for whom the division was not a great emotional issue. A former Education Minister who had also served as Minister of Industry and Commerce, he did not wish to interfere, but was forced to make gestures, such as sending medical teams to the frontier to aid refugees. His party was returned by the electors, with fewer votes but more seats, in 1969, before the troubles really got under way. He was embarrassed, in 1970, and forced to sack two of his key ministers, Charles Haughey and Neil Blaney, on suspicion of arms running to the North. In an effort to show he would, nevertheless, work for unity by peaceful means, he sponsored the removal of the controversial clause of the Catholic Church's 'special position' from the Constitution, in theory making the Republic more acceptable to Protestants. On a turnout of only 51 per cent, the voters approved the amendment in December 1972. The move did little to impress the hard-line Republicans in the South or the extreme Unionists in the North. Also approved was the reduction of the voting age from 21 to 18.

Lynch set his next date with the electorate for March 1973. This time he was to be disappointed. Inflation and a feeling that it was time for a change resulted in Fianna Fáil's replacement by a Fine Gael–Labour coalition. The two parties had fought the election together as a potential coalition. Liam Cosgrave, a deeply religious barrister and strong pro-American,[12] had taken over the leadership of Fine Gael in 1965, at the same time that Lynch became leader of Fianna Fáil. Now he became Taoiseach, remaining head of government until 1977. Garret FitzGerald, a university economics lecturer, was appointed Foreign Minister. He was the son of Southern Ireland's first External Affairs Minister. A fluent French speaker, he helped to give his country a more positive image abroad. He wanted to pursue a policy of active reconciliation with the North. Labour's Connor Cruise O'Brien was given Post and Telegraphs, which also put him in charge of the state broadcasting system, RTE. Through a Broadcasting Amendment Act (1976) he strengthened the curbs on IRA propaganda. He also angered some by asserting that the South's claim to the North was a kind of imperialism.[13] The Fine Gael–Labour coalition abolished the requirement that a pass in Irish was necessary to gain the school-leaving certificate. Irish was also dropped as a requirement for entry into the civil service.

The new government was hit by the quadrupling of oil prices at the end of 1973, which brought about a massive increase in borrowing. Inflation worsened, rising higher than in most European countries. Unemployment rose from 7.9 per cent in March 1973, to 12.5 per cent in March 1977.[14] Native Irish businesses continued to decline under the impact of foreign competition.

The IDA went on, largely independent of government, encouraging foreign investment, especially in chemicals and electronics.[15] During this period, the farmers started to benefit from the EEC's Common Agricultural Policy but consumers fared less well, with higher food prices. In the election of 1977, the electors ruthlessly cut down the government parties. O'Brien lost his seat. Cosgrave accepted responsibility for the defeat and resigned, being replaced as Fine Gael leader by FitzGerald. Labour's leader, Brendan Corish, also resigned, his successor being Frank Cluskey.

Ireland: Unrest in the North

In theory, a Conservative government should have been in a better position than a Labour government to restore peace to Northern Ireland. The Ulster Unionists had always been regarded as the Northern Ireland wing of Conservatism at Westminster. Eleven of the twelve Westminster MPs from Northern Ireland were Ulster Unionists. The Conservative leaders, it might be thought, could have prevailed on their Ulster friends to moderate their position. But the old structures were breaking up in Ulster and the accession to power of Heath was soon followed by a sharp deterioration in the situation.[16] Maudling was seen as a failure in an admittedly difficult situation. Chichester-Clark saw the solution largely in terms of law and order. The only good news from Northern Ireland, in 1970, was the formation of the Social Democratic and Labour Party (SDLP), a moderate party designed to appeal to the great majority of Catholics and, hopefully, some non-Unionist non-Catholics. The veteran Republican and moderate socialist, Gerry Fitt, was elected leader. John Hume and Ivan Cooper, from the civil rights movement, were also among the leading members. Fitt, a former merchant seaman, had been Republican Labour MP for Belfast West since 1966. He had been a Belfast city councillor since 1958, and member of the Stormont parliament since 1962.

Throughout 1971 the situation worsened. On 6th February, the first British soldier was killed by the IRA in Belfast. Chichester-Clark resigned in March, to be replaced by Brian Faulkner, who, at least, had slightly increased credibility because of his Ulster accent. In April, the Provisionals started their systemic campaign of bombing and assassination. After the killing by British troops of two young Derry men in July, the SDLP decided to boycott the Stormont parliament. They had been refused a public enquiry into the killings. As the violence mounted, so did the calls for the internment of known IRA sympathisers. Faulkner converted Maudling and Heath to this policy, which senior army officers thought would exacerbate the situation. Over 300 men were interned, most of them Catholics, and most of them either innocent or inactive. The IRA leaders had escaped over the border.[17] This began on 9th August, but it seemed to make the situation worse. Rioting and a campaign of civil disobedience, including a rent and rates strike, followed. Talks in September, between Heath, Faulkner and Jack Lynch, brought no relief. A new low was reached on 30th January 1972, when British paratroopers shot dead thirteen unarmed civilians during a civil rights march in Derry. This 'Bloody Sunday' only made the position of Catholic moderates more difficult. In an attempt to restore credibility with the Catholics, Heath suspended the Unionist-dominated Northern Ireland Stormont parliament and imposed direct rule, on 24th March 1972. William Whitelaw was appointed to the new post of Secretary of State for Northern Ireland, with a seat in the Cabinet, to rule the Province. He took the bold initiative of meeting (June–July) with the Provisionals but the talks ended in failure. The next major outrage was the bombing of central Belfast, carried out by the Provisionals, on 21st July ('Bloody Friday'), in which nine people died. Ten days later, the British Army launched Operation Motorman, to bring 'no-go' areas back under control. Sectarian killings continued, with the illegal (Protestant) Ulster Volunteer Force 'claiming responsibility' for its share.

On 20th March 1973, the government published its White Paper on Northern Ireland, which subsequently became the Northern Ireland Constitution Act. It provided for an Assembly and a power-sharing Executive. They were given fewer powers than the old parliament. The Act also called for the establishment of a Council of Ireland, with only vague consultative functions. After the election, towards the end of 1973, a power-sharing Executive was formed from the SDLP, the moderate Unionists under Faulkner, and the small non-sectarian Alliance Party. This development was welcomed in both London and

Dublin, but bitterly opposed by anti-Faulkner Unionists. In December 1973, politicians from London, Belfast and Dublin met at Sunningdale to move towards setting up the proposed Council of Ireland. Some thought this was the beginning of the beginning.

Uganda Asians

In their election manifesto the Conservatives had promised to tighten up on immigration and Maudling introduced a new Immigration Act (1971) which sought to eliminate the distinction between aliens and New Commonwealth citizens and also to link future immigration to economic necessities. Immigrants would, in future, no longer be considered permanent residents on arrival, and they would need to be doing work considered by the Home Office as useful. There was also provision for repatriation. Commonwealth citizens with patrial status were allowed unrestricted entry.[18] Something like panic broke out, at least in Powellite circles, in 1972, when the dictator of Uganda, Idi Amin, announced the expulsion of the Asians living in that country. An estimated 50,000 of them held British passports and the government made it clear that those who wanted to come would be admitted. Powell attacked this, and he sought to embarrass the government by raising the issue at the Conservative Party conference in October 1972. Robert Carr, who had succeeded Maudling as Home Secretary, with the help of the Young Conservatives, took on Powell whose critical resolution was heavily defeated in a vote which followed.[19] It must be admitted, however, that Powell had a strong influence on immigration policy before and after 1972. He had articulated the fears of many ordinary voters, and a considerable minority of MPs, and the result of his campaigns was a speeding up of the process of restriction and control, which would have happened sooner or later.

Liberal Revival

In 1950 Clement Davies, the Liberal leader (1945–56), told the electorate: 'If you want a Liberal Government this time, you can have one.' The Liberals increased the number of their candidates from 306, in 1945, to 475. The electorate rejected his offer and the Liberals lost 319 deposits. Not surprisingly, they put up only 109 candidates, in 1951, and 110, in 1955; the majority of them lost their deposits. Talk of the death of Labour, in the 1950s, led to a Liberal revival under Jo Grimond (leader 1956–67). He saw the party as a radical non-socialist alternative to the Conservatives. This was based on changes taking place in society with the decline of the old working class and the rise of the white-collar classes who, it was supposed, judged parties on their teams and programmes rather than on class loyalties. The Liberals made a great effort in 1964, with 365 candidates (216 in 1959) gaining 11.2 per cent of the vote, their highest since their 23.6 per cent in 1929. Despite putting up 311 and 332 candidates in 1966 and 1970 respectively, their percentage vote fell to 8.5 and 7.5.[20] For a time, the electorate appeared to be returning to the two main parties; but disillusionment, first with Wilson and then with Heath, gave the Liberals a chance as the respectable party of reform. In the second half of the 1960s, under Jeremy Thorpe (1967–76) – like his predecessor, an old Etonian – they even attracted some for whom Labour was too orthodox, too much part of 'the system'. They led the way in calling for the abandonment of Britain's bomb, opposition to South Africa's apartheid régime and Britain's entry into the EEC. Their domestic policies included co-partnership in industry, a fairer electoral system, devolution in Scotland and Wales and a less rigid immigration policy. They appealed to the electors as the party free of big business and free of big unions. The Young Liberals went much further, advocating policies which lined them up with left-wing socialist and Marxist groups. To some extent, this must have cost them some votes. Usually, Liberal voters were to the right of Liberal MPs and policies. Influenced by liberal, socialist and civil rights groups in the USA, the Liberals pioneered 'community politics' in the 1960s. This was an attempt to build up their strength by identifying grass roots causes and mobilising local people to solve them. It helped them to win local council seats and score at by-elections by attracting protest votes, usually in suburban middle-class or farming constituencies. In Scotland and Wales, the nationalist parties were more likely to be the recipients of protest. In June 1969, the Liberals won a spectacular victory with a 32 per cent swing against Labour, in Ladywood, Birmingham. This was a personal triumph for Wallace Lawler, who had developed his brand of community politics there. He lost the seat in the general election in the following year.

Between 1972 and 1979, the Liberals won six outstanding by-election victories, four against the Conservatives and two against Labour, with large swings. Even if, in many cases, the seats subsequently reverted to the original party, these victories helped to keep the fighting spirit of the Liberals alive. Cyril Smith, who won Rochdale from Labour in October 1972, held on to the seat. He had been Labour Mayor of Rochdale before becoming a Liberal. He was a local man with a small business, who built up a personal following in what was an industrial town. The advance of the Liberals was, of course, held back by Britain's 'first-past-the-post' electoral system, by lack of finance and lack of organisation. Like their rivals, the Liberals did not avoid the whiff of scandal. Thorpe was associated with London and County Securities, a secondary bank, that collapsed. He was also accused of having an affair with a former male model. He was forced to resign in May 1976. Grimond then resumed his leadership role to allow time for a new leader to be elected under a new constitution. This gave every ordinary constituency Liberal Party member a vote, something new in British politics. In July 1976, David Steel was elected by 12,541 votes to 7,032 for John Pardoe, MP for Truro. The son of a Scottish missionary, educated at Edinburgh University, Steel was a TV journalist. He was the youngest MP (aged 27) when he was elected to Parliament in 1965, having won the Roxburgh, Selkirk and Peebles (Scotland) seat in a by-election. He was left of centre and believed the way forward for the Liberals was by co-operation with the other political parties. He remained leader until 1988.

Oil Crisis and Miners' Strike

On 6th October 1973, Egyptian and Syrian forces attacked Israel, with the intention of regaining territory lost in June 1967. They surprised Israel, attacking on the Jewish religious holiday of Yom Kippur. The war ended in a truce on 24th October, the Israelis once again having got the better of the Arabs. Yet the

Arabs had another weapon which proved to be more effective than their armed forces. This was the oil of such countries as Algeria, Iraq, Kuwait, Libya, Saudi Arabia and Syria. They persuaded the OPEC states, meeting on 15th–17th October, to cut back oil supplies to the industrial states and increase the price four-fold. In fairness, it should be mentioned that their prices had fallen behind Western inflation and thus they had been getting less and less for their produce, in real terms. This dramatic move immediately led to a re-evaluation of fuel in general and coal in particular. Coal had faced years of downgrading and the industry was in a constant battle to increase productivity. Uneconomic pits were closed under both Conservative and Labour governments and thousands of miners were encouraged to take early retirement. In 1964, there were 517,000 miners employed in 576 pits. In that year 40 pits were closed. By 1970, there were only 305,100 men employed in 299 pits and nineteen were closed. The workforce fell to 268,000 in 281 pits, by 1973, with eight pits closing in that year.[21]

With the industry withering and their place in the industrial pay league dropping, the miners were becoming more militant. They had beaten the government in 1972, and in September 1973 they put in for a 40 per cent pay claim. The oil crisis strengthened their resolve. After the failure of talks with Heath in Downing Street, they introduced an overtime ban on 12th November. The following day, the government declared a State of Emergency. On 2nd December, William Whitelaw was recalled from Northern Ireland to take over as Secretary of State for Employment. He was regarded as having the necessary negotiating skills and conciliatory approach necessary to find a solution. The miners' leader, Joe Gormley, was certainly a moderate too. Yet no settlement could be found. By 30th December, the government was forced to put industry on a three-day week because of energy shortages, to reduce heating and lighting in offices and shops, introduce a 50 m.p.h. speed limit and force television to close down by 10.30 p.m. The TUC was prepared to give the government guarantees that, if it treated the miners as a special case, other unions would not seek increases beyond the government's pay norms. Apparently, Heath remained unconvinced by such offers. On 4th February 1974, 81 per cent of the miners voted for strike action. Three days later, Heath called a general election. It is not entirely clear why a settlement was not reached. Some say there was a misunderstanding between Heath and Gormley,[22] others point to Heath's stubbornness. As for the public, they were showing sympathy for the miners rather than for Heath.[23]

Heath Out, Wilson In

The election campaign, which ended with polling on 28th February 1974, was fought by Heath asking the return of a strong government to fight inflation, a government which would not be forced to give in to one particular powerful group of workers. He called on the voters to say to the extremists, 'We've had enough.' Wilson claimed his rival was using the miners' dispute to distract the electors from the real issues: high prices, the collapse of the house-building programme, high mortgage rates and the disastrous terms negotiated by Heath for entry into the EEC.[24] Thorpe called for moderation and industrial partnership as an alternative to confrontation. There was little distraction from abroad during the brief campaign and the weather was good for electioneering. Powell was almost a one-man party; having decided to give up his seat as a Conservative, he intervened in the election by making a statement on the EEC issue, on 25th February, urging Conservatives opposed to the Common Market to vote Labour. The following day he revealed that he had used his postal vote to support Labour. He got front-page coverage on five of the 21 days of the campaign. On 25th February, there had been other bad news for Heath – horrendous balance-of-trade figures. A similar situation was thought to have helped sink Wilson in 1970.

The country had a long wait to see who was going to be the next Prime Minister. On a turnout of 78.1 per cent (72 in 1970), the Conservatives gained 37.8 per cent (46.4), Labour 37.1 per cent (43) and the Liberals 19.3 per cent (7.5). Together, PC and the SNP doubled their share of the vote from 1.3 to 2.6 per cent. In Wales, PC gained 10.7 per cent, and, in Scotland, the SNP attracted 21.9 per cent. These percentages produced 297 seats for the Conservatives, 301 for Labour, fourteen for the Liberals, seven for the SNP and two for PC. In Northern Ireland, the anti-Sunningdale Unionists won eleven seats and the SDLP one. In addition, Dick Taverne was returned as Independent Democratic Labour for Lincoln, on a platform close to that of the Liberals, and Eddie Milne was returned as Independent Labour MP for Blyth, on a manifesto to the left of Labour. Both were sitting MPs. The National Front (NF), whose main platform was anti-immigrant and anti-EEC, put up a record 54 candidates. Their average vote was 3.3 per cent, compared with an average of 3.6 for NF candidates in 1970. There was evidence that some of their voters were would-be Liberals for they did better where Liberals did not stand. To a slightly lesser extent, the same was true of the small Communist vote.[25] A handful of votes brought disaster for Heath. Labour beat PC at Carmarthen by three votes, and the Conservative candidate at Bodmin was beaten by the Liberal by nine votes. The last blow for the Conservatives was the fall of Argyll to the SNP, which was announced after the other results.

Heath sought a coalition with the Liberals on the basis that his party had gained more votes than Labour, and that he and the Liberals agreed on Europe and on incomes policy. The Liberals refused this, thus sealing the fate of Heath. Wilson then formed the first minority government since 1929.

'a kind of archaism of the society and national psychology'

Those concerned with Britain's future at this time were shocked by the publication of *The United Kingdom to 1980*, by the (US) Hudson Institute, in 1974. Although it praised various past achievements of Britain, it was immensely pessimistic about Britain's present and future. 'The present reality is that it is Britain that is the unstable and socially divided nation, economically depressed. Today, the continental states overall have not only a vastly better economic performance but also superior popular standards of living and amenity.' It saw Britain as in a worse situation than Italy, 'the other "sick man of Europe"', because, although Italy suffered from out-of-date institutions, it was at least economically dynamic. 'Britain's problems consist of a decline in both governmental competence and economic performance: a universal loss of dynamism.' The authors of the

Hudson Report felt Britain's social and psychological evolution had been in abeyance for nearly a century. It called for a deep shift in psychology, in will – in short, in style. 'For style is the habit of action and decision that derives from those assumptions about political and economic reality. We would argue that Britain's present economic difficulties and social difficulties derive ultimately from a kind of archaism of the society and national psychology.'[26] The Report caused anger as well as approval when the BBC gave it publicity. No doubt both Heath and Wilson agreed privately with many of the findings of the Hudson Report, but given the nature of democratic politics, they were greatly circumscribed in what they could achieve to reform Britain.

10 Trouble and Strife, 1974–79

Election October 1974

Wilson had a daunting task. The new Labour government was in a worse situation than in 1964. It had no clear majority, it was faced with a much worse trade deficit than the large one of 1964, with higher inflation (19 per cent compared with 3 per cent), declining production, national disputes awaiting settlement, rising nationalism in Wales and Scotland, the issue of the EEC unresolved, and the conflict in Northern Ireland getting worse. Moreover, Labour was itself divided on many issues. Wilson had four advantages. First, he could claim that he had once again inherited a Tory mess. Second, he knew the electorate would not take kindly to a party which forced his government out of office without giving it a chance. Third, he could claim that the world economy, and not just Britain's, was suffering from the oil-price explosion. Fourth, his team was largely an experienced one. No less than thirteen out of the 21 members of the new Cabinet, including Wilson, had previous Cabinet experience. There were a record number of women members – two; Barbara Castle, Secretary of State for Social Services, and Shirley Williams, Secretary of State for Prices and Consumer Protection. The aim was to act, giving the public the conviction that the new government meant business. Denis Healey presented a Budget which raised income tax and corporation tax and extended VAT to sweets and petrol. James Callaghan, Foreign Secretary, won praise from the Left by cancelling naval visits to Greece and Chile, because of their authoritarian régimes. Anthony Crosland (Environment) also won two cheers at least from the Left, by discouraging the sale of council houses. Reg Prentice, Secretary for Education, encouraged the establishment of comprehensive schools. Shirley Williams projected a caring image. Bread, butter, cheese and milk were subsidised. Wilson had appointed Michael Foot, Secretary for Employment, and he moved quickly to end the miners' dispute and repeal the Industrial Relations Act. Things were moving. Wilson was not prepared to preside over a lame-duck government.

Within a month or so of taking office, Wilson faced scandal in his party. The Poulson affair, which had struck down Maudling, now threatened Labour. Two Labour figures, Alderman Andrew Cunningham, who had served on Labour's NEC, and T. Dan Smith, who had been lionised as a local government entrepreneur in Newcastle-upon-Tyne, were sent to prison, for five and six years respectively, on corruption charges. Smith accused Edward Short, Lord President, of having accepted £250 in expenses from him. There were other whiffs of scandal, but they were largely shown to be lies, and Wilson sought to dispel any doubts by setting up a Royal Commission on Standards of Conduct in Government. Labour lost one of its MPs in July, when Christopher Mayhew joined the Liberals. Clearly the government could not hold out for long before presenting itself to the electors once again.

The shortest Parliament since 1681[1] came to an end on 18th September, when Wilson announced that the election would take place on 10th October. The campaign was a re-run of the previous one and lacked colour. The weather was bad, with more rainfall throughout the country than in any previous campaign.[2] On balance, this was more of a hazard for Labour than for the Conservatives. Strikes at seven Ford plants were certainly a danger for Labour. An IRA bomb outrage at Guildford possibly harmed the Liberals slightly, as the party appearing less tough towards the terrorists, but an eve-of-poll break-in at their headquarters would, if anything, have helped them. Lord Chalfont, who had served in Wilson's 1964–70 government as Minister for Disarmament (outside the Cabinet), left the Labour Party to support Dick Taverne at Lincoln. He claimed there was too much left-wing influence. An obscure Labour Peer, Lord St Davids, got momentary publicity by defecting to the Liberals. Much worse was the outburst by Shirley Williams, that she would leave politics if the proposed referendum on the EEC went against Britain remaining a member. Labour was very much at twos and threes over the issue.

The electors had a wide choice from a record number of candidates. The Liberals fielded more candidates than ever before, with only Lincoln and three Scottish seats left without Liberal contenders. The Nationalists fought all the constituencies in Scotland and Wales and the National Front total rose from 54 to 90. The number of women candidates – 161 – and the proportion – 7.1 per cent – were the highest ever. On the same electoral register as in February, the turnout was 72.8 per cent (78.7 in February). Perhaps rain, boredom and deaths explain the lower attendance in October. With a slightly smaller vote, Labour gained 39.2 per cent (37.1 per cent in February), Conservatives 35.8 (37.8) and the Liberals 18.3 (19.3). PC attracted 10.8 per cent (10.7) in Wales, and the SNP 30.4 per cent (21.9) in Scotland. The National Front percentage was 0.4, its strongest support being in the East End of London. Labour candidates were returned in 319 constituencies (301) and the Conservatives in 277 (297). The Liberals won thirteen (fourteen) seats, PC three (two) and SNP eleven (seven). The SNP gains were from the Conservatives. Dick Taverne and Eddie Milne lost their seats to Labour. Mayhew failed to get re-elected as a Liberal. In Northern Ireland, Enoch Powell was elected as a Unionist, but with a lower vote than his predecessor. Of the twelve seats there, the Unionists held ten. Overall, Labour was back with enough seats to run the country.

Anti-terrorism

The provisional IRA got bolder in 1972 and subjected mainland Britain to a sustained campaign of violence. It culminated in the worst terrorist attack, up to then, in British history, when 21 people died in explosions at two Birmingham pubs, in November 1974. Roy Jenkins, Home Secretary, himself a Birmingham MP, then had the distasteful task of introducing the Prevention of Terrorism Bill, which went through all its stages in an eighteen-hour marathon. It was meant to be temporary and expire after six months. Jenkins resisted the growing demands for the

introduction of the death penalty.[3] Free votes on capital
punishment defeated the demands in 1974 and 1975. The Act
made the IRA illegal, gave the Home Secretary power to exclude from mainland Britain persons suspected of involvement
with terrorism, and gave the police power to hold a suspect for
up to seven days, with the permission of the Home Secretary. In
1972, the IRA killed seven people in mainland Britain. In 1973,
one died, in 1974, 45, and in 1975, ten. In the same period,
1,033 were injured. More deaths and injuries followed. Among
the later cases was the murder of the Conservative spokesman
on Northern Ireland, Airey Neave, in London, in 1979, and the
assassination of the British Ambassador, Christopher Ewart
Biggs, in Dublin, in July 1976.

National Enterprise

In 1974, the Labour Government published its White Paper,
The Regeneration of British Industry. Its main proposal was the creation of a new National Enterprise Board. This was included in
the Industry Bill, finally enacted in November 1975. The idea
behind it was to ensure that top technological companies were
not put out of business by foreign competition. They would be
given the chance to become competitive with state assistance.
There were also strategic (defence) and social reasons for helping
such firms. As we saw, Heath had been forced to do this, for all
three reasons, in the case of Rolls-Royce. The NEB took over
companies already state-owned, like Rolls-Royce, and acquired
shares in a number of companies, among them Ferranti, the
troubled electronics firm heavily involved in defence work, which
finally went bankrupt in the 1990s. The NEB also took over
International Computers and the machine tool company, Herbert
Samuel. Rescue operations were mounted in the vehicle industry, including the take-over of British Leyland, the only
substantially British-owned motor company, and the American-
owned Chrysler. Leyland employed 130,000, with many more
relying on it for their livelihoods. Chrysler had 27,000 on its
payroll. Industries which were not directly under government
control could also seek assistance.

At a meeting of the National Economic Development Council

at Chequers, on 5th November 1975, the government presented its White Paper *An Approach to Industrial Strategy*. According to this analysis, Britain's industrial decline resulted from: (i) low and inefficiently deployed investment; (ii) low productivity, reflecting poor management, restrictive practices, overmanning and disruptive industrial action; (iii) frequent shifts in government policy; (iv) the pre-emption of resources by the public sector and by personal consumption. The government was to give priority to industrial growth over private consumption and even social objectives. There was to be a sector by sector development of industrial strategy, identifying over 30 key sectors. The government also submitted a second document, setting the criteria for government assistance to individual companies. Essentially it was looking for winners. The strategy must be viewed against a background of industrial collapse. Britain did appear to be deploying its capital badly, with defence, nuclear energy, space and civil aeronautics accounting for about two-thirds of total investment in research and development in the first three decades after the war.[4] These were sectors with far less commercial promise. Remarkably, the White Paper did not identify the shortage of skills as a major problem. Historically, Britain lacked a trained workforce at all levels. At this time, for example, 60 per cent of all German workers, but only 30 per cent of all British workers, had attained intermediate or vocational qualifications – that is, qualifications equivalent to an apprenticeship or full secretarial training.[5] The Wilson/Benn (Secretary of State for Industry, 1974–5) strategy was influenced by developments in other countries such as Austria, France, Taiwan and Japan where it proved more successful.

Irish Cauldron

Hopes of a fresh start in Northern Ireland through power sharing soon proved to be a mirage. Faulkner felt obliged to resign as Unionist leader after his party rejected the Sunningdale Agreement. Harry West took over. In the South, hard-line Republicans challenged the Agreement, claiming the Dublin government was breaching the Republic's constitution by seeming to recognise partition. The Irish government's rejection of this gave ammunition to extreme Unionists in the North, who argued that this revealed Dublin's lack of honesty. At another level, the IRA stepped up its campaign of violence. In the British general election, in February 1974, the anti-power-sharing Unionists set up the United Ulster Unionist Coalition (UUUC), which won eleven of the twelve seats, with 51 per cent of the votes. The incoming Labour administration then faced a new challenge. A new organisation, the Ulster Workers' Council, called a province-wide general strike against the power-sharing Executive and the Sunningdale Agreement. The strike began on 14th May 1975, and lasted fifteen days. On 29th May, the Unionist members of the Executive resigned and Northern Ireland's five-month-old power-sharing Executive collapsed. The Labour government had no alternative but to re-impose direct rule. It launched a new initiative with a constitutional Convention, but elections by proportional representation to this body were won by the anti-power-sharing parties, which then produced unacceptable recommendations. Merlyn Rees, the minister responsible, dissolved the Convention, on 5th March 1976, and direct rule continued.

Deaths through bombs or bullets had become almost a daily occurrence: in 1970 there were 25 deaths (23 civilians); in 1971, 173 (114); in 1972, 467 (322); in 1973, 250 (170); in 1974, 216 (166); in 1975, 246 (216) and in 1976, 296 (244). In the 1970s, the number of injured each year was, on average, well over 2,000.[6]

The South of Ireland was not spared entirely by the bombers. 'Bloody Friday' in the Republic was 17th May 1974, when loyalist terrorists from the North attacked Dublin and Monaghan. Twenty people died when car bombs went off in crowded Dublin streets, and many more were injured. The attacks were believed to be protests against the Sunningdale Agreement.

'she has never looked prettier'

Writing in her diary, on 5th February 1975, Barbara Castle commented, 'What interests me is how blooming she looks – she has never looked prettier . . . She may have been up late on the Finance Bill Committee; she is beset by enemies and has to watch every gesture and word. But she sails through looking her best . . . If we have to have Tories, good luck to her!' This was a remarkable tribute from a Labour politician to Margaret Thatcher, who was fighting for the leadership of her party. Heath had never been all that popular, in or out of his party, and now he had to pay the penalty for three lost elections. He was challenged by Thatcher, who gained 130 votes to his 119, on the first ballot. His other challenger was right-winger Hugh Fraser, who collected sixteen. This result was not enough to avoid a second ballot, but enough to cause Heath to resign. On the second ballot, Thatcher scored an easy victory with 146 votes to 79 for William Whitelaw, nineteen each for Sir Geoffrey Howe and James Prior and eleven for John Peyton. Few had expected Thatcher to win and it was later said that her victory was more a rejection of Heath, on both political and personal grounds, than a positive endorsement of the Lady.[7] Another strong contender, Keith Joseph, had put himself beyond the pale by making a speech on 19th October 1974, in which he referred to 'the high and rising proportion of children . . . being born to mothers least fitted to bring children into the world'.[8] Benn was not the only one to think it was 'bordering on Fascism'.[9]

Margaret Thatcher was still a relatively unknown politician and had cultivated a south of England, public school, housewife image. She appeared hard and ruthless because of her abolition of free school milk (see above). She had no experience of the great offices of state and her party had shown itself to be reluctant to select women as parliamentary candidates. Like Heath, she was an outsider in that she did not belong to one of the aristocratic Conservative families. She had made her way by academic success (chemistry at Somerville College, Oxford), marriage to a wealthy older man and sheer determination. Her father, a grocer, had encouraged her interest in politics and learning. He served for many years on the local council, becoming Mayor of Grantham. Thatcher was mother of twins and a qualified barrister. Ideologically, she emphasised self-help and individualism.

EEC: 'Parliament should take that decision . . .'

On 28th May 1970, Wilson, speaking on BBC television, insisted that 'Parliament should take that decision [on the EEC] with a sense of full responsibility, with a sense that reflects national

views and national interests.' Many other leading members of
his party, like the future leader Michael Foot, agreed. They
claimed referenda were not in the British tradition. Continuing
divisions within the Labour Party forced a rethink. In government, Wilson and Foreign Secretary, James Callaghan, renegotiated
the terms Heath had agreed. They won concessions, but they
did not win fundamental changes in the package. Perhaps the
most significant concession was that a new mechanism was established containing provision for a refund to any member state
whose net contribution to the Budget went significantly beyond
what was fair, in relation to its share of EEC GNP. This resulted
in an unexpected net profit in 1975. A special conference of
the Labour Party actually rejected the new terms on 26th April
1975. The Referendum Bill was given a second reading in the
Commons, by 312 votes to 248, on 10th April. It received the
Royal Assent on 8th May and the referendum was held on 5th
June 1975. The Cabinet was divided on the issue, having voted
by sixteen votes to seven, in favour of recommending continued
membership, on the renegotiated terms. Among the opponents
in Cabinet were Castle, Foot, Benn and Peter Shore. The Commons had accepted the terms by 396 to 170, on 9th April 1975.
The referendum campaign was not fought on strictly party lines.
The majority of Conservative MPs, virtually all the Liberals and
a significant minority of Labour MPs, were in favour of remaining in the EEC, so was much of industry and commerce and
the media. In most cases, the opponents were on the Left of
the Labour Party and on the Right of the Conservatives. As Roy
Jenkins has pointed out, 'there was a great weight of establishment opinion in favour of Britain staying in the Community.
This was not due to a conspiracy, but to the fact that for once
the establishment was spontaneously on the more sensible side.'[10]
The all-party 'Britain in Europe' organisation led the fight to
stay in. Roy Jenkins, William Whitelaw, Edward Heath and Jo
Grimond led this. Vic Feather, TUC General Secretary (1970–4),
was also prominent in the pro-EEC campaign. John Davies,
Director General of the Confederation of British Industries
(1965–9), also campaigned for a 'Yes' vote. Their most prominent opponents were 'fluent and persuasive',[11] Tony Benn, Enoch
Powell, Barbara Castle and Peter Shore. Among the key opponents in Wales, was the young Labour MP, Neil Kinnock, future

Labour leader and EEC commissioner. He called the EEC 'the robber of the real sovereignty of the people'.[12] The government sent the pro and anti arguments in leaflet form to every household and paid £125,000 to each side in the campaign. Both sides got equal time on television. Many people found the arguments confusing and simply followed the line of their favourite politicians. When the votes were counted, on 5th June 1975, 67.2 per cent were for Britain remaining in the EEC and 32.8 against. The turnout was 64.5 per cent. Every area of the UK voted 'Yes' except for the Shetland Islands and the Western Isles.

Elizabeth's Silver Jubilee

On 7th June 1977, a Thanksgiving Service to commemorate the Queen's Silver Jubilee, held at St Paul's Cathedral, was attended by 32 heads of Commonwealth governments and representatives from other states. It was just one of the many official functions the Queen had to attend or host over the year, as she had been doing since the early 1950s. Of this period Callaghan wrote, 'But arduous though her duties were, she seemed to thrive on the constant procession of visitors and never once did I see her less than sparkling.'[13] Some would find it remarkable that Callaghan, and Wilson before him, got on well with the Queen. Both were socialists but both were supporters of the monarchy. Crossman had mellowed in his attitude to the monarch during his period in government. On leaving office, he recorded, on 22nd June 1970, that the Queen 'doesn't make all that much difference between Labour and Conservative'. From the Queen's experience of governments, there probably had not been much difference. In 1969, there had been a fuss in Cabinet about the royal finances. The Duke of Edinburgh had made a remarkable statement on American television claiming that he and the Queen were hard up. Barbara Castle called for a Select Committee to examine the royal finances. Wilson set up one, passionately defending the royals in the Commons.[14] The Committee reported in 1971, recommending a doubling of the Queen's income. Prime Minister Heath accepted this. In addition, government departments were discreetly taking over royal expenses. Although a Gallup poll revealed a majority in favour of an increase for the Queen, a majority complained about the size of the increase. At the same time, a poll showed the Queen as equal first with Indira Gandhi, the Indian Prime Minister, as the most admired woman in the world. Prince Philip came second to Wilson, as the most popular man, Heath coming third.[15]

Television and press, in competition with each other, brought ever more material on the royal family, who were persuaded that they needed to have a high profile. The success of the Coronation, in media terms, helped to make this inevitable. There were ever more royal occasions. One was the annual Trooping of the Colour ceremony; another was the annual State Opening of Parliament. There was the Investiture of the Prince of Wales at Caernarfon Castle in 1969, which was, in part, genuflexion to growing Welsh nationalism. Bombs, planted by the self-styled Free Wales Army, had gone off in North Wales and the police thought there was a major security threat.[16] There was the drama and tragedy of the murder of Lord Louis Mountbatten, together with his fourteen-year-old grandson and Irish boatman, at the hands of the IRA, in 1979. The royal weddings attracted great attention, especially that of Prince Charles and Diana Spencer in 1981. This was watched on television by 750 million, with a further million lining the processional route.[17] Other occasions were the Queen's 60th birthday celebrations and the Queen Mother's 80th and 90th!

By the 1970s, the royal family was becoming soap opera. It was a method of keeping what Prince Philip regarded as a family business solvent. The first family was seen as an aid to maintaining stability in an increasingly changing world with changing values. This kind of publicity both fed and created curiosity. The need to feed the swelling demand for 'news' led to ever more intrusive journalism. Princess Margaret was subjected to this, though it seemed to lessen after her divorce, in May 1978. In the decade to follow, the situation was to get far worse.

Sex Discrimination

Under both Heath and Wilson, there were further moves to end discrimination against women. The Attachment of Earnings Act (1971) required husbands who were liable for maintenance payments to inform the court when they changed employment, so that the maintenance order might be carried over from job to job. The Criminal Justice Act (1972) ended the property qualification for jury service, thus enabling many more women to be called to serve on juries. The Guardianship of Children Act (1973) gave mothers equal rights with fathers to make decisions about a child's upbringing, whereas previously the father's rights were paramount. The Sex Discrimination Act (1975) made it unlawful to discriminate on grounds of sex in the field of employment, or in the provision of educational facilities, housing, goods, services and facilities; it also made it unlawful to discriminate in advertisements in these areas. The Act gave individuals who believed they had been discriminated against access to courts and, where appropriate, industrial tribunals. Under the Act, an Equal Opportunities Commission was created with investigative powers. Welcome though these measures were, they could not, by themselves, transform the situation. For one thing, it remained difficult, in many cases, to prove discrimination. There was also the fear of being branded a troublemaker.

Wilson: 'sagacity and sangfroid'

On 16th March 1976, the public got two surprises. The first was the news from Buckingham Palace that the Queen's sister, Princess Margaret, and her husband, Lord Snowden, were separating. The second, of greater political significance, was the announcement by Harold Wilson that he was retiring. Wilson had given the Queen advanced warning of his departure, enabling her to make her announcement on the same day, thus reducing its impact. Wilson's resignation came shortly after his 60th birthday, after he had led Labour for thirteen years, nearly eight of them as Prime Minister. Callaghan later commented, 'When we were in difficulties his sagacity and sangfroid were beyond doubt, as was his kindness to his colleagues.'[18] Jenkins agreed regarding his kindness and wrote that his resignation 'came as a great shock and marked the end of an era'.[19] Writing in his diary of that day, Benn's impressions were that his colleagues were stunned, but without emotion, because Wilson did not arouse affection in most people. Wilson's press secretary, Joe Haines, wrote of his 'complete lack of self-importance'.[20] Most students of the period find the reasons for his resignation unsatisfying. He was still a young man by the standards of political leaders. He was not under pressure from his Cabinet colleagues. Nor was he ill at the time. The resignation becomes more dramatic, when one recalls that at this time George Brown had announced that he was leaving the Labour Party, and Liberal Leader Jeremy Thorpe was forced to resign, because of accusations against him. Labour's majority was wafer thin and there was talk of a coalition. Haines commented that Wilson resigned 'for a variety of reasons'.[21] Peter Wright, the former Assistant Director of MI5, suggested there was a plot to remove Wilson, in 1968, and again, in 1974. In the first case, *Daily Mirror* tycoon Cecil King hoped, with the aid of some members of the intelligence community and some public figures, to bring down the Wilson government and replace it by a coalition led by Lord Mountbatten. In the second case, 'altogether more serious' according to Wright,[22] the plotters were MI5 officers, sympathetic journalists and some prominent personalities. Chapman Pincher, the expert on security matters, was convinced of MI5's interest in Wilson and some of his friends. In the second case, at least one investigator claims that it was after a confrontation with Sir Michael Hanley, head of MI5, that he decided to resign. This was some time before his actual resignation.[23] Remarkably, in his book *The Governance of Britain* (1977), Wilson's chapter on 'The Prime Minister and National Security' is just over a page in length! The full story of Wilson and the security services is likely to be denied the public for some time to come.

Wilson's resignation honour's list was also a matter of great controversy. To say the least, it was idiosyncratic. It caused a furore, especially in the Labour Party. Many of those included were business tycoons of some kind or another. Among them was Sir Joseph Kagan, manufacturer of the Gannex raincoat, who later, as Lord Kagan, was convicted of fraud and sent to prison. He was suspected of being a Soviet agent and, as such, inter-

ested MI5. Prime Minister Thatcher advised the Queen to withdraw his knighthood.[24] Many of those honoured were of Jewish
background and some believed this 'kindled a covert anti-
Semitism'.[25] Anyone who had much to do with Eastern Europe
during the Cold War was both a target (of intelligence services)
and a suspect. Most of those concerned kept clear of intelligence activities and by building cultural, trading and political
links did useful service.

Wilson remained Prime Minister until Labour MPs chose their
new leader. Technically, he had only resigned as Labour leader.
Once the election was over he went to the Palace to formally
tender his resignation. 'The Queen was sorry to see him go, for
she had liked him and his wife, Mary.'[26]

Six candidates stepped forward to replace Wilson as Labour
leader. On the first ballot, Michael Foot polled 90 votes,
Callaghan 84, Jenkins 56, Benn 37, Healey 30 and Anthony
Crosland seventeen. In round two, Callaghan attracted 141, Foot
133 and Healey 38. In the final contest, Callaghan gained 176
to Foot's 137. Foot's vote showed the strength of the Left, though
doubtless he secured a few personal votes. Callaghan was regarded as a compromise candidate between Left and Right. He
had unrivalled experience, being the only postwar Prime Minister to have held all three great offices of state – Foreign, Home
and Exchequer. At 64, he was older than the man he was replacing. He had not been to university and had made his way
through the union movement, having been an official of the tax
inspectors' union. His father was a coastguard, who had died
young, and Callaghan was the first Prime Minister since
MacDonald to have known childhood poverty. In the war, he
had served in the Royal Navy, gaining a commission after a
period below decks.

'people of different cultures'

By 1974, election analysts were noting the growing importance
of the ethnic vote. They identified 50 seats with relatively high
New Commonwealth populations. The highest was Birmingham,
Ladywood, where 29.6 per cent were either born in a New Commonwealth state – mainly India, Pakistan or the Caribbean – or

had a parent who was born there. The lowest of this group was Manchester, Ardwick, with 9.3 per cent. There were 25 seats with significant numbers of inhabitants born in Ireland. Brent East had the highest, with 4.8 per cent.[27] The potential significance of the Irish ties was much higher than those figures suggest, because of the continuing immigration from Ireland over a very long period. The 'coloured' population from the New Commonwealth had not yet gained any significant influence, even though a small number of candidates from these states had stood in a number of elections. In the case of the Irish, pro-Republican Irish Catholics had a certain influence in the Labour ranks. The Jews too were well represented. Although there were estimated to be only 400,000 Jewish electors, there were 45 Jewish MPs, 33 of them Labour.[28] For historical and sociological reasons, most Jewish voters supported Labour after 1919. Disenchantment with Labour had started to take hold because of the Attlee government's policy on Palestine. The Suez affair had further weakened Labour's influence in the Jewish community. Upward social mobility of Jews also played a part in this. However, local Conservative Associations had not been welcoming to Jews even in the 1950s.[29] Some thought anti-Semitism was a factor, by no means the only one, in the loss of the normally safe Conservative seat at Orpington in March 1962. In the postwar period, there were, until 1970, only two Jewish Conservative MPs, Sir Henry d'Avigdor Goldsmid (elected 1955) and Sir Keith Joseph (elected 1956).[30] During the 1973 Arab–Israeli war, only two out of nine Jewish Conservative MPs voted for their government's ban on arms to Israel. At the elections of 1974, many Jewish voters looked more carefully at the attitude of candidates to the Middle East.

By the mid-1970s, several MPs, mostly Conservative, became 'prisoners' of their Jewish voters: John Gorst at Hendon North; Geoffrey Finsberg at Hampstead; Tom Iremonger and Milly Miller (Labour) at Ilford North; Tim Sainsbury at Howe; J. Callaghan (Labour, not to be confused with Prime Minister Callaghan) at Middleton and Prestwich; and, most intriguing of all, Margaret Thatcher at Finchley. Some 16 per cent of all voters in Finchley were Jewish.[31] In an attempt to create a more receptive attitude towards Conservatism, the Conservative Friends of Israel was established in 1974. Thatcher was an early adherent of this group.

The death of Milly Miller caused a by-election at Ilford North, in October 1977. Thatcher, in a television interview, called for stronger immigration controls, warning that Britain might become 'swamped' by peoples who lacked 'fundamentally British characteristics'. The Conservatives won the seat on a swing of 6.9 per cent, but the swing amongst Jewish voters was 11.2 per cent. It is thought that a speech by Keith Joseph, targeting Jewish voters, helped to produce this result. He commented: 'There is a limit to the number of people from different cultures that this country can digest. We ignore this at our peril . . . Therefore I say that the electors of Ilford North, including the Jews . . . have good reason for supporting Margaret Thatcher and the Conservative Party on immigration.'[32] Increasingly, all political parties were targeting the immigrant groups.

A new Race Relations Act was introduced in 1976, replacing those of 1965 and 1968. It dealt with racial discrimination in employment, training, education, in housing and in the provision of goods, facilities and services. It extended the law to cover discrimination by private clubs. A new body, the Race Relations Commission, replaced the earlier bodies. The Bill was passed with all-party support, though a few Conservatives, and three UUUC MPs, including Powell, voted against it. The Conservatives continued to emphasise their worries about numbers. Between 1966 and 1976, 507,000 immigrants came to Britain from the 'Old' (largely white) Commonwealth and another 780,000 from the New Commonwealth (including Pakistan). There were 987,000 immigrants from other areas, making a total of 2,275,000. This figure excluded a considerable number from the Irish Republic.[33]

Ireland in Transition

Since the late 1950s, Southern Ireland had been undergoing changes which were at least as great as those in Britain. These were the results of the development of the Irish economy, which in turn was the consequence of both domestic economic policies and world economic developments. Most people were engaged in manufacturing and more people were living in an urban environment. Thus, the old dependence on agriculture was lessening and the old way of life was disappearing. In 1951, 41.44 per cent of the population lived in towns; by 1966, it was 49.2 per cent; and in 1971 it was 52.25 per cent. By the 1970s, over one-third of the population lived in the Dublin area.

During this same period, great cultural changes had been taking place. The generations that had witnessed the independence struggle were being replaced by others who had other, more practical concerns. The importance of the Gaelic (Irish) language continued to decline. This was due to social changes on the west coast but also to declining interest in the rest of Ireland. Most people learnt Gaelic at school as they would learn a foreign language. There was pressure to abolish Gaelic as a compulsory examination subject and requirement for the civil service. The Fine Gael–Labour coalition of 1973 responded to this, removing the requirement that pupils should pass in Irish in order to gain the secondary school leaving certificate. The necessity for a pass in leaving-certificate Irish as an entry for the civil service was also abolished. Television must be reckoned as one of the key factors in stimulating this and other changes. British television was available to those on the east coast, and even Irish television broadcast largely British or American material. Education was another factor. In the 1960s and beyond, there was considerable expansion of secondary, vocational and higher education. And although Ireland remained one of the countries most faithful to the Catholic Church, a process of secularisation could be observed. The numbers of those entering the priesthood or other forms of religious service were in decline. No doubt this was, in part, due to the other opportunities available. This, in turn, reduced the clerical influence in schools. The total bans on contraception and abortion started to be challenged. After much debate, a Fianna Fáil bill, in 1979, permitted the sale of contraceptives to married persons in chemists' shops on doctors' prescriptions. These debates owed a good deal to the changing place of women in Irish society. Many more women were seeking gainful employment and many more were going into the white-collar sectors. Women were no longer, as in the past, largely confined to labouring on the family farm, seeking domestic work, joining a religious community or emigrating. This was reflected in the Employment Equality Act (1977), which made it illegal to discriminate against women in employment. Previously, women in the civil service, local government and health boards had been forced to give up their jobs on marriage. Despite all these changes, Ireland still had a long way to go to be like the other small, modern states of Western Europe.

The Social Contract and Industry Democracy

Labour's policy towards the unions was known as the Social Contract. The government would do all it could to introduce socially just measures, especially to help the poorer sections of society, and the unions would operate a system of voluntary wage restraint. In his July 1974 Budget, Healey introduced policies in line with the Social Contract, including the extension of food subsidies, a mitigation of increases in council house rents and so on. Healey issued a number of warnings that a lack of restraint would lead to rising prices and unemployment. In June 1975, at the initiative of Jack Jones, leader of the Transport and General Workers Union, the TUC approved a set of guidelines, a modified form of which the government accepted. Despite the opposition of some left-wing Labour MPs, these seemed to work in 1975–6, but Britain remained behind the other main industrial states in its progress to emerge from the recession, with more unemployment and inflation and less production than most others. In October 1975, unemployment topped a million for the first time since the war. In his 1976 Budget, Healey offered tax concessions, with more to come if the unions would accept a new pay ceiling, equivalent of 3 per cent on wage increases. In fact, the agreement with the unions set wage increases at about 4.5 per cent. The tax concessions went ahead.

A new threat appeared to be the vanishing pound. Confidence in sterling collapsed and, in an effort to restore it, severe spending cuts were announced in July. The outflow was not halted and Healey was forced to turn back at London airport, cancelling a trip to an IMF conference in Malta, to take personal charge of the developing crisis. As before, the IMF came to the rescue, but the price was that Britain should swallow the medicine it ordered, in the shape of massive cuts in public spending. On 15th December 1976, Healey announced cuts of

£1,016 million in 1977–8, and £1,513 million in the year to follow. The government was forced, among other measures, to sell a £500 million block of BP oil shares. Alcohol and tobacco were to cost more and food subsidies were to be phased out. An understanding with the Liberals was needed to get Parliament to agree to the package (see below). The position of sterling then rapidly improved; so much so that, by the beginning of 1978, $1 billion was repaid to the IMF.[34] This rapid improvement was based on the fact that North Sea oil was starting to flow, with the promise of British self-sufficiency by 1980. By the end of 1977, the balance of payments was in surplus. But the government then undid the progress by miscalculation. There followed the winter of discontent: 'Those events that were to shatter our hopes and antagonise the country beyond recall', as Callaghan himself put it.[35] Callaghan wanted a further round of incomes policy, starting in the summer of 1978, which would offer wage settlements aiming for 5 per cent (though knowing they would go somewhat higher). This was totally opposed by the new leader of the TGWU, Moss Evans, and rejected by the TUC annual conference and the Labour Party conference in 1978.

As autumn turned to winter, the government was faced with increasing industrial action. The Ford motor workers started, with a successful strike, and were followed by truck drivers and oil-tanker drivers, backed by the TGWU. Soon everyone seemed to be striking – though the great majority of trade unions never went on strike – with the press and television giving a great deal of publicity to such actions. Some cases undoubtedly brought the unions into disrepute. As Callaghan later wrote, 'One of the most notorious was the refusal of Liverpool grave-diggers to bury the dead, accounts of which appalled the country when they saw pictures of mourners being turned away from the cemetery. Such heartlessness . . . rightly aroused deep revulsion and did further untold harm to the cause of trade unionism.'[36] Such scenes tipped the balance against the Labour Party in the coming election.

In an effort to give a new framework to industrial relations, the government had set up a committee on industrial democracy, headed by Lord Bullock, which reported in January 1977. Influenced by the German example and by the success of the

German economy, it recommended that workers in plants with over 2,000 employees should appoint a number of trade union directors equal to the shareholder directors, plus a smaller group agreed by the first two. No concrete proposals could be passed through Parliament because of opposition from employers and key trade union figures.

Lib–Lab Agreement

Callaghan faced a 'No Confidence' motion on 23rd March 1977. If he lost it, he would have been forced to call an election. The problem was that he no longer had a majority. Labour had been subjected to by-election defeats in 1975, at Woolwich, and in 1976, at Wallsall North and Workington, thus losing its parliamentary majority. To remain in office, it had to rely on the votes of the minor parties, including two Catholics from Northern Ireland, and two MPs who had broken with Labour to form the Scottish Labour Party.

The Liberals had been doing badly in by-elections, a normal trend during a Labour government, and they were not anxious for an early election. In addition, an arrangement with Labour could give them greater importance. Callaghan and Steel came to an agreement under which they would meet regularly to discuss legislation. The deal was agreed in Cabinet by twenty votes to four (including Benn).[37] This maintained the government until August 1978, despite opposition within both the Labour and the Liberal parties to the agreement. After this, the government could have fallen at almost any time. In the end, it was the adverse results of the two referenda, on devolution for Scotland and Wales that brought the government down.[38]

The government had tried to placate demands for Scottish and Welsh assemblies by offering referenda on the issue. Such demands were less strong in the Labour and Conservative parties than they were among the Liberals and, of course, the nationalists. Indeed, many in the two major parties were actually against, including the future Labour leader, Neil Kinnock. After much discussion, referenda took place on 1st March 1979. In Wales, there was a heavy defeat for a Welsh assembly; in Scotland, a 'Yes' vote of 51.6 per cent. But, as only 63 per cent had voted, this meant that only 32.9 per cent of the electorate had voted for an assembly. As the Scotland Act required a minimum 'Yes' vote of 40 per cent of the electorate in Scotland, the bid to set up an assembly had failed.

On 28th March 1979, the government was defeated by 311 to 310 on a 'No confidence' motion brought in by the SNP. Labour lost because one of their MPs was dying in hospital and Gerry Fitt, who usually voted with them, opposed the government. He opposed the increase in the number of seats in Northern Ireland, justified on the grounds of population, because it would favour the UUUC. It was the first time that any government had been defeated on a vote of confidence since MacDonald's minority Labour government was defeated in 1924. The election followed on 3rd May.

Conservative Victory

Despite the tremendous problems Labour had faced since 1974, its defeat in 1979 was not a foregone conclusion. Healey produced a Budget in 1978 regarded by 68 per cent of those questioned by Gallup as fair. This made it the most acceptable Budget since the question was first asked in 1952.[39] As Prime Ministers, Wilson and then Callaghan were far more popular than Heath had been, and far more popular than Thatcher as Opposition leader or later as Prime Minister.[40] In July 1978, the polls showed Labour and the Conservatives running neck and neck.[41] The government lost ground during the winter of discontent, with trade union popularity falling, from 57 per cent of the public thinking unions a good thing in 1978 to only 51 per cent in 1979, their lowest popularity rating between 1952 and 1987.[42] There was also a continuing majority who, although they opposed left-wing policies in favour of more nationalisation, union power and so on, were in favour of more NHS improvements and better education. On the other hand, such Conservative policies as selling council houses and tighter immigration controls were also popular.[43]

The Conservative election campaign was fought effectively with the help of the public relations firm Saatchi and Saatchi. The two brothers sought to give Thatcher a softer image. She was persuaded to tone down her rhetoric and even to embrace a calf in Suffolk! With a highly successful poster they attacked Labour's record on unemployment. The Conservatives promised lower taxes and a return to law and order. The assassination of Airey Neave on 30th March, mentioned above, could not have done the government's credibility in this field much good nor could the (entirely legal) strikes of often low-paid public sector workers. Even 10 Downing Street was hit by the strike.[44] Gordon Reece, a television producer, and Harvey Thomas, who had organised rallies for the American evangelist, Billy Graham, gave expert advice including the decision not to risk a television debate with Callaghan. Paul Johnson, former *New Statesman* editor, joined Lord George-Brown, Lord Chalfont, Reg Prentice (former Labour Cabinet minister) and other converts from socialism to work for a Thatcher victory.[45]

Seventy-six per cent of the voters turned out on 3rd May 1979, often in bad weather, to record their verdict. This compared with 73 per cent in October 1974. They gave Labour slightly more votes in absolute terms, though its percentage fell from 39.2 to 37 – its lowest since 1931. The Conservative percentage rose from 35.8 to 43.9, which was good, but still below what Heath had achieved in 1970. As had happened before when Labour was in office, the Liberal total slumped from 18.3 to 13.8 per cent. The PC and SNP votes declined. In terms of seats, the Conservatives leapt up from 277 to 339; Labour fell from 319 (in October 1974) to 269, while the Liberals dropped from thirteen to eleven. The SNP only held on to two of its eleven seats, with PC falling from three to two. The only other MPs were the twelve from Northern Ireland. There were more women candidates than before but fewer were elected, reducing the numbers to eight Conservative and eleven Labour – the lowest number since 1951. Shirley Williams lost her seat. All three parties fielded ethnic candidates: two Asians stood as Conservatives; Labour and the Liberals put up one West Indian each. They were all unsuccessful.[46] The number of Jewish MPs fell, with 21 returned as Labour (35 in 1974) and eleven as Conservatives (nine). The anti-immigration National Front put up a record 303 candidates, but where a comparison could be made with 1974, their average share (1.4 per cent) went down. Standing in mainly Conservative seats, the Ecology Party nominated 53 candidates, their average vote being 1.5 per cent. This was better than either the Communists (38 candidates, average vote 1.1 per cent), or the Trotskyist Workers' Revolutionary Party (60, 0.5).[47]

Once again, with better management of the timing of the election, Labour would have stood a good chance of winning a further term of office.[48] Then, with the help of North Sea oil revenues and with the moderates remaining in the party, British politics in the 1980s could have been very different. This is in no way to deny that developments in British society were bringing changes in the political thinking and aspirations of the electorate. Broadly speaking, the old working class was in decline and the Conservatives were increasing their share of that class. On the other hand, Labour was improving its position among the middle classes. Perhaps a Labour victory would have speeded up the modernisation of Labour and of Britain in a social democratic direction. However, some changes, due rather more to technology than to ideology, would have been introduced irrespective of which party was in power.

There had been dramatic changes in the world during the 1970s. US President Nixon had been forced to resign in 1974, narrowly missing being impeached. In the same year, Turkey had invaded Cyprus, while in neighbouring Greece the military dictatorship was overthrown. After a coup, democracy came to Portugal in 1975; it came to an end, however, in Bangladesh. The new régime in Portugal moved quickly to end its colonial rule in Africa, which, in turn, made the position of the white minority régime in Rhodesia, untenable. Black majority rule followed in Rhodesia in 1979. In 1975, the long Vietnam War ended in the victory of the Communists. In Spain, Franco died and his régime quickly disintegrated. Israel and Egypt signed a peace treaty at Camp David in the USA. In Iran, in 1979, the Shah, who had been a well-known figure on the international scene for many years, was ousted and an old mullah, Ayatollah Khomeini, was soon as well known as the Shah had been. In Pakistan, the elected leader, Dr Bhutto, was overthrown and executed in February 1979. Britain had no influence on any of these events. Symbolic of the twilight of Britain as a world power was the final withdrawal of the Royal Navy from Malta, on 31st March 1979.

Few on either side of the political divide would have predicted, in May 1979, that Thatcher would be at the centre of the British political stage until 1990. In personal terms, her tenure was a remarkable achievement. But was her triumph in good measure a case of time and chance, the inadequacies of her opponents both domestic and foreign, and the changing fashion in world politics and economics?

11 The Thatcher Era, 1979–87

The Road to Serfdom

Norman St John Stevas, a Thatcher minister, recorded that the bones of Thatcherism revealed 'a fairly repellent skeleton'.[1] Surprisingly, it was the Left that did Margaret Thatcher the honour of giving her policies the coherence of an ideology by inventing the term. One could say that Thatcher's policies were simply the platform of the Reaganites adapted to Britain. Ronald Reagan was elected President of the USA in 1981, but long before this he had campaigned, as Governor of California, on a robustly free-market and anti-welfare agenda. This agenda sought to roll back the state, reducing its activities drastically by privatisation and de-regulation. Private bodies, it was argued, subject to market forces, were better suited in virtually every case to produce positive results. De-regulation was meant to increase competition and release the creative energy of individuals. The encouragement of private business would further this process. For the same reasons, individuals should be weaned off welfare dependence and encouraged to provide for themselves. This implied measures to gradually reduce eligibility for state benefits, in order to get people back to work. As important was the fight against inflation. Little, or preferably nil, inflation would encourage people to save and would enhance confidence in the economic system. It was also part of this platform to proclaim 'Victorian values' – thrift, hard work, self-reliance and moral rectitude, though the arguments for the economic agenda were not necessarily dependent on these values. Finally, the Reagan/Thatcherites were strong on law and order. The Austrian economist, F. A. Hayek, and the American economist, Milton Friedman, first put these ideas into systematic form. Hayek, whose book, *The Road to Serfdom*, was published in 1944, in London, was in part reacting

224

against the statism of the Nazis and Austro-Fascism. He was not very successful in getting his ideas implemented in his own country, where, as in the other states of Western Europe, there was traditionally a positive view of the state as a regulator, arbitrator, innovator, leader, provider and guide. By contrast, in the Anglo-Saxon states, there existed a deep-rooted suspicion of the state. The two world wars and the interwar slump led to a partial modification of this view. This revision had been made into a systematic theory by (Lord) John Maynard Keynes (1883–1946), especially in his *General Theory of Employment, Interest and Money* (1936). Now it was under attack. One reason for this was increasing public indebtedness. Western economies, it was argued, would not be able to cope with rising demands for welfare due to ageing populations, the increasing costs of health care and growing unemployment.[2]

Thatcher's Cabinet

Thatcher came under the influence of Sir Keith Joseph after becoming leader of the Conservative Party. Joseph was one of the main intellectual standard bearers of what later became known as Thatcherism. She found these ideas appealed to her gut feelings, her prejudices about economics,[3] which she had, to a degree, suppressed in the earlier period of Macmillan and his *Middle Way*. However, when she entered Downing Street in 1979, she had to face the fact that it was necessary to include in her Cabinet colleagues who held on to the Macmillan/Keynsian inheritance. Most of her colleagues had served in Heath's government and had far more experience of government than she had. She was in no position, therefore, to simply impose 'Thatcherism'.

Among Thatcher's key appointments in her 1979 Cabinet of 22 were: Lord Carrington (Foreign Secretary), William Whitelaw (Home Office), Norman St John Stevas (Leader of the Commons), Patrick Jenkin (Health and Social Security), James Prior (Labour), Michael Heseltine (Environment) and Angus Maude (Paymaster-General). She attempted to reserve the economic departments for her allies, thus Howe was appointed Chancellor and Joseph was given Industry, John Nott went to Trade, John Biffen was appointed Chief Secretary to the Treasury (in charge of public spending) and Nigel Lawson was appointed Financial Secretary. Heath was offered the post of British Ambassador to Washington, which he declined.[4] There were no women members of the Cabinet apart from Thatcher.

Howe: 'threat of absolute decline'

Howe, who served as Chancellor for four years, had, as his Permanent Secretary, Sir Douglas Wass, 'intellectual, austere but eager'.[5] Wass had occupied this post since 1974 and was considered unsympathetic to the Thatcher agenda. Although he had been on Thatcher's transfer list, he kept his job.[6] Howe's first Budget revealed a monetarist tendency, to which Howe had been converted in the 1970s. It is only fair to say that Healey had also, to a degree, adopted this position as Labour Chancellor and had fallen foul of his party by so doing. The aim was to bring down public spending, which had greatly expanded as a result of growing welfare, education and defence programmes, and the oil price explosion. In June 1979, Howe introduced a package, which included the sale of public assets to finance public spending, cash limits on such spending, a sharp increase in the public lending rate and in VAT, from 8 to 15 per cent, but a (more modest) reduction in income tax. In a controversial move, the link between the rise in average earnings and the rise in pensions was cut. In future, pensions would only increase in line with inflation. The plan, according to Howe, was to swing from pay as you earn to pay as you spend.[7] Exchange controls were first further relaxed and then abolished.

Much of this was part of a trend throughout the Western world, to a greater or lesser degree. Public pay awards already in the pipeline were one of several factors helping to fuel inflation. High interest rates, North Sea oil, the removal of exchange controls and preference for a Conservative government among foreign investors all helped to strengthen the pound, which in turn encouraged imports and discouraged exports. By January 1981, sterling was 25 per cent higher than two years earlier.[8] World demand was failing due to a threefold oil price rise after the Khomeini revolution in Iran, in 1979. This, the strong pound and deflationary policies, pushed the economy into recession, with mounting bankruptcies and unemployment rising to unprecedented postwar levels of over 10 per cent (more than 3 million, the highest level since 1933). The aim of full employment was abandoned as an unrealistic goal in a changed economic world. Incomes policy, which had been tried by previous Labour and Conservative administrations, was abandoned for a market-driven policy of *laissez-faire*, at least for the private sector. Unemployment, it was believed, would help to curb wage inflation and so would the destruction of union militancy. Tight monetary policy in the USA also contributed to the worsening recession.

As one member of the Thatcher government later wrote, by 1980, the government 'had caused much the biggest slump since 1929–31'.[9] No wonder that, as Thatcher herself put it, the summer of 1980 was one of 'government leaks and rifts'.[10] But she told the party conference in October there would be no U-turns.

In his first Budget speech Howe mentioned the progress of France and Germany and how they had overtaken Britain in manufacturing since 1954. 'In the last few years the hard facts of our relative decline have become increasingly plain, and the threat of absolute decline has gradually become very real.'[11] Yet there was a new vogue in economic thinking, which claimed that it did not matter too much if manufacturing industry declined, because this was part of the nineteenth-century inheritance. The future lay in the service sectors: advertising, banking, information technology, insurance, leisure, property, retailing, tourism and the caring professions. Why work in the pits if you can be a professional footballer? Why work in a steel plant if you can be a pop star? Why make clothes in a dingy workshop if you can sell them in a pleasant department store? Why shuffle papers as a civil servant if you can make a million in the City? There was an element of truth in this, but much oversimplification. It was correct that some of the so-called 'smoke stack' industries were in decline worldwide – change was inevitable. However, in the two strongest major economies, those of West Germany and Japan, the manufacturing base was very strong and the newly industrialised states were taking on the challenge of the most modern technological sectors. Moreover, even in banking, Tokyo and New York had long been more important in terms of volume than London. This view of the future of the economy overestimated the importance of the banking skills of the City of London in bringing permanent investment and ensuring for itself a larger share of the world financial sector. The 'de-industrialisation' of Britain, which gathered pace in the early Thatcher years, brought dismay and disappointment even among the Conservative Party's traditional allies such as the CBI. Britain lost nearly a quarter of its manufacturing capacity between Thatcher taking over and the first half of 1981.[12] What of the debris from this shake-up, the rising number of the unemployed? Most would find it difficult to retrain and find new employment. They often lived in areas dominated by one declining industry. Their basic education was often deficient which limited their options. Housing problems and family circumstances made it difficult for them to 'get on their bikes' as the rising Conservative star, Norman Tebbit, advised them.[13]

By the end of 1981 Thatcher had become the most unpopular Prime Minister since Neville Chamberlain in 1939.[14] Howe was the most unpopular Chancellor since Gallup first posed this question in 1949.[15] The Labour Party, which had quickly regained popularity after Thatcher's 1979 victory, was by then also unpopular.

Labour Elects Foot

Callaghan remained, in defeat, more popular than Thatcher did. When he decided to retire, in October 1980, Denis Healey and Mrs Shirley Williams were the public's favourites to replace him. Within the Labour Party these three were by no means as popular as they were with the general public. The Wilson and Callaghan governments had disappointed substantial elements within the Labour camp that felt they had not been socialist enough. Many did not realise that British governments were no longer entirely in control of what they did, because of the sickly British economy and its relative smallness and because of Britain's alliances. They also forgot that in a democracy there has to be a minimum of agreement to disagree. On the moderate wing of the party, there were substantial numbers who thought that Labour was still trying for an out-of-date agenda. The party's electoral successes in the 1960s and 1970s had, to a considerable degree, forced the different wings to work together. In opposition, they could renew their old antagonisms more openly.

Surprisingly, the Parliamentary Labour Party elected Michael Foot (67) as the new leader with a ten-vote majority over Healey. Thus, they ignored the evidence of public opinion polls showing that Foot was unpopular. Healey was then elected Deputy Leader. Foot (b. 1913) was an Oxford-educated radical journalist who had first stood for Parliament, unsuccessfully, in 1935. He had served as Deputy Leader of the Labour Party (1976–80), and had been editor of the Left-Labour weekly, *Tribune*. He was an opponent of the EC, supporter of CND and, though not a Marxist, stood for full-blooded socialism. Apart from a break of five years, he had been in the Commons since 1945. He had served as Leader of the House (1976–9) and Secretary of State for Employment (1974–6).

The Left, whose main vehicle was the Campaign for Labour Democracy (CLPD), scented power in the party and at a special conference in Wembley, January 1981, their proposals were adopted. In future an electoral college, rather than just the Parliamentary Labour Party, would elect the Leader and Deputy Leader. This college would comprise the Parliamentary Labour Party (30 per cent of the votes), the affiliated unions (40 per cent) and the constituency parties (30 per cent). The decision revealed the suspicion felt by the constituency activists for the parliamentarians. In 1979 and 1980 the annual conference had agreed that, in future, all Labour MPs would face reselection procedures during the life of each Parliament. Although ostensibly democratic, this put MPs' careers in the hands of often very small numbers of activists. According to Healey, many constituencies 'were easy prey to penetration and capture by a handful of conspirators who knew what they wanted'.[16] In April 1981, Benn announced his intention to challenge Healey for the deputy leadership. Benn represented all the Left forces in the party. Healey was subjected to a hurtful campaign of abuse.[17] The Left split and Kinnock led a campaign against Benn supporting John Silkin. In the second round, Kinnock and his followers abstained. The result was Healey 50.426 per cent and Benn 49.574 per cent. 'By the hair of an eyebrow Kinnock's action enabled Healey to spare the Party from Benn's deputy leadership.'[18] By this time, however, the party had split.

The Social Democrats

The special Wembley Conference (24th January 1981) and Labour's decisions to advocate withdrawal from the EC, and, to a lesser extent, its ambivalent attitude on defence, led to the Social Democratic secession from the party. The day after the conference, 'the gang of four' – Roy Jenkins, who had just re-tired as President of the EC Commission, David Owen, former Foreign Minister, Shirley Williams and William Rodgers, former ministers of Education and Transport respectively – issued the Limehouse Declaration and established the Council for Social Democracy. In it they proclaimed support for NATO, multilat-eral disarmament, the EC and the mixed economy. Messages of support poured in, with many small donations, and the gang of four found themselves at the head of 'a pulsating popular move-ment'.[19] On 26th March, there followed the setting up of the Social Democratic Party (SDP), represented in Parliament by thirteen MPs, twelve ex-Labour and one ex-Conservative. They announced their intention of negotiating an electoral alliance with the Liberals. The prospects for the Alliance grew almost daily. In October, the Liberals won the normally safe Conserva-tive seat at Croydon North and, in November, Williams won the equally safe Conservative seat of Crosby. Thus, she became the first MP to be elected as a Social Democrat. By that time nine more Labour MPs had transferred to the SDP. By the end of 1981, support for the Liberal–SDP Alliance rose to 50.5 per cent in the Gallup poll, as against only 23.4 per cent for Labour and 23 per cent for the Conservatives. In January 1982, Jenkins won the Conservative seat at Hillhead in Glasgow. In the follow-ing month, an Australian homosexual Marxist lost Bermondsey, which Labour had held since 1918, to the Liberals. Why was this happening? First, because the SDP gang of four and the Liberal leader David Steel were attractive personalities, who gained much media attention. Second, because of the deep recession which Britain faced. Third, because a number of Labour's policies, especially concerning the EC and nuclear disarmament, appeared totally unrealistic. Fourth, because Labour appeared to be more and more the party of the old working class, unrepresentative of the newer, white-collar employees. Fifth, both major old parties seemed to have failed and many thought a new approach was needed. The Alliance called for consensus and co-operation instead of confrontation in politics and the economy. This seemed very attractive in strife-torn, rioting Britain.

Riots on a Summer Day

On 11th April 1981, riots broke out in Brixton, south London. They continued over the weekend with pitched battles between the police and black youths. Since the 1950s, Brixton had become an area settled by immigrants from the West Indies. It suffered from social deprivation, drug gangs and poor relations between the newcomers and the police. The government was taken by surprise, but there had been rioting in the St Paul's area of Bristol, in April 1980. Lord Scarman was asked to investigate the situation, but the riots soon dropped from the headlines. On the weekend of 4th July, however, riots spread like a rash across the country to Toxteth, Liverpool; Moss Side, Manchester; Wood Green and Southall, London; and several other towns in the north and the Midlands. They went on in fits and starts until 26th July.[20] They were a horrible shock for the great British public: the television pictures of burning cars and police baton charges, then their own experiences of shops boarded up, fear on the streets and distant fires in a Midlands town lighting up the night sky. The worsening prospects for youngsters, especially black youngsters, were the main reasons for the riots, with the media attention encouraging 'copy cat' disturbances. The hot weather and late sunset are also thought to have contributed to the turmoil. According to *The Times* (14th October 1982), about 4,000 people were arrested, two-thirds under twenty years old. Less than half those arrested were unemployed. Two-thirds had criminal records. The Home Office published statistics on the 'ethnic appearance' of those arrested: in London, two-thirds were of 'ethnic appearance', but only one-third in Toxteth and Moss Side. The Scarman Report condemned the rioting but drew attention to the social and economic difficulties which beset the inner-city areas. Similar rioting occurred in Handsworth, Birmingham, in September 1985.

Lack of job opportunities was undoubtedly a factor in the deteriorating situation. Technological advances and the recession had reduced the demand for unskilled and semi-skilled labour, which many young people with few educational qualifications had traditionally gone into. It was estimated that between 1978 and 1985, the number of semi-skilled and unskilled jobs available would fall by nearly 1 million.[21] In 1982–3, the under 25s made up 40 per cent of the unemployed. Only 50 per cent of Britain's school leavers were trained, compared with 90 per cent in Germany and 80 per cent in France. Over 33 per cent of school leavers entering jobs received no training at all. Partly as a result of the riots, the Youth Training Scheme (YTS) was announced at the end of 1981. Under the scheme, all young people were guaranteed training and would receive payments while being trained. Employers taking on trainees got financial inducements. Everyone accepted that the scheme was an improvement, but there was continuing criticism of the standard of training, especially in small businesses. Heseltine also set about regenerating the inner cities with a special scheme of aid based on public–private partnerships.

War with Argentina: 'shocked disbelief'

When Thatcher's Cabinet gathered on the evening of 2nd April 1982, there was an atmosphere of 'shocked disbelief'.[22] News had arrived that one of the last outposts of the British Empire, the Falkland Islands, had been invaded by Argentine forces, and that the British garrison of Royal Marines had surrendered. How had Britain got itself into this embarrassing position? Britain had established a post on these desolate, uninhabited, South Atlantic islands in 1770, and had been in continuous possession since 1832. Most of the 2,000 or so inhabitants were of British origin. However, Argentina claimed the islands, which were relatively close to its territory, and had been occupied by the Spanish/Argentinians between 1810 and 1832. Britain and Argentina had been negotiating about the future of the islands since the 1960s. In March 1967, the Wilson government had formally expressed its readiness to give up sovereignty to Argentina under certain conditions.[23] The Foreign Secretary, Lord Carrington, and Thatcher's right-wing ally in her government, Nicholas Ridley (junior minister at the Foreign and Commonwealth Office), had earlier recommended to her that sovereignty should be ceded to Argentina, which would then lease the islands back to Britain.[24] This proposal fell after a cross-party revolt of the Labour left and the Conservative right: 'The former were remarkably bigoted and the latter were narrow and nostalgic.'[25] The islanders also opposed any compromise. In a cost-cutting operation, Thatcher agreed with her Defence Secretary, John Nott, to withdraw Britain's only naval vessel in the area, HMS *Endurance*, an icebreaker. This sent the wrong signals to the ruling Argentine military junta. Also on grounds of cost, the government announced it was to scrap one of the fleet's remaining aircraft carriers. This would further reduce the Royal Navy's ability to defend the islands. These moves greatly tempted the Argentine government, which was desperate for cheap success abroad to boost its declining support at home. Carrington later claimed that he had warned Thatcher in February about the situation.[26] Nevertheless, after the invasion, he faced 'a sulphurous meeting'[27] of the 1922 Committee of Conservative MPs and decided to resign. Francis Pym replaced him. Pym continued to negotiate while Thatcher prepared for war. The UN and the EC condemned the Argentine invasion and urged Argentina to withdraw. The USA were anxious not to offend their Latin American allies – including Argentina – by open support for Britain, their NATO ally. They were also concerned about their big investments in the area. American Secretary of State Haig, and President Reagan therefore continued to urge compromise on Britain. Reagan, however, told his military to give Britain covert support, especially invaluable intelligence.[28]

The Chiefs of Staff advised Thatcher's War Cabinet that a military operation would be, 'one of extreme difficulty, much more likely to fail than to succeed'.[29] Thatcher was prepared to take the risk, and on 5th April, a British carrier group sailed from Portsmouth. The uninhabited island of South Georgia was retaken on 26th April. At the beginning of May, air and sea operations commenced against Argentine positions on the Falkland Islands. Three weeks later British forces landed, forcing an Argentine surrender on 14th June. The risks involved had been high – sending a task force to fight in appalling weather conditions, a long, long way from the nearest British bases, with only sketchy intelligence to guide it, pitted against a well-armed (with British and French equipment) opponent – but were questioned by few. Those who did so were dismissed as defeatists or appeasers. One minister said to another, 'We have gone out of our collective mind.' Many were 'apprehensive'.[30] Most informed opinion thought the shooting would not start, until the news came, on 1st May, that a single, elderly, Vulcan bomber had attacked the airfield at the Falklands capital, Port Stanley, after an epic flight from Ascension Island. On the same day, there followed air and naval bombardment of the Argentine positions. The sinking of the ageing Argentine cruiser, *General Belgrano*, on the following day, by the British submarine *Conqueror*, with the loss of 368 Argentine crew members out of 1,000, caused shock and elation, and brought home more clearly that a shooting war had started.[31] Controversy continues about the action, as no state of war existed between the two countries, and the ship was well out of the Total Exclusion Zone, established by the British around the islands. On 4th May, the appalling news came through that HMS *Sheffield*, with a crew of 268, had been sunk. By the end of the campaign, six British ships had been sunk and ten others more or less badly damaged. It cost Britain 255 lives and 777 wounded, some maimed for life. This was three times the number of casualties in the anti-EOKA campaign in Cyprus, but only about one-third of those lost in Korea. The government put the cost of the operation at £1,600 million.[32] The cost of holding the islands since then has proved to be enormous. The dangers were tremendous – what of the benefits?

To Britain as a whole, it is difficult to think of any. But the action must be seen against the background of increasingly aggressive confrontations by non-democratic régimes. Argentina was ruled by a 'common or garden dictator'.[33] The Soviets had invaded Afghanistan in 1979, and it was some time before they were forced to pay for this folly. Poland was a sort of military régime where the workers' movement, Solidarity, had been crushed, in December 1981. It was beginning to look as though the 'bad guys' could do what they liked. In that sense the Falklands campaign was a kind of warning that they could not.

The Argentine military dictatorship fell after losing the campaign in the South Atlantic. It would probably have fallen anyway but not as suddenly.

In terms of British domestic politics, the campaign totally transformed the situation for Thatcher. Overnight the government became very popular. A six-point lead for Labour in March, became a three-point Conservative lead in April. By mid-May, the Conservatives had a 12.5-point lead over the Alliance, with Labour in third place. The Alliance had backed the government actions throughout the emergency, but Labour was less consistent. Around Benn and Tam Dalyell, there were about 33 MPs opposed to the military option.[34] Benn thought that, 'the real interest there is the oil. There is oil around the islands.'[35]

Hong Kong, southern Africa

Toughness was not seen as a realistic option when dealing with Communist China over Hong Kong. It was to be returned to China in 1997, as agreed under the original treaty with the Chinese Empire. It would, however, retain a special status, with its own market economy and political system, for a further 50 years. Most of its 5.7 million population (in 1987) would fall under the régime many of them had fled from. Parliament agonised about who, and how many, should have the option of coming to Britain, if they so desired. The Alliance was prepared to give all of them this right, an unrealistic policy. In the end, the Commons agreed to the government's proposal to admit 50,000 Hong Kong residents, plus their families. This meant that immigration to Britain was restricted to those with money, special skills, or who had served the Crown. It was never made clear why resettlement in Taiwan was not an option, considering that Taiwan regarded itself as the only legitimate Republic of China, and was a rapidly developing semi-democracy.

Thatcher also favoured a softly, softly approach to southern Africa. On gaining office in 1979, she was ready to accept the régime of Bishop Muzorewa, who had emerged as the black leader favoured by the whites, in Rhodesia/Zimbabwe. Commonwealth opposition, leading to its possible break-up, and the likelihood of embargoes on British goods around the world,[36] helped Carrington to persuade her otherwise. In November 1979, a settlement was reached at a conference chaired by Carrington in London. To avoid further bloodshed, a small British and Commonwealth force then brought in 22,100 heavily armed guerrillas from the bush, together with 35,000 refugees.[37] A general election was held in February 1980, which brought Robert Mugabe to power. Most of the whites remained, including Ian Smith.

In the case of South Africa, since the days of Macmillan's 'Winds of Change' speech (3rd February 1960) at Cape Town, in which he urged the white parliament of South Africa to recognise African nationalism, Britain had distanced itself from Pretoria's Apartheid policies. However, Conservative governments had been opposed to economic sanctions against South Africa. The argument was that sanctions would hit blacks more than the white minority. Everyone believed that the fact that British companies were heavily involved there was also an important consideration. Britain continued its arms sales, making a distinction between those for external defence, and those that could be used for internal repression. The Cold War too was an important factor. With pro-Soviet régimes in neighbouring states (Angola and Mozambique), there was the fear that the riches of South Africa and its strategic naval bases, could fall to the Soviets. Finally, many who wanted a speedy transformation in South Africa, usually in the Labour and Liberal parties, often neglected that fact that it was a multicultural society with sharp antagonisms, in addition to the black and wide divide. There were also the relatively small Asian and mixed-race groups to consider. Hence the preference in London for a slow evolutionary process of reform. This started under President P. K. Botha after 1978. Thatcher welcomed it. This approach appeared as appeasement of an evil régime, and indeed, the UN, the Commonwealth and the EC, did not accept the advice of the British government on the issue in 1985. Reagan took a similar view to that of Thatcher, but Congress overruled him in 1986, when it voted, by a majority of two-thirds, for new economic measures against South Africa.

It is convenient to mention here that the independence of first Zimbabwe and then Namibia (South West Africa) in March 1990, were two more nails in the coffin of the Apartheid régime, increasing its isolation and providing yet another base from which it could be attacked by guerrillas. The end of the Cold War, after 1989, was also decisive. The release of Nelson Mandela, the leader of the African National Congress, in February 1990, after 25 years in prison, marked both the culmination of a reform process and the beginning of much more fundamental change under President F. W. de Klerk. De Klerk announced on 1st February 1991 that legislation would be introduced to end Apartheid.

1983: Thatcher Returned

In spite of the continuing high unemployment, but falling inflation, the Conservatives remained popular in 1982–3 and speculation mounted about an early election. A government-induced mini-boom was in progress, 'a prime example of "electoral Keynesianism"', as a former minister called it.[38] After analysis of the local government elections of May 1983, Thatcher set the date for the election – 9th June. Labour went into the election with an unpopular leader, Foot, and an election manifesto which Gerald Kaufman, a member of the shadow cabinet, described as 'the longest suicide note in history', being too detailed in parts and too ambiguous in others.[39] The Conservatives even bought 1,000 copies to distribute among their major supporters 'so that they would realise what they were in for if Labour won'.[40] Healey believed Labour's confused defence policy lost his party some traditional supporters. He and Callaghan were saying one thing and Foot was saying another.[41] He stumbled himself, when he said that Thatcher had gloried in slaughter during the Falklands campaign. He apologised the following day. As usual, the great majority of the voters were reading Conservative-supporting newspapers. Labour's organisation was in worse shape than normal. Their General Secretary, Jim Mortimer, 'was contemptuous of state-of-the-art electioneering methods',[42] and there were still 150 constituencies in which candidates had to be selected when the election was announced.[43] On the other hand, the Conservative machine, in the hands of Chairman Cecil Parkinson, was 'in top gear' by April 1983.[44] Parkinson was assisted once again by Saatchi & Saatchi and Gordon Reece. The Alliance suffered from apparently having *three* leaders – Jenkins, Owen and Steel. No one expected the Conservatives to lose and from the first result it was clear they had won. Interest focused on the size of their majority and on whether the Alliance would replace Labour as the main opposition. With 43 per cent, the Conservatives actually gained 1 per cent fewer votes on a lower poll of 73 per cent (76 in 1979). Labour just managed to beat the Alliance into third place, with 28 per cent to 26 for the Alliance. It was Labour's lowest percentage since 1918. In Scotland, the SNP vote fell from 17.3 per cent to 11.8 and, in Wales, PC's percentage fell from 8.1 to 7.8. The Conservatives won 397 seats (339 in 1979), Labour 209 (268) and the Alliance 23 (eleven) The SNP held on to two seats as did PC. Among the defeated candidates were Benn, Shirley Williams and William Rodgers. A Boundary Commission redistribution of seats earned the Conservatives approximately 30 seats.[45]

Having won so decisively, Thatcher reshaped her Cabinet. Pym, Carrington's replacement at the Foreign Office, was dropped in favour of Sir Geoffrey Howe. Nigel Lawson followed Howe as Chancellor. Lawson (b. 1932) was an Oxford-educated financial journalist from Hampstead. He had served as Secretary of State for Energy (1981–3) and as Financial Secretary to the Treasury (1979–81). Also on the move was William Whitelaw, who left the Home Office to become Deputy Prime Minister, sitting as Viscount Whitelaw. This was the first hereditary peerage to be conferred since 1964, but was of little practical significance, as Whitelaw had no male heir. The new Home Secretary was Leon Brittan (b. 1939), a Cambridge-educated barrister, who had served as junior minister in the Home Office. Like Lawson, he was of Jewish background. Prior was shunted off to Northern Ireland. Parkinson, who had held the chairmanship of the Conservative Party since 1981, took on Trade and Industry. The son of a railwayman from Carnforth in North West England, Parkinson (b. 1931) was a Labour Party member before going to Cambridge and into accountancy. He had served as Secretary of State for Trade (1979–81), and was spokesman for the War Cabinet during the Falklands war. He resigned just after the 1983 election, because of his tangled personal life.

Labour's New Leader, Neil Kinnock

Immediately after their election defeat, both Foot and Healey stood down as Leader and Deputy Leader respectively. Neil Kinnock was elected Leader and Roy Hattersley Deputy. Educated at the University of Wales, Kinnock (b. 1942) was the son of a Welsh miner and had made his way in the Labour ranks as a left-winger. Elected to Parliament in 1970, he had very little experience either inside or outside Parliament. His youth and flexibility offered his colleagues hope. Foot had backed Kinnock and the Association of Scientific, Technical and Managerial Staffs (ASTMS) and other unions followed. The organising ability of newly elected MP, Robin Cook, was placed at his disposal. Because he had lost his seat, Benn was out of the race. The election was held at the Labour conference at Brighton, in October 1983. Kinnock won 71.3 per cent of the votes, Hattersley 19.3 per cent, Eric Heffer 6.3 per cent and Peter Shore 3.1 per cent. Heffer had been the 'Benn' candidate. In the deputy leadership contest, Roy Hattersley, the Healey-backed moderate, romped home with 67.3 per cent against three other candidates. 'The soft Left "dream ticket" had been achieved.'[46] Hattersley (b. 1932), from Sheffield and educated at Hull University, was in virtually every respect Kinnock's superior. He had served in Callaghan's Cabinet as Secretary of State for Prices and Consumer Protection (1976–9), having started his ministerial career in 1969. He had been a Gaitskellite in his early days in the Labour Party.

The new leaders set about the task of reviewing Labour's policies, organisation and communications. They soon persuaded their colleagues that opposition to EC membership should be dropped. Kinnock took on the Militant Tendency, a Trotskyist 'party within the Party', and a number of expulsions followed.

Under Kinnock, Labour looked set to make a dramatic comeback. In 1984 it greatly improved its position in the second elections to the European Parliament, gaining 33 seats (seventeen in 1979). The Conservatives won 46 (61 in 1979). The Alliance was deprived of seats because the old British 'first-past-the-post' system continued to operate. Despite this success, Kinnock did not seem to grow with the job. An opponent, Parkinson, who saw him daily in the Commons, thought, 'Thatcher outgunned him week after week'.[47] David Steel has commented, 'I consider his qualities of vigorous compassion to be more important than his alleged defects of verbosity.'[48] Yet a not unfriendly observer thought he seemed like 'an ageing schoolboy debater' whose Welsh accent irritated.[49] He also had a tendency to make newsworthy gaffes.

After the 1983 election, Jenkins resigned as Leader of the SDP after an ultimatum from David Owen, who replaced him unopposed. The party, which preached against the politics of confrontation, suffered many damaging confrontations in its higher echelons.

Industrial Relations and the Miners

The winter of discontent, under Callaghan, had finally convinced large sections of British opinion that the trade unions needed reforming. Thatcher was determined to do it.[50] It was left to James Prior, Secretary of State for Employment until September 1981, to introduce the Employment Act of 1980. This modified Acts of 1974 and 1976 brought in by the previous Labour administration, which in turn had modified Heath's Industrial Relations Act of 1971. The new Act restricted lawful picketing to the pickets' own place of work. Thus, in future, it would be illegal for 'flying pickets' to go to other enterprises to win over workers for strike action. It provided compensation for individuals unreasonably excluded from a union in a closed shop, where union membership was necessary to remain in employment. New closed shops could only be established after a secret ballot in favour by four-fifths of the workers covered. It made it more difficult to sack a conscientious objector to union membership or policies, and restricted legal immunity for sympathy strikes, blacking and blockading. The Act made funds available for ballots of trade union members on strikes, union elections and so on. It also removed those provisions of the Employment Protection Act, which, it was claimed, damaged small businesses. Among these was the obligation to reinstate employees after maternity leave.[51] Prior did not go far enough for Thatcher. She looked round for a replacement and decided Norman Tebbit was her man. Tebbit (b. 1931), the son of an Enfield (London) retail salesman, after a grammar school education became an airline pilot and an official of the pilots' union. A staunch Conservative from his youth, he was elected to the Commons in 1970. As a backbencher, he painted a dramatic picture of the 'enemy within'. 'Inside Britain there is a parallel threat from the Marxist collectivist totalitarians . . . Small in number, those anti-democratic forces have gained great power through the trades union movement.' Such 'colourful language' as he himself later called it,[52] helped him to get promotion to the Cabinet, in September 1981, when he took over from Prior at Employment. Under Tebbit's 1982 legislation, union legal immunities were eroded and the closed shop was further undermined.

The bulk of the unions in the TUC rejected the legislation *in toto*, calling for at least token industrial action. The lonely figure of the 1982 TUC President, Frank Chapple, urged his colleagues not to challenge a democratically elected government by such methods, but to work to change the government.

Emboldened by their 1983 victory, the Conservatives introduced the 1984 Trade Union Act, which required unions to ballot their members on the retention of their political funds, which in the bulk of cases went to the Labour Party. Given that in 1983, a record number of trade unionists had not voted Labour, they expected to reduce drastically Labour's finances, whilst they continued to cash in record sums from industrial and commercial backers. The move backfired as union after union voted to continue their support for Labour. However, unemployment, the decline of the smokestack industries, geographical change and technological innovation, as well as the poor image of unions, all played their part in reducing the influence of trade unions. Between 1979 and 1983 TUC membership dropped from over 12 to below 10 million; at the same time, the number of workers in stoppages fell from 4.6 million to 574,000.[53] In July 1982, a rail strike was defeated. It could be argued that even without legislation there would have been a weakening of unionism, as happened in other industrial countries.

The number of strikes fell to a 50-year low, yet in 1984, there occurred perhaps the last attempt to defend the old-style unionism, which was already regarded as obsolete by many in the TUC and the Labour Party. This was the miners' strike, which dragged on throughout most of 1984. The National Coal Board (NCB) announced further cuts in the mining industry to rid itself of uneconomic pits. There was to be a loss of 20,000 jobs when 21 pits were closed. The NCB seemed to be taking a tough line and the executive of the National Union of Mineworkers (NUM) voted for a tough response. In quick stages they unleashed a national strike. The miners' President, since December 1981, Arthur Scargill, played a decisive part in making this disastrous choice. Summer was approaching, coal stocks were high, demand was low, cheap imports were available. Perhaps because he knew many miners, not just in the prosperous Nottinghamshire pits, were against a strike at this time, Scargill failed to carry through a national strike ballot. However, traditional union loyalty prevailed in most areas. The miners' cause was further weakened by some cases of violence against non-striking miners and members of their families. This made it more difficult for Labour MPs to speak up for these traditional supporters. Yet Labour MPs like Stan Orme worked for a negotiated settlement.[54] At first Walker, Energy Secretary (1983–7), kept a low profile, but worked hard behind the scenes. Months into the strike Scargill turned down a compromise, which even the Communist Vice-President of the NUM, Mick McGahey, regarded as a victory.[55] In the end, Thatcher was able to impose what amounted to unconditional surrender on the NUM. The strike ended officially on 3rd March 1985, having started on 12th March 1984. The Welsh miners made a sad but impressive sight on television, as they marched back to their pits, heads held high behind their banners and brass bands. Out of 22 pits in operation at the time of the strike, only one survived to the 1990s.[56] All that Scargill achieved was embarrassment for the Labour Party, damage to the economy and the mining industry, hardship for his members and a split in the NUM. Based mainly on the Nottinghamshire and Leicestershire coal fields, the Union of Democratic Miners was established as an alternative to the NUM. There was less public sympathy for well-paid printers opposed to the move of Rupert Murdoch's papers from Fleet Street to Wapping, where new technology could be used. Murdoch offered to pay off the redundant printers, but the offer was rejected. This embarrassed Kinnock, who deprived Labour of badly needed publicity by banning contact with Murdoch journalists (most of whom were not Thatcher fans).

A Bomb in Brighton

As the Cabinet slept at the Grand Hotel, Brighton, venue of the Conservative Party annual conference, an IRA bomb went off. In all, five people, including one MP, were killed and 31, including Tebbit and his wife, were injured. The incident, on 12th October 1984, was the most dramatic of many, which revealed that the Provisional IRA sought to escalate murder and mayhem. In July 1982, IRA bombs were detonated in Hyde Park and Regents Park, London. In July 1983 the IRA burnt out the home of Gerry Fitt, former SDLP MP. In September, they had staged a spectacular escape from the Maze Prison (Northern Ireland) killing a guard. On 6th December 1983, Official Unionist, Edgar Graham, was shot dead at Queen's University, Belfast. A bomb exploded at Woolwich RA barracks on 10th December. Six Christmas shoppers were killed and many others injured by a bomb outside Harrods department store, in London, on 17th December. The deputy governor of the Maze Prison was shot dead outside his home, in January 1984. In May, four members of the security forces were shot dead. In February 1985, nine policemen were killed by an IRA bomb in Newry. The government had been faced with the self-imposed martyrdom of imprisoned IRA terrorists, led by Bobby Sands, who, in August 1981, died of hunger.

In an effort to change the situation in Ireland, Thatcher and Dr Garret FitzGerald, the Irish Taoiseach, signed the Anglo–Irish (Hillsborough) Agreement on 15th November 1985. It was the result of fifteen months' secret negotiations and established an intergovernmental conference concerned with Northern Ireland, relations between the two parts of Ireland, legal matters and cross-border co-operation. The British government was at last recognising the legitimate concern of the South with the North. The Unionists met it with a sharp rebuff. They all resigned from the Commons to force by-elections. They retained fourteen of their seats on 24th January 1986, but lost one to the SDLP.

FitzGerald led a Fine Gael–Labour coalition in the South after the election of November 1982. With 86 seats out of 166, their majority was regarded as safe.[55] FitzGerald attempted to nudge the establishments of both South and North nearer together and, in the Republic, to take on board the Protestant, as well as the Catholic, traditions. Progress was slow.

Although Charles Haughey opposed the Hillsborough Agreement in opposition, he did not repudiate it when his Fianna Fáil formed the government after the close-run February 1987 election. He was elected Taoiseach by the casting vote of the Speaker of the Irish Parliament.

Privatisation

In the first eight years of the Thatcher administration, fourteen large companies and many smaller ones, employing a total of 600,000 people, were privatised. The state sector was cut by a third and the Treasury collected more than £11 billion in funds. In most cases, these were profit-making holdings or undertakings such as British Airways, Cable & Wireless, the airports, Britoil and the public utilities – gas, electricity, water – and British Telecom (BT), and BP shares. The sale of BT in 1984, brought in almost £4 billion. Initially, the share issue attracted 2.2 million investors, but the number dropped to 1.7 million after some sold their shares for a quick profit. The sale cost the government over £3 billion, as a result of under-pricing the share issue and a lavish advertising campaign. The disposal of the Trustees Savings Bank (TSB), was also under-priced and attracted 3 million investors, falling to 2.5 million later. In 1986, British Gas attracted 4.5 million, of whom about 4 million remained after profit-taking.[57] There were similar numbers involved in the other big privatisations such as electricity. Privatisation was not as popular as these figures suggest. A Gallup survey, in October 1983, found that only 39 per cent of those interviewed thought the proposed privatisation of BT was a good idea, while 46 per cent were against. Those in favour said they believed in private enterprise, thought it would bring more competition and a better service, and would lead to price stability, or even a lowering of prices. Opponents of privatisation felt the service would deteriorate, prices would rise, and that profits should go to the public as a whole and not just to shareholders.[58]

The Conservative Manifesto of 1979 had said little about privatisation,[59] but the Conservative appetite for it grew with each successful privatisation and with each electoral victory. Initially, Treasury officials had seen it as an expedient means of raising funds to reduce the public debt. It was, however, a once-and-for-all intake of funds instead of recurring profits over an indefinite period. Something of the sort was done in the 1980s in many countries, by governments of different political complexions, for this reason. The Thatcherites also believed in it ideologically. There had always been competition between gas and electricity. Water was a natural monopoly in any given area. The Conservatives were criticised for not increasing competition in the privatised utilities. In the case of BT, limited competition was introduced by the new company, Mercury. To meet such criticism each industry was subject to a watchdog. To the extent that the Conservatives ever believed in the idea of creating popular capitalism, they met with very limited success. Most of the shareholders had only small amounts of shares in one or other of the privatised undertakings. They would find it difficult to break into the wider market as the commission charges remained a deterrent, most companies were less secure than the familiar utilities, and few knew how to seek out a reliable stockbroker. Finally, the small shareholders could exercise no control over the companies in which they had invested, faced as they were with the representatives of the big institutional investors. It remained to be seen how the natural conflict between the concern of consumers about prices and services and the expectations of profits by shareholders would be resolved.

For the Conservatives, the privatisations were a good thing. Given the British electoral system, they needed to convince only a relatively small number of voters that their privatised shares would be at risk, if Labour won, to have a considerable impact in marginal constituencies. The same was even more true of the results of the 'right to buy' legislation.

The 'right to buy' legislation was of greater significance politically and perhaps socially. This offered council tenants the right to buy, at substantial discounts, the homes they were renting. Initially, tenants of three years' standing received a discount of 33 per cent off the market value of their homes. There were higher discounts for tenants of longer standing, rising to 50 per cent for those of twenty years' standing or more. The upper limit for mortgage tax relief was also increased from £25,000 to

£30,000. By 1988, the number of homeowners increased by nearly 3 million compared with 1979. It was estimated that more than 1 million of them were former tenants buying their council homes.[60] Home ownership increased from around 57 per cent to about 64 per cent of households. Thatcher believed this had been one of the government's greatest successes.[61] These measures found critics, who argued that enough reasonably priced homes were being built for sale to those people who wanted to buy their own homes, and that council house sales reduced the stock of homes available for the genuinely needy. Councils were being forced to sell properties at below cost, in the case of newer properties, and ratepayers would have to go on paying for these for a long time in the future. Moreover, the government froze the receipts councils gained from the sales, making it very difficult to build new homes (indeed, the number fell dramatically). For whatever reason – as Thatcher herself later admitted – under her régime the number of people, especially young people, 'sleeping rough' grew.[62]

Defence Problems

In the 1980s, British defence policy was torn between the increasing realisation that the UK could not afford to maintain higher levels of expenditure than its trade rivals, and the pressure from NATO to increase expenditure. The Callaghan government committed Britain to spending an extra 3 per cent in real terms for NATO purposes until 1986. However, economic problems and the spiralling costs of new weapons and service pay, caused the government to think again. Howe, when he took over as Chancellor in 1979, wanted to prune defence expenditure, but was resisted by Defence Secretary Francis Pym. Thatcher backed Pym. 'She retained this ambivalent attitude towards defence spending for some years to come.' She agreed to 'cut back extravagant plans for the new Trident base and knocked out the fifth submarine'.[63] Although the Royal Navy was seen as a target for expenditure cuts, the Falklands War forced the government to postpone its plans for this service. It also saddled itself with the extra costs of that campaign and the maintenance of the British garrison on the islands. Between 1979 and 1985, defence expenditure rose by 18 per cent in real terms, which was higher than that spent on defence by any other European NATO state.[64] As much as 95 per cent of expenditure was said to be going to NATO commitments. According to the White Paper on Public Spending, in January 1988, defence expenditure looked set for modest reductions in real terms. The end of the Cold War was not yet in sight, nor were such events as the Gulf War.

One area of continuing controversy was Britain's and NATO's nuclear policies. The government was faced with the fact that Britain's Polaris submarines were becoming obsolete. In December 1979, President Carter offered Britain the new Trident system as a replacement. In the following year, Thatcher announced the acceptance of this at a cost of £3 billion, spread over ten years. Britain was to build five new submarines with the USA supplying thirteen Trident missiles per submarine. As we saw, the fifth submarine was cancelled. Some of the old arguments were revised about whether Britain's nuclear fleet really was independent and a deterrent. Further controversy was fuelled by the government's decision to station 96 radar-evading cruise missiles at US bases in Britain. This was part of a NATO decision agreed by the previous government, taken in response to Soviet deployment of SS20 medium-range nuclear missiles in Central Europe.[65] The missiles were divided between the Greenham Common and Molesworth bases, and helped to inject new life into the Campaign for Nuclear Disarmament (CND), with women CND members campaigning outside the bases. This presented the Labour leaders with a difficulty, especially after the replacement of Foot by Kinnock. The same issue had been a factor in the break up of Helmut Schmidt's Social Democratic-led government in West Germany, in 1982. It was impossible to ignore the increasingly aggressive moves of the Soviet military and their proxies. The Falklands War also gave the government more credibility on defence, in spite of its mistakes in this area.

Tory Revolts

As Thatcher got farther into what was to become her record-breaking run as Prime Minister, it was only natural that there were increasing numbers of her ex-ministers scattered around.

Such individuals often became the leaders of revolts over one policy or another. Some had suppressed their views, either out of ambition or because of collective responsibility, whilst in office; others were just disappointed men. Heath was the most consistent of her critics, taking up a left-wing (in Conservative terms), Tory or 'wet' position on many issues. He led a spirited opposition to the demolition of the Greater London Council (GLC), and he was a constant critic over the government's policy towards European Community. Pym, who had been sacked as Foreign Secretary after the 1983 election, formed a new Conservative group, Centre Forward, but little was heard of this. James Prior (Secretary of State for Employment, 1979–81; Secretary of State for Northern Ireland, 1981–4) and Sir Ian Gilmour (Lord Privy Seal, 1979–81) were also 'wet' critics of the government's 'dry' policies on unemployment, the economy, cuts in overseas aid and other matters. In the long run, the resignation of Michael Heseltine, Secretary of State for Defence (previously Environment Secretary), was to be more significant.

Heseltine resigned over the 'Westland Affair'. Basically, the ailing Westland Helicopters sought government approval to agree a rescue deal with the American firm Sikorsky. Heseltine favoured a European partner and in disgust walked out of a Cabinet meeting, in January 1986. Another dramatic revolt by 72 Conservative MPs, in April 1986, concerned opposition to the legalisation of Sunday trading. Thatcher was able to withstand all these revolts, and looked with increasing confidence to the next election providing she chose her moment well. Before she did, she went off on a highly successful visit to Moscow, to meet the reforming Soviet leader Mikhail Gorbachev. By contrast, Kinnock's visit to Washington to build a bridge to the White House was rebuffed by President Reagan.

Election 1987

In February 1987, Labour suffered a stunning defeat at the Greenwich by-election. A Labour majority of 5,000 was turned into an SDP majority of 6,000. Candidates are so much more important at by-elections than at general elections, and Labour had made the mistake of choosing Deirdre Wood of the 'hard left'. She was beaten by Rosie Barnes (b. 1946), a graduate of Birmingham University and market researcher. It was a harbinger of Labour's coming defeat. Labour strategists like Peter Mandelson, since 1985 Labour's head of campaigns and communications, admitted the election was about the 'survival of Labour as the major opposition party in British politics'.[66] After good local election results, and a two pence cut in income tax, Thatcher decided to call a general election for 11th June 1987. Labour did well on television, climaxing with romantic footage of Kinnock and his wife, Glenys, walking along windswept cliffs. Kinnock's ratings went up 16 per cent overnight.[67] Then Kinnock slipped up in an interview, when answering a question on defence, Hattersley stumbled on taxation and Healey fumbled on private health care.[68] Thatcher scored her hat-trick with 42.2 per cent of the vote (42.4 in 1983); Labour gained 30.8 (27.6) and the Alliance 22.6 (25.4). Labour did slightly worse than the polls predicted and the Alliance slightly better. In Wales, PC's vote declined from 7.8 per cent to 7.3. In Scotland, the SNP increased its share from 11.8 per cent to 14. Turnout had risen from 72.7 per cent to 75.3. In terms of seats, the Conservatives fell from 397 to 375, Labour rose from 209 to 229 and the Alliance lost one seat. In Wales, PC increased its representation from two to three, as did the SNP in Scotland. In Northern Ireland, the moderate SDLP added one extra seat to its existing two; Sinn Féin held its one seat and the various shades of Unionist returned thirteen (fourteen).

Women did relatively well in the election, with more women candidates than ever before. The total of 41 returned (Labour 21, Conservative seventeen, Alliance two, SNP one) was also a record. The first black woman, Diane Abbott (b. 1953), a Cambridge graduate and journalist, was elected as Labour MP for Hackney North and Stoke Newington. Three other Labour MPs were of black or Asian origin. These were solicitor Paul Boateng, who was born in Ghana, Bernie Grant from Guyana, a local government community worker, and barrister Keith Vaz, an Asian born in Aden. At Tottenham, Grant had replaced the de-selected Labour MP, Norman Atkinson, a chief design engineer and former member of Labour's NEC. Prominent among Labour's new recruits was the man the Conservatives loved to hate, Ken Livingstone, former leader of the abolished GLC. Among the notable election casualties were Roy Jenkins (SDP) and Enoch Powell (OUP). Rosie Barnes held on to her seat. Perhaps Thatcher was relieved to see no less than eight of her former ministers retire and one current minister. Eighty-seven MPs from both sides had decided not to stand again, which represented the largest exodus since 1935.[69] Would this make it easier for Thatcher to control her MPs?

Labour had picked up seats from the Conservatives, the Alliance and the SNP, but had lost seats to the Conservatives in London and the Midlands. The North–South divide seemed to be strengthening. The Conservatives were in danger of becoming merely an English party. They lost eleven of their 21 seats in Scotland. Labour had improved its performance, but it still frightened some voters with its taxation and non-nuclear defence policies, and many people had never had it so good!

12 Thatcher in Decline, 1987–90

SDP Ends in 'loveless meetings'

The Alliance challenge to Labour was routed in 1987 and many thought having two leaders – Steel and Owen – had hindered the Alliance's progress. Many felt too that it was logical that the two parties should merge. Continental experience showed that this was not necessarily so. Two separate, but allied, parties could often attract a wider spectrum of voters than one party. However, the longer two parties remained, the more likely they were to start bickering – the more so if they were not as successful as they had hoped. In the 1987 election, there had been voters who were put off by Owen's 'Thatcherism'.[1] Some Owenites suspected the Liberals of being soft on defence and perhaps much else. But a majority in both parties was looking for a merger. Steel voiced these wishes immediately after the 1987 election without having fully consulted Owen. However, once it was in the open there was no going back. It took three 'horrible'[2] meetings of the SDP executive before a membership ballot was held, which voted by 57.5 per cent in favour of a merger, with 42.3 against. Negotiations with the Liberals then followed, after which the SDP was brought to an end with the final 'loveless' meeting of the executive. Owen resigned from the leadership before the end, being replaced by Bob Maclennan, who took the majority into the new party – the Social and Liberal Democrats (SLD). Launched in March 1988, the SLD eventually became known simply as the Liberal Democrats. Of the original 'gang of four', Jenkins, Williams and Rodgers joined the SLD. Owen refused to endorse it. A few Liberals left the party and attempted to set up a new Liberal party without success. More dangerous were the activities of Owen's followers, who clung to the SDP title. They helped to destroy the earlier enthusiasm and idealism of many in the Alliance. As the election approached, they became less of a challenge and more of an irritant to the Liberal Democrats. In July 1988 Steel and Maclennan stepped down as joint leaders of the party and Paddy Ashdown (b. 1941) was elected leader. A former Royal Marines Commando officer and later diplomat, he also had commercial experience. He was elected MP for Yeovil in 1983, increasing his majority in 1987.

The SDP adventure was over. Historians will be left to debate whether it changed anything in British politics. Had the SDP defectors remained with Labour, they could have made a significant contribution to that party's early reform, and Labour's defeat in 1983 would not have been as certain. In the end the SDP made little difference to the Liberals.

Stock Exchange's 'Black Monday'

Monday 14th October 1987 became known as 'Black Monday', and with good reason. On that day, £50 billion were wiped off City stock values and by the end of the week nearly £102 billion. Many thousands of small savers saw their funds decimated. Up to the 1990s, their values had still not recovered. The crash originated in New York, where billions were lost. The crash came because the speculative boom of the 1980s could not be sustained. Britain's prosperity had been fed by speculative funds flowing in, the massive expansion of credit and a whole range of new consumer products – many of them in electronics – which made people eager to buy. Sterling had become a currency based on North Sea oil. The opening up of the City of London, through de-regulation, encouraged foreign banks to come to London. By the 1990s about half the banks were foreign-owned.

The crash of British and Commonwealth, the conglomerate, in 1990, thought to be the biggest crash in the City to that date, led to 27,000 investors having their investments frozen. This was apparently due to bad advice being taken, but it did nothing to give confidence to small investors.

Perhaps inevitably, the sleazy side of the financial world was attracted by the opportunities in London. The long-running Guinness case resulted in convictions for fraud and theft, as did that which followed the collapse of the Barlow-Clowes financial empire, which cost many small investors their savings. Investigations following the death of Robert Maxwell, the media and publishing tycoon, in November 1991, revealed he had been plundering the pension fund of his employees. In July 1991, the Bank of Credit and Commerce International (BCCI) was closed down after massive fraud was discovered in its operations. The bank, owned by one of the ruling families of the United Arab Emirates, was active in 70 states. Thousands of small investors, many of them Asians, were hit. A US Senate report by Senator John Kerry, accused the Bank of England of not acting early enough to stop the rot, and the Serious Fraud Office was called in to investigate the alleged bribing of Bank of England officials. The BCCI was believed to be involved with organised crime and with various secret service agencies. These, and many other scandals and collapses in the late 1980s, damaged the City and the Bank of England. Between March 1990 and September 1992, over 100,000 jobs were lost in the financial services industry in London. The 1990s brought expansion of Frankfurt, Germany's main financial centre, with the prospect of it eventually overtaking London in importance.

The Rise and Fall of the Poll Tax

The system of financing local government had long been a matter of controversy in Britain. While central government grants had long since become the major source of council finance, a significant amount of money was still raised by levying rates based on property values. This system had survived because no more acceptable or fairer method had ever been given serious attention. Some socialists attacked the rates, claiming that this way of raising money took no account of the needs of actual families and their ability to pay. Some right-wing critics, Thatcher among them, felt this method did not bring home to individuals the true cost of local government. Accordingly, the old system was to be replaced by a community charge, levied by local authorities on all residents within their boundaries. Such a charge would 'maximise the pressure for efficiency and low spending'.[3] Under the legislation, due to come into operation in England

and Wales in April 1990, students, the unemployed and certain others, qualified for a reduction. The charge was regressive in that it was not related to the size of income or the value of individual properties. Businesses were subject to a separate rate fixed by the government, thus further reducing the area of responsibility and initiative open to local authorities. Thatcher and her allies did not much care for local councils, as electors seemed to be forever electing 'loony left' councillors. Under separate legislation, the Local Government Act (1988), Nick Ridley (Department of Environment) required local authorities to put out various services – refuse collection, street cleaning, catering services, etc. – to tender. Local authorities were seen, at best, as regulators not owners of businesses, which would compete with private business.[4]

The community charge 'generated the most oppressive volume of correspondence'[5] to MPs. Its opponents dubbed it the 'poll tax', and it is a measure of their success that it became generally known by this, rather than by its official name. Over 100 Conservative MPs were said to have their doubts about the measure[6] that was opposed by Labour, the Liberal Democrats, PC and the SNP. The SNP and PC and the far left urged their supporters not to pay; Labour rejected this tactic, confining its opposition to parliamentary pressure and peaceful protests. It was after such a peaceful demonstration that a riot occurred in Central London on 30th March 1990. In the end, under a new Prime Minister, the community charge was abolished, in March 1991. A great deal of parliamentary time and taxpayers' money had been expended attempting to explain and enforce it. On 1st April 1993, a new council tax was introduced based on property values and the assumption that each home contains two adults. Those with only one received a discount of 25 per cent.

From New Brutalism to Post-modernism

Private sector housing experienced a great boom in the second half of the 1980s followed by the most dramatic slump since the 1920s. The housing boom was based on easy credit, two salaries and mortgage interest tax relief. Chancellor Nigel Lawson belatedly attempted to cool 'the frenzied housing market' by cutting tax relief. Even so, 'the bill to the taxpayer for this middle-class handout was £7 billion in 1989, and by delaying the change until August, provoked a last-minute scramble among house-buyers'.[7] What were the new homes like? Usually they offered central heating and the slightly larger ones a downstairs lavatory. Most were houses rather than flats, though more flats and 'town houses' for singles were being offered. In external appearance, the modernism of the 1960s was replaced by neo-Georgian, mock Tudor and, a new departure, neo-Victorian embellishments. This seemed to fit the Thatcherite view of the 'good old days', a view of the past projected by some television advertising. It was also a reaction to the New Brutalism[8] of the 1950s and 1960s, local housing projects of concrete-slab tower blocks and fortress-type blocks of flats, and other buildings influenced by the ideas of the French architect Le Corbusier. They were found from Edmonton Green (London) to Liverpool, Sheffield and beyond to Newcastle-upon-Tyne and Glasgow.[9] Some of the modernist public buildings, including some at new universities, were exciting and successful; Nottingham Playhouse and Stirling University are among many examples. Sometimes little consideration was given to the other surrounding buildings and the modernist newcomers seemed totally out of place. The least successful ones were public housing. Designed by well-meaning 'revolutionaries', they were often hated by those who had to live in them, and were soon found to be defective in their materials. The corrupt architect John Poulson had a hand in some of them (see above). Although often associated in the public mind with Labour councils, in fact, as Alan Clark pointed out,[10] the tower blocks and the sink estates, 'housing estates seemingly modelled on the morally debasing aesthetics of the Eastern European Communist bloc received Macmillan's enthusiastic backing'. This was when he was in charge of housing. When he opened Park Hill, 'a monstrous concrete jungle in Sheffield, into which 2,000 council-house dwellers were herded', Macmillan said it would, 'draw the admiration of the world'.[11] The collapse of the Ronan Point (London) tower block, in 1968, forced a rethink. Public and commercial buildings started to take on a new look which became known as 'post-modernist', a return to more traditional, even romantic, forms and materials creating an expression of harmony and proportion which most people found more reassuring. The Hillingdon (London) Civic Centre, completed in 1978, marked an important move in this direction. Of it one critic has written: 'From a distance it sprawls like a huge brown marquee . . . one becomes aware, after the lights go on, that behind its geometrical complexities of brown brickwork is another concrete-framed office building got up in an elaborate, if necessarily cost-conscious fancy dress.'[12] Prince Charles, who by this time had developed a keen interest in architecture, aided the attack on modernism. He thought Hillingdon 'pioneered the departure from the nuclear-fallout-shelter look'.[13] By the mid-1980s, everything from new office blocks and hotels to old people's homes, hospitals and the many shopping complexes being erected on the outskirts of towns were post-modernist – Meadowhall (Sheffield), for example. The danger was that post-modernism would become the *only* style and descend into dull conformity.

Increasingly over the 1970s and 1980s much greater emphasis was put on conservation in the centres of towns and cities. The shells of familiar old buildings were renovated and the interiors redesigned for modern usage. New buildings had to be in keeping with the scale of the buildings around them. Stratford upon Avon and Ludlow (Shropshire), for example, have successfully ensured this. Pedestrian precincts became widespread, with easier access for the handicapped provided. The growth of tourism was another factor encouraging inner-city renewal. York and Durham benefited from this and held their places as top tourist attractions. Much was done in Glasgow, Bristol and other centres. Heavy cuts in local government expenditure in the late 1980s and 1990s impeded this work. In 1991, the government intro-duced its City Challenge scheme to encourage local authorities to make detailed bids for central funding for renovation projects in rundown inner-city areas. Great progress was made in the 1980s and 1990s in providing more shopping, leisure and eat-ing facilities in British town centres. Money from the European Union helped, as with the promenade at Southport and the train station at Chesterfield. Lottery money assisted as well in the 1990s. Despite the progress, they were still untidy and shabby by the standards of Germany and some other Western European countries.

Welfare 'safe with us'

Ideally some Conservatives would have liked to privatise the NHS, the education system and many aspects of welfare. Public opinion consistently favoured the NHS and gave Labour better ratings on health, education and dealing with unemployment. Thatcher was forced to defend herself by claiming the NHS 'is safe with us'. Many were not convinced, whichever party they voted for. Britain spent less on health than any Western European country and far less than the USA. Many hospitals were shabby and much equipment was inadequate. Many nurses, doctors and ancillary staff felt underpaid and even more undervalued. In any case, there were not enough of them. There was a widespread view that patients had to wait too long for treatment. The NHS had not been able to shake off a condescending attitude towards patients. Moreover people were expecting more than ever before from the NHS and specialists were anxious to perform operations unimagined even in 1968 let alone when the NHS was established in 1948. Looking after the growing number of elderly patients was also expensive. All this was not the fault of any one government alone, but most aspects of the NHS did not improve under the stewardship of the Conservatives. They attempted to make patients pay whenever possible and to encourage private health care. There was a massive rise in prescription charges over the 1980s and dental services were virtually private by 1990. Doctors were expected to prescribe cheaper, non-generic medicines rather than well-known brands. Patients were kept in hospital for shorter periods after operations. There was a great deal of emphasis on putting in managers who would encourage 'market forces' in the NHS. At the end of the 1980s, the government could argue that there were more nurses and doctors at work treating more patients then ever before. Yet there was a general feeling that the NHS was massively underfunded. Changes brought in by Kenneth Clarke, at the end of the 1980s, were very controversial and were opposed by many in the NHS at all levels. He attempted to create a market for health care. The regional NHS authorities became self-governing trusts, free to buy and sell health services to each other and anyone else prepared to pay. General practitioners were made responsible for their own budgets and were supposed to give their patients the best possible care for the lowest possible price.

Education in the 1980s

As discussed in Chapter 7, there had long been criticism of Britain's educational system. This continued throughout the 1970s. Some Conservative critics believed discipline had broken down and that this was a cause of academic failure. Many more focused on what they believed to be poor teacher training, informal styles of teaching, failure to give due attention in the early years to the '3 Rs', poor standards of numeracy among school leavers, failure to test the progress of pupils at different ages, lack of streaming and so on. Many of these 'evils' they associated with comprehensive schooling. In the Conservative Party, Sir Keith Joseph led the way, supported by former head teacher Dr (later Sir) Rhodes Boyson, MP, and Caroline (later Baroness) Cox. The right-wing 'think tank', Centre for Policy Studies, founded by Joseph and Thatcher, interested itself in this as in other aspects of society. These critics often forgot that up to the 1970s, most children left school without any qualifications, because no academic or other courses leading to qualifications were in place in most schools, the secondary moderns. As for discipline, despite the use of corporal punishment, there had always been problems in both the public and the private sectors, but they had rarely been highlighted in the past. Left-wing critics put more emphasis on underfunding, the problems of inner-city schools, the problems of immigrant children, the failure to ensure that more girls took science, the divisive nature of an education system based on well-endowed and well-connected private schools, and the under-financed schools with large classes attended by most children. Moreover, it was still true in the 1970s and the 1980s that most MPs chose to send their children to private schools, not those attended by the bulk of their constituents' children. In addition to these criticisms, there were those critics who straddled the political divide, who believed Britain's education failure was helping to produce economic failure. Increasingly those were heard who believed greater account should be taken of the needs of industry and commerce when constructing curricula. Despite all the criticism, more young people were leaving school with 'O' levels/GCSEs, more were completing 'A' levels and more were entering higher education. However, by the early 1990s, according to Department of Education figures, Britain still faired badly in an international survey of the participation of 16–18-year-olds in education and training (see Table A 11). In a famous, and controversial, speech at Ruskin College in October 1976, Premier James Callaghan had voiced many of these concerns. He signalled that changes would have to be made and that education could not be left to the teaching profession alone. He saw the goal of education as equipping 'children to the best of their ability for a lively constructive place in society and also to fit them to do a job of work . . . not one or the other, but both'.[14]

Had Labour remained in office it is almost certain that they would have introduced a national curriculum and other changes. As it was, it was the Conservatives who introduced this in the Education Reform Act, 1988. For the first time this laid down that all pupils must learn maths, English and science as core subjects, and, as foundation subjects, history, geography, technology, music, art, physical education and, at the secondary stage, a modern foreign language. As in the past, religion remained part of the curriculum, and was strengthened. The Act set up two Curriculum Councils (one for England and one for Wales) all members of which were appointed by the Secretary of State for Education. Previously, in practice, the senior staff at schools had been responsible for the curriculum – often influenced, in upper schools, by the pressure to prepare for external examinations. The Act introduced testing and assessment of pupils at seven, eleven, fourteen and sixteen. Another aspect of the Act, emphasised by Kenneth Baker, the Secretary of State, was the formal increase of parental choice. Within a given area, parents had a right to choose the school to which they wanted their child to go. The Act transferred control of budgets from local authorities to school heads. No provision in the Act caused greater controversy than that allowing schools to opt out of local-authority control to become 'grant-maintained'.[15] Such schools would then be funded directly by the Secretary of State and run by their governors. A simple majority of a secret ballot of parents could achieve this status. Without doubt, part of this development was due to a deep-seated prejudice among Conservatives against local education authorities (LEAs) and against teachers. Many teachers, especially in local authority schools, were not Conservative and many LEAs were Labour-controlled.

The Act also changed higher education in a number of ways. Polytechnics were removed from local-authority control and would in future get their funds through a new body – the Polytechnics and Colleges Funding Council. This proved to be preparatory to allowing them, from 1992, to award their own degrees and call themselves universities. This was to be welcomed, as most departments in most polytechnics had achieved high standards for years, but had been regarded as second class because of their origins, names and the fact that they could not award their own degrees. The government liked the polytechnics because they were often doing more 'relevant' work, such as business studies or textile design, and the average cost per student was lower. The universities tended to be unfairly judged by the standards of Oxbridge, where many Conservative cabinet ministers had studied. The University Grants Committee, a body dominated by university professors, which distributed public money to individual universities, was abolished. It was replaced by the Universities Funding Council, on which representatives of industry, commerce and the professions played a large part, together with professors. The Act abolished tenure for new academic staff and for those who changed their jobs or who were promoted. Academics could be made redundant like anyone else. 'For nearly a century governments have struggled to insulate universities from political pressure. Now this policy has been stood on its head. Universities are to be paid for doing what the Government tells them to do, or not be paid at all.'[16]

Main Churches Face Decline

Former Methodist chapels which had been turned into furniture warehouses, as in Matlock, or Anglican churches which had been transformed into Hindu temples, as in Archway, North London, had become an increasingly familiar sight since the 1950s. They reflected the decline of the main churches since the interwar period (see Chapter 1). According to a Gallup poll, in January 1973, only 40 per cent of those questioned accepted church authority, although 50 per cent said they accepted the Bible. By 1984, the Bible too seemed to have lost ground. Asked about the miracles described in it, only 25 per cent felt they were mainly historical fact, 38 per cent regarded them as interpretations by the writers concerned and 28 per cent thought they were mainly legends. Two-thirds of those surveyed did not think the churches should take sides in politics. However, over the 1980s churchmen like Robert Runcie, Archbishop of Canterbury (1980–91), felt compelled to speak out more and more in favour of the disadvantaged at home and abroad. His predecessor, Michael Ramsey, supported the abolition of capital punishment (1965) and the de-criminalisation of homosexuality (1967) and favoured widening the grounds for divorce and abortion. He spoke out strongly against racism.

In decline, the churches became more tolerant of each other. Joint services caused no embarrassment, except for the Catholics. However, attempts at unification failed. Yet Rome and Canterbury were closer than in the past. The Second Vatican Council (1962–5), summoned by Pope Paul, set in motion liberal reforms in the Catholic Church which, among other things, made relations with other Christian communities easier. Ramsey, Archbishop of Canterbury (1961–74), took the initiative in reaching out to Catholic, Protestant and Orthodox leaders alike. In 1982, Pope John Paul II, making the first papal visit to Britain, joined Dr Runcie in Canterbury Cathedral to celebrate Christian unity. Yet there were sharp controversies within the churches. Many Catholics were disappointed by the Pope's rejection of artificial birth control and/or the right of priests to marry. In the Church of England, a determined minority was prepared to abandon Canterbury for Rome because they rejected women clergy. In 1992, the Church of England General Synod voted narrowly in favour of the ordination of women. Some other Christian denominations already had women ministers (the first women being ordained to the Methodist ministry in 1974). There were also sharp differences between Conservative members of the Synod and pacifist-inclined Christians, who propagated support for unilateral nuclear disarmament.

The churches lost the argument in favour of keeping Sunday special. For several years some big retailers had been prepared to risk being fined for opening on Sundays. The law was not clear on the issue. In 1993, the Commons voted in favour of a compromise under which small shops could open as they wished, but big stores could open for six hours only. This was part of a long-term trend against the British Sunday. Even after 1945, in many towns, cinemas and even public playgrounds for children, were closed on Sundays – pubs were not. By the 1950s, cinemas were open throughout England. Tourism, the fact of both partners working in many households – thus having little time to shop in normal hours – and ethnic shopkeepers (from non-Christian traditions) opening, helped to force change. The drift away from the churches made it easier to bring this about.

By the 1990s, it was possible to envisage a time when Islam would have more adherents in Britain than the Church of England. According to *Social Trends* 23 (1993), the Anglican Church of England claimed 1,840,000 members among the adult population of the UK, as against 2,270,000 in 1975. On the other hand, the numbers professing Islam had risen from 400,000 to 990,000 (probably an underestimate). With 2,530,000 members in 1975, the Catholic Church had overtaken the Church of England. By 1990, it estimated membership had fallen to 1,950,000. The Methodists and Baptists, who had played an important role in nineteenth-century reform and in the twentieth-century Liberal and Labour parties, counted 720,000 members combined, down from 880,000. The Presbyterians, mainly in Scotland and Northern Ireland, were down from 1,650,000 to 1,290,000. Of course, millions of others had been baptised, but they were likely to use the churches only for marriage and burial. The Jewish religious community had remained stable at 110,000, although the wider Jewish community was in decline. It was estimated to be 300,000 in 1992. The Jewish religious community had split, the main force being the United Synagogue, which competed for membership with the Reform and Liberal Synagogues. There was also a small, ultra-orthodox group, mainly in Stamford Hill (London). The religious communities based on recent immigrants – Sikhs, Hindus, Muslims and Afro-Caribbeans – had increased. As they had many more young people in their ranks (often seeking partners from their countries of origin), this trend seemed set to continue. Small groups like the Mormons, Jehovah's

Witnesses and Spiritualists had expanded (to 330,000 in 1990). This was the result of their resources (often from the USA), active recruitment campaigns and the disillusionment of some Christians with 'organised' religion.

Irish Parties in the 1980s

Fianna Fáil had remained the largest party in the Republic of Ireland since 1932. It continued to draw its support from all social classes but was stronger among the working class and small farmers. Its appeal was a mixture of nationalism and conservatism on social/church issues such as divorce. In the European Parliament, it was allied to the French Gaullists. Fine Gael remained the second largest party. More middle class, more conservative, especially on economic issues, than Fianna Fáil, it appeared more conciliatory on the border, relations with the North and so on. From 1976, it was allied with the Christian Democrats in the EC Parliament. Under the leadership of Garret FitzGerald (1977–87), it had become more liberal. Alan Dukes served as Fine Gael leader between 1987 and 1990 when he was replaced by John Bruton. The Labour Party was traditionally the third largest party, allied to the Socialists in the EC Parliament, and usually the junior partner in any Fine Gael government, as in 1981 and again, 1982–7. It leader from 1992, Dick Spring, was a barrister who had followed his father into politics. His career had been helped by his success on the rugby field. In December 1985, Des O'Malley, a former Fianna Fáil minister, founded the Progressive Democrats Party. It took a more liberal view on contraception, was more conciliatory on national issues and more Thatcherite in economic terms. Its supporters were the better off. Briefly, in 1987, the Progressive Democrats did well, emerging from the election as the third largest party, having taken votes from Fine Gael and Fianna Fáil. In the EC Parliament, they joined the Liberals. To the Left of Labour, there were the Workers' Party and Sinn Fein. The Workers' Party lined up with the French and Portuguese Communists in the EC Parliament. Although it remained the biggest party in the 1970s and 1980s, Fianna Fáil found itself on the opposition benches, in an increasingly volatile situation (see Table A 25).

In the 1980s, there were no less than five elections with three changes of government. Changes in the parties' electoral strength reflected the increasing secularisation of society, the influence of television, EC membership, economic changes and the weakening of the border issue. Attempts to cut taxes, to cut government expenditure and to privatise, in the 1980s, generally lowered support for the government parties among the working classes, but secured middle-class voters. Labour, as a government party, lost votes to the Workers' Party because of this in 1987. By 1989, Labour had regained its position, but the Workers' Party advanced farther (see Table A 25). Fianna Fáil gained middle-class votes at the expense of the Progressive Democrats, whose appeal seemed to be ephemeral. In the end, these two parties, led by bitter rivals, formed a coalition, which lasted until 1992.

Thatcher's 'embarrassing anti-Europeanism'

Up to the 1990s, Britain had an uneasy relationship with its partners in the European Union (EU). There were all the problems connected with a latecomer. The officials of the original six had built up an organisation for roughly twenty years to suit their needs; they were at home in it. The British could only slowly find their way. The European Commission found it difficult to recruit enough qualified Britons to work for it. As Roy Jenkins, the British President of the Commission (1977–81), found, there was a strong Franco–German friendship.[17]

By the time he had become Foreign Secretary in 1979, Lord Carrington had come to the conclusion 'that militarily as well as economically we were pretty small'. He felt that only within the EC could Britain find a role. 'But we had missed our tide.'[18] Like Jenkins, Carrington found the EEC, as it then was, had been 'shaped to suit the interest and to advance or protect the economy of France. Of Germany to some extent; but primarily of France.'[19] He was ashamed of Britain's relative poverty. He rightly believed Britain was paying too much in its EEC contribution in 1979. The issue dominated the EEC meetings during this period, making them 'disagreeable and wearisome'.[20] Luckily for Britain, Thatcher was 'no bad hand at conducting rows . . . bluntly saying, "I want my money back" . . . Margaret's firmness and intransigence were the key factors in getting us a proper settlement.'[21] That was in the period 1979–82.

This was a 'proper settlement' which few could quarrel with, involving as it did, a huge rebate for Britain. Before British entry in 1975, French President Pompidou had succeeded in stitching up an EEC arrangement which favoured France to the disadvantage of Britain.[22] Some criticised Thatcher's style and urged the Prime Minister to follow up this success with a constructive approach to the EC. Unfortunately, Thatcher was basking in the smile of Ronald Reagan, US President (1981–9), with whom she had a 'special relationship'. They agreed on defence, and most aspects of foreign policy, and were ideological soul mates. She foolishly believed closeness with Reagan could counter the growing closeness of the Franco–German entente, and the realisation by the USA that Germany was Western Europe's major power.

The Premier of Luxembourg, Pierre Werner, had in 1970, proclaimed economic and monetary union as a priority for the EEC. This was the position when Britain joined. It gradually became reality as the partners traded increasingly with each other, but formal steps were few. In 1977, Jenkins, as President of the EEC, backed by West German leader, Helmut Schmidt, resurrected this objective. Premier Callaghan felt it would undermine the US dollar/pound alliance as the lynchpin of the international monetary system.[23] Callaghan also opposed it because he claimed it would prevent him dealing with unemployment. Thatcher, on gaining office, opposed it, saying she feared it would prevent her dealing with inflation. As Jenkins recorded, Britain remained faithful to 'our national habit of never joining any European enterprise until it is too late to influence its shape'.[24]

Despite her scepticism, Thatcher took Britain deeper into the EC by agreeing the Single European Act in 1986, which meant unrestricted movement of labour, capital and goods between member states by 1992. It was the work of Lord (Arthur) Cockfield, former Conservative Cabinet Minister, Vice-President of the EC (1985–8),[25] supported by French socialist Jacques Delors, President of the EC. Delors, favoured by Howe and Thatcher (among others),[26] served from 1985 to 1995

On 21st September 1988, Thatcher made a speech at Bruges, in Belgium, in which she came out clearly against political and economic union within the EC. This pleased the 'Euro-sceptics' in the Conservative Party, but informed opinion was increasingly worried that Britain would be isolated in Europe. This was undoubtedly a factor in Labour's victory in the elections to the European Parliament on 15th June 1989. During the campaign she had 'found it impossible to conceal her contempt for the European Parliament itself. Her own Quasi-Gaullist pronouncements increasingly imprinted on our campaign a crudely embarrassing anti-Europeanism.'[27] At the Madrid EC summit on 27th June, Thatcher was forced to admit that one day the UK would join the Exchange Rate Mechanism (ERM). Sir Geoffrey Howe, Foreign Secretary, and Nigel Lawson, Chancellor, had threatened to resign if she did not make this statement of intent.[28] Many thought Thatcher had at last turned to a more constructive policy on Europe. This was not to be.

Thatcher was to cause some of her colleagues further embarrassment over her attitude to German re-unification. From the summer of 1989, the East German Communist régime started to unravel. This process was speeded up, after the opening of the Berlin Wall and East Germany's frontiers, on the night of 9th–10th November. Thatcher told Soviet leader Gorbachev that she was rather 'apprehensive' about the possibility of a reunited Germany. She repeated this to all who would listen, including President Bush, on 24th November.[29] In the end, her views did not count. Bush and Gorbachev, and Gorbachev and West German leader, Helmut Kohl, sorted out the fundamentals, at separate meetings, and Germany was united after further negotiations, on 3rd October 1990. By that time, Thatcher's days were numbered.

Thatcher Falls: 'sick at heart'

On the morning of 24th July 1989, Howe was called to Thatcher at Downing Street and dismissed from the Foreign Office. He was asked to take over as Leader of the Commons, which he accepted. Thatcher also offered the 'sullen' Howe the title of Deputy Prime Minister, which she had 'held in reserve as a final sweetener'.[30] The relatively unknown John Major replaced him. Lawson, whom Thatcher was also anxious to be rid of, resigned in October 1989 over the position of Alan Walters, Thatcher's economic guru. Major was then moved again to become Chancellor of the Exchequer. He was replaced by Douglas Hurd, who had previously served as Home Secretary (1985–9). Hurd (b. 1930) was an old Etonian, former President of the Cambridge Union and member of the diplomatic service (1952–66).

Quite apart from Howe, Lawson, Heseltine and Heath, Thatcher had made many political enemies by the time she celebrated ten years as Prime Minister. Some, the 'wets', disagreed with her views over a wide range of issues; others over particular areas of policy. Many more did not like her style of leadership. She paid more attention to a small group of advisers than to her Cabinet colleagues. These included Charles Powell, senior civil servant and Thatcher's Private Secretary (1984–91), Bernard Ingham, her press secretary and Sir Alan Walters, the 'unelected Chancellor'.[31] 'Their combined influence was resented by many Tory MPs.'[32] By the end of the year, Thatcher was challenged to a leadership contest by the strongly pro-EC, but relatively obscure, Sir Anthony Meyer. This was the first challenge to her since taking over in 1975. Meyer did not expect to win, but 33 MPs were persuaded to vote for him, 25 spoilt their papers and three abstained.[33] Junior minister and Thatcherite, Alan Clark, believed 'the Party in the House has just got sick of her'.[34]

Thatcher faced another blow, in July 1990, when her ideological soul mate, Nicholas Ridley, incautiously described the EC as a 'German racket', when speaking to the editor of *The Spectator*. He was forced to resign from the Cabinet in which he served as Energy Secretary. Meanwhile, Major and Hurd pressed Thatcher to say 'Yes' to the ERM and Britain finally joined, on 4th October 1990. This was the day after German unity was restored. On 28th October, Thatcher was again isolated as the EC summit in Rome set a 1994 deadline for the second stage of European Monetary Union. Thatcher denounced this in the Commons as 'the back door to a federal Europe', which she opposed. She appeared to be undermining her own Chancellor, John Major, who was trying to work out an acceptable alternative to a common currency. Thatcher's manoeuvre was the last straw for Howe, who resigned on 1st November 1990.

Howe's forceful attack on Thatcher, in his resignation speech, set in motion the leadership contest in the Conservative Party.

Heseltine was under pressure to stand, and was challenged by Ingham to do so.[35] Although most of the declining number of Conservative activists still admired Thatcher, by-elections in 1990 showed cause for concern. On 22nd March, Labour had gained Staffordshire Mid from the Conservatives on a 21.3 per cent swing. There were swings to Labour in four Labour seats, and, on 18th October, the Liberal Democrats captured Eastbourne from the Conservatives on a 20 per cent swing. Even Thatcher loyalists had to have doubts about their future under her leadership. Perhaps Thatcher seemed too dismissive, too over-confident, for when the election took place she was in Paris, not rallying her supporters in the Palace of Westminster. When the result was known, on 20th November, Thatcher 204 votes to Heseltine's 152, the Prime Minister realised that under the Party's complicated electoral rule, there would have to be a second ballot. There were sixteen abstentions. With two more votes she would have been home and dry! She had won 55 per cent of the vote as against the 53 per cent she achieved when she was first elected.[36] She announced she would stay in the ring. However, under pressure, she called in her ministers one by one. Kenneth Clarke went in first and told her she could not win. However, he said that he would be happy to support her for another five or ten years.[37] Norman Lamont told her the position was 'beyond repair'. At the end, Thatcher was 'sick at heart', grieved by the desertion of her friends and 'the weasel words whereby they had transmuted their betrayal'.[38]

Thatcher had been turned out by a revolt without parallel, though the revolt against Chamberlain in 1940 had similarities. Thus ended the longest Premiership of the twentieth century. Given the vicious in-fighting from its start in 1979, it is remarkable that it survived so long. One reason was because the 'power of a modern Prime Minister is awesome, particularly when it comes to the power of appointment and dismissal of ministers'.[39] Because of her strong personality, strong views and the support she enjoyed among the grassroots of her party, Thatcher must have enjoyed more power, *vis-à-vis* her colleagues, than almost any other postwar Prime Minister. Given the rather brief tenure of ministers, one can justifiably ask how much influence individual ministers really had. Kenneth Clarke, for example, moved six times in eleven years.[40] During those years, Thatcher shuffled her ministers around often for party reasons rather than for their efficiency or lack of it. She had only three Chancellors but four Home Secretaries, four at the DSS and five Foreign Secretaries. Defence, Education, Energy and Northern Ireland all had five ministers each, while Employment and Transport managed six each. Yet the record must go to Trade/DTI, which had no less that ten ministers between 1979 and 1990. On the other hand, there were only two Permanent Secretaries to the Cabinet, Sir Robert Armstrong (1979–88) and Sir Robin Butler, from 1988. These able and experienced civil servants, and others like them, must have enjoyed considerable influence even under Thatcher.

In personal terms, Thatcher's career was a remarkable achievement. The girl from a small shop in Grantham had become an 'empress'.[41] What had she left behind? Her party was divided and was to remain so, and Britain had declined further in terms of relative wealth and influence. It was a more divided country. As one of her former colleagues wrote later, 'a redistribution of wealth from the poor to the rich in the name of "incentives"' had taken place. The 'standard of living for the top 10 per cent rose by 60 per cent in real terms; for the poorest 10 per cent, it either stood still or even fell by 14 per cent'.[42]

13 Major's Avalanche of Problems

'He's a nice enough fellow'

John Major readily admits that one of the reasons why he got so much early support after the fall of Thatcher was that, 'I was not Michael Heseltine, but was the person best placed to defeat him.'[1] In the second contest for the leadership of the Conservative Party Heseltine, therefore, faced John Major. He also faced Douglas Hurd, who could split the anti-Heseltine vote enough to ensure victory. Held on 27th November 1990, the election produced 185 votes for Major, 131 for Heseltine and 56 for Hurd. Major had attracted 49.7 per cent, which was two votes short of an outright win – Heseltine and Hurd then withdrew in his favour.[2]

With the exception of Cecil Parkinson, Major retained all his colleagues in his new Cabinet of 23 (including the Prime Minister). Hurd remained at the Foreign Office, John MacGregor remained Leader of the Commons, Tom King retained Defence and Kenneth Clark Education. Major's campaign manager, Norman Lamont, was given the Treasury and Kenneth Baker got the Home Office. Heseltine was brought back and given Environment. Chris Patten was appointed Conservative Party Chairman with a seat in the Cabinet as Chancellor of the Duchy of Lancaster. There were no women in the Cabinet.

Some papers had presented Major as the 'boy from Brixton', who had taken on the toffs in the Conservative Party and won. This was true. Major (b. 1943) was from a humble background. He had left Rutlish Grammar School at sixteen and had taken on a number of makeshift jobs before a fairly brief career in banking. He climbed the political ladder via local politics in Lambeth. Elected to Parliament in 1979, he had advanced with some help from Thatcher, joining the Cabinet in June 1987.

He was Britain's youngest twentieth-century Prime Minister with the least previous ministerial experience of any Conservative Prime Minister since Baldwin replaced Bonar Law in 1923.[3]

Major started his term of office with a higher personal rating in the polls than Thatcher had scored during the Falklands conflict. People liked his mild-mannered ordinariness. Kinnock said of him, 'He's a nice enough fellow.'[4] This was the eve of the Gulf War. The other key problems he inherited were the poll tax which, as we saw, was sorted out by Heseltine. There were fears about law and order, including the terrorist bombs which were still going off. Britain's place in the EC was still a matter of controversy, although Major signalled a more positive attitude when, in Bonn, in March 1991, he said he wanted Britain, 'At the very heart of Europe. Working with our partners in building the future.'[5] At the end of January 1991, he had become the most popular Prime Minister for 30 years, since Macmillan's heyday.[6] This was due to victory in the Gulf War.

Conflict in the Gulf

When British troops were dispatched to Saudi Arabia, in 1990, to take part in the liberation of Kuwait, there can be no doubt that, as with the Falklands, few Britons had more than a vague idea where Kuwait was. It had been a British-protected state until 1961, and threatened by Iraq since the British withdrawal in that year. The reason for Iraqi and Western interest in this small Arab kingdom was its oil. In 1990, it was thought to possess 13 per cent of the proven world resources of oil. On 2nd August 1990, when most of the world's media were watching the breakup of the Soviet Union and the reunification of Germany, Iraqi troops invaded Kuwait. On 8th August, the Iraqi dictator, Saddam Hussein, formally annexed it. The UN first agreed economic sanctions against Iraq and then set a deadline for withdrawal. Thatcher was prominent in calling for tough action. Soon an American-led military coalition was put together with troops from Saudi Arabia, Egypt, Morocco and some other Arab states, joining American, British, French and Italian units. With 45,000 British service personnel in the Gulf, Britain's contribution was second only to that of the USA. As Saddam did not respond to the entreaties of personalities such as the UN Secretary General, President Waldheim of Austria, Edward Heath and others who made the trip to Baghdad, Iraq and Kuwait were subjected to massive aerial bombardment. Once the coalition troops moved forward, the Iraqis were effectively demoralised and fell back. Saddam then saved his own position by quickly agreeing to UN demands, and the coalition forces were halted.

By the time the shooting started, Thatcher had been replaced by Major, whose stock rose during the brief war. The Labour and Liberal leaderships backed the government, but a few MPs raised questions about the feudalistic nature of the Kuwait state, and the civilian deaths in Iraq, caused by coalition bombing. There were also questions about the morality and wisdom of Western military aid to Saddam's régime during the Iran–Iraq war in the 1980s. Some of Britain's part in this was later exposed in the official Scott Inquiry (1993–4).

Trouble with Law and Order

After seventeen years of imprisonment and vilification as terrorists, the 'Birmingham Six' were declared innocent, on 14th March 1991. It had taken three appeals to produce this judgement, based on new evidence. Their original convictions were secured on the basis of confessions obtained by force, and forensic evidence, which had not explored all the possibilities. The 'Guildford Four', who had been convicted for the Guildford pub bombing in 1974, were released in 1989. These were two of the most dramatic cases in a series of similar miscarriages of justice, which had been revealed since 1989. By no means all were connected with terrorism. They exposed police corruption and incompetence and were a powerful argument against capital punishment, which was once again rejected by the Commons in 1988. Under the Police and Criminal Evidence Act (1984), an independent Police Complaints Authority was set up. The tape-recording of interviews was introduced. The Crown Prosecution Service was established in 1986. Under the Prosecution of Offences Act (1985), it decides whether prosecutions initiated by the police should go forward.

There was a rise in crime over the 1980s. Most classes of

crime increased: numbers of sexual offences rose relatively modestly, contrary to popular belief; robberies, burglary and white-collar crime increased to a much greater extent. Despite the increase in police personnel – 138,543 in 1981 and 147,434 in 1991 – the clear-up rate for these, and other categories of crime, fell. Experts differed in their assessments of the causes of the rise. Some of it was explained by a greater readiness to report crime, as insurance companies demanded this if claims were made. Some of it was due to increased opportunities, from open shelves in supermarkets, computer and credit card crime, and theft of motor vehicles. Some of it was due to unemployment and social deprivation, especially when committed by youngsters. The sale of illicit drugs, and other drugs-related offences, were also on the increase. The police believed that secondary schools throughout the land were venues for drug pushers as well as drugs users. Others linked increasing crime to the decline of the nuclear family, the decline of moral standards and the decline in the respect for authority. Alcohol abuse and drug abuse were linked to crime. Violence on television was widely regarded as being responsible for increasing violence in real life. However, the police got much support from television, with such programmes as *Crimewatch UK* and fictional detective series like *Inspector Morse, Taggart, The Ruth Rendell Mysteries* and, from the USA, *NYPD Blue* and many others.

Publicity given to a number of gruesome homicides led to outrage and helped to push crime close to the top of the political agenda. Each decade seemed to produce one or two particularly nasty murderers, such as the 'acid bath' killer, George Haigh, and Neville Heath, who preyed on women in the 1940s; John Christie, in the 1950s, whose victims were also women; the 'Moors murderers', who massacred children in the 1960s; the 'Black Panther', Donald Neilson, in the 1970s; 'Yorkshire Ripper' Peter Sutcliffe, and Dennis Nilson, the serial killer of young men in the 1980s. By 1993, the new decade had reached a new low. In Nottingham, a nurse was convicted of killing several children in her charge. In Liverpool, two ten-year-old boys were sentenced to be 'detained at her Majesty's pleasure' for abducting and battering a toddler to death. In 1994, a house in Gloucester yielded police investigators the remains of at least nine murder victims – all women. In Manchester, six men and women were convicted of imprisoning, torturing and killing a teenage girl. They had doused her with petrol and set her alight. Drugs and video 'nasties' played a part in the last case – for them, horror fiction became reality. However, the number of convictions for murder and manslaughter remained, in 1991, roughly around the same level as 1981 – 4,000.

By the 1990s, the public perception of the crime problem was so bad that vigilante groups were springing up all over Britain. A Gallup survey, published in the *Daily Telegraph* (30th August 1993), revealed that 75 per cent of those asked felt that vigilante action could be justified. 'Confidence in the ability of the police, courts and government, to tackle rising crime, has fallen so dramatically that the vast majority of the public now supports taking law into its own hands . . . nearly half expressed little or no confidence in the police.'

In an attempt to bring 'market forces' to the police service, the government set up the Sheehy Committee, chaired by industrialist Sir Patrick Sheehy. The fundamental premise of the report, presented in July 1993, was that differences in responsibilities, the circumstances of police roles (exposure to risk, long hours, unpopular assignments), differences in skills and performance, should be formally recognised in the pay scheme.[7] The report provoked the biggest protest rally in police history, when over 20,000 off-duty officers, from Britain's 52 forces, packed the Wembley arena, on 20th July, to voice their opposition to the report. The police, who had done well under the Conservatives in terms of pay, believed that the proposal to introduce appraisal and performance-related pay would destroy the ethos of policing as a public service.[8] The Labour Party supported this criticism.

The rise in crime in Britain was part of an international trend. However, the International Crime Survey, which compared crime in fourteen countries, revealed that the number of people who experienced robberies, sexual offences and assault was lower in England and Wales than in many other similar countries: Belgium, Finland, Norway, West Germany, the Netherlands, Canada, the USA, Spain and Australia. Surprisingly, Northern Ireland joined Switzerland, Scotland and France in being safer in this respect. England and Wales, and Northern Ireland, suffered fewer burglaries than most of these states. Car thefts were, on the other hand, higher in Britain.

One other aspect of law and order was the place of the security services in a democratic society. In Britain, MI5, which, like the American FBI, dealt with internal security, and MI6, which like the American CIA, was responsible for information-gathering abroad, never had to account for their activities to Parliament. At the official level, even the names of their respective heads and their addresses remained secret. This looked increasingly foolish, as ex-operatives like Anthony Blunt were exposed as traitors, and ex-officers like Peter Wright published their memoirs or leaked damaging accounts of their activities. As the Cold War was over, John Major decided that less secrecy was called for, and many petty restrictions surrounding these bodies were lifted.

Maastricht

In 1987, Maastricht was just a medium-sized Dutch town with a population of about 115,000, which earned its living from pottery, glass, textiles, brewing and tourism. Some people remembered it had been in the path of the German invasion, in May 1940, but that was almost a lifetime ago. A few British people had visited it, usually *en route* for somewhere else. By 1992, it was famous, and it was to remain so. There the leaders of the twelve EC states signed a treaty, on 7th February 1992, which became known as the Maastricht Treaty.[9] It was designed as a 'new stage in the process of creating an ever closer union among the peoples of Europe, in which decisions are taken as closely as possible to the citizen'. So ran the opening words of the Treaty. It set up a European Union based on the EC, which would, in addition to economic functions, have 'a common foreign and security policy and a common interior and justice policy'. In the economic sphere, economic and monetary union was the aim and 'Ultimately this will included a single currency'. A 'common defence' was also seen as a future possibility.

Britain had objected to any idea that the aim was an eventual federal state and this term was, therefore, omitted from the final version of the treaty. Britain had also opted out of the Social Chapter of the Treaty, which was based on the 1989 Social Charter of the EC. Britain and Denmark had the right to opt out of the

Social Chapter; they also had the right to opt out of the single currency, if they eventually decided to do so. Most Conservatives had argued for these opt-outs. Labour had supported the Social Chapter and most in the Labour Party accepted a single currency. There was some doubt about an open espousal of federalism. Other European businessmen argued that if Britain opted out of the Social Chapter, which set out certain minimum rights for employees, it would amount to giving British business an unfair advantage. British firms would be able to offer poorer terms and conditions to their employees than those prevailing in the rest of the EC. British Conservatives argued that the Social Chapter would 'add to employers' costs and push up unemployment'.[10] Most British businessmen favoured a single currency, as it would eliminate the uncertainties of fluctuating exchange rates between European currencies. Thatcher, and some of her close associates, attacked the Treaty on the grounds that it was federalism by the back door. The Yugoslav imbroglio revealed the need for an EC security strategy, but Britain was more inclined to leave such matters to the existing NATO structures and the UN. France and Germany led those who wanted to prepare EC structures that could deal quickly with such 'forest fires' without Europe being forced to rely on the Americans. The Treaty plagued the Conservative Party for over a year, leading to the near defeat of Major's government, in the Commons, on several occasions. To ensure firm majorities, Major came to an understanding with the Ulster Unionists.

Election 1992

In the run up to the election, the economic outlook continued to appear gloomy. Unemployment grew in 1991 from 1.9 million in January to 2.6 million in December. Interest rates were cut but the housing market remained far more depressed than at any time since 1945. Business and consumer confidence remained poor. Constant attempts to reduce stocks by sales failed to relieve the retail trade. There were record numbers of business failures and record numbers of house and flat repossessions as borrowers fell behind with their loan repayments. The balance-of-trade deficit fell because of lack of demand for foreign goods, but

Britain's trade balance remained in the red. Inflation fell but was higher than in most other industrial nations. What was bad for Britain should have been good for the opposition parties.

By-election results, opinion polls, the 'natural' swing – all pointed to a Conservative defeat in the April 1992 election. The Conservatives suffered seven by-election defeats between 1987 and 1992, four to Labour and three to the Liberal Democrats. As late as 3rd–4th April, an NOP poll gave Labour 41 per cent to 35 for the Conservatives and 20 for the Liberal Democrats. On the day before the election, an ICM poll put the two main parties at 38 per cent each and the Liberals at 20 per cent.[11] The actual result in Great Britain – that is excluding Northern Ireland – was 42.8 per cent going to the Conservatives, 35.2 for Labour and 18.3 for the Liberal Democrats. The Conservatives gained 336 seats (375 in 1987). Net, they lost 39 constituencies to Labour and two to the Liberal Democrats. They also won one newly created constituency. Labour won 271 (229 in 1987), winning three seats formerly held by the SDP, in addition to the 39 from the Conservatives. The Liberal Democrats took twenty seats, as against 22 that the Alliance had won in 1987. In Wales, PC with 8.8 per cent (7.3 in 1987) won four seats (three in 1987) and in Scotland, the SNP increased it share of the vote from 14 to 21.5 per cent, but stayed on three seats. Unexpectedly, the Conservatives staged a slight recovery in Scotland, achieving 25.7 per cent (24 in 1987). Labour's vote in Scotland fell to 39 per cent (42.4 in 1987) and the Liberal Democrats' vote also fell from 19.2 per cent to 13.1. The four Labour MPs of Asian or black backgrounds were all re-elected and one additional Asian Labour candidate was returned. Under the Conservative colours, an Asian was returned at Brentford and Isleworth. At Cheltenham, however, the black barrister, John Taylor, lost a Conservative seat to the Liberal Democrats on a higher than average swing. Taylor's candidature had been subject of controversy in the local Conservative Association.

In Northern Ireland, the SDLP increased its representation from three to four, ousting Gerry Adams (Sinn Féin) in Belfast West. This victory for moderation was due to tactical voting by Protestants. The Official Unionists gained nine seats, Democratic Unionists three, and one Independent Unionist was re-elected. The Conservatives, contesting for the first time, attracted only

5.7 per cent of the vote but no seats. The non-sectarian Alliance Party gained 8.7 per cent, a drop of 1.2. It won no seats.

Labour: 'too American, too glitzy'?

The British electoral system makes every vote in the marginal constituencies count. Of the 651 MPs elected in 1992, 170 had majorities of 10 per cent or less, compared with 151 in 1987.[12] The Conservatives' overall majority of 21 rested on their eleven most marginal seats, all secured with majorities of under 600 votes.[13] The Conservatives had won more seats more 'cheaply' in terms of votes than any of the other parties. Clearly, in this situation, organisational factors cannot be ignored, and the Conservatives were best placed to win. In addition, the 700,000 poll-tax evaders, who were not on the register, must have harmed Labour rather than the Conservatives, even if we admit that many of them would not have bothered to vote, had they been on the register.[14]

The attention given to television at election time, the fact that most voters get most of their information from that source, should not lead to an underestimation of the press. If the three tabloids which campaigned most vigorously against Labour – *The Sun* (circulation 3.6 million), the *Daily Mail* (1.7 million) and the *Daily Express* (1.5 million) – had persuaded a couple of thousand of their readers to vote Conservative that would have virtually done the trick for Major. Of the dailies, seven out of eleven backed the Conservatives, and only three backed Labour. Newspapers accounting for 67 per cent of sales backed Major, corresponding exactly to the 1987 election.[15] By contrast, television was more even-handed. The Conservatives got 15,000 seconds, Labour just under 14,000 and the Liberal Democrats about 9,000 during the election campaign.

The campaign was fairly low key as there was less to argue about than in the past. As all three leaders agreed broadly on foreign affairs, the main issues became the state of the economy, taxation and welfare. The Conservatives did not seem to be doing all that well, but could Labour do any better? Many people doubted that they could.[16] Labour's campaign was badly flawed. Misled by the favourable polls, Labour campaigners 'allowed ourselves to become the incumbents: to take on the attributes of the government, rather than the opposition ... the Conservatives ... fought like tigers and behaved like the opposition'.[17] Apparently, after ugly scenes in the streets of Southampton, in the south, and Bolton, in the north, Major insisted on more street campaigning, including a soapbox! For him, it worked better than any 'toothpaste photo-opportunity' could have done.[18] Major also had behind him Norman Lamont's Budget and his own *Citizen's Charter*. Just before the election Lamont announced a tax cut of 5 pence for the first £2,000 of income. This would benefit all taxpayers but would be of proportionately greater benefit to those on low incomes. Shadow Chancellor, John Smith, foolishly produced an alternative Budget, which did not stand scrutiny. The *Citizen's Charter* obliged the NHS, British Rail and other public bodies to offer certain guaranteed services. Major sought to win over wavering SDP and Liberal voters. He got a little help from David Owen and some other former SDP figures. Maybe one other factor was that so many Labour figures, who dealt with key issues, were from either Wales (Kinnock) or Scotland (John Smith, Gordon Brown, Robin Cook); Margaret Beckett and John Cunningham, Labour's campaign co-ordinator, were exceptions. Finally, Labour slipped up with a rally at Sheffield on 1st April, just over a week before polling day. As one of their strategists later wrote, 'it looked over-confident ... and it was too American and glitzy'.[19]

After the election Kinnock and Hattersley resigned. They had brought about great changes in Labour policy but had failed to lead their party into government. In the final week of the campaign, the *Daily Express* (6th April 1992) had asked its readers, 'Dare we really trust this man?' It mentioned that Kinnock had been, 'Wrong on Europe: Wrong on privatisation: Wrong on nuclear deterrence: Wrong on the Cold War'. In his favour, it could be argued that Kinnock had prepared the ground for his successor by ditching untenable positions.

John Smith (1938–1994) and Margaret Beckett, replaced Kinnock and Hattersley. Smith was the son of a Presbyterian minister who, after graduating from Glasgow University, had turned to law. He had the advantage of ministerial office (1974–9) behind him, having served in the Cabinet (1978–9). Mrs Beckett (b. 1943), who had been educated at Manchester

College of Science and Technology, was MP for Lincoln (1974–9), and after working for Granada Television, was elected MP for Derby South in 1983. Whereas Kinnock (and Beckett) had started on the left of the Labour Party, Smith was more centre-right. As befitting a Queen's Council, he had a considerable presence in the Commons and on television.

Labour still claimed to be a party committed to democratic socialism but it was unsure what this was. Although British Labour had quite a different view of socialism from that of the Soviet Communist Party, the collapse of East European 'socialism' made it more difficult to salvage anything from the socialist tradition. Their comrades in the other democratic socialist parties had the same problem, though most of them had 'modernised' and many of them were in government, mostly in coalitions, in the early 1990s.

Just when Labour's morale was soaring, it was struck a potentially serious blow by the sudden death of John Smith, a week after the party's victory in the local elections of 5th May 1994. Margaret Beckett was given temporary custody of the party's top chair. All watched the European election on 9th June. Labour scored again, increasing its vote from 40.1 to 44.24 per cent. The Conservative vote fell from 34.7 to 27.83 per cent. There was also a surge in the Liberal Democratic vote, up to 16.72 from 6.7 per cent. Labour took 62 (previously 45) of Britain's 84 seats, the Conservatives eighteen (32) and the Liberal Democrats two (nil). The SNP pulled in 32 per cent of the vote in Scotland, increasing its seats from one to two. PC garnered 17 per cent of the vote in Wales but no seats. The Green Party vote collapsed. Labour had campaigned more on domestic than European issues, the Conservatives played a Euro-sceptic tune, and the Liberal Democrats were overtly pro-EC. On the same day, Labour held four seats in by-elections with greatly increased majorities, and the Liberal Democrats snatched Eastleigh from the Conservatives with a 21.4 per cent swing.

Tasting victory, Labour had the delicate job of electing a new leader without allowing old divisions to re-appear. Beckett competed with Tony Blair and John Prescott. Blair won easily. In the election for the deputy leadership Prescott won against Beckett. The son of a Conservative university law lecturer and barrister, Blair (b. 1953) was someone to appeal to the middle-class suburbs.

A barrister, he was educated at public schools and Oxford. He adhered to Christian socialism and had embraced the orthodox 'left-wing' policies of Foot and Kinnock on his way up. Prescott was a former merchant seaman, who had later studied politics at Ruskin College, Oxford, and Hull University. Like his leader, he had moved with the times. At Labour's annual conference in October 1994, Blair introduced the slogan 'New Labour, New Britain'. Labour's stock rose in the opinion polls. At a special conference in London, on 29th April 1995, Labour replaced the old Clause IV of its constitution, which had caused so much controversy. Labour proclaimed it no longer stood for 'common ownership', that is, public ownership of the economy, but wanted, 'A dynamic economy serving the public interest' in which 'the enterprise of the market and the vigour of competition are joined with the forces of partnership and co-operation'.

Women in Parliament . . . and Elsewhere

A record number of women candidates stood in 1992, and a record number, 60 (as against 41 in 1987) were elected. Labour led as usual with 37 women MPs (21 in 1987), the Conservatives elected twenty (seventeen), the Liberal Democrats two (two) and the SNP one (one). Women achieved another first when the Labour MP Betty Boothroyd was elected, by 372 to 238, Speaker of the House of Commons. She served until 2000. Two women were among Major's 22 Cabinet colleagues. Virginia Bottomley took over as Minister of Health and Gillian Shephard as Minister of Employment. Despite the progress, the number of women in Parliament in 1992 represented a smaller percentage than those elected to the German Bundestag (see Table A 4) and many other European parliaments.

Women had achieved great advances over the 1980s and into the 1990s, especially in the media, advertising, publishing, the civil service, the NHS and the legal profession. The number of women solicitors, for example, rose from 5,175 in 1983–4 to 12,683 in 1989–9. The decline of areas previously the sole domain of men, such as iron and steel, coal, the merchant marine and shipbuilding, also helped to change the perception of the roles of the sexes in society. Women were also gaining a more important place in the armed forces, the police and the prison service. Under Major, the internal security service, MI5, got its first woman head, as did the Customs and Excise Service, and Barbara Mills, QC, was appointed Director of Public Prosecutions. Britain's first astronaut was a woman, Helen Sharman, who flew on a Soviet space mission. For the first time, women were being appointed editors of newspapers in the 1990s. In April 1998 Rosie Boycott was appointed editor of the *Express* and, in June 1999, Janet Street-Porter was appointed editor of the *Independent On Sunday*. By that time most other national dailies had women in senior positions.

More and more women were entering higher education. The proportion increased from 42 per cent in 1979 to 46 per cent in 1992. In medicine, dentistry and health just over 40 per cent of the full-time students for first degrees in 1979–80 were women. By 1987–8, the proportion had risen to nearly 60 per cent.

By 1992, women made up 44 per cent of the British labour force, by which time Britain had a higher percentage of women in employment outside the home than any other EC country. Because of falling population this percentage was expected to go on rising in the 1990s. The need for more women in employment would, it was believed, increase the choices offered to women.[20] Despite this progress, women often occupied the lower-paid jobs in the economy and lack of nursery places made it difficult for mothers to pursue careers outside the home. To a degree, that was a reason why more educated women were looking for opportunities to work from home. By the beginning of the 1990s, there were still few women academics, but women writers – Anita Brookner, Beryl Bainbridge, A. S. Byatt, Angela Carter, Maureen Duffy, P. D. James, Iris Murdoch, Fay Weldon – were ever more prominent. Germaine Greer, the Australian-born academic and feminist, whose *The Female Eunuch* (1970) had influenced generations produced *The Whole Woman* in 2000.

Economic changes appeared to be favouring women, as employers replaced full-time, expensive male employees with women working part-time, who were often denied benefits enjoyed by full-time staff. In terms of maternity leave women were worse off in Britain than in other EC states.[21]

Attitudes to the role of women were changing in the 1980s. A Mori poll, in 1992, revealed that only 20 per cent of Britons believed a woman's place was in the home, compared with more than 33 per cent in 1982.[22] In 1987, an EC poll revealed that Denmark, followed by the Netherlands, the UK and France, scored higher than the EC average on questions to do with equality between the sexes and the role of women. Well below average were Germany, Luxembourg and Ireland.[23] Despite the changes in attitude, many of the old ways were retained in practice. At the Conservative Party conference in October 1993, there were strong attacks on single women parents. Yet although the numbers had increased dramatically since 1971, out of 19,036,000 households in 1991, a lone parent headed only 1,891,000. Most of them were women, but about two-thirds of them had been married.

The Press: 'dangerously scurrilous'

The press proprietors – Conrad Black, Robert Maxwell, Rupert Murdoch and Lords Rothermere and Stevens – controlled fifteen national newspapers representing over 90 per cent of national sales.[24] Four out of five of them strongly supported Thatcher and three out of five of them had come from abroad. As we have seen, in the 1980s they introduced modern technology and left Fleet Street, the traditional location of most of the press, for Wapping. They fought bitter circulation wars, with the tabloids seeking to outbid each other with gossip and scandal to boost circulation. Conrad Black commented: 'The London tabloid journalist ranges from the saucy to the completely, dangerously scurrilous and, frankly, far worse than anything I've seen in any other English-speaking place.'[25] This, in turn, brought increasing criticism in the 1980s for what was seen by many as intrusive reporting on the private lives of prominent individuals. Often the articles published were about the sexual indiscretions of prominent individuals, such as Conservative ministers Cecil Parkinson and David Mellor and the Liberal leader Paddy Ashdown. The troubles of the royal family made good copy for the popular press but resulted in increasing calls to curtail it. The Calcutt Committee into Privacy and Related Matters was set up in response to criticism of the press. Although it strongly criticised the press, it rejected legislation to protect privacy, and it called for the Press Council to be replaced by a Press Complaints Commission (PCC). Unlike the Press Council, the PCC was simply a complaints body and it did not have the role of defender of the press. On 1st January 1991, the PCC commenced operations. It appeared to have been ambushed when Lord McGregor, its chairman, issued a stern rebuke condemning journalists who dabbled 'their fingers in the stuff of other people's souls', only to retract it later. This came after the *Guardian* (12th January 1993) disclosed that Prince Charles and Princess Diana had in fact recruited rival newspaper groups to carry their own accounts of their marital rifts. The government was forced to shelve any plans for legislative curbs on the press.

In an attempt to break the stranglehold of the existing proprietors, Andreas Whittam Smith founded a new daily, *The Independent*, in 1986. The two main shareholders (18 per cent each) were the liberal newspapers of Italy and Spain, *La Repubblica* and *El País*. It rapidly established a niche for itself in the quality market, appealing to the growing number of people who had no firm party political commitment. However, by 1993 it was in difficulties, with falling circulation and rising debts. It staggered on to be bought by the Irish proprietor Tony O'Reilly. In the first half of 1999, its circulation was 222,064 compared with the *Guardian*'s 308,938, *The Times*' 742,595 and the *Daily Telegraph*'s 1,091,852. An attempt to found a left-wing Sunday paper, the *Sunday Correspondent*, failed after a few months. Circulation of the national dailies fell from 17 million in 1990 to 13 million in 1999,[26] due to the continuing expansion of television, the growth of the number of radio stations and the expansion of the Internet.

There were, by the end of the century, over 120 titles aimed at Britain's ethnic communities. These ranged from the old-established weekly, *Jewish Chronicle*, to many, more recently founded publications such as the monthly *Asian Hotel & Caterer*.

Electronic Media

The Conservatives introduced great changes in television and radio after 1979. Many local radio stations were established, including ethnic channels. In 1982, Channel 4 was established as a second independent television channel, financed by the

ITV companies from advertising revenue. The Annan Committee on Broadcasting, which reported in 1977, had recommended its founding. It gave more attention to minority interests, sexual as well as ethnic, put on television's most in-depth news programme, and the 'thinking man's soap', *Brookside*. It was also an important contributor to ensuring that the British film industry survived, as many films were made for early exhibition on Channel 4. Many of them analysed recent British experience. *Wish You Were Here* (1987), though about the problems of a teenage girl in the 1950s, had much to say about British attitudes and society. *My Beautiful Laundrette* (1985) was a sympathetic look at the problems of a young Asian gay in contemporary Britain.

The BBC was under attack throughout the period, particularly from Conservative critics who saw it as a hotbed of liberals and radicals. The aim was to reduce the influence of the BBC by increasing competition and starving it of funds. It had continued to compete with commercial television in all areas of broadcasting and not without success. In January 1993, its soap *Eastenders*, set in an East London square, was attracting 23.18 million viewers, as against ITV's *Coronation Street*, which had an audience of 21.46 million. By comparison *Brookside* pulled in 6.66 million. The success of the BBC's Australian soap *Neighbours*, and similar Australian offerings, seemed to indicate the longing of many Britons to get away to a classless, informal, sunny environment. An increasing number of young people were visiting Australia. The only news programmes that got into the top twenty programmes in January 1993 were those of the BBC.[27]

The government changed the structure of ITV. The Independent Broadcasting Authority, which had regulated both independent television and radio, was abolished and replaced by two separate authorities, the Independent Television Commission and the Radio Authority. The tendency was towards less regulation. ITV companies were not only forced to show they had the resources to put on a full range of programmes in their regions, but were also forced to compete on price by bidding for the franchises. This system was introduced in 1991, when four out of sixteen franchise-holders lost their licences. It was claimed the old system tended to exclude new talent and restrict the growth of independent programme-makers.[28] The new system weakened the unions and gave less security to those in the television industry. Both ITV and the BBC were facing a new challenge in the 1990s: satellite television was slowly coming in, offering more choice to those prepared to pay the subscription.

By the end of the 1980s cinema audiences had been rising for some years but, as in the past, most of the films screened were from Hollywood. In 1992, *Basic Instinct*, a violent thriller starring Michael Douglas and Sharon Stone, was the biggest box-office success. The only British film to score was *Howards End*, adapted from the novel by E. M. Forster. In box-office terms it came 35th, after 34 American films. It earned £2.67 million compared with £15.5 million earned by *Basic Instinct*.[29] Among the acclaimed British films was Richard Attenborough's *Gandhi* (directed by David Lean, 1982), which dealt with the life of the Indian nationalist and pacifist. In 1994, *The Remains of the Day*, a romance, with Anthony Hopkins and Emma Thompson, which had much to say about pre-war British society and social attitudes, was widely acclaimed as was *Four Weddings And A Funeral*, a comedy about the difficulty of finding a partner in contemporary Britain. *Brassed Off* looked at the fate of a mining community and its brass band after the miners' strike of 1984. A number of American movies were attacked for taking liberties with British history. These included the blockbusters *Braveheart* (1995), about the Scots' struggle to remain free of England, and *Titanic* (1997), about the ill-fated liner. These led to more calls for financial aid to the British film industry, which received some assistance from the EU.

Although some, who claimed to approve of 'Victorian values', would have liked to experience a 'clean up' of television, the tendency towards 'permissiveness' could not be reversed. Fear of the rising tide of deaths from AIDS in the 1980s forced the government to initiate an educational campaign on television in 1988. The condom was praised nightly in a variety of ways as a method of achieving 'safe sex'. At about the same time the ban on advertisements for women's sanitary towels was lifted and such adverts became normal. The arrival of Channel 5 in 1998 opened the door widely to much more 'adult material' on television. A survey showed that the number of those believing in pre-marital sex to be wrong continued to fall, from 28 per cent in 1983 to only 25 per cent in 1987. Perhaps television had played a part in this change.

ERM Exit: 'a great defeat'

After his dramatic, nail-biting win, in 1992, nothing seemed to go right for Major. He got little gratitude for taking the party to victory. The Maastricht controversy grew in intensity within the Conservative camp. After much talk about the 'green shoots of recovery' by Lamont, the economy remained depressed. The housing market remained stagnant and large numbers of house-buyers found their properties were worth less than what they paid for them. Major had fought the election on the basis that Britain's membership of the Exchange Rate Mechanism (ERM) was central to his economic policy. As Chancellor in Thatcher's government, he had taken Britain into the ERM, in October 1990, with an overvalued pound. Membership involved defending the fixed exchange rate, within certain narrow limits, of the pound against other ERM currencies headed by the German mark. Speculation against the pound, caused by currency dealers doubting the stamina of the Conservative government, resulted in a flight from sterling. On 'Black Wednesday', 16th September 1992, interest rates were dramatically increased to 15 per cent but, as Lamont put it, 'We were losing hundreds of millions of pounds every few minutes.'[30] Britain was still forced to leave the ERM. This represented a *de facto* devaluation of the pound and 'unleashed havoc in the Conservative Party'.[31] The government had lost £3–4 billion in hours in a vain effort to defend the pound. Major called it later 'a great defeat',[32] Lamont survived as Chancellor but the government lost much of its credibility for economic management.

Bosnia: War and 'ethnic cleansing'

A significant number of British people had taken holidays in Yugoslavia in the 1970s and 1980s. They were shocked to see television pictures of the beautiful old towns they had visited going up in flames. This happened in the early 1990s with the break-up of Yugoslavia. First Slovenia and then Croatia declared their independence with some fighting. This was after efforts by Lord Carrington, the EC envoy, to mediate between the constituent republics had failed. There was controversy over the hasty recognition of Croatia and Slovenia in December 1991, which Germany had urged. But this recognition offered them a degree of protection from the powerful, Serb-dominated, Yugoslav armed forces controlled by President Slobodan Milosevic. The process was even more painful in Bosnia, which declared its independence after a referendum, in April 1992. There Muslims made up just under half the population with the remainder being 17 per cent Croat and one-third Serb. The Serbs, most of whom were farmers, lived on a disproportionate amount of Bosnian territory before the war. The Muslim and Croat populations were concentrated in the towns and cities. By late March 1992, nationalist groups from all three ethnic groups were at war. The Bosnian Croat militia was armed by the government of Croatia, while the Serb nationalists, led by Radovan Karadzic, were armed and assisted by the Yugoslav army. The Croats initially fought the Karadzic Serbs alongside the Bosnian army, but later aimed to join with Croatia.

While the various efforts at peace negotiations were in progress between 1992 and 1995, other efforts were being made to minimise the violence in Bosnia. At the beginning of the conflict, in September 1991, the UN imposed an arms embargo on the former Yugoslavia. While aimed at lowering the destructiveness of the war, it served to maintain the military advantage of the Serb forces, who inherited the bulk of the Yugoslav army arsenal, putting the Muslims at a severe disadvantage. Also, the UN authorised NATO to enforce a no-fly zone in Bosnia in April 1993, and to conduct airstrikes to protect six UN safe-havens and UN Peacekeepers. With memories of their heavy casualties in Vietnam, the Americans were cautious about getting involved on the ground.

The under-armed and poorly organised Bosnian army was defeated by the Karadzic Serbs and Croatian militia. The Serbs engaged in campaigns of murder and rape designed to drive out non-Serbs. Thus the term 'ethnic cleansing' entered the vocabulary. The Bosnian army was not blameless, but its actions were never as systematically criminal. The Serbs were soon in possession of 70 per cent of Bosnia. Sarajevo, the capital of Bosnia-Herzegovina, was surrounded and under siege by April 1992. UN Peacekeepers, including 1,800 British troops and contingents from France and Canada, charged with the escort of refugees and the delivery of humanitarian aid, arrived in Bosnia. This was opposed in the Commons by Benn, Heath and right-wingers like George Gardiner.[33] Within the Cabinet Major and Hurd stood for intervention, Clarke and Portillo were 'uneasy', and Defence Secretary Rifkind was 'dubious'.[34] In the meantime David Owen, who had been appointed EC representative, and former US Secretary of State Cyrus Vance, the UN's envoy, negotiated with all sides.

February 1994 saw increased Western action in Bosnia. In response to a particularly bloody mortar attack on a Sarajevo marketplace, which killed nearly 70 people and injured over 200 others, NATO demanded the withdrawal of all Serb artillery from around Sarajevo. The Serbs responded, on the condition that Russian troops joined the UN mission. Later that month, NATO jets shot down four Bosnian Serb aircraft violating the no-fly zone. In October 1994, the Muslims captured Bihac with Croat assistance, and the Serbs responded with a fierce counter-attack. NATO bombed the Serbs in support of Bihac, a UN Safe Area. The Serbs then took UN Peacekeepers hostage and used them as 'human shields' that November. They were eventually released.

In spring 1995, NATO escalated its air campaign, which resulted in the Serbs taking more Peacekeepers, including British servicemen, hostage. These hostages are also all eventually released. In July, however, the Serbs overran the UN Safe Area of Srebrenica. Bosnian Serb military commander Ratko Mladic appeared in person to assure the civilians and the media that all Muslims would be safely conducted out of danger. This was shortly followed by the mass execution of thousands of military age Muslim men. Zepa was also taken. NATO responded by threatening to bomb the Serbs to protect the remaining four Safe Areas. In August and September, NATO lived up to this threat, launching an intensive campaign of airstrikes against the Serbs. There was considerable controversy over the fall of the Safe Areas and the conduct of airstrikes.

In May 1995, the Croats launched an offensive into Western Slavonia, a small territory in the Serb-held Krajina. US mercenaries had trained the Croats. Milosevic abandoned the Croatian Serbs in the Krajina to their fate. The Croat move proved to be a rehearsal for the larger offensive in August, which completely cleared out the Krajina, sending almost 200,000 Serbs fleeing into Bosnia. There were reports of attrocities. The success of this offensive shifted the balance of power in the region away from the Serbs, by clearly demonstrating the effects of Croatia's military build-up, and also eliminating the support of the Krajina Serbs for their brethren in Bosnia. In the summer of 1995, an Anglo–French Rapid Reaction Force of 1,700 was dispatched to defend Sarajevo but this did not stop the mortar attacks.[35]

During the early autumn of 1995, US envoy Richard Holbrooke began a period of round-the-clock, shuttle diplomacy negotiations with all the Bosnian factions, Croatia and Serbia. This produced a tenuous cease-fire in October, and the peace talks in Dayton, Ohio, where a peace agreement was concluded, on 21st November 1995. It left Bosnia as a single state comprising a Muslim–Croat Federation, and a Serb Republic.

Why did Milosevic become more amenable to a peace settlement? A split had developed between Milosevic and the Serbs in Bosnia, particularly Bosnian Serb leader Radovan Karadzic, a potential political rival. Furthermore, Serbia had been suffering greatly under UN economic sanctions imposed in May 1992, which exacerbated the ongoing economic crisis from before the war. Milosevic also knew that time did not favour the Serbs. The Serbs had been successful early on in the war because they had superiority in arms, they inherited the bulk of the Yugoslav Treasury, and the West was divided. Milosevic knew that these advantages would not last.

National Heritage, National Lottery

Major broke new ground, after the 1992 election, by establishing a Department of National Heritage whose minister, David Mellor, had a seat in the Cabinet. The new ministry was responsible for promoting the arts, sport and the national heritage. To augment the rather meagre funding these areas traditionally received in Britain, Major introduced legislation to set up a National Lottery. This was normal in the rest of Europe but met with some opposition from the clergy. It was feared that, in desperation, poorer people would spend more than they could afford on this activity and that, once again, people were being given dreams of winning easy money rather than earning money by hard work.

The National Lottery was established by Parliament in autumn 1993 and came into operation in November 1994. Its purpose was raise money for good causes. A commercial firm, Camelot, was awarded the contract to operate the Lottery. The 'good causes' were defined as: arts, sports, charities, heritage, celebrating the millennium and the new health, education and environment causes. Appropriate bodies like the Arts Council of England distributed monetary grants. Out of every pound spent on the National Lottery, some 28 pence went to the six 'good causes'. The government got 12 pence in Customs and Excise, 5 pence went to the traders selling tickets, 5 pence to Camelot and 50 pence to prizewinners. This changed on 31st December 2000: the Millennium Commission ceased to exist and the New Opportunities Fund received 33.13 per cent. By September 1998, £4.86 billion had been allocated to projects, many of which were community-based schemes helping to improve the quality of life for everybody by building and strengthening communities. The money distributed helped deprived groups, saved buildings and national treasures, enabled more people to enjoy sports and the arts, and supported initiatives to celebrate the new millennium.

The Lottery proved to be highly successful with an estimated 30 million taking part either as individuals or as members of syndicates. In February 1997, a mid-week draw was introduced. The Lottery drew funds away from the traditional football pools and other sectors of the gambling industry. Some believed that charities were also affected as people turned away from draws held by such bodies for the more spectacular prizes of the Lottery.

Major: 'back to basics' and 'the bastards'

Major's first Heritage Secretary, Mellor, lasted but a few months. He was brought down after the press published details of an affair he, a family man, had had with an actress. As Major later wrote, stories like this became 'a routine'.[36] In May 1993, Michael Mates, a minister at the Northern Ireland Office, resigned over his involvement with Asil Nadir.[37] Nadir, a Cypriot businessman, had given generously to the Conservative Party but fled the country when under investigation by the Serious Fraud Squad. Junior minister Tim Yeo resigned on 5th January 1994, after it became known that he had fathered a child outside his marriage.[38] Lord Caithness, transport minister in the Lords, stepped down after his wife killed herself. In February 1994, Stephen Milligan, MP, died 'in a bizarre ritual'.[39] On 10th July 1994, two Conservative MPs were exposed for agreeing to take payment in return for asking questions in Parliament.[40] The *Guardian* (20th October 1994) accused two ministers, Tim Smith (Northern Ireland) and Neil Hamilton (Consumer Affairs), of taking cash for questions as backbenchers. Smith confessed[41] and resigned, Hamilton was forced out.[42] Some of this was trivial but the problem was that Major had given a speech at the Conservative annual conference in 1993 in which he had urged, 'We must go back to basics ... and the Conservative Party will lead the country back to these basics right across the board'. He later claimed that he was not primarily thinking of private morality, but he did include 'respect for the family and the law. And above all, lead a new campaign to defeat the cancer that is crime.'[43]

It is worth mentioning at this point that Major's régime pushed the trend towards greater acceptance of gays. With his encouragement, on a free vote, in February 1994, Parliament voted to lower the age of consent for gays from 21 to eighteen. This was a move which a segment in his own party strongly disapproved of.

Major continued facing open and muted criticism, leaks and rumours, from within his party over Europe, over his leadership competence and over the general direction of things. In an unguarded remark, on 23rd July 1993, 'utterly exhausted and drained of all energy',[44] he had referred to his Euro-critics as 'bastards' but denied he was referring to Lilley, Redwood or Portillo. He decided to challenge his opponents to 'put up or shut up' by taking the brave step of resigning from the party leadership, an unprecedented act, on 22nd June 1995. Nevertheless, the move had been well planned.[45] Major's opponent in the contest was John Redwood, who had been the Welsh Secretary. In the days that followed, Major came under attack from the traditionally Conservative press and on the day of the vote, 4th July, the *Daily Mail* thought it was 'Time to Ditch the Captain'. Despite some gloomy predictions, Major won a clear victory with 218 to Redwood's 89. There were eight abstentions and twelve spoiled papers.[46] However, he knew that the size of Redwood's vote meant that there would be storms ahead.[47] He reshuffled his Cabinet. Heseltine became Deputy Prime Minister, Malcolm Rifkind replaced Hurd at the Foreign Office and Portillo went to Defence. As the Euro-sceptic right continued to criticise, Major suffered a defector to the left. Former junior minister, Alan Howarth, announced he was joining Labour on the eve of the 1995 Conservative conference. At Christmas, Emma Nicholson, MP, defected to the Liberal Democrats. This reduced Major's parliamentary majority to three. It fell to one on 11th April 1996, when the Conservatives lost the Staffordshire South East by-election to Labour.

Education, Health and Transport

Traditionally, apart from the economy and taxation, very many voters give a high priority to education and health. On both issues Labour kept its lead throughout the period 1992–7. MPs of all parties beat their breasts from time to time about the failure of the British education system, its inability to provide a general education and appropriate vocational training, on a par with those available in other West European countries. That British schools were underfunded could easily be demonstrated. In 1993–4 of the twelve states in the European Union, only four spent less, per student, on primary and secondary education. Ireland spent most, followed by France and Belgium. Over seven years there were three ministers responsible for education: Kenneth Clarke (1990–2), John Patten (1992–4) and Gillian Shephard (1994–7). The uncertainty about policy was revealed by the fact that Clarke was responsible for education and science, Patten for just education and Shephard for education and then, from 1995, for employment as well. All three were products of selective schools and Oxbridge. Shephard, however, had been an Education Officer and Schools Inspector. Most MPs, especially Conservatives, did not use the state system but sent their children to private schools, which generally enjoyed better facilities and more staff. Clarke, like Major, subscribed to a classless society, but after 'classic Fabian agonies' sent his children to fee-paying secondary schools.[48] Blair had presumably gone through the same agonies before sending his son to the grant-maintained Oratory School. The Conservatives sought to undermine local-authority control of the 'state sector' by encouraging opt-outs of schools after ballots by parents. In the period 1992–3 555 did so, but then enthusiasm disappeared. In 1995–6, only 32 voted to leave local authority control and 31 voted against. Arguments continued about the National Curriculum, tests in primary schools (which were introduced by Shephard), standards, teaching methods and provision for the almost non-existent nursery places. Under the Education Act (1993), a national system of inspection under the Office for Standards in Education was introduced. Clarke, under the Further and Higher Education Act (1992), had given the polytechnics and larger higher education colleges the opportunity to call themselves universities.

The Conservatives honoured their 1992 election pledge to award above-inflation increases in NHS funding. However, the electorate remained sceptical about their achievements. The fact was that Britain spent less, relative to population, than other advanced countries. The theory was advanced that Britain could deliver more for less expenditure because the NHS was efficient. This was probably true in relation to the USA, where great disparities existed. It was not true relative to Western Europe, whose services were often better than those in Britain. On 16th May 1996, the British Medical Association warned that hospitals across the country faced financial meltdown and that patient care was being put at risk. Under the National Health Service and Community Care Act (1990) hospitals had the right to become self-governing trusts, outside health authority jurisdiction. GPs became fundholders, that is, they were responsible for their own budgeting. Local authorities were given more responsibility for care in the community. There was concern that there were not enough qualified staff in all areas of health care and that the new trusts would result in higher administrative costs. The new trusts were, as one Conservative critic put it, 'stuffed with Conservative businessmen'.[49] NHS dentistry was gradually dying out as fewer and fewer dentists took NHS patients.

Between 1992 and 1997 Labour had a massive lead over the Conservatives on transport policy. The voters' perception was that private motoring, public buses and rail travel were getting more expensive and the roads and the railways seemed to be deteriorating. Neither government nor opposition would go against the car lobbies. Relative to population, Britain had fewer cars than many European countries, but Britons were more inclined to go by car to work. Labour and the Liberal Democrats advocated taxing car usage rather than car ownership. The two major initiatives by the government were supporting the building of the Channel Tunnel, which was opened on 6th May 1994, and rail privatisation. Under the Railways Act (1995), British Rail was broken up for sale. Twenty-five Passenger Train Operating Companies (TOCs) were awarded franchises to run services. Railtrack Group plc, owned the lines, signalling and control equipment and the main stations. The policy faced much opposition. 'Tory backbenchers, particularly those from the south-east marginals, blanched at the idea',[50] but the policy was pushed forward under Malcolm Rifkind (1990–2), John MacGregor (1992–4), Dr Brian Mawhinney (1994–5) and George Young (1995–7). There was increased anger as several of the new owners sold out to make quick profits on assets they had bought cheaply.

After massive opposition, from some within their own ranks, the opposition, the unions and the public, plans to privatise the Post Office were abandoned.

Northern Ireland: 'into the mists'

On 7th February 1991, when Major was leading a Cabinet committee discussion on possible Iraqi terrorism in London, there was a 'tremendous explosion' outside the window. It was not the work of the Iraqis, but of the IRA. In all, three mortar shells hit Downing Street. There were no causalities. The continuing violence led to pressure from all sides to negotiate a settlement.

On 31st August 1994, the Provisional IRA announced an immediate cease-fire. This was the culmination of a process of open and secret negotiations and followed the Downing Street Declaration of December 1993. The Declaration was signed by Major and Albert Reynolds (the Irish Taoiseach), who pressed ahead despite the scepticism of some of their colleagues.[51] Essentially, both sides recognised that there would be no constitutional changes to the status of Northern Ireland without the consent of its people. Britain recognised that the people of

Ireland alone, by agreement between the two parts, had the right to self-determination on the basis of consent, to bring about a united Ireland, if they wished to do so. The Declaration offered those associated with paramilitary violence a route into the political process through democratically mandated parties, which were committed to peaceful methods. The Protestant 'Combined Loyalist Military Command' followed with a cessation of military operations, on 13th October 1994. The next step was the publishing of *A New Framework for Agreement* by John Bruton, who had replaced Reynolds, and Major on 22nd February 1995. The two governments committed themselves to comprehensive negotiations involving the Northern Ireland parties, the outcome of which would be submitted for democratic ratification through referenda in both parts of Ireland.

Within the Ulster Unionist community, these moves heightened fears that the Province was being handed, inch by inch, to the South. James Molyneaux, Deputy Grand Master of the Orange Order, who had led the (main) Ulster Unionist Party since 1979, had a difficult task holding his party together. Aged 75, he was ousted, in August 1995, and was replaced by David Trimble, a law lecturer at Queen's University, Belfast. There were rumblings about the increasing role of the government of the Irish Republic and of the USA.

In December 1995, the British and Irish governments established an international body, to provide an independent assessment of the problems involved in 'decommissioning' the weapons held by the IRA and the Loyalist militias. This body was chaired by US Senator George Mitchell of Maine, assisted by Former Finnish Prime Minister, Harri Holkeri, and retired Canadian General, John de Chastelain. Mitchell was President Clinton's 'economic envoy' to Northern Ireland appointed in August 1994. In November 1995, Clinton and his wife, Hilary, visited both parts of Ireland and were warmly received. This was the first visit of a US President to the North. Between the cease-fires and that visit, the IRA had carried out 148 'punishment' attacks, and the Loyalists 75.[52] There had been nine fatalities due to the 'Troubles' in 1995, compared to 61 in 1994 and 84 in 1993.[53] Peace was a relative term.

On 9th February 1996, the IRA announced an end to its cease-fire and within an hour a lorry packed with explosives detonated at Canary Wharf in London, killing two people and injuring over one hundred.[54] Nevertheless, the search for a peace settlement acceptable to all went on, and all the parties in Northern Ireland, except for Sinn Féin, started talks with the British and Irish governments for an election to a forum. The election took place on 30th May 1996, with Sinn Féin having dropped its boycott and gaining its best result of 15 per cent. John Hume's SDLP gained 21 per cent. On the Loyalist side, Trimble's UUP attracted 24 per cent and Paisley's DUP, nearly 19 per cent. Mitchell and his two colleagues then held talks with all the parties, except Sinn Féin, which had been excluded because its lack of a complete and unequivocal cease-fire. Meanwhile the violence continued. On 15th June 1996, the commercial heart of Manchester was destroyed by a 3,300 lb IRA bomb, which injured 220 people. The British military HQ in Northern Ireland was attacked on 7th October 1996, causing one death and injuring 30 people.

Both Major and Bruton were running out of time. From 1993 Major had found Northern Ireland the most time-consuming problem of his premiership,[55] which, in a way, is outrageous. It was also extremely costly to the British taxpayer and to the economy. Major had gone 'into the mists'[56] of Northern Ireland and did not find his 'bright hopes' fulfilled.

Economic and Political Change in Eire

Like Britain, Southern Ireland had changed enormously over the previous 30 years. In 1966, half the population was still rural. By the mid-1980s, nearly two-thirds lived in towns. Only 5 per cent of the labour force were women in 1961. By 1990, it had risen to 32 per cent. According to the EC publication *Social Europe* (3/93), the share of women among computer professionals and related occupations, in 1990, was 27 per cent, compared with only 20 and 22 per cent in the UK and Germany respectively. However, in general, activity rates for women remained below the EC average. Symbolic for the changing place of women was the election of Ireland's first woman President in 1990. This was Mary Robinson (b. 1944) who was also Ireland's youngest president. A professor of law at Trinity College Dublin, she stood as an independent backed by the Labour Party. When Robinson retired to take up a UN job, Mary McAleese (b. 1951) replaced her. President McAleese was also a law professor, well-known television presenter and mother of three. She was inaugurated on 11th November 1997 as eighth President.

The shape of the economy was changing as old labour-intensive industries such as clothing and textiles declined, and computing, electronics and chemicals expanded. Foreign firms accounted for two-thirds of output and 40 per cent of employment. After easing in the 1960s and then being reversed in the 1970s, net emigration had resumed in the 1980s. In the 1990s, Ireland started to hold on to its population and by the end of the century there was a labour shortage. By this time, Ireland was Europe's leading exporter of computer software accounting for about 60 per cent of PC software and nearly one-third of PCs sold in Europe.

After the election of 1992, Fianna Fáil formed a coalition with Labour. Labour had gained 31 seats, its highest number ever. But this coalition broke up in December 1994, partly due to the personal antagonism between Labour's Dick Spring (Foreign Minister) and Taoiseach Albert Reynolds. Spring then led his party into a coalition with Bruton's Fine Gael and the small Democratic Left. This coalition felt reasonably confident about its re-election on 6th June 1997; however, this hope was dashed. Labour, in particular, lost heavily. Was this due to disillusionment within its broad constituency that it was merely opportunist, having partnered both main parties within the life of a single parliament? Perhaps potential Labour voters abstained. Turnout was only 66.8 per cent, that is, 2 per cent lower than in 1992. On the other hand, Fine Gael benefited from its time in government, gaining ground. Broadly speaking, Fianna Fáil and its small would-be partner, the Progressive Democrats, came out as the tax-cutting parties. The Progressive Democrats pushed the idea that they were the party of the enterprise culture. Fianna Fáil came out strongly on law and order at a time of concern over rising crime. Northern Ireland entered the election, with Fianna Fáil attacking Bruton for alleged leadership failure over the national issue. Bertie Ahern met Gerry Adams at the start of the campaign. Sinn Féin garnered enough votes to gain one seat in the Dáil. The election resulted in the formation of a

Fianna Fáil–Progressive Democrat government with Ahern as the new Taoiseach. He was elected by 85 votes to 78. His majority included three maverick independents. Progressive Democrat leader, Mary Harney, emerged as Minister for Enterprise and Employment. History was made in that Harney was also appointed Deputy Prime Minister, the first woman to hold this post. Altogether, 23 women were elected to the 166-seat chamber, the same as in the outgoing Dáil. Dick Spring, the hero of 1992, resigned as Labour leader. He had led the party since 1982. Ruairi Quinn (b. 1946) replaced him. Quinn was a former finance minister and an architect by profession. Labour accused the new government of neglecting public services, which were in need of renewal. EU figures showed that, in 2000, government expenditure as a percentage of GDP would be only 33.2 per cent in Ireland as compared with 45.2 per cent in Holland, 54.2 per cent in Denmark and 56.4 per cent in Sweden.

Election 1997: Conservatives in 'dreadful tangle'

As he went into the election, Major could claim he had not just coasted along after Thatcher's departure. He had ditched the detested poll tax, introduced the *Citizen's Charter*, established the Heritage Department and the National Lottery. He had granted the polytechnics university status. He had attempted to bring more women into top jobs in public life. All of these steps proved popular. He had also lifted the veil just slightly on the security and intelligence services. Abroad he had signed the Maastricht Treaty and allied Britain with the UN on Kuwait and Bosnia. He had played a positive role in negotiations on Northern Ireland. Finally, despite Britain's fall in the international wealth table, the economy appeared to be doing well. Would this be enough to see him through? The boy from Brixton must have known that he had done nothing to change the great disparities in wealth and income during his and his party's period in office. The top 5 per cent of the population had owned 36 per cent of the marketable wealth in 1981, 35 per cent in 1991 but 39 per cent in 1996.

Major hung on to 1st May 1997, the last possible day allowed by the constitution.[57] He hoped that a long campaign would expose Labour's policy weaknesses[58] so he fought the longest campaign in living memory. However, according to one leading Conservative, the electorate 'wanted the Tories out' and by hanging on they made the actual outcome worse.[59] Major later admitted his party was afflicted with 'bickering, squabbling and back-stabbing', which did more damage than Blair.[60] According to another Conservative, Ian Gilmour, Major tarnished still further his government's reputation by announcing that Parliament was to be prorogued two weeks before it was dissolved. This pre-vented the publication of Sir Gordon Downey's Report on the allegations of sleaze made against a number of (mainly Conser-vative) MPs. 'As a result, the first two weeks of the campaign were almost entirely concerned with sleaze, an issue which could only do the Government harm.'[61] By refusing to stand down at Tatton, Neil Hamilton gave the opposition parties plenty of am-munition. Their candidates withdrew, when the much-respected BBC war correspondent, Martin Bell, opposed Hamilton as an independent. This was possibly a factor encouraging tactical voting elsewhere by Labour and Liberal Democratic voters to vote for candidates most likely to defeat the Conservatives. In Scotland, Allan Stewart was forced to resign as candidate following allega-tions about his private life. As Major later wrote, 'Further blows followed.'[62] The candidate at Beckenham, Piers Merchant, aged 46, seeking re-election, was exposed for having an affair with a seventeen-year-old Soho hostess. He refused to give up and won by a narrow margin. He returned to the hostess 'and did – at last – resign.'[63]

According to Lamont,[64] the Conservatives had got themselves into a 'dreadful tangle' over Europe. In principle, their posi-tion 'was formally no different from that of Labour.'[65] Both leaders sounded more sceptical about Europe than they had previously, but neither Major nor Blair would commit their parties to Euro-scepticism. Under pressure from the Referendum Party, Con-servative candidates broke ranks and many issued manifestos at variance with official policy. Paul Sykes, a Yorkshire millionaire, announced that he would give £2,000 to every Conservative Association whose candidate undertook to vote against a single currency.[66] There are differing views about the importance of Europe as a campaign issue, but it certainly helped to expose continuing Conservative divisions, and voters traditionally punish divided parties. Labour was keen to focus on education, the NHS and pensions – three areas where normally it scored high marks among the electors. As the economy was doing relatively well, these issues gained more attention during the campaign. Another, secondary, issue, was the state of the privatised railways. South West Trains, which had cancelled numerous services because they had sacked too many drivers, had come in for much adverse publicity. 'London voters were unimpressed by a promise to privatise the Underground.'[67]

With the rise of the mass media, party organisation is not regarded as important as in earlier times, but organisation should not be underestimated especially when small numbers of votes can make a big difference. Labour usually suffered from a poorer organisation than the Conservatives. However, there were reports of Conservative organisations having 'atrophied'.[68] As Labour's proposals were very moderate, there was an absence of the 'Fear Factor,'[69] which on many occasions had put off middle-class voters from supporting Labour. Labour committed itself to Conservative spending plans for the first two years of a Blair administration. Labour also took a tough stance on law and order, traditionally a weak area for Labour. Labour did commit itself to introducing a minimum wage and accepting the Social Chapter of the EU. Labour had made election gaffes in the past and Major kept his figures crossed. Blair obliged when he likened a future Scottish parliament, which Labour advocated, to an English parish council.[70] Luckily for Labour, this was of little importance south of the border. Gordon Brown seemed to advocate widespread privatisation by announcing he would draw up a list of all public assets with a view to disposing of 'inessential' elements.[71] This was not popular with the electors and even less so with Labour activists.

Most people in Britain get their information from television – television had to be impartial. No less than thirteen parties qualified for a national television broadcast by putting forward more than 50 candidates.[72] All three political leaders – Major, Blair and Ashdown – performed well. The press was a different story. Labour had courted, and been courted by, the media tycoons, Rupert Murdoch and Lord Rothermere. Murdoch's *Sun* came out for Labour, reversing its 1992 position, his *Sunday Times* for the Conservatives and his *Times* for Euro-sceptics of all parties. Rothermere's London *Evening Standard* supported Labour but his *Daily Mail* took a strongly Euro-sceptic line.[73] The *Mirror* retained its traditional pro-Labour stance and the *Daily Telegraph* stayed with the Conservatives. The *Guardian* supported Labour. The press was more pro-Labour than at any previous election.

Apart from a rogue poll in the *Guardian*, the polls consistently pointed to a Labour victory. Labour had to fear apathy among it own voters in these circumstances. When the polls closed on 1st May 1997, only 71.4 per cent of those eligible had recorded their votes in mainland Britain. This represented the lowest turnout since 1935. Those who did vote inflicted on the Conservatives their worst defeat since 1832 and gave Labour its best ever win in terms of seats – it won even more than in 1945. However, it was not quite the landslide in popular opinion that it appeared to be. Labour got fewer votes, in absolute terms, than the Conservatives did in 1992 (see below). And Labour actually gained higher percentages of the vote in 1951, 1955 and 1959 (48.8, 46.4 and 43.8 respectively), and on higher turnouts, lost those elections. As the winning party, it also gained higher percentages in 1964 and 1966 (44.1 and 47.9), without gaining nearly as many seats. With 43.2 per cent (34.4 per cent in 1992), Labour had massively increased its share of the vote in 1997. The Conservative share had dropped as dramatically, from 41.9 to 30.7 per cent. The Liberal Democratic share actually declined slightly, from 17.8 to 16.8 per cent. The Labour wave swept through the whole kingdom. The mood of the country seemed to have been a strong desire to get rid of the Conservatives. From the seats the Liberal Democrats won, it is clear that some Labour supporters voted for them in an effort to defeat the Conservatives. On the same basis, some Liberal Democratic voters had given Labour the benefit of the doubt. The Conservatives suffered from some of their own people staying at home. Labour also suffered from apathy especially where Labour looked certain to win. In absolute terms, the Labour vote had increased from 11.5 million to 13.5 million. The Conservative vote declined, from over 14 million to 9.6 million. The Liberal Democratic vote slipped from just under 6 million to 5.2 million. The Conservatives had lost ground everywhere. They had been completely ejected from Scotland and Wales, and also lost in the south of England. The SNP and PC had attracted 782,580 votes as against

783,991 in 1992. Yet the SNP doubled the number of its seats.

What of the alternatives to the big three? The Referendum Party was completely routed. It did, however, attract the most votes – 810,778 – of the minor parties. Its rival, the UK/Independence Party received 106,019. With 2.7 per cent of the poll, the Referendum Party did better in England than Scotland or Wales. Its best result was 4,923 votes (9.2 per cent) at Harwich. Many of its candidates collected more votes than their leader, Sir James Goldsmith, who attracted only 1,518 (3.45 per cent) and lost his deposit at Putney. There were few places where the Referendum Party could have influenced the result. If, as seems likely, it attracted more Conservative than Labour votes, it *possibly* influenced the outcome at Harwich, where Labour's majority was only 1,216 and in six other constituencies won by Labour. It possibly helped the Liberal Democrats win Eastleigh, Lewes and Winchester. That Goldsmith's cash had some impact is revealed by the UK/Independence Party's results. Its candidates usually garnered fewer votes than those of the Referendum Party. It probably attracted the same sort of voters, though its stand on Europe was clearer than that of the Referendum Party. Nigel Farage gave it its best result at Salisbury – 3,302 votes (5.72 per cent). The Referendum Party did not field a candidate there. Only at Torbay did it possibly affect the outcome. Without competition from the Referendum Party, it took 1,962 votes (3.68 per cent). The Liberal Democratic victor's majority was just twelve.

The Greens did poorly, their best vote being 2,415 (5.48 per cent) at Stroud, as did the Liberals, a splinter party, whose best result was at Liverpool West Derby (4,037 or 9.58 per cent). The far-right BNP made little impact, its best results being in the 1930s hunting grounds of the British Union of Fascists. In Bethnal Green, it attracted 3,350 votes or 7.5 per cent. On the left, the most important challenge came from Scargill's Socialist Labour Party, nine of whose 57 candidates got into four figures. The best result was Imran Khan in East Ham. He gained 2,697 votes (6.78 per cent), probably helped by the Asian community. In Scotland, the Scottish Socialist Alliance (SSA) gained 3,639 votes (11.09 per cent) in Glasgow, by far its best vote.

The number of women MPs doubled from 60 to 120, 101 of them Labour, fourteen Conservative, three Liberal Democrat and two SNP. Would this massive increase of women prove to be some kind of turning point for the future of politics and society?

The Commons had become much younger. Labour's Clair Ward (Watford) was only 24. For the first time, two openly gay candidates, Ben Bradshaw and Stephen Twigg, were elected in the Labour interest, which reflected changing attitudes in society. The ethnic minorities secured increased representation. All outgoing Labour MPs from ethnic minorities were re-elected. They were joined by Marsha Singh (Bradford West), Dr Ashok Kumar and the first Muslim, millionaire businessman, Mohammed Sarwar (Glasgow Gowan). The only Asian Conservative MP, Nirj Deva, was defeated at Brentford and Isleworth. Labour's Oona King (Bethnal Green and Bow) became the second black woman MP. According to the *Jewish Chronicle* (9th May 1997), a survey of 'the 20 known Jewish MPs' revealed thirteen Labour (eight in 1992), six Conservative (eleven) and one Liberal Democrat (one).

In Northern Ireland Sinn Féin achieved its best result in 40 years, gaining 16.1 per cent. Gerry Adams seized West Belfast from the SDLP and Martin McGuiness defeated the DUP in Mid-Ulster. This result would put pressure on Blair to grant concessions.

Major saw his Cabinet colleagues – Forsyth, Lang, Newton, Portillo, Rifkind and Waldegrave – and former colleagues, Lamont and Mellor, cut down. He took the blame and concluded, 'When the curtain falls it is time to get off the stage, and that I propose to do. I shall advise my parliamentary colleagues to select a new leader of the Conservative Party.' With that he left Downing Street to tender his resignation to the Queen and then go on to the Oval to watch some cricket.[74]

14 New Labour in Office

Blair's Government

In forming his Cabinet of 22, Blair appointed his colleagues to the posts they had shadowed. This was more important given their lack of ministerial experience and it also avoided controversy. Prescott was styled Deputy Prime Minister with responsibility for the environment, transport and the regions. Gordon Brown was appointed Chancellor of the Exchequer, Robin Cook took over at the Foreign Office and Jack Straw at the Home Office. Lord Irvine became Lord Chancellor. As expected, David Blunkett took over Education and Employment, and George Robertson Defence. The sensitive post of Health Secretary went to Frank Dobson. Dr Jack Cunningham was given another sensitive post – Agriculture, Food and Fisheries. Another key appointment, given Labour's pledge on devolution, was Donald Dewar at the Scottish Office. Five women were appointed – a record – compared to two in Major's Cabinet. Blair's women took over posts usually reserved for men. Thus Ann Taylor was appointed Leader of the Commons, Dr Mo Molam, Secretary of State for Northern Ireland and Harriet Harman Social Security Secretary. Only Clare Short, at International Development, took over a post previously occupied by a woman. The most senior appointment which went to a woman was Margaret Beckett as President of the Board of Trade and Secretary of State for Trade and Industry. Nineteen women were ministers (out of 89) outside the Cabinet, which was also a record. Another big difference with the outgoing régime was that no less than nine members were Scots, as against four in Major's Cabinet, and two were Welsh. And whereas seventeen members of the Major team of 23 were Oxbridge graduates, only five of the new Cabinet were. Eleven Blair members were graduates of provincial English universities or polytechnics and six had graduated from Scottish universities. No less than sixteen members of the outgoing

Cabinet were products of public schools, four of them Eton, but only nine members of the new Cabinet had studied at Head-masters' Conference (HMC) public schools. However, at least sixteen had attended selective schools (see Table A 15). In terms of their education, Blair's Cabinet could be seen as more representative of the provincial middle classes than the outgoing régime, but they were not so representative of the broad masses of the people who had elected them.

MPs from the new immigrant communities were not included in Blair's Cabinet, but Paul Boateng was appointed as a junior minister at the Department of Health. Keith Vaz, who came from Aden, served as Minister of State at the Foreign Office from October 1999. One other difference from previous governments was that there were open gays in it. Heritage Secretary, Chris Smith, had publicly proclaimed his homosexuality years before. Outside the Cabinet, Peter Mandelson, Minister without Portfolio, and Nick Brown, were the most prominent gay ministers. Both joined the Cabinet later. Labour's most prominent gay woman was Angela Eagle, Under-Secretary of State in the Department of Social Security.

The Parliamentary Labour Party was less working class, in terms of occupation, than ever before, and relied heavily on recruits from the public sector, especially teaching and local government. A record number of Labour MPs, 66 per cent, were graduates, and, in terms of the nation's universities, the Parliamentary Labour Party was more representative than the majority party in previous parliaments. Out of 418 Labour MPs, 192 had no pre-vious parliamentary experience, which must have made it easier for the leadership to keep their followers 'on message'. In any case, Blair had a government, which included nearly 90 MPs, giving him a relatively large inner circle of core supporters.

Having gained office Blair and his team had to address the problem areas they had campaigned so vigorously about: the NHS, education, constitutional reform including devolution, 'fighting crime and the causes of crime', and the transport system. Like his predecessor Blair faced the continuing problem of Britain's role in the EU, the Balkans and Northern Ireland. The government's hands were tied on many issues because it had agreed to keep to the spending plans of the previous government.

William Hague and his Team

With the announced departure of John Major the Conservatives had to elect his replacement as soon as possible. Given other retirements and the defeat of so many leading Conservatives, the choice was limited. Five candidates decided to let their names go forward and, after three ballots, William Hague defeated Kenneth Clarke by 94 to 70 votes of Conservative MPs. In Conservative terms Hague appeared in the centre compared to Clarke's 'left-wing' image and the other key contender, John Redwood's, 'right-wing' image. Hague was not very well known among the public, having served briefly in Major's Cabinet as Welsh Secretary. He had the advantage of youth, being only 36. Another possible advantage was his Yorkshire background. The son of a local businessman, he went from Wath-on-Dearne Comprehensive School to Magdalen College, Oxford, from where he went to INSEAD Business School, France, and then on to a post with Shell UK. Elected to the Commons in 1989, he had held a number of junior ministerial appointments under Major. His election was a remarkable personal achievement. However, Hague found it difficult to make an impact on the public in spite of his sometimes powerful performances in the Commons. Some thought his physical appearance, including his baldness, did him no good; others found his voice irritating. He had his work cut out for him to construct an able and balanced shadow cabinet. Among his key appointments in the run up to the general election were: Michael Portillo (b. 1953), Shadow Chancellor; Ann Widdecombe (b. 1947), Home Office; Francis Maude (b. 1953), Foreign and Commonwealth; Michael Ancram (b. 1945), Conservative Party Chairman. They all had previous ministerial experience. In fact, Hague's team had considerable experience both of government and outside politics. Nevertheless, they came across as a bit stuffy. Perhaps it helped a little that eight of them admitted, in autumn 2000, to having tried cannabis. This threw Widdecombe, who had been proposing 'zero tolerance' for drugs users, but made them appear a little more human.

Hague continued to face divisions within his party, which did appear to tilt to the right especially on Europe and asylum seekers. It was criticised by former leader Major and by Clarke and Heseltine. Hague had also to put up with ghosts from the past and defections. Jonathan Aitken, the former Cabinet Minister, was sent to prison for perjury and perverting the course of justice. Lord Archer had to withdraw from the race to become the Conservative candidate in the London mayoral elections after being exposed as a liar. Former minister and MP, Neil Hamilton (see Chapter 13), lost his law suit against Harrod's owner Mohamed al-Fayed and was left with over £1m to pay in costs. Al-Fayed had alleged that Hamilton had corruptly taken money from him to put questions in Parliament and the jury believed him. In December 1999, it was announced that a former Conservative front-bench spokesman for London had defected to Labour. This was Shaun Woodward, MP for Witney, a former BBC producer, who had masterminded Major's 1992 electoral victory. Woodward claimed that Hague had thrown away John Major's 'sensible' wait-and-see policy on the euro and described the party's guarantee to cut the tax burden as 'reckless'. He was also critical of the party's stance on gays.

Despite the criticism of Hague, the Conservative Party did improve its standing in the local government elections of May 1999 and in the election to the European Parliament in June (see Table A 3). Although the Conservatives recovered only about half the representation lost to them in the previous elections for the same seats in 1995, the results were seen as strengthening Hague's hand against his critics. Hopes of a revival because of the government's difficulties over the asylum problem, the 'revolt' against the tax on fuel in September 2000, the EU and Blair's problems within his party, gave only temporary success. By the end of 2000, Hague did not seem able to make enough progress to win the election to come. The trouble was, his party had been in office for over eighteen years during which time public services had got worse. The voters were not too impressed by Blair's efforts but could they forget the Thatcher/Major legacy?

NHS: 'Blair in the doghouse'?

Under Dobson and then Alan Milburn, the NHS remained beset by problems and controversy just as it had done under Major and earlier administrations. Britain had simply not been investing enough in the NHS to enable it to remain a modern service

on a par with the rest of Western Europe. A conference of top
specialists, in 1999, claimed that Britain's cancer treatment
programme was poor relative to other advanced countries.[1] The
Office of National Statistics reported that in 1998–9, winter deaths
of the elderly were the highest for ten years.[2] A real test of the
situation came in the winter of 1999–2000 with the outbreak of
a flu epidemic. The NHS could not cope. Scotland seemed to
be hit harder than England and Wales but everywhere there
were reports of operations being cancelled so that beds could
be re-allocated for incoming flu patients. The outbreak led to
renewed argument about the inadequate funding of Britain's
much-vaunted NHS. Lord Winston, the fertility pioneer and
Labour peer, was severely critical of the way the health service
was going. 'Do we want a health service that is steadily going to
deteriorate and be more and more rationed and will be inferior
on vital areas such as heart disease and cancer, compared to
our less well-off neighbours?' A poll published in *The Observer*
(16th January 2000) revealed that 'Blair [was] in the doghouse
on waiting lists'. Only 47 per cent of those polled trusted the
government to develop the right policies for the NHS while
49 per cent did not trust the government. This did not help
the Conservatives very much as only 25 per cent trusted them
and 69 per cent did not trust them. As the paper pointed out,
the NHS compared badly with those in other developed countries.
Britain had one doctor for every 625 people. In France it was
one for every 344. In 1997, Britain spent £869 per head
on health, compared with £1,245 in the Netherlands, £1,490 in
Germany and £2,559 in the USA. Women with breast
cancer had a 67 per cent chance of living more than five years,
compared with 80 per cent in France, Sweden or Switzerland.
Blair told television viewers on 16th January that his aim was
to increase British spending on health to reach *the EU average*
within six years. This was not a firm commitment but based on
the assumption that the economy would continue to grow. If
realised, it would still leave Britain behind France, Germany
and other more affluent European states. In another blow to the
credibility of the NHS, figures showed that over 5,000 patients
died each year from infections they picked up in hospital.[3] By
September 2000, it was reported that 2 per cent of hospital
beds had been lost in the previous year. Nearly 4,000 beds had

gone because of a lack of nurses or funds. The British Medical Association believed the hospital building programme actually involved bed losses. Hospitals built with private funds would see to this.[4] The trouble was that nurses and doctors could not be trained overnight. The government was forced to search countries where nurses and doctors were worse off than in Britain in an attempt to recruit more staff. This usually meant countries like India, Pakistan, the Philippines and so on. As Labour's first term drew to a close, Blair and Milburn had to hope the electors would put the blame on eighteen years of neglect by the Conservatives.

'Dr Death' – What's News?

In addition to the shortage of staff, several cases of faulty diagnoses, fatal mistakes and malpractice increased fears about the trustworthiness of medical staff. The worst case that came to light was that of general practitioner, Dr Harold Shipman, who was found guilty, on 31st January 2000, at Preston Crown Court, of murdering fifteen of his patients, all elderly women, at Hyde in Cheshire. He denied all the charges. It was believed he had killed many others. Shipman was the worst serial killer in British history and the most unusual. Police and fellow practitioners were baffled by the doctor's motives, as he appeared a normal, well-liked individual. Questions started to be asked about the freedom of doctors to sign death certificates for their own patients, the role of coroners and so on. On the following day, the case momentarily swept everything else from the headlines and this could lead one to ask, 'What is news?' *The Times*'s factual headline was, 'Britain's worst serial killer'. The *Daily Telegraph* speculated, 'Evil GP may have killed 150'. *The Sun* claimed to know, 'He killed 141'. Equally certain, The *Daily Mail* claimed, '150 The Chilling Death Toll of Dr Shipman'. The *Daily Record* out-did them both, '1000 That's the true murder toll of Doctor Death warns coroner'. Not to be out-done, The *Express* asked, 'Shipman: Did He Murder 1,500?' By comparison, *The Mirror* was almost staid, 'Dr Death'! *The Independent* avoided speculation about figures, 'The serial murderer who had no motive, save the desire to play God'. And the *Financial Times*? 'Weak euro troubles ECB', and 'EU warns Austria over talks with far right party'. The *Financial Times* report on the worries by the European Central Bank about the euro currency carried implications for every person in Britain in that if interest rates went up in Euroland there could be problems for the British economy. One other important news item was the renewed crisis in Northern Ireland, which was stoked up on that day by the publication of the official report on the decommissioning of weapons by the paramilitary groups there. It revealed, as expected, that no weapons had been handed over to the official body responsible for their destruction. This put pressure on the Ulster Unionist leader, David Trimble, to leave the Ulster government and posed the threat of renewed violence. Obviously, the Shipman case was of great interest and a cause for public concern. But did it merit such blanket coverage to the exclusion of other important issues? By the beginning of 2001 Shipman was in the news again when an official report estimated that over 25 years he had killed up to 300 of his patients.

Education: Standards Improving?

> Primary schools are improving dramatically after the Government's insistence that standards will rise only if schools get the basics right in the early years. Test results for 11-year-olds show a leap of 10 per cent in the proportion of pupils reaching the expected standards in maths (up to 69 per cent) and a rise of 5 per cent in English (to 70 per cent) . . . Ministers explain the big improvement by pointing to the new literacy hour, the daily period of reading and writing based on what the Government calls 'tried and tested methods', which was introduced just over a year ago.   (David Blunkett)

Blunkett believed that the numeracy hour, which went nation-wide in 2000 but was in use in most schools in the previous year, had done wonders for children's mental arithmetic. Some were less sure about the claims because science results went up by 9 per cent even though there was no dedicated hour and no target.[5] By the end of the twentieth century, the British government seemed to be more test orientated than ever before. Much of this was due to the work of Chris Woodhead, Chief Inspector of Schools, who retired in 2000. In his final week, a school branded a failure by his inspectors mounted the first legal challenge to the verdict and won 'a historic victory'.[6] In 1999–2000 there were 300 complaints, of which 116 were formal written ones, to the Office for Standards in Education (OFSTED). Of these complaints, 32 were partially upheld and five were totally upheld. OFSTED had inspected 4,520 schools. That much still needed to be done was brought out by a report revealing that British adults were behind those in German-speaking Switzerland and Canada in both reading a newspaper and calculating the advantages of a sale advertisement. The mathematician, Professor Margaret Brown, believed such poor standards among adults had been a cause of the decline of the British car industry compared to that of Germany.[7]

Classroom stress, with an increasing number of reports, exams and outside inspections, was said to be leading to an increase in teacher suicides and there were fears that pupils also were being driven to take their own lives. Such worries were expressed at the conference of the Association of Teachers and Lecturers in 2000.[8]

Blair's government was criticised for not reversing the trend of selling off school land and playing fields to make up the shortfall of funds as parents were expected more and more to raise money for their children's schools. However, unlike previous governments, Labour stipulated that money so raised had to be ploughed back into sport or education.[9]

. . . but not in Maths?

In 2000 a report, *Measuring the Mathematical Problem*, revealed an alarming decline in maths education and blamed the 'dumbing-down' of A levels and GCSE maths exams over the previous ten years. It surveyed 120 university science departments and found half of them needed to give remedial lessons. It claimed that many undergraduates' maths knowledge was, in 2000, equivalent to that of a fourteen-year-old, in 1990. Part of the problem was a lack of qualified maths teachers in schools. However, the *Third International Maths And Science Study* (2000) reported an improvement in England's performance, though it was still placed twentieth out of 38 countries. Science produced better news with England coming ninth out of 38.[10]

In the 1990s, universities around the country were looking increasingly to non-EU students to boost their incomes as they were expected to find ever more funds from non-governmental sources. They worked hard to recruit students from far-away lands. Another variation of securing income from overseas was to set up satellite campuses abroad. Nottingham University reported, in 2000, success in establishing the first branch campus of a British university in Malaysia. It also reported close ties with China, Egypt, Japan, Mexico and Turkey, whose Interior Ministry was planning to send 25 experienced provincial administrators to gain masters degrees.[11] On the positive side, such contacts gave British academics and students a wider vision, helped developing countries to gain skills, enriched universities by bringing gifted foreign scholars to Britain, and, not least, brought in foreign currency. There were dangers too. In 1999, Manchester University stopped selling degree courses to Israel after criticism from an education watchdog, the Quality Assurance Agency (QAA).[12] Another potential problem was that admissions tutors were under pressure to admit foreign students even when, in some cases, their qualifications were below those required of British students. Having accepted foreign students, academics were under strong pressure to ensure that they got their degrees. A third problem was that British host universities could become dependent on political régimes which fell below UN standards on human rights and other issues. The same problem of dependency arose with big donations from business interests. In 2000, Nottingham University accepted a gift of £4.5 million from British American Tobacco plc to fund a school of business ethics. Former Chancellor of the Exchequer, Kenneth Clarke MP, vice-chair of this company and a local MP, negotiated the deal. As a result, the university lost some of its cancer research funding.

In January 2000, it was announced that MIT and Cambridge University were to link up using both public and private funds.[13] British critics of the scheme thought other British universities had been insulted as the deal by-passed the normal competitive bidding procedures. That universities were under enormous pressure is shown by the fact that nearly a third were running 'continuing deficits'.[14] The financial difficulties of students appeared to be increasing. The numbers taking up loans had increased from 28 per cent in 1990–1, when the scheme began, to 64 per cent in 1997–8.[15] Universities did not appear to be opening their doors to those from the lower socio-economic groups.

Scotland and Wales get their Parliaments

High on Blair's agenda was the setting up of a Scottish Parliament and a Welsh Assembly and the reform of the House of Lords. These had been talked about for decades and were approved by referenda in both countries, in the Welsh case by the narrowest of margins. Elections to both bodies took place in May 1999 using a modified proportional representation system similar to that in Germany. This ensures that the parliaments that emerge are roughly proportionate to the votes of each party unlike the old, first-past-the-post system. Had the old system still been in force, the Conservatives would have got no seats in Scotland and only one in Wales despite getting substantial votes.

Under Blair the voting system for the European Parliament was brought into line with that of the other EU countries. But the traditional system was retained for elections to the House of Commons. Although Scotland had retained its own legal, educational and police systems, bank-notes and religion, decisions about Scotland would be made in future more clearly, and openly, by elected Scots politicians. The same was true in Wales. Especially in Scotland, there was a sudden surge of interest in the Scottish identity. Given this, the relative success of the SNP and the achievements of the Irish Republic, it seemed likely that at some point in the future Scotland would go for full independence. As an independent member of the EU, Scotland would have a higher profile without any of the risks involved in being independent. The new Scottish executive decided it wanted to spend more on teachers' pay and help for the elderly, than the central government was prepared to spend in England and Wales.

Lords, 'Czars' and Task Forces

The large, unelected assembly which is the House of Lords played a useful function in the Labour Party in that everyone (almost) could unite in attacking it. This had been so since Labour was founded in 1900. Its abolition had been promised on many occasions. It never happened. In 1998 it comprised 507 life peers, 633 hereditary peers, 26 Lords Spiritual (the archbishops of Canterbury and York and 24 Church of England bishops) and a similar number of Law Lords. The life peers, since 1958 elevated by the Queen on the recommendation of the Prime Minister, were made up of 172 Conservatives, 148 Labour, 44 Liberal Democrats, 120 cross-benchers and 24 others. The hereditary peers reinforced the Conservatives by 300. Only eighteen of them were Labour and 24 admitted to being Liberal Democrats; another 202 sat as cross-benchers. Finally, another 89 admitted to no classification. The Lords could still make a nuisance of themselves to any government by amending non-monetary bills and delaying them for a year. Negotiations between Irvine, the Lord Chancellor, and Cranbourne, Conservative Leader in the Lords,[16] led to the hereditary peers losing their sitting and voting rights except for 92 of their members whom they could elect. This still left Labour outnumbered (see Table A 17) even after Blair had been generous with the creation of new life peers.

Few thought the new composition of the Lords was satisfactory, and Blair promised his reform was just an interim measure. Some of those in it saw it as a source of influence rather than legislative power. The life peers were widely different in their backgrounds and current interests. Some, like Lord Marsh (cross-bencher, 1981), the former Labour minister, were enmeshed in business. He was chairman of British Income Growth Investment Company, Business Newspapers (UK) Ltd, China & Eastern Investment Trust (Hong Kong) and Lopex plc (holding company and media conglomerate). He also had other business interests.[17] The Hong Kong Shanghai Bank Corporation, better known simply as HSBC, was well represented in the upper chamber. Baroness Dunn (cross-bencher, 1990) was its deputy chair and listed six other businesses among her interests. Lord Marshall of Knightsbridge was also a director of

HSBC. Both were members of the Hong Kong Association. At that time Marshall (cross-bencher, 1998) was Chairman of British Airways and listed 24 interests, eight of which he was chairman. Cross-bencher Powell of Baywater (2000) ran neck and neck with Marshall as one of the busiest members of the Lords. He held twenty directorships ranging from Hong Kong Land Holdings and J. Rothschild Name Co. Ltd, to Mandarin Oriental International Ltd and the National Westminster Bank. He also held five 'voluntary posts' including President of the China–Britain Business Council. Lord Paul (Labour, 1996) was another very busy man. He listed 24 interests, some of which were public sector appointments connected with the police and Foreign Office. He was Vice-President, Engineering Employers' Federation and Director, Indo–British Association. By contrast, his fellow Asian colleague, Lord Alli (Labour, 1998) listed 22 directorships in media, property, public relations and music publishing. Also in the media, were Labour's Lord Hollick (1991), chief executive, United News and Media plc and Bragg (Labour, 1998) of London Weekend Television fame. Baroness Mallalieu (Labour, 1991), a practising barrister, was President of the Countryside Alliance, which had been mobilised against proposed legislation to ban fox-hunting.

Blair used life peerages to bring more leaders from the ethnic communities into public life. For example, he nominated the first Sikh, Tarsem King, managing director of Sandwell Polybags and leader of Sandwell Borough Council, to be elevated to the Lords in 1999. Also on the Labour benches was Lord Nazir Ahmed of Rotherham, a well-known member of the Muslim community, who became Chairman of the All-Party Libya group.

What happened to Major's former ministerial colleagues who went to the Lords? Baker listed ten paid interests from printing to chemicals. Forsyth became a Director of Robert Fleming International Ltd and a member of the Council of Aims of Industry. Freeman was appointed Chairman, Thomson (UK) Holdings Ltd and a consultant, PricewaterhouseCoopers. He mentioned three other business interests. Among Howe's many interests were Chairman, Framlington Russian Investment (Luxembourg) and membership of the advisory council of J. P. Morgan and Co., the American bank. Hurd was Deputy Chairman of Coutts and Co., the top people's bank. He had other business interests including acting as advisor to Nippon Life Insurance (Tokyo). Howe's fellow Conservative, Earl of Home, was Chairman of Coutts. Perhaps surprisingly because of his Euro-scepticism, Lamont's business interests stretched across Europe, but he was also chairman, Indonesia Fund and director, Balli Group plc. Lang's business interests took in chairmanship of British American Film Academy Inc., Thistle Mining Inc., European Telecom plc and China Internet Ventures Ltd. He listed other interests as well. Newton listed fifteen bodies that he was associated with. Some of these were clearly charities. Patten was a director of five companies and an adviser to a sixth. Prior ran his family farm but had business interests in India, Kenya, China and the USA. Lord Wakeham listed nineteen interests, most of them commercial. Finally, Lords Waldegrave and Walker were both farmers and both directors of Dresdner Kleinwort Benson and both had other pecuniary interests.

Other members of the Lords, like Morris of Manchester (Labour, 1997), dedicated themselves to unpaid activities. He was President of the Society of Chiropodists and Podiatrists, a director of the British Youth Opera and parliamentary advisor to the Royal British Legion (the war veterans' association). Ashley of Stoke, the former MP, had a number of unpaid appointments like his presidency of the Hearing Research Trust. He suffered from deafness himself.

It is unlikely that the Lords ever had such a large and varied business interest represented within its chamber. In terms of business experience and interests the Lords would seem to be more important than the Commons. This importance would surely be brought to bear in committees of all kinds both, official and unofficial, within and outside the Palace of Westminster.

Lord Marshall was a member of the Chancellor's Task Force on the Industrial Use of Energy and a member of his Standing Committee on European Monetary Union. He was also Chairman of Britain in Europe, the pro-EU/single currency, cross-party group. Under Blair, military images were conjured up as 'task forces' were sent forth to investigate problems. They covered everything from the health hazards from using mobile phones to nutritional standards for school lunches. Some felt these bodies were undermining the authority of the Commons. By December 2000, the government was reported to have set up more than

200 task forces and advisory bodies since taking over. Another way of dealing with a problem was to appoint a 'czar' to sort it out. Most notably Keith Hallawell, a senior police officer, was appointed 'drugs czar'.

Under Attack from Organised Crime

As we saw in the last chapter, there was a widespread perception in Britain that crime was getting out of hand in the 1980s and 1990s. Would Labour's Jack Straw be able to do more than his predecessors to combat it? Most people wanted more 'Bobbies on the beat'. This was easier said than done. Without big, rather than marginal, increases in pay and conditions, the profession was not so attractive. Housing was a particular problem in London for police officers, nurses, teachers and many other public sector workers. Like other public sector employees, the police were constantly in the spotlight, which, even when they had nothing to hide, was often stressful. The police had to face, and rightly so, the Police Complaints Authority, which started work in 1985. The number of complaints was rising. Protection of minorities also enhanced the call for greater transparency, the setting up of a proper system of redress, and recruitment of more police officers from the ethnic communities. In 2000, Tarique Ghaffur was appointed to one of the most senior posts in the Metropolitan Police, Deputy Assistant Commissioner, after a 'meteoric rise' through the ranks of the police service in Leicestershire and Lancashire. From a Punjabi family, Ghaffur came to Britain as a fifteen-year-old from Uganda.[18] Relatively poor pay, constant criticism and the pressure to get results could tempt some officers into corruption, taking short cuts or, alternatively, ignoring crime incidents.

Two murder cases in London brought into question the attitude of the Metropolitan Police to racism. One was the murder of Stephen Lawrence in April 1993, while he was standing at a bus stop in south east London. The other was the killing of Michael Menson, in north London, in 1997. Lawrence was a teenager, Menson was 30, both were black. In the first case, the police were forced to admit they had bungled the investigation. In the second case, they refused at first to regard it as anything other than suicide. The Metropolitan Police's investigation of the Lawrence case was strongly criticised by Sir William Macpherson, who concluded in a report published in February 1999 that, 'The investigation was marred by a combination of professional incompetence, institutional racism and a failure of leadership by senior officers.' Menson's three attackers were eventually tracked down, tried and convicted. In both cases, the families of the victims were responsible for them gaining wide public attention.[19]

When Jack Straw reported on the crime situation in January 2000, he was forced to admit that violent crimes, including mugging, had increased for the first time for some years. Straw said that the Metropolitan Police were afraid to use their right to stop and search suspects, since the Stephen Lawrence Inquiry, for fear of being branded racist.[20] The Police Federation Chairman Fred Broughton agreed. He commented that 'stops and searches are down, street crimes are up. Cause and effect'.[21] Straw took comfort from figures showing a reduction in car theft and burglary.

Britain, like other EU countries, was under attack from beyond its borders. This involved 'people trafficking', drugs, fraud, money laundering, computer crime, contraband, trafficking in stolen vehicles and other crimes. In 1999, the number of people seeking political asylum in Britain topped 71,000, a record and over 50 per cent up on 1998. The backlog of applications awaiting a decision reached 100,000 for the first time. There was growing concern about illegal immigration. In 1991 only 61 people were detected entering the UK clandestinely. In 1996, 616 were detected. By 1999 the figure was 16,000.[22] The number of those not detected was probably much higher. Often they arrived hidden on freight trains or in trucks or with fraudulent documents or false identities. In the summer of 1999, in one incident, immigration officials spotted a group of 50 refugees trying to escape from Willesden freight terminal in north London.[23] In another, 18th June 2000, 58 Chinese were found suffocated in a truck. Such illegal immigrants came mainly from the Indian subcontinent, former Yugoslavia, Romania, China, Congo, Angola, Colombia and Ecuador. 2000 was a record year for asylum seekers. In 2000 Chinese headed the list.

Illegal immigration was usually the result of organised crime and brought crime with it. 'Yardie' gangs, dealing in crack and cocaine, had brought violence to the streets of London, Birmingham, Bristol and Manchester. Their leaders were often Jamaican-born and in 1999 they were responsible for the deaths of thirteen people, with many others injured.[24] These incidents were part of the growing trend of offences in which firearms were reported as having been used. In 1983 there were 7,962 such incidents. The figure had grown to 10,373 in 1990 and 13,951 in 1993. The police used firearms three times in 1983, three times in 1990 and six times in 1993.[25] According to *The Observer* (31st December 2000) figures revealed more than 15,000 firearms offences in 2000, which the paper thought was an under-estimate because of reluctance to involve the police.

The National Criminal Intelligence Service (NCIS) was struggling to cope. Clearly, only closer international co-operation could combat crime. To this end, the NCIS was a member of Interpol and the EU's Europol set up in 1994. According to the NCIS, 'Ethnic Turkish crime groups are believed to be responsible for 90% of all heroin found in the UK.'[26] Most of this came from the 'Afghani area'. The NCIS also reported that West African organised crime groups were mainly active in fraud and drugs. They cost Britain an estimated £3.5 billion a year from fraud. The NCIS believed that Chinese Triads were mainly responsible for trebling credit fraud between 1994 and 1998.[27] Between 20,000 and 40,000 stolen vehicles were exported annually by the end of the century. In 1999 the NCIS received over 14,500 disclosures of suspicious financial transactions.[28]

Rich and Poor

The death, in December 2000, of Nigerian schoolboy Damilola Taylor, who died after being attacked on his way home from school, focused attention again on street crime and social deprivation as a cause of crime. The ten-year-old lived on a North Peckham estate. In the 1991 census, the Camberwell and Peckham constituency had the highest number of council or new town tenants out of 569 constituencies in England and Wales. It came second for the number of unskilled residents, ninth for unemployment, fourth for lone-parent families and had the highest percentage of black population (26.5).[29] There were many such places in the UK where the police got little co-operation for fear of reprisals. It was not just the north–south divide. Glasgow was very much the poor relation of Edinburgh, for instance, and there were wide differences within the greater Manchester area, and within London, between boroughs like Hackney, and Kensington and Chelsea, or in Birmingham, between Edgbaston, and Sparkbrook and Small Heath.

In 1996, 10 per cent of the adult population owned 52 per cent of the marketable wealth (see Table A 10). This gap increased in the first year of Blair's government with a million more people earning less than two-fifths of the national average income. This was the finding of a report commissioned by the Joseph Rowntree Foundation and conducted by the New Policy Institute. The government's reaction was to blame it on the developments under the Conservatives over the previous eighteen years.[30] At the same time, according to the *Independent on Sunday* (12th December 1999):

> The rich got richer last week. City bonuses went through the roof, with 2,500 staff at investment bankers Goldman Sachs sharing £100m in salary top-ups. The extraordinary wealth of celebrities was also highlighted when Manchester United's captain, Roy Keane, broke his team's pay ceiling with a salary of £50,000 a week. Elsewhere in Britain, 2 million children are living in homes where no one has a job ... There are 14 million people living below the poverty line.

In the EU, in the mid-1990s, Britain had one of the highest percentages of people with incomes below 60 per cent of the median.

The government, like its predecessor, put much emphasis on benefits fraud and individuals taking benefits they did not need. According to a government-funded report published in 1999, three-quarters of the 1.7 million people on incapacity benefit were capable of work. Professor Stephen Fothergill of Sheffield Hallam University, who compiled the report, stressed that he was not accusing claimants of fraud, but insisted that most could work. The research revealed that in Britain, 2.5 million people, or 7 per cent of the working-age population, were on incapacity or other sickness benefits. The comparable figure for Germany was 4 per cent, and for France was less than 2 per cent. Only Italy among the large European states had an inferior record, with 11 per cent. In 1999, incapacity benefit was being paid to three times more people than the number twenty years ago. The figures were highest in areas of high unemployment. Previous governments had taken a relaxed attitude to the problem in order to reduce the numbers of officially registered unemployed.

Benefits experts have calculated that money lost to benefit cheats in 2000 could have paid for 100,000 new nurses, 56 new hospitals or 21,000 new homes. On the other hand, it was often forgotten that thousands of people, often retirement pensioners, entitled to benefits were not claiming them. In 1998–9, it was thought that between 13 and 21 per cent of those eligible were failing to claim, leaving more than £4 billion unclaimed.[31] This was not new. Thousands of pensioners were also on reduced pensions because of the failure of the new computer system installed at the Benefits Agency. Many within Labour's ranks thought Gordon Brown was mean not to reinstate the link, cut by Thatcher, between the rise in average earnings and the rise in pensions. Pensioners' organisations lobbied their MPs. By 2001, Brown promised more but not the restoration of the link.

The 'Carnival Against Capitalism', in June 1999, in the City caused shock and fear, apparently taking the police by surprise. It was organised on the Internet to attract environmental pro-testers and opponents of capitalism. The organisers made good use of mobile phones. Similar events took place at the World Trade Organisation meeting in Seattle, in 1999, and again in Prague, in 2000. Would this become a growing movement in the future or would the organisers remain fringe transient groups?

Good Friday Deal in Northern Ireland

Under Blair, the search for peace in Northern Ireland, initiated under Major, gained a new momentum. The popular Dr Mo Mowlam was appointed as Secretary of State for Northern Ireland. In 1999 Peter Mandelson replaced her. On 10th April 1998, Good Friday, the parties in Northern Ireland and the British and Irish governments, reached a comprehensive political agreement. Voters of Northern Ireland and the Republic approved it in simultaneous referenda on 22nd May. In the North 80.95 per cent of those eligible voted and 71.2 voted in favour. In the Republic, on a turnout of 55.59 per cent, 94.39 per cent were in favour. The combined 'Yes' vote in both parts of Ireland was 85 per cent. Blair and Irish Prime Minister, Bertie Ahern, assisted by Major and Clinton, had worked hard for the 'Yes' campaign. However, six of the ten Ulster Unionist MPs opposed this deal, which was backed by their leader David Trimble. The deal led to the setting up of the Northern Ireland Assembly, elected on the basis of proportional representation. The Unionists gained 28 seats, the SDLP 24 and Sinn Féin eighteen. It, in turn, elected a power-sharing government with ministers from all parties represented in the Assembly. Sinn Féin had reversed its long-standing policy of boycotting elected institutions in the North as 'partitionist'. Long negotiations were needed to thrash out the details of the agreement. In December 1999 the new government took office headed by David Trimble with Seamus Mallon (SDLP) as his deputy. Sinn Féin was represented by two ministers out of ten. Martin McGuiness, Sinn Féin's chief negotiator, was appointed Minister of Education. Gerry Adams, Sinn Féin's President since 1983, did not join the government.

Throughout 1998 and 1999, there were minor incidents such as revenge beatings and killings. Drumcree remained a flashpoint. The Protestant Orange Order insisted on its right to parade along the Garvaghy Road, a largely Catholic area, as it had done since 1807. Violence occurred, when the march was banned, in 1996, and again, in 1997. In 1998, the new Parades Commission also banned the march, and more violence erupted. The march passed off peacefully in 1999. Overall, optimism prevailed and economic aid poured into the province. Northern Ireland looked set to have its own parliament and government as it had from 1921 to 1972, when Heath suspended them. The difference was that the new institutions would be inclusive not sectarian.

General John de Chastelain, Canadian head of the disarmament commission set up under the Good Friday Agreement, was increasingly frustrated as no weapons were being handed over. Blair had given assurances that politicians linked to paramilitaries who refused to hand over weapons would not hold office. Trimble had promised his party that he would resign from the Assembly if there was no IRA decommissioning by 31st January. The Unionists had been persuaded to co-operate in the new assembly on the basis that the IRA and other paramilitary groups would 'decommission' their weapons. This did not happen and it led ultimately to the collapse of the Good Friday Agreement.

On 9th January 2000, Mandelson announced his programme of reform for law enforcement in Northern Ireland. Over five years the police force was to become evenly divided between Catholics and Protestants instead of being 90 per cent Protestant. The most controversial measure was the proposal to change the name of the police from the Royal Ulster Constabulary to the Police Service.

After only nine weeks, on 11th February 2000, Mandelson suspended the North Ireland Assembly because of the lack of progress on 'decommissioning'. This largely referred to the IRA, which was supported by Sinn Féin. Sinn Féin would not give any unequivocal assurances that the IRA would ever hand over its weapons to the international commission and refused to say 'the war is over.' There were some that agreed with the Sinn Féin view that as the devolved assembly had been working 'why collapse it?' The SDLP disagreed with the decision.

Given the progress made, few expected renewed violence but this happened in Omagh on 15th August 1998. A car bomb went off which killed 29 people and was the worst atrocity in the history of the postwar 'Troubles'. The bomb was planted by a Republican splinter group calling itself the Real IRA. It was condemned by both sides. Gerry Adams condemned it 'without any equivocation whatsoever'. Other acts of violence followed. According to official figures, a total of 49 people were killed in Northern Ireland after the Good Friday Agreement. A total of 2,422 were injured as a result of terrorist attacks between April 1998 and 10th February 2000.[32] The British government continued its policy of scaling down the military presence in the North, reducing security installations and releasing those convicted of terrorist attacks. By 2001, it was clear that the Real IRA planned a campaign of violence in Britain. In March 2001, it attacked the BBC in London.

Irish in Britain and Elsewhere

One complication for British governments, in relation to Northern Ireland, are the large numbers of people around the world who claim Irish ancestry and an interest in the old country. These are mainly in Australia, Canada, New Zealand, South Africa and, above all, the USA and Britain. Over 40 million Americans claim an Irish connection and organised groups there, such as the Friends of Ireland, seek to influence American actions over Ireland. Speaker Tip O'Neill, Senators Edward Kennedy and Daniel Moynihan, and Governor Hugh Carey of New York took a keen interest in developments in Northern Ireland. In 1977, President Carter was the first US President to promise aid once a settlement had been reached. President Reagan supported the establishment of an International Fund for Ireland, which was set up in 1986 by the Irish and British governments, to promote economic regeneration and reconciliation. President Clinton took a pro-active interest in Ireland, appointing Senator Mitchell his 'economic envoy'. He angered the British government when he granted a visa to Gerry Adams, in January 1994. Adams was fêted as a celebrity.[33] Under the leadership of Speaker O'Neill, the USA pledged an initial contribution of $85 million to the International Fund for Ireland. Along with the financial support provided by the EU, Canada, New Zealand and Austalia, the Fund to 2000, had committed $475 million to some 3,500 projects in largely disadvantaged areas. These projects attracted additional private and public funds totalling $950 million, so that total investment in Fund projects amounted to $1.4 billion by 2000.[34] The IRA also secured funds from private groups the USA.

According to the 1991 census, there were 582,020 people born in the Republic living in Britain. Countless others were from Northern Ireland. Many more were members of families that originated in Ireland. All were potential voters whose views had to be taken into account. Traditionally, they were more likely to be involved with the Labour Party than with the Conservatives. Among the recent examples of Irish success in Britain was the elevation of Baroness Crawley, an 'unpretentious, forthright Wicklow woman' who retained 'her love of Ireland and all things Irish' to the Lords in 1998, and her appointment as chair of the Cabinet Office-based Women's National Commission. A former teacher, she had been a Labour MEP.[35] Another example was the election of Councillor Nick Nolan as leader of Labour-controlled Coventry City Council, in May 2000. A former Lord Mayor of Coventry, he was congratulated by two other Irish-born former Lord Mayors, David Cairns and Don Ewart.

Irish activities in Britain included the 2000 Easter Rising Commemoration in Liverpool which attracted more than 100 people to the Fenian monument outside the city. Brendan Magill gave the oration and criticised the Good Friday Agreement. He said: 'This new Stormont is a British institution and those who sit in it or hold office are lackeys of the people who have ruled Ireland for 800 years.' The commemoration was organised by Republican Sinn Féin.[36]

In various parts of England, there were St Patrick's Day celebrations. The Irish in London were hoping for a parade similar to the one in New York. They hoped that the new Mayor, Ken Livingstone, whose election they welcomed, would inaugurate one. The Federation of Irish Societies said the Irish community in London, 'the biggest in the world outside Ireland,' should lobby together as one organisation. PRO Father Jerry Kivlehan said: 'It is important that we speak with one voice on all issues that matter.'[37]

The Irish in Britain have contributed greatly to British life over the generations. In the arts and in the media, people of Irish birth living in Britain in the period under review, include great actors such as Kenneth Branagh, Michael Gambon and Peter O'Toole, writers such as Edna O'Brien, Sean O'Casey, C. S. Lewis, George Bernard Shaw and William Trevor. In radio and television, it started with Eamon Andrews in the 1950s and then came Terry Wogan, Gay Byrne, Brian Inglis, Frank Delaney, Anthony Clare, Dave Allen, Val Doonican, Gloria Hunniford and Henry Kelly[38] and, of course, Des Lynam.

Very many others from Ireland worked at more humble levels and had a variety of attitudes to their adopted country. As Mary McAleese put it, 'It is not uncommon for the second and third generation Irish people to struggle with the dual identities of being both British and Irish, often finding themselves psychologically at home neither in Ireland nor in Britain.'[39] Surely many agreed with Michael Mannix in his letter to the *Irish Post* (13th May 2000):

I have been reading in the *Irish Post* about no free travel for pensioners who visit Ireland. I am an Irish OAP and have been in Britain most of my life, not because of choice, because Ireland could not give me a living, as a disabled man. I am grateful to Britain for taking me in and giving me a better life and free travel. Only because of Britain millions of Irish who had to leave Ireland have a better life today.

There were thought to be 6 million people of Irish descent in Britain.[40]

Death on the Railways

Concern about safety on Britain's privatised railways continued to grow as a result of four major accidents. Four people were killed and 34 injured when a high-speed train went off the tracks just north of London, on 17th October 2000. In October 1999, there were 31 fatalities at Ladbroke Grove, London, in a rail crash when a train went through a red light. In September 1997, seven people were killed and 150 injured in Southall, London, in a rail collision. There were five fatalities and twelve injuries, in October 1994, when a driver ignored a red light near Cowden, Kent. In the first incident, defective rails were found. Britain's railways were in poor shape. The tracks were often in need of attention, the signalling equipment was no longer modern. In addition, trains on some lines were often delayed or cancelled, coaches were old and fares were high relative to standards on Western European railways. No wonder that the number of passenger complaints of poor service and delays passed the one million mark in 1998. This was an 8 per cent rise on the previous year, Tom Winsor, the Rail Regulator, reported.[41] The tragedy of October 2000 brought near panic and Railtrack, the company owning the lines and signalling equipment, announced a blitz examination of the track throughout the country. The result was rail chaos with cancellations and massive delays. These in turn caused more cross-country road traffic on the already congested highways and byways and even a dramatic increase in internal air travel. There was criticism that nobody at the top of Railtrack had significant railway operating experience.[42] There were also calls for the renationalisation of the railways or parts of them. The disaster of rail privatisation did not deter Blair's government from pushing through part privatisation of Britain's air traffic control system in spite of widespread opposition both within the Labour Party and among the public at large. A rail crash at Selby, Yorkshire, 28th February 2001, causing thirteen deaths and 70 injuries, was not the fault of the rail companies but was caused by a car plunging on to the track from the nearby motorway.

Blair and his Party

Despite a few hiccups Blair had a relatively peaceful term at 10 Downing Street. There were few changes in the Cabinet. In terms of public opinion, he and his party held on to their lead in the polls as no previous party in government had done. He even got the blessing of a fourth child in 2000, becoming the first Prime Minister to increase the size of his family whilst in office. The pundits thought this could only help the Prime Minister. After 1,000 days in office, by early 2001, Blair was in a much stronger position than his three predecessors as Prime Minister, at a similar stage in the political cycle. Within the Labour Party there had been rumblings of discontent especially in 1999 and into 2000, but by traditional standards these were relatively minor.

The biggest revolt Blair faced in the Commons was over reform of the disability benefits system. Despite this revolt Blair suffered much less dissension than earlier Labour Prime Ministers. He brushed aside the resignation of Peter Kilfoyle, a junior defence minister, and long-standing Blairite, in January 2000. Kilfoyle claimed that the government was neglecting its traditional working-class voters.[43] There was also trouble for the Prime Minister in Wales. There he had pushed his man, Alun Michael, to take over as the Welsh Assembly's First Secretary. Michael was voted down in February 2000 and replaced by Rhodri Morgan, a more traditional Labour figure. One of the issues in Wales and the North West was that these and other regions were in danger of loosing EU funds because the Chancellor, Gordon Brown, refused to confirm the matching funds that would trigger payments from Brussels.[44] In another case, many felt that Blair had unfairly supported Frank Dobson, the former Health Secretary, to be Labour's candidate for the new post of Mayor of London and had been unduly hostile to Ken Livingstone, MP and former GLC leader. Worse still for Blair, Livingstone, without organisation, beat Dobson, the Conservative Steve Norris, the Liberal Democrat and an array of other candidates. Livingstone offered a 'left-wing' alternative to Blair, opposing the government's determination to privatise the London underground.

There was also unease in some sections of the party when news came, in January 2001, of three donations of £2 million each from Lords Sainsbury and Hamlyn, and from Christopher Ondaatje. Ondaatje had previously given money to the Conservatives. By this time, Labour had received donations from Lords Levy, Alli and Paul and other entrepreneurers. Worried about this trend, Clive Soley, chairman of the Parliamentary Labour Party, called for state funding of parties as in several other democracies. Blair introduced the Parties, Elections and Referenda Act, which required parties to give details of all gifts of £5,000 or more. The urgency of such legislation was highlighted by the surprise resignation of Blair-associate Peter Mandelson, Northern Ireland Secretary, in January 2001. He was accused of lying about an intervention to the Home Office, to help the billionaire Indian businessman, S. P. Hinduja, in his application for a British passport. An official enquiry exonerated Mandelson. But the Indian received his passport in a much shorter time than was normal after agreeing a £1 million gift for the Millennium Dome, then Mandelson's responsibility. Earlier, another Hinduja brother had received his passport in a shorter than normal period. Both were under investigation for corruption in India about an arms contract. According to *The Times* (1st February 2001), they had employed a previous Conservative immigration minister and Labour's Keith Vaz had close ties with the brothers. The Indians' connections with the Labour élite dismayed many rank-and-file MPs and activists. The brothers did not discriminate against members of any of the three British parties in seeking high-level contacts.

Outside his party Blair was rattled by the fuel tax revolt in September 2000. This started with road hauliers and farmers, influenced by similar events in France, blockading the terminals of the oil companies like that at Ellesmere Port, Cheshire. Some taxi drivers and small businessmen joined the protesters. With the police taking a 'softly-softly' approach and the oil companies not ordering their truck drivers to defy the protesters, the country was very soon on the verge of economic collapse and shortages of food were expected. The government, police and oil suppliers, appear to have been taken totally by surprise. The 'revolt' revealed just how vulnerable modern Britain was to disruption by small groups aiming at strategic targets. The government armed itself with special powers to deal with the situation. After Blair, Prescott and Straw said they would speak with everyone concerned but would not allow the country to be held to ransom, the protesters realised they were in danger of the public loosing patience with them. The revolt subsided as quickly as it had started. Brown refused to make any immediate fuel tax concessions.

What did the voters think about the government's record? In sixteen by-elections held in Great Britain between the general election in 1997 and December 2000, there was only one seat that changed hands. This was due to the defeat of the Conservative candidate in Romsey, 4th May 2000, by the Liberal Democrat. The Conservatives held on to their four other seats where by-elections were held. Labour held its eight seats where it faced by-elections. PC and the Liberal Democrats retained one seat each in by-elections. What was sad about these, and other voting opportunities, was that so many voters failed to use their ballots. As everyone speculated about an election in the spring of 2001, Blair's main fear was that apathy and over-confidence would be greater dangers than Hague's Conservatives.

Liberal Democrats: Goodbye Paddy

The victory of Sandra Gidley in the Romsey by-election, 4th May 2000, was also a victory for Charles Kennedy who was elected Liberal Democratic leader in August 1999. There was surprise and even some sadness when the charismatic Paddy Ashdown announced his retirement as Leader of the Liberal Democrats. He had led the party since 1988. He had guided it from the fringes to the centre of the political stage. In 1987, the Liberals and the SDP had 22 MPs, in 1997 46 Liberal Democrats were elected – ten in Scotland, two in Wales and 34 in England. Blair had treated Ashdown as a serious political partner, having secret conversations with him before the 1997 election, and invited him to join a Cabinet Council after it to discuss constitutional reform. Under Ashdown, the party had fought its way into the European Parliament in 1994 and, helped by the new proportional representation system, increased its membership in 1999 from two to ten. In Scotland the Liberal Democrats joined Labour in a coalition government.

Charles Kennedy was the youngest MP when first elected as an SDP MP in 1983. Educated at Glasgow University and Indiana University (USA), he had worked as a journalist for BBC Highland in Inverness. Kennedy was strengthened by the relative success of Liberal Democratic candidates in the local government elections held on the same day as the Romsey by-election. However, his difficulty was to position his party so that it could appeal to new voters in a positive way, as well as attracting tactical voters from both big parties who would vote Liberal Democrat as the lesser of two evils. One target group was pro-European Conservatives. In November 2000, Bill Newton Dunn, a Conservative MEP, defected to the Liberal Democrats. As the election approached, Kennedy was at pains to emphasise his party's independence of Labour.

Kosovo, NATO and the EU

After spending more than it could afford on defence for decades Britain, like many other states, reduced its defence expenditure after the end of the Cold War in 1990. By the end of the century, its forces had many deficiencies in terms of planning, manpower and equipment. The intervention in Kosovo highlighted both the strengths and weakness of Britain's forces.

The conflict in Kosovo (1998–9) was similar to that in Bosnia. Kosovo was part of Serb-dominated Yugoslavia and in historical/cultural terms very important to the Serbs. However, the bulk of the 1.6 million population were ethnic Albanians and wanted at least internal self-government within Yugoslavia, something they had enjoyed until 1990. The Belgrade régime of Milosovic refused to accept this and resorted to repression, which provoked

resistance by a guerrilla group calling itself the Kosovo Liberation Army (KLA). After the KLA attacked a police patrol, the
Yugoslav security forces killed up to 30 Kosovars in Drenica.[45]
UN, NATO and EU diplomatic activity failed to bring an end to
sporadic fighting and individual killings by both sides, which
occurred throughout 1998 and into 1999. Thousands of refugees
crossed into Albania and Macedonia reporting Serb atrocities
and ethnic cleansing. After repeated warnings from NATO, on
24th March 1999, NATO airstrikes began against Yugoslav military and economic targets continuing until 10th June – the day
before, the Yugoslav military and police had signed an agreement with General Sir Mike Jackson, British Commander of the
NATO Kosovo Force (KFOR). Under the agreement, Yugoslav
forces were to withdraw from Kosovo. KFOR units then occupied
the area. Between 24th March and 25th May 886,000 refugees
left Kosovo,[46] many of them going to Albania and Germany with
smaller numbers going to Britain and other countries. It was
hoped most would return home as conditions improved.

There was criticism of the NATO strikes. Some said NATO
was usurping the functions of the UN even though UN resolu-
tions had expressed concern about 'indiscriminate use of force
by Serbian security forces and the Yugoslav Army which have
resulted in numerous civilian casualties'. Critics also believed
that the damage and casualities caused by NATO could not be
justified. Among the unintended hits were a refugee convoy
near Prizren (14th April), the Chinese Embassy (7th May), the
ethnic Albanian village of Korisa (13th May), a Belgrade hospital,
the Swedish and Swiss ambassadors' residences (19th May) and
a train on Varvarin bridge (30th May).[47] Other critics thought
NATO ground troops should have been sent in earlier. British
pilots had flown 9.6 per cent of NATO's strike sorties and provided a total of 41 of the 829 aircraft used in all operations.[48]
The Defence Committee of the Commons concluded, 'UK pilots
and other aircrew and support staff discharged their mission
with distinction. But aside from its tanker fleet, UK aircraft were
(even compared to their other European Allies) relatively few
in number, delivered few munitions relative even to their small
numbers, and were not well-equipped for the task they faced.'[49]
The Committee also commented, 'Despite some success in
bottling-up Serbian forces, the strikes against fielded forces in

Kosovo unarguably failed in their declared primary objective of averting a humanitarian disaster. The limitations of airpower in pursuit of such humanitarian goals were clearly demonstrated.'[50] The Committee pointed to the importance of the Territorial Army, which was being further reduced in size. It also criticised the deficiencies in NATO's 'information campaign'. The campaign also drew attention to the need for greater EU defence co-ordination. In 2000, Milosevic was forced from office after demonstrations against rigged elections. Democratic elections followed and his party was voted out. Were these events totally unconnected with the NATO campaign? The EU immediately recognised the new leadership and help was given to restore the war damage.

'the greatest threat . . . the idea we ignore the EU'?

In the period 1997–2000 the major developments in the EU were the Amsterdam (1997) and the Nice (2000) treaties, the introduction of the euro, single currency (1st January 1999), the EU reaction to Kosovo and the BSE crisis.

The Amsterdam Treaty discussion started under Major and ended under Blair. The Treaty committed the signatories to granting their citizens more rights as citizens and as consumers, involving their parliaments more closely in EU affairs, and closer co-operation on external affairs.

Major had left Britain unprepared for euro entry and Blair and his colleagues did not push the matter. They set up Britain in Europe with Heseltine, Clarke and Charles Kennedy, but then did nothing to promote the euro. They were opposed by millionaire Paul Sykes and his Democracy Movement and other bodies. Blair's government took a 'wait and see' stance – wait and see whether the euro was a success. This had the disadvantage that Britain was excluded for many of the EU-wide pre-parations and consultations and would still be forced keep in step with the euro-zone states with little say in policy. Britain also appeared cynically opportunist in only wanting to be a fair weather friend to the other twelve euro zone states. Inevitably, Britain was slipping from the inner core of the EU headed by Germany and France. For British business there was uncertainty about the future. The pound gained against the euro in its first year, which led sceptics to believe the euro experiment was flawed. But the low exchange rate of the euro helped exports from the euro states. British industry suffered from the strong pound and around 56 per cent of British exports went to the EU as against about 14 per cent to North America. John Cushnaghan, managing director of Nissan UK, warned that Britain had 'the worst of all possible worlds, as we are competing outside a major currency bloc. The greatest threat lies with the strength of sterling and the idea we can ignore the EU. We need to move closer, and not, as some would have it, move away.' Cushnaghan warned that jobs in the motor trade were at risk. Shadow Chancellor, Michael Portillo, disagreed. *The Times* (19th April 2000) reported him as saying that, since the euro launch, Britain had continued to do well and inward investment had poured in. Unemployment was higher in euro countries like Germany. 'There is no case for the UK to give up the pound.' In fact, Rover collapsed in March 2000, Ford announced it was stopping vehicle production at Dagenham (May) and Vauxhall signed the death warrant for its Luton plant in December 2000. In each case, the management claimed the high strength of the pound was one of the factors involved. Other manufacturers were in difficulties as Britain's de-industrialisation continued.

The Nice Treaty (December 2000) must be seen against the growing Euro-sceptical tone of the Conservative leadership which, to a degree, put Blair and his colleagues on the defensive. They had been dealt a psychological blow earlier in the the year by the rejection of entry into the single currency system by Denmark. After gruelling negotiations ending at 5 a.m. on 11th December, the EU leaders reached agreement on the issues necessary to pave the way for enlargement of the EU. The summit agreed to extend qualified majority voting (QMV) to 29 policy areas and six personnel appointments that previously required unanimity. However, Blair and Cook got what they wanted in that QMV was not extended to the politically sensitive areas of taxation and social security, immigration and border controls, culture, broadcasting, health and education.

The level to which the debate had fallen was revealed when Nice was debated in the Commons on the same day, 11th December. Robin Cook assured the Commons, 'Before the European Council,

Britain had double the votes of Belgium; we now have two-and-a-half times its votes. We had two-and-a-half times the votes of Sweden; we now have three times its votes. We had three times the votes of Denmark; we now have four times its votes – and we have done all that while keeping parity with the four larger countries.' The big five were Britain, France, Italy, Germany and Spain. But these agreed that they would lose one of their two commissioners in 2005. They also agreed that eventually enlargement would lead to an EU of 27 states. The newcomers would be mainly from the former Soviet bloc plus Cyprus, Malta and Slovenia.

Blair told the Commons that day that Britain expected to make a proportionately smaller contribution to the EU budget by 2006. This would be roughly equivalent to those of France and Italy. The question of the much-talked-about rapid reaction force, a proposal made after the crises in Bosnia and Kosovo, was also settled to the satisfaction of the British. It would 'operate only when NATO chooses not to be engaged; secondly, that it be limited to peacekeeping, humanitarian and crisis management tasks; and thirdly . . . the commitment of national assets to any EU-led operation will be based on "sovereign national decisions". Collective defence will remain the responsibility of NATO.' Blair and Cook had disarmed Hague and his colleagues and done so by agreement with their EU partners.

Although all EU states were agreed in principle on enlargement, there would be much hard negotiating ahead before it became a reality. The question of reform of the Common Agricultural Policy (CAP) was still to be resolved and this was vital as several of the proposed new members such as Bulgaria, Poland and Romania had large agricultural sectors.

BSE Attacks Europe

The crisis caused by the outbreak of BSE or 'mad cow disease' showed just how important EU agreement was on standards and regulations in the single market. The 'mystery' disease struck in 1987 causing 446 cases. The number rose rapidly to 2184 in 1988, 7137 in 1989 and 14,407 in 1990. There was a further massive increase in the following years of the century. Ireland,

Switzerland, Portugal, France and Denmark had all registered cases by 1992. Later cases were registered in Belgium, Denmark, Italy and Germany, and outside Europe. As was usual with infections, whole herds were slaughtered. But the Conservative government, the farming community and the meat industry, did not want to admit the scale of the crisis. Ministers like John Gummer dispatched their scientists to the media to reassure the public. Pessimistic scientists such as Richard Lacey, who sought to warn about the possible transmission of the disease to humans, were dismissed as cranks. Later the pessimists were proved right and it was recognised that humans were suffering from a new variant of BSE, Creutzfeldt Jakob Disease (CJD, named after two German scientists). CJD attacked the brain, killing its victim after months of agony. By the end of 2000, there had been 80 known deaths in Britain, mainly of young people. It was thought later that perhaps there had been more but these had been missed due to faulty diagnosis in elderly patients thought to have died of dementia.

The official assurance in Britain stirred up bad feelings when British beef was banned in the other EU states. It helped the Euro-sceptics case to claim discrimination against Britain. Even after Brussels lifted the ban, the French were reluctant to import British beef. However, it was later revealed that French firms secretly continued to import British cattle food after the ban on British meat products had been imposed. By 2000, French beef faced bans in many states and French citizens were dying from CJD. There were even claims within France that the danger had been played down there too. One of France's leading scientific advisers on BSE believed that her country had thousands of undiagnosed cases, and infected animals could have entered the food chain. Professor Jeanne Brugère-Picoux said that although France had officially registered 75 cases of BSE in the past ten years, she believed the real figure to be 'far higher than that'. Infected French beef could have entered Britain.[51] It was again a case of putting public health at risk to appease vested interests.

In February 2001, British farmers were dealt another savage blow when an outbreak of foot-and-mouth disease, the first since 1967, was registered. The outbreak, which engulfed the land, led to renewed doubts about intensive farming and its propensity to spread diseases more rapidly than old-style farming.

Into the Twenty-first Century

It was only to be expected that as the new century got nearer there would be greater hopes and greater fears about the new millennium. At the official level, the government went ahead with the Millennium Dome project, commissioned by the previous government. It was built on wasteland in south London. It was supposed to celebrate Britain's spiritual, intellectual and material achievements, and reveal its creativity. Of course, it was also hoped to enlighten and entertain the millions of expected visitors. It ran into difficulties from the start. It went well over budget and failed to attract enough visitors. Critics thought the money would have been better spent on more projects (of which there were many funded by Lottery money) up and down the kingdom. The Dome was a disappointment for the government but not a disaster. Another disaster which did not occur was the millennium bug. There was widespread fear in official circles that there would be computer failures due to machines not being able to cope with the change in date. The government co-ordinated a programme to deal with this problem and disaster was avoided in Britain and elsewhere. Britain took its annual Christmas break earlier, and for longer, except that is, for those in essential services and those preparing computers for the new century. There was plenty to celebrate. For the third year in succession Christmas was cheaper.[52] Unemployment was lower than it had been for twenty years and mortgage interest rates were relatively low. Those who had any raided their savings and those who had not used their credit cards as never before to fund the festivities.

Increased attendance at Christian services over Christmas could not mask the decline of the Christian churches. One sign of this was that the number of churches in service had further declined. In 1989 there were 38,607 churches of all denominations in England. In 1999 the number had fallen to 37,717.[53] Figures revealed that attendance at Sunday schools continued to fall. It is estimated that 33 per cent of the child population (under fifteen) attended in 1945. This fell to 14 per cent in 1970, 9 per cent in 1980 and 7 per cent in 1990. It was estimated at 4 per cent in 2000.[54] The trouble was that it was not just the Bible stories which were being forgotten, it was that the ethical principles behind them were not being implanted by other agencies. On the other hand, the number of mosques increased from 40 in 1960 to 350 in 1990 and 660 in 2000.[55] Other minority faiths had also increased. Materialism, which had gained momentum in the 1980s, continued to grow over the 1990s. The media reflected this and fuelled it especially in magazines such as *Hello!* and *OK!*. Following the success of the National Lottery, ITV put on, in 1999, the successful quiz show 'Who Wants To Be A Millionaire?'

On 13th January 2000, the Samaritans revealed that they were inudated with calls from the lonely and the depressed during Christmas and New Year. Some 246,000 callers phoned their helpline over the period starting 25th December and ending 7th January, 18 per cent more calls than the previous year. The Samaritans believed that high expectations and 'millennium hype' were responsible for a sense of anti-climax and depression.[56] Loneliness was a growing problem. In 1961, in Britain, the proportion of households occupied by just one person was 10 per cent. In 1999 it was 30 per cent. The Department of the Environment estimated that by 2010 it would be 40 per cent.[57] Divorce was a factor in this, putting off marriage was another. Some believed that many successful young women, and men, were consciously deciding to remain single. They did not want to make the compromises necessary for a long-term commitment or/and bringing up a family. Another worrying trend was the increase in suicides, especially among the young. No one seemed to know why. Happily, suicide among the over 65s had declined (see Table A 21).

Loneliness, isolation, lack of beliefs and media hype, were probably the reasons behind the extraordinary scenes of grief which afflicted the nation when Princess Diana was killed in a car accident, in Paris in August 1997. In a television interview, she had admited adultery and being a Prozac (anti-depressant) user. A divorcee, she had attempted suicide and in her last years had devoted time to good causes. She had been built up into a larger than life figure by the media. Was it a sign of national malaise that so many people could be affected in this way? After all, many of them would not feel such sorrow when deaths occurred nearer home. Even Blair felt compelled to say, 'I am utterly devastated. We are a nation in a state of shock, in mourning, in grief.'[58]

Was Britain gradually dying like Italy, Germany, Japan and Russia were doing? Old Britain was dying. Analysis of official figures, indicated, according to one source, that whites would become an ethnic minority in Britain by 2100. This would happen in London by 2010. 'It would be the first time in history that a major indigenous population has voluntarily become a minority, rather than through war, famine or disease.'[59] Did it matter? It would not necessarily mean the decline of British culture and values. It could be argued that British culture had been enhanced by outsiders over many years. V. S. Naipaul, from Trinidad, starting in the late 1950s, became respected as one of Britain's leading novelists. Kazuo Ishiguro wrote the supremely English novel *The Remains of the Day*, which gained the Booker Prize in 1989, and other works. Arundhati Roy won the same prize in 1997 for *The God of Small Things*. There were others. The same was true in music, television and the cinema. Would it be so awful if Sir Trevor MacDonald were Minister of Education or Foreign Minister? Or a Nelson Mandela-type figure were Prime Minister? On the other hand, few would want to see a Robert Mugabe as one of our leading politicians. As Blair had emphasised, Britishness is about values not skin colour. However, it would be foolish to underestimate the problems caused by mass migration from many different countries and cultures.

Progress and Decline?

Where was Britain going under Blair? How much progress had it made in the late twentieth century? As it went into the delayed election of June 2001, the government pronounced itself optimistic about the future. Yet Britain witnessed a collapse in its rail system in 2000, something unprecedented in Western Europe. Its roads needed substantial investments. Unlike its neighbours, its health service appeared near breakdown. Britain had top cancer researchers but the NHS offered poorer care than many European states. According to the British Heart Foundation, Britain lagged behind other EU states on both preventing and dealing with heart disease. Britain's system of education and training was patchy, to say the least. This was a long-term problem, which must have been a key element in its decline and contrasts with the situation in Germany and France. As one former Conservative education minister admitted, 'The economic cost of the endemic failure of our education system to eradicate functional illiteracy is high.'[60] Britain faced a growing teacher crisis in 2001. It had such unenviable records as the highest rate of teenage pregnancies,[61] the highest rate of asthma sufferers[62] and one of the highest rates of drug abuse in Western Europe. TB had reappeared and HIV infections were rising. What had happened to the 'English rose'? British women were the second most obese in the EU. Their menfolk were the fourth most obese.[63] Britain sent more people to prison than other West Europe states.[64] It was one of the most unequal societies in the EU,[65] with mounting consumer debt. A report published in October 2000 pronounced Britain as one of the least family-friendly countries in Europe. In spite of increasingly flexible working arrangements, parents were left struggling with long hours, poor childcare facilities and inadequate state benefits.[66] Britain had declined in terms of its standard of living relative to those of its neighbours. It enjoyed fewer public holidays. The OECD predicted that in 2001 Britain would have the lowest growth rate in the EU except for Denmark. Ireland was expected to have the highest.[67] In 2000 manufacturing industry suffered what *The Observer* (31st December 2000) described as 'annus horribilis' with losses of jobs and capacity. The economy's 'underlying inefficiency is actually getting worse in relation to the rest of the world'.[68] Britain suffered a huge balance of trade deficit in 2000, it was not paying its way, but this seems to cause little concern. London was by far the most expensive city in the EU.[69] Britain, which used to be famous for its civilised travellers, was becoming notorious for its hooligans.[70] Admittedly, it was not alone in this.

How had we reached this rather sorry state of affairs? Clearly, although Blair and Major bore some responsibility for this situation, it was part of a longer trend. Under-investment in roads and rail, relative to countries like France and Germany, and even health care, probably goes back to the years before 1914.

The gap has never been closed. The same can be said for education and training. Britain had devoted more of its GDP to defence over the whole period, since 1945, than its richer allies (see Table A 22). Much of the cult of the amateur criticised, by the Hudson Institute in 1974 (see Chapter 9), and the 'archaism of the society and national psychology' remained in 2001. Britain still suffered from short-termism, a patch-and-mend mentality and complacency born, in part, by having 'muddled through' in two world wars. In 1998, Britain was still under-investing in its future, in research and development, compared with the USA, France, Germany, Japan and other countries (see Table A 19).

On the positive side, more Britons were more prosperous than ever before and unemployment was at its lowest for a generation. Britons also enjoyed greater personal freedom especially in terms of sexual orientation than in earlier times. More Britons were attending university than ever before. At the Sydney Olympics in 2000 Britain won 11 gold medals, an 80-year best. Despite the constant battle to get funding, the arts flourished in Britain as never before and British architects had world-wide respect.

At the commencement of the 2001 election campaign, Labour enjoyed a great lead, but Blair knew that apathy was a traditional problem for his party. Since 1997 apathy, the decline in political interest, had continued to grow. This was apparent by the low turnout rate at by-elections, local elections and elections to the European Parliament. Why did voters, especially young ones, find politics boring? Did they believe that the differences between the parties were so small that it did not matter who held office? Was it because the prosperity Britain was enjoying reduced discontent? Was it due to the continuing emphasis in the media on rich young celebrities? Who were the role models for Britain's youth? There were celebrities such as footballer Rio Ferdinand, who at 22 was earning an estimated £30,000 a week. Ex-footballer Gary Lineker was not doing badly either. He signed a contract to endorse Walkers Crisps for £1.5m. There was Madonna and there were the Spice Girls. There were the 'heroes' of C4's *Big Brother* 'who know very well that the celebrity they crave is directly proportionate to the exhibitionism they display'. *Daily Express* (20th July 2000) writer, Mark Jagasia, thought the show, 'is designed to pander to the worst elements of voyeurism in all of us'.

Writing in the *New Statesman* (4th December 2000), the left liberal weekly, Jason Cowley reflected on our progress. He referred to the figure of Leonard Bast, in E. M. Forster's, *Howards End* (1910), 'a lonely autodidact who longed to be part of the world of learning and high culture'. Bast was 'humiliated not so much by his lack of money but by what money can buy – in this instance, the time to read, listen to music and to think. It is impossible to believe that anyone would create such a character in today's decadent Britain'. Yet Bast-like characters still abounded in the Britain of the 1950s.

2001: a Historic Election

Just before 3 a.m. on 8th June 2001, Labour knew that it had once again gained an absolute majority of Commons seats. The polls had got it right by predicting a Labour victory from the start of the campaign, a campaign that had been postponed from May to June because of the foot and mouth crisis. Labour had successfully focused its campaign on the economy, the NHS and education. The Conservatives attempted to mobilise fears about asylum seekers, the single currency, Labour's alleged mishandling of rural affairs, and, towards the end, fears of a Labour landslide. The Liberal Democrats fought on the NHS, education and honesty in politics and Charles Kennedy emerged as the most popular of the three leaders during the campaign. For the first time, the majority of newspapers supported Labour; even *The Times* backed Blair. *The Economist* commented, 'Our instincts remain closer to William Hague's . . . [But] Tony Blair is the only credible conservative currently available.'

Blair's victory was historic in that this was the first time that Labour had gained enough seats for a second full term and no party had previously won such a large majority for its second term. The only disappointment for Labour was the low turnout. This was traditionally a feature of constituencies which Labour held with large majorities. But this time it was a common feature across the land. Only 59 per cent of eligible voters decided to vote. This was the lowest turnout since 1918 and risked posing a threat to the democratic system. Labour attracted 41 per cent of the vote, the Conservatives 31.9 and the Liberal Democrats

18.4. This translated into 413 seats for Labour (419 in 1997), 166 for Conservatives (165) and 52 (46) for the Liberal Democrats. The SNP held on to five seats (six) and PC four (four). The Conservatives could take some slight comfort from their gains in the local elections, mainly at the expense of the Liberal Democrats, held on the same day, and from the fact that they captured a seat in Scotland from the SNP, regained Newark and Romford from Labour and Tatton, the seat Martin Bell had vacated. Excluding Northern Ireland, fewer seats changed hands than at any time since 1910.

Among the interesting results were Ludlow, captured by the Liberal Democrats from the Conservatives, Torbay, where the Liberal Democrats increased their previous majority of 12 to 6,708, and Edgbaston, where minister Gisela Stuart held the seat for Labour. All three constituencies were traditionally Conservative constituencies and were typical of many other former Conservative seats. In Chesterfield, the Liberal Democrats took the seat held by Labour since 1935 until the retirement of Tony Benn in 2001. Among the other interesting results were those in the traditional working-class constituencies of Hartlepool, Leicester East and St Helens South. In all three cases the successful Labour candidates, Peter Mandelson, Keith Vaz and former Conservative Shaun Woodward, had been subjected to strong critical reporting by the media yet they all romped home easily. They saw off challenges from a wide variety of candidates including socialists. In Hartlepool, Arthur Scargill (Socialist Labour) attracted only 912 votes. The *Morning Star* (9th June 2001) reported that of the 113 Socialist Labour candidates only one kept his deposit. The left-wing vote was split between several parties in many constituencies. The rival Socialist Alliance saved two deposits, one at St Helens South. In Scotland the Scottish Socialist Party gained 3 per cent of the vote but in Glasgow Pollok its vote reached 9.98 per cent. The Green Party fielded 145 candidates and saved 10 deposits. Its best results were in Brighton Pavilion, where it secured 9.3 per cent and Leeds West, with 8 per cent. The most remarkable result of the election was at Wyre Forest. There, Dr Richard Taylor gained a 17,630 majority standing as an independent. He defeated the Labour junior minister David Lock, who had previously held the seat, as well as Conservative and UKIP candidates. Sixty-six-year-old Dr Taylor,

who had received little national media attention, harvested discontent over the closure of Kidderminster hospital, where he
had worked as a consultant, and the state of the NHS. The
results which gave very many politicians in all three parties cause
for concern were in Oldham East & Saddleworth and Oldham
West & Royton. Although Labour held on to these seats the
anti-immigrant British National Party gained 11.2 and 16 per
cent respectively. Oldham suffered several nights of violence
between Asian and white youths in the period leading up to
polling day. There was also rioting by Asian youths in Leeds on
5th June. Oldham is a town with a considerable Asian population where housing conditions are poor. Elsewhere the BNP
achieved very poor results. The UKIP failed to make any impact. Perhaps the anti-euro stance of Hague's Conservatives and
fear of a Labour landslide put off Conservative Eurosceptics from
risking a vote for the UKIP.

There was bad news for those seeking peace and reconciliation in Northern Ireland. Trimble just managed to scrape back
into Parliament, but his UUP lost four seats. Paisley's DUP, which
opposed the Good Friday Agreement, won five seats (two in
1997). Although it lost no seats, Hume's SDLP was overtaken by
Sinn Féin, which gained 4 Commons seats to 3 for the SDLP.
The DUP and Sinn Féin each took 21 per cent of the vote, with
the UUP vote falling to 22 per cent and the SDLP's to 19 per
cent. Meanwhile in the Republic, 54 per cent of voters rejected
the Nice Treaty in a referendum held on the same day as the
UK election. Turnout was under 35 per cent. Support for the
Treaty came from the main parties and the Catholic hierarchy
but was opposed by a disparate alliance including Sinn Féin,
the Green Party, Catholic anti-abortion groups and pacifists. The
result was a blow to the enlargement of the EC, which needs a
unanimous decision by all the member states. On the same day,
voters also decided by a majority of over 60 per cent to remove
all mention of the death penalty from the constitution and pro-
hibit its reintroduction. The last execution in the Republic was
in 1954 and the death penalty for ordinary crime was abolished
in 1964.

According to the *Irish Post* (16th June 2001), 'a host of Irish MPs'
(not including Northern Ireland) were elected to the Commons.
The paper listed 25 Labour and 3 Conservative. All 5 Asian MPs

were re-elected and they were joined by 2 others. However, the resignation of Keith Vaz from the government 'has overshadowed the historic number of Asian MPs' commented *Eastern Eye* (15th June 2001). Six 'ethnic minority' candidates were elected, all of them Labour. The *Jewish Chronicle* (15 June 2001) recorded that 21 Jewish MPs had been elected: 13 Labour, 7 Conservative and 1 Liberal Democrat. These figures represent an inadequate measure of the influence of these (and other groups) on New Labour. According to *The Guardian* (9th June 2001) 8 'openly gay or lesbian' candidates were returned. The new Parliament had 23 fewer women than the outgoing one but surprisingly 3 from Northern Ireland were elected – one each from UUP, DUP and SF.

Hague was the first Conservative leader since Austin Chamberlain (1921–2) not to become Prime Minister. He followed the example of his predecessor and resigned immediately after the election results were declared. Most thought his party faced an enormous task of remoulding itself to be an effective opposition to Blair's government.

The decline of female membership of the Commons was to some degree offset by the increase of women in the new Cabinet. Blair's new government (see Table A 27) included 7 women, which was a record. Nine members of the Cabinet retained their posts, most notably Gordon Brown as Chancellor. Blair's most important change was to move Cook from the Foreign and Commonwealth Office to become Leader of the House. Straw replaced him Straw replaced him, to the dismay of many Europhiles who remembered Straw's earlier Eurosceptic background but, so the *Jewish Chronicle* commented, it was 'heralded as good news (?) by Jewish leaders'. Blunkett moved from Education to the Home Office. Estelle Morris, a former schoolteacher, took over at Education.

The second Blair government faced enormous tasks. It had to deliver on promises regarding the NHS, education, crime and transport, at the same time maintaining prosperity. It faced difficult decisions over Europe, a continuing crisis in Northern Ireland and crises beyond its control in the Middle East and the Balkans. The economic situation looked less rosy. On past performance, it seemed unlikely that it would prevent Britain's further relative decline.

Appendix Tables

Table A 1   *Key British Ministers since 1918*

Prime Minister	Foreign Secretary	Chancellor of Exchequer	Home Secretary
D. Lloyd George (1916–22)	A. Balfour Earl Curzon	A. Bonar Law A. Chamberlain Sir R. Horne	Sir G. Cave E. Shortt
A. Bonar Law (1922–3)	Earl Curzon	S. Baldwin	W. Bridgeman
S. Baldwin (1923–4)	Earl Curzon	S. Baldwin N. Chamberlain	W. Bridgeman
J. R. MacDonald (1924)	A. Henderson	P. Snowden	J. Clynes
S. Baldwin (1924–9)	Sir A. Chamberlain	W. Churchill	Sir W. Joynson-Hicks
J. R. MacDonald (1929–31)	A. Henderson	P. Snowden	J. Clynes
J. R. MacDonald (1931–5)	Marquis of Reading Sir J. Simon	P. Snowden N. Chamberlain	Sir H. Samuel Sir J. Gilmour
S. Baldwin (1935–7)	Sir S. Hoare A. Eden	N. Chamberlain	Sir J. Simon
N. Chamberlain (1937–40)	A. Eden Viscount Halifax	Sir J. Simon	Sir S. Hoare Sir J. Anderson
W. Churchill (1940–5)	Viscount Halifax A. Eden	Sir K. Wood Sir J. Anderson	H. Morrison Sir D. Somervell
C. Attlee (1945–51)	E. Bevin H. Morrison	Dr H. Dalton Sir S. Cripps H. Gaitskell	C. Ede
W. Churchill (1951–5)	Sir A. Eden	R. A. Butler	Sir D. Maxwell-Fyfe G. Lloyd George
Sir A. Eden (1955–7)	H. Macmillan S. Lloyd	R. A. Butler H. Macmillan	G. Lloyd George
H. Macmillan (1957–63)	S. Lloyd Earl Home	P. Thorneycroft D. Heathcote Amory S. Lloyd R. Maudling	R. A. Butler H. Brooke

Table A 1 *Continued...*

Prime Minister	Foreign Secretary	Chancellor of Exchequer	Home Secretary
Sir A. Douglas-Home (1963–4)	R. A. Butler	R. Maudling	H. Brooke
H. Wilson (1964–70)	P. Gordon Walker M. Stewart G. Brown M. Stewart	J. Callaghan R. Jenkins	Sir F. Soskice R. Jenkins J. Callaghan
E. Heath (1970–4)	Sir A. Douglas-Home	I. Macleod A. Barber	R. Maudling R. Carr
H. Wilson (1974–6)	J. Callaghan	D. Healey	R. Jenkins
J. Callaghan (1976–9)	A. Crosland Dr D. Owen	D. Healey	R. Jenkins M. Rees
Mrs M. Thatcher (1979–90)	Lord Carrington F. Pym Sir G. Howe J. Major D. Hurd	Sir G. Howe N. Lawson J. Major	W. Whitelaw L. Brittan D. Hurd D. Waddington
J. Major (1990–7)	D. Hurd M. Rifkind	N. Lamont K. Clarke	K. Baker K. Clarke M. Howard
T. Blair (1997–)	R. Cook J. Straw	G. Brown	J. Straw D. Blunkett

Table A 2   *British general elections, 1918–97 (percentage share of votes and seats)*

Turnout	Conservative		Labour		Liberal		SNP	PC	(NI)	Others
%	%	seats	%	seats	%	seats	seats	seats	seats	seats
1918 59	39	383	24	73	26	161			90+	0
1922 71	38	344	30	142	29	115			3	11**
1923 71	38	258	31	191	30	158			3	5
1924 77	48	412	33	151	18	40			1	11**
1929 76	38	260	37	287	23	59			3	6
1931 76	59	521	32	52	7	37			2	3
1935 71	54	429	39	154	6	21			2	9**
1945 73	40	213	48	393	9	12			4	18**
1950 84	44	299	46	315	9	9			2	0
1951 83	48	321	49	295	3	6			3	0
1955 77	50	345	46	277	3	6			2	0
1959 79	49	365	44	258	6	6			1	0
1964 77	43	304	44	318	11	9			0	0
1966 76	42	253	48	364	9	12			1	0
1970 72	46	330	43	288	8	6	1	1	6	4
1974 78 (Feb)	38	297	37	301	19	14	7	2	12	2
1974 73 (Oct)	36	277	39	319	18	13	11	3	12	0
1979 76	44	339	37	269	14	11	2	2	12	0
1983 73	42	397	28	209	26*	23*	2	2	17	0
1987 75	42	376	31	229	23*	22*	3	3	17	0
1992 78	42	336	34	271	18	20	3	4	17	0
1997 73	31	165	43	419	17	46	6	4	18	1
2001 59	33	166	42	413	19	52	5	4	18	1

+ Includes *all* Irish MPs in 1918; ** includes 1 Communist in 1922, 1924, 1935 and 2 in 1945; * includes SDP

Table A 3 *British elections to the European Parliament since 1989*

	1989	*1994*	*1999*
Labour	45	62	29
Conservatives	32	18	36
Liberal Democrats	0	2	10
Scottish National	1	2	2
Plaid Cymru	0	0	2
Green	0	0	2
UKIP	0	0	3
SDLP	1	1	1
Unionist	1	1	1
Democratic Unionist	1	1	1

Source: 1999: *Daily Telegraph* (15th June 1999)
1994 and 1989: *The Times Guide to the European Parliament, June 1994*

Table A 4 *Women members of parliaments of EU states 1998 (percentage)*

Sweden	43
Denmark	35
Finland	34
Netherlands	31
Germany	30
European Parliament	30 (1999)
Austria	24
Spain	20
Luxembourg	18
Belgium	17
Portugal	13
Britain	12
Ireland	11
France	8
Greece	6

Source: *Das Parlament* (21st January 2000)

Table A 5   *Population of UK in millions*

	1951	1961	1981	1991
England	41.6	43.5	46.2	46.1
Wale	2.6	2.6	2.8	2.8
Scotland	5.0	5.2	5.1	5.0
Northern Ireland	1.4	1.4	1.5	1.6
UK	50.2	52.7	55.7	55.5

Source: Adapted from *Social Trends*, 22 (1992), 26

Table A 6   *Expectation of life at birth (by sex) in UK*

	1931	1961	1981	1991
Males	58.4	67.9	70.8	73.2
Females	62.4	73.8	76.8	78.8

Source: Adapted from *Social Trends*, 22 (1992), 123

Table A 7   *Full-time students enrolled in the academic years*

	1938–9			1951–2		
	men	women	total	men	women	total
England	29,192	8,241	37,433	49,275	14,309	63,584
Wales	2,041	728	2,779	3,546	1,317	4,863
Scotland	7,324	2,710	10,034	11,149	3,862	15,011

Source: Professor K. B. Smellie, *The British Way of Life* (London, 1955)

Table A 8   *Shares of world trade (percentage)*

	1938	1950	1951	1959	1962
UK	22	25	22	17	15
USA	20	27	26	21	20
West Germany	23*	7	10	19	20
Japan	7	3	4	7	7

*whole of pre-war Germany

Source: *Board of Trade Journal*

Table A 9   *British overseas trade, 1950–62*

	British exports (% of total)			British imports (% of total)		
	1950	1960	1962	1950	1960	1962
Commonwealth	48	42.2	45.8	35.8	38.4	37.2
EEC	14	14.6	18.9	12.3	14.6	15.8
EFTA		12.1	13.6		12.3	13.5

Table A 10   *Distribution of marketable wealth in UK*

	1976	1981	1986	1991	1996
Percentage of wealth owned					
by adults (18 and over)					
Most wealthy 1%	21	18	18	17	19
Most wealthy 5%	38	36	36	35	39
Most wealthy 10%	50	50	50	47	52
Most wealthy 25%	71	73	73	71	74
Most wealthy 50%	92	92	90	92	93

Source: Adapted from *Social Trends*, 30 (2000), 97

Table A 11   *Participation in education and training of 16–18-year-olds in selected countries, 1990 (percentage)*

	full-time	part-time	all
Canada	78	–	78
Denmark	79	–	79
France	82	–	82
Germany	89	–	89
Japan	76	3	79
Netherlands	77	10	87
Spain	61	–	61
Sweden	73	–	73
UK	40	31	71

Source: Department of Education: *Statistical Bulletin* (August 1993)

Table A 12   *Complaints to the Police Complaints Authority*

Year	1985	1986	1987	1988	1989	1990	1991	1992	1993	1994
Completed cases	3581	6646	5566	5516	5283	7273	7953	9200	9047	9853
Complaints	7897	15865	13147	12523	11155	16712	18065	19289	17991	19118
Percentage of fully investigated cases leading to disciplinary action	11.1	10.4	9.2	9.4	9.7	8.2	8.5	8.7	10	11

Table A 13   *Elections to Scottish Parliament, 1998*

party	first (% vote)	second (% vote)	constituency	seats top-up	total
Labour	38.8	33.8	53	3	56
SNP	28.7	27.0	7	28	35
Conservatives	15.6	15.4	0	18	18
Liberal Dems	14.2	12.5	12	5	17
Others	2.7	11.4	1	2	3

Table A 14   *Elections to Welsh Assembly, 1998*

party	first (% vote)	second (% vote)	constituency	seats top-up	total
Labour	37.6	35.4	27	1	28
Plaid Cymru	28.4	30.5	9	8	17
Conservatives	15.9	16.5	1	8	9
Liberal Dems	13.4	12.6	3	3	6
Others	4.7	5.1	0	0	0

Table A 15   *Education of the Cabinet formed in May 1997*

	School	University
Blair	Fetes (HMC)	Oxford
Prescott	Secondary Modern	Ruskin/Hull
Brown	Kirkcaldy High	Edinburgh
Cook	Aberdeen Grammar	Edinburgh
Irvine (1940)	Hutcheson's Grammar (HMC)	Glasgow
Beckett	Notre Dame High School, Norwich	Manchester College of Science and Technology
Strang	Morrison's Academy (HMC)	Cambridge
Straw	Brentwood School (HMC)	Leeds
Dobson	Archbishop Holgate	London (LSE)
Darling	Loretto (HMC)	Aberdeen
Cunningham	Bede, Jarrow Grammar	Durham
Dewar	Glasgow Academy (HMC)	Glasgow
Blunkett	Sheffield School for the Blind	Sheffield/Huddersfield
Robertson	Dunoon Grammar	Dundee
Taylor	Bolton School (HMC)	Bradford/Sheffield
Smith	George Watson's College (HMC)	Cambridge
Harman	St Paul's (HMC)	York
Mowlam	Comprehensive	Durham/Iowa
Davies	Bassaleg Grammar	Portsmouth Polytechnic/ Wales
Short	N/A	Keele/Leeds
Lord Richard	Cheltenham College (HMC)	Oxford
David Smith	Windermere Grammar	Manchester/Sheffield

HMC denotes member of Headmasters' Conference 'public school'

Table A 16   *Educational backgrounds of Shadow Cabinet as at February 2000*

	School	University
Hague	Wath-on-Dearne Comprehensive	Oxford/INSEAD
Portillo	Harrow Grammar	Cambridge
Ancram	Ampleforth (HMC)	Oxford
Widdecombe	La Sainte, Bath	Birmingham/Oxford
Maude	Abingdon (HMC)	Cambridge
Young	Eton (HMC)	Oxford
Norman	Charterhouse (HMC)	Harvard/Cambridge
Heathcoat-Amory	Eton (HMC)	Oxford
Smith	N/A	Sandhurst/Italy
Lord Strathclyde	Wellington College (HMC)	East Anglia/Aix-en-Prov
Mackay	Solihull School (HMC)	
Willets	King Edward, Birmingham (HMC)	Oxford
Fox	St Brides HC	Glasgow
Ainsworth	Bradfield College (HMC)	Oxford
Streeter	Tiverton Grammar	London
Yeo	Charterhouse (HMC)	Cambridge
Browning	Reading College of Techology	Bournemouth College of Technology
May	Wheatley Park Comprehensive	Oxford
Lansley	Brentwood School (HMC)	Exeter
Jenkin	Highgate School (HMC)	Cambridge
Arbuthnot	Eton (HMC)	Cambridge
Lord Henley	Clifton (HMC)	Durham

HMC denotes member of Headmasters' Conference 'public school'

Table A 17   *House of Lords, 1st November 2000*

	life		*hereditary*			
			+	*		
Conservative	181	42	9	1		**233**
Labour	197	2	2			**201**
Liberal Democrats	58	3	2			**63**
Cross-bench	133	28	2	1		**164**
Archbishops and Bishops					26	**26**
Other	6					**6**
TOTAL	**575**	**75**	**15**	**2**	**26**	**693**

NB Excludes 3 life peers on leave of absence. + elected office holders: * appointed royal office holders

By type

Archbishops and Bishops		26
Life Peers under the Appellate Jurisdiction Act 1876		28
Life Peers under the Life Peerages Act 1958	(107 women)	550
Peers under House of Lords Act 1999	(4 women)	92

TOTAL 696

Source: www.parliament.uk

Table A 18   *Gross Domestic Product per head: EU comparison, 1991 and 1997*

	Index (EU = 100)	
	1991	*1997*
Luxembourg	156	172
Denmark	107	118
Belgium	107	114
Austria	107	113
Netherlands	101	108
Germany	104	107
France	111	104
Irish Republic	75	102
Italy	103	102
Sweden	103	102
United Kingdom	95	100
Finland	92	98
Spain	80	80
Portugal	64	72
Greece	60	69

Source: Eurostat

Table A 19 *Research and development as percentage of GDP 1998*

Sweden	3.9	Denmark	1.9
Finland	2.9	Britain	1.9
Japan	2.9	Norway	1.7
USA	2.8	Belgium	1.6
Switzerland	2.7	Austria	1.6
South Korea	2.3	Czech Rep	1.3
Germany	2.3	Italy	1.0
France	2.2	Spain	0.9
Netherlands	2.1	Poland	0.8

Source: Adapted from OECD and *Das Parlament* (2nd and 9th February 2001)

Table A 20 *Personal computers per 100 inhabitants in 2000*

USA	65
Sweden	63
Switzerland	51
Norway	51
Denmark	48
Netherlands	42
Finland	38
UK	36
Germany	36
Japan	32
France	29
Belgium	27
Spain	16
Italy	16

Source: *Das Parlament* (23rd February 2001)

Table A 21 *Suicide rates, by gender and age (UK rate per 100,000 population)*

	1971	1976	1981	1986	1991	1997
Males						
15–24	6.9	9.6	10.6	12.7	15.9	16.4
25–44	13.5	15.0	19.5	20.1	24.3	21.8
45–64	19.8	21.0	23.1	22.6	20.4	17.5
65 and over	25.4	23.8	23.7	26.4	18.4	15.4
Females						
15–24	3.3	4.6	3.4	3.4	4.0	4.0
25–44	7.7	8.9	7.7	6.6	5.9	6.2
45–64	15.9	14.3	15.0	12.0	8.2	6.9
65 and over	16.5	15.0	15.5	13.6	8.6	6.3

Source: *Social Trends*, 30, 119

Table A 22 *Defence expenditure as percentage of GDP*

Country	1975–9	1980–4	1985–9	1990–4	1995	1996	1997	1998
Belgium	3.2	3.3	2.8	2	1.6	1.6	1.5	1.5
Denmark	2.3	2.4	2.0	1.9	1.7	1.7	1.7	1.6
France	3.8	3.9	3.8	3.4	3.1	3.0	2.9	2.8
Germany	3.4	3.4	3.0	2.2	1.7	1.7	1.6	1.6
Greece	5.6	5.4	5.1	4.4	4.4	4.5	4.6	4.8
Italy	2.1	2.1	2.3	2.1	1.8	1.9	2.0	2.0
Netherlands	3.1	3.1	2.9	2.4	2.0	2.0	1.9	1.8
Norway	2.8	2.7	2.9	2.8	2.4	2.2	2.1	2.3
Portugal	3.4	3.0	2.7	2.6	2.0	2.4	2.3	2.2
Spain		2.3	2.2	1.7	1.5	1.5	1.4	1.4
Turkey	4.4	4.0	3.3	3.8	3.9	4.1	4.1	4.4
UK	4.9	5.2	4.5	3.8	3.0	3.0	2.7	2.7
NATO Europe	0	3.5	3.2	2.7	2.3	2.2	2.2	2.2
Canada	1.9	2.0	2.1	1.9	1.5	1.4	1.2	1.2
USA	5.0	5.6	6.0	4.7	3.8	3.5	3.4	3.2

Source: *NATO Review* (Spring/Summer 2000)

Table A 23 *Irish Prime Ministers from 1922*

Year	Name	Party
1922	Michael Collins	Sinn Féin
1922–32	William T. Cosgrave	Fine Gael
1932–48	Eamon de Valera	Fianna Fáil
1948–51	John A. Costello	Fine Gael
1951–4	Eamon de Valera	Fine Fáil
1954–7	John A. Costello	Fine Gael
1957–9	Eamon de Valera	Fianna Fáil
1959–66	Sean Lemass	Fianna Fáil
1966–73	Jack Lynch	Fianna Fáil
1973–7	Liam Cosgrave	Fine Gael
1977–9	Jack Lynch	Fianna Fáil
1979–81	Charles Haughey	Fianna Fáil
1981–2	Garrett FitzGerald	Fine Gael
1982	Charles Haughey	Fianna Fáil
1982–7	Garrett FitzGerald	Fine Gael
1987–92	Charles Haughey	Fianna Fáil
1992–4	Albert Reynolds	Fianna Fáil
1994–7	John Bruton	Fine Gael
1997–	Bertie Ahern	Fianna Fáil

Table A 24 *Strength of the parties in the Dáil after each general election since 1933*

	FF	FG	Lab	Others	Government
1997	77	54	17	18	FF
1992	68	45	33	20	FF/Lab
					FG/Lab/DL
1989	77	55	15	14	FF/PD
1987	61	51	12	14	FF
1982 (2)	75	70	16	5	FG/Lab
1982 (1)	81	63	15	7	FF
1981	78	65	15	8	FG/Lab
1977	84	73	14	4	FF
1973	69	54	19	2	FG/Lab
1969	75	50	18	1	FF
1965	72	47	22	3	FF
1961	70	47	16	11	FF
1957	78	40	13	16	FF
1954	65	50	19	13	FG/Lab
1951	69	40	16	22	FF
1948	68	31	19	29	FG/Lab
1944	76	30	8	24	FF
1938	77	45	9	7	FF
1937	69	48	13	8	FF
1933	77	48*	8	20	FF

FF = Fianna Fáil, FG = Fine Gael, Lab = Labour,
PD = Progressive Democrats, DL = Democratic Left
* 1933 = forerunner of Fine Gael
1982 (1) and (2) election due to government crisis

Table A 25 *Irish elections, votes and seats, 1987 and 1989*

	1987		1989	
	% votes	seats	% votes	seats
Fianna Fáil	44.1	81	44.1	77
Fine Gael	27.1	31	29.3	55
Labour	6.4	12	9.5	15
Progressive Democrats	11.8	14	5.5	6
Workers' Party	3.8	4	5.0	7
Green Party	0.4	0	1.5	1
Sinn Féin	1.9	0	1.2	0

Source: Michael Gallacher: 'Irish Politics after the 1989 Election', in *Parliamentary Affairs* (July 1990)

Table A 26   *Irish elections to the Dáil, 1992 and 1997*

party	seats 1997	seats 1992
Fianna Fáil	77	69
Fine Gael	54	43
Labour	17	31
Progressive Democrats	4	10
Democratic Left	4	4
Greens	2	1
Sinn Féin	1	0
Socialist Party	1	0
Independents*	6	5
Total	166	162

* includes 2 ex-Fianna Fáil and 1 ex-Fine Gael

Table A 27   *The Cabinet after Tony Blair's post-election reshuffle, June 2001*

Office	Holder
Prime Minister	Tony Blair
Deputy Prime Minister	John Prescott
Chancellor of the Exchequer	Gordon Brown
Foreign Secretary	Jack Straw
Home Secretary	David Blunkett
Education and Skills	Estelle Morris
Trade and Industry	Patricia Hewitt
Transport, Local Government and the Regions	Stephen Byers
Environment, Food and Rural Affairs	Margaret Beckett
Health Secretary	Alan Milburn
Work and Pensions	Alastair Darling
Defence Secretary	Geoffrey Hoon
Chief Secretary to Treasury	Andrew Smith
Scottish Secretary	Helen Liddell
Welsh Secretary	Paul Murphy
Northern Ireland	John Reid
International Development	Clare Short
Cabinet Office Minister	John Prescott
Chief Whip	Hilary Armstrong
Culture, Media and Sport	Tessa Jowell
Leader of the House of Commons	Robin Cook
Lord Chancellor	Lord Irvine
Leader of the Lords	Lord Williams of Mostyn
Party Chairman	Charles Clarke

Notes

(The place of publication is London unless otherwise stated.)

Notes to Introduction

1. Michael Dintenfass, *The Decline of Industrial Britain, 1870–1980* (1992)

Notes to Chapter 1: Interwar Britain, 1919–39

1. William Ashworth: *An Economic History of England, 1970–1939* (1972), 285. K. Middlemas: *Politics in Industrial Society: The Experience of the British System since 1911* (1979) is a thoughtful analysis.
2. Leslie Halliwell: *Seats In All Parts* (1986), 100.
3. Jeffrey Richards: 'Controlling the Screen: the British Cinema in the 1930s', *History Today*, March 1983.
4. David Childs: 'Stefan Lorant', in *Politics and Society in Germany, Austria and Switzerland*, vol. 1, no. 1 (1988).
5. John Stevenson: *The Penguin Social History of Britain: British Society, 1914–45* (1990), 406. Of the press lords, Beaverbrook's life is covered by A. J. P. Taylor, *Beaverbrook* (1972) and Anne Chisholm and Michael Davie, *Beaverbrook: A Life* (1992).
6. Roy Jenkins: *Baldwin* (1987), 120.
7. David Sinclair: *Two Georges* (1988), 49.
8. J. Stevenson, op. cit., 301.
9. Henry Pelling: *A Short History of the Labour Party* (1992) can be read with great interest. See also his *A History of British Trade Unions* (1963).
10. Robert Blake: *The Decline of Power 1915–1964* (1983), 113, writes of the 'panic' at the thought of Labour in office.
11. See Lewis Chester *et al.*: *The Zinoviev Letter* (1967) for the details.
12. Keith Middlemas (ed.): Thomas Jones' *Whitehall Diary, vol. II 1926–1930* (1969). Jones was Deputy Secretary to the Cabinet and gave a full account of the strike from the government side. He commented on the 'impressive trade union loyalty only equalled by the orderly behaviour of all concerned', 53.

For a history of the strike see Margaret Morris: *The General Strike* (Harmondsworth, 1976); A. J. P. Taylor: *A Personal History* (1983) has some interesting memories of the strike.

13. According to Noreen Branson: *Britain in the Nineteen-Twenties* (1975), 203, the number of women on the electoral register rose to 14.5 million compared with 12.25 million men. Labour had attempted to introduce this in 1924.

14. Roy Jenkins: *The Chancellors* (1998), 277.

15. Alan Ereira: *The Invergordon Mutiny* (1981), 166.

16. Gregory Blaxland: *J. H. Thomas: A Life For Unity* (1964), 255.

17. R. Jenkins, *The Chancellors*, op. cit., 299.

18. Trevor Wilson: *The Downfall of the Liberal Party, 1914–1935* (1966) records the decline of the Liberals. Andrew Thorpe: *Britain in the 1930s* (Oxford, 1992), 33–41, gives a succinct account of the Liberals. His *The British General Election of 1931* (Oxford, 1991) attempts a modern analysis with the limited data available.

19. Philip John Stead: *The Police of Britain* (New York, 1985), 73–5.

20. J. B. Priestley: *English Journey* (1934); see also his *Our Nation's Heritage* (1939).

21. Noreen Branson and Margot Heinemann, *Britain in the Nineteen-Thirties* (1971), 190.

22. J. Stevenson, op. cit., 110.

23. Jack Ashley: *Acts of Defiance* (1992) records his personal experience of workers in 1939 being 'submissive', 27.

24. David Butler and Jennie Freeman: *British Political Facts, 1900–1968* (1969), 219.

25. Sidney Pollard: *The Development of the British Economy, 1914–1980* (1983), 68.

26. S. Pollard, op. cit., 69.

27. S. Pollard, op. cit., 75.

28. E. J. Hobsbawm: *Industry and Empire* (Harmondsworth, 1969), 242.

29. E. J. Hobsbawm, op. cit., 222.

30. E. J. Hobsbawm, op. cit., 213.

31. Martin Gilbert: *Winston Spencer Churchill, vol. V: 1922–1939* (1976), 226. In 1933 Churchill called Mussolini 'the greatest lawgiver among living men' and 'the Roman genius', 457.

32. Ben Pimlott (ed.): *The Political Diary of Hugh Dalton, 1918–40, 1945–60* (1986), 170 and 174–5. See also Ben Pimlott: *Hugh Dalton* (1985), 216. Labour's economic policy in 1935 owed 'some of its inspiration to Italian Fascism'.

33. Richard Thurlow: *Fascism in Britain: A History, 1918–1985* (1987); D. S. Lewis: *Illusions of Grandeur: Mosley, Fascism and British Society 1931–1981* (Manchester, 1987). For Mosley see, Robert Skidelsky: *Oswald Mosley* (1990).

34. Charles Higham: *Wallis: Secret Lives of the Duchess of Windsor* (1988).

35. J. A. Morris: *Writers and Politics in Modern Britain* (1977), 48.

36. Hugh Thomas: *John Strachey* (1973).

37. Margaret Thatcher: *The Path To Power* (New York, 1995), 28.

38. Chapman Pincher: *Their Trade is Treachery* (1982).
39. N. Branson: *History of the Communist Party of Great Britain, 1927–41* (1985) is written from the Communist point of view. Henry Pelling: *The British Communist Party: A Historical Profile* (1958) is a straightforward outline; see also H. Dewar: *Communist Politics in Britain: The CPGB from its Origins to the Second World War* (1976). A. J. P. Taylor: *A Personal History*, presents some colourful sketches of left-wing interwar politics.
40. Keith Middlemas and John Barnes: *Baldwin: A Biography* (1969), 746, remind us that in 1933–4 Labour looked like winning because of by-election victories.
41. Trevor Baridge: *Clement Attlee: A Political Biography* (1985).
42. R. Jenkins, *Baldwin*, op. cit., 146.
43. D. Sinclair, op. cit., 217–8.
44. James Obelkevich: 'Religion', in F. M. L. Thompson (ed.): *The Cambridge Social History of Britain 1750–1950, vol. 3: Social Agencies and Institutions* (Cambridge, 1990), 352.

Notes to Chapter 2: Britain and the World, 1919–39

1. Martin Gilbert: *The Arab-Israeli Conflict: Its History in Maps* (1976), 5.
2. Rex Taylor: *Michael Collins* (1970).
3. Among the books on Ireland covering this period are: J. C. Beckett: *A Short History of Ireland* (1958); D. G. Boyce: *Englishmen and Irish Troubles* (1972); D. G. Boyce: *The Irish Question and British Politics 1868–1986* (1988); Tim Pat Coogan: *The IRA* (1980); T. Ryle Dwyer: *De Valera: The Man and the Myths* (Dublin, 1991); Tony Gray: *Ireland This Century* (1994); Earl of Longford and Thomas P. O'Neill, *Eamon de Valera* (1970); Francis MacManus (ed.): *The Years of the Great Test, 1926–39* (Cork, 1967); Frank Pakenham [Lord Longford]: *Peace by Ordeal: The Negotiation of the Anglo-Irish Treaty 1921* (1991).
4. Maurice Manning: *The Blueshirts* (Dublin, 1987).
5. Michael Farrell: *The Orange State* (1980) gives the history. See also Steve Bruce: *God Save Ulster* (Oxford, 1989) and Patrick Buckland: *The Factory of Grievances: Devolved Government in Northern Ireland 1921–39* (n.d).
6. David Dilks: *Neville Chamberlain, vol. 1: 1869–1929* (Cambridge 1984) gives a convincing picture of his early life.
7. F. L. Carsten: *Britain and the Weimar Republic* (1984).
8. G. C. Peden: *British Rearmament and the Treasury, 1932–1939* (Edinburgh, 1979) frees the Treasury from undue blame in this matter.
9. Frank Roberts: *Dealing with Dictators: The Destruction and Revival of Europe, 1939–70* (1991), 35. Roberts was a key figure in the Foreign Office throughout the period. Among the classic books on appeasement are: Martin Gilbert and Richard Gott: *The*

Appeasers (1963); Maurice Cowling: *The Impact of Hitler* (1975); Keith Middlemas, *The Strategy of Appeasement* (Chicago, 1972).

10. H. G. Nicholas: *The United States and Britain* (Chicago and London, 1979), 86–7.
11. Gerald D. Nash: *The Great Depression and World War II: Organizing America, 1933–45* (New York, 1979), 94.
12. G. D. Nash, op. cit., 95.
13. John Charmley: *Chamberlain and the Lost Peace* (1989), 38.
14. Robert J. Wybrow, *Britain Speaks Out, 1937–87: A Social History as Seen Through the Gallup Data* (1989), 53.

Notes to Chapter 3: Britain at War, 1939–41

1. Letter to the author.
2. John Charmley: *Chamberlain and the Lost Peace* (1989), 209.
3. Letter to the author.
4. Ray Whitney, MP, letter to the author.
5. Michael Foot: *Aneurin Bevan*, 1945–1960 (1973), 304.
6. Roy Jenkins: *Mr Attlee: An Interim Biography* (1948), 202.
7. Nigel Nicolson (ed.): *Harold Nicolson: Diaries and Letters, 1930–39* (1966), 421.
8. See comments of Robert Boothby, House of Commons, 20th September 1939, and broadcast by Churchill quoted in D. N. Pritt: *Light on Moscow* (1939), 421.
9. Noreen Branson: *History of the Communist Party of Great Britain, 1927–41* (1985), 267.
10. Willie Thompson: *The Good Old Cause British Communism 1920–1991* (1992), 68.
11. J. McGovern, House of Commons, 3rd September 1939. For an interesting account of what it meant to be a conscientious objector, see Willie Hamilton: *Blood on the Walls* (1992).
12. Nicolas Mosley: *Beyond the Pale: Sir Oswald Mosley 1933–1980* (1983), 159–60.
13. Anne de Courcy: *1939 The Last Season* (1989), 28.
14. A. de Courcy, op. cit., 141.
15. Anthony Howard: *RAB: The Life of R. A. Butler* (1987), 89.
16. A. Howard, op. cit., 89–90.
17. Tim Pat Coogan: *The I.R.A.* (1980), 169.
18. T. P. Coogan, op. cit., 167.
19. Frank Roberts: *Dealing with Dictators: The Destruction and Revival of Europe 1939–70* (1991), 42.
20. William L. Shirer: *The Rise and Fall of the Third Reich* (1964), 763.
21. Correlli Barnett: *The Audit of War: The Illusion and Reality of Britain as a Great Nation* (1986), 130.
22. Lord Hailsham: *A Sparrow's Flight Memoirs* (1990), 131.
23. The *Daily Telegraph*, 30th August 1999. Lord Carrington, a pro-

fessional Guard's officer, later admitted that his colleagues were over confident and 'not well trained'. See *Reflections on Things Past: the Memoirs of Lord Carrington* (1988), 32.

24. Michael Colvin, letter to the author.
25. John Terraine: *The Right of the Line: The Royal Air Force in the European War 1939–45* (1988), 110.
26. Willy Brandt: *My Life In Politics* (New York, 1992), 109.
27. Andrew Roberts: *The 'Holy Fox' The Life Of Lord Halifax* (1991), 208, tells how Halifax went to the dentist rather than face those who wanted him to agree to take on the job. Churchill was not favoured by the Royals because of his support for Edward VIII.
28. Clive Ponting: *1940: Myth and Reality* (1990), 91–2. Nicholas Harman: *Dunkirk* (New York, 1990), 71–3.
29. Baroness Shreena Flather: *Saga Magazine*, March 2001.
30. N. Harman, op. cit., 105–6.
31. N. Harman, op. cit., 117.
32. Liddell Hart: *History of the Second World War* (1973), 89.
33. Noel Barber: *The Week France Fell* (1979), 178–9.
34. L. Hart, op. cit., 79.
35. N. Barber, op. cit., 287–8.
36. A. J. P. Taylor: *The Second World War: An Illustrated History* (1976), 62.
37. Charles Cruickshank: *The German Occupation of the Channel Islands* (1975), 59.
38. Madeleine Bunting: *The Model Occupation* (1995), 13, 34.
39. M. Bunting, op. cit., 13.
40. M. Bunting, op. cit., 12.
41. M. Bunting, op. cit., 100–3.
42. L. Hart, op. cit., 93.
43. W. Shirer, op. cit., 903.
44. A. J. P. Taylor, op. cit., 66.
45. A. Howard, op. cit., 96.
46. John P. Duggan: *A History of the Irish Army* (Dublin, 1991). An excellent book on this period is Kevin B. Nowlan and T. Desmond Williams (eds): *Ireland in the War Years and After, 1939–51* (Dublin, 1969).
47. WP (40), 402, 8th October 1940, on Subversive Newpaper Propaganda (PRO). Morrison distinguished between papers like the *Daily Mirror*, which attacked government measures but was not subversive, and the *Daily Worker*, which was. According to Paul Addison: *Churchill on the Home Front* (1993), 343, Churchill would have detained the Communists but this was opposed by MI5 as likely to provoke working-class hostility.
48. Francis Selwyn: *Hitler's Englishman: The Crime of Lord Haw-Haw* (1987) tells the story of William Joyce, who was not, of course, English.
49. Gerhard Hirschfeld (ed.): *Exile in Great Britain* (Leumington Spa, 1984), 176.
50. Colin Holmes: *John Bull's Island: Immigration and British Society 1871–1971* (1988), 202–3.

51. J. Terraine, op. cit., 207. Martin Gilbert: *Second World War* (1990), 121.
52. J. Terraine, op. cit., 219.
53. A. J. P. Taylor, op. cit., 78; Robert Blake: *The Decline of Power 1915–1964* (1985), 245.

Notes to Chapter 4: From European War to World War and Victory, 1941–5

1. F. H. Hinsley with E. E. Thomas, C. F. G. Ransom and R. C. Knight: *British Intelligence in the Second World War,* vol. 1 (1979), 481–2. It was estimated that the Germans would reach Moscow in three to four weeks and would attempt an invasion of Britain four to six weeks after that.
2. Margaret Thatcher: *The Path To Power* (New York, 1995), 33.
3. William Roger Louis: *Imperialism at Bay: The United States and the Decolonization of the British Empire 1941–1945* (New York, 1978), 125.
4. John Dower: *War without Mercy: Race and Power in the Pacific War* (1986), 84.
5. Quoted in W. R. Louis, op. cit., 8.
6. P. S. Gupta: *Imperialism and the British Labour Movement* (1975), 272.
7. W. R. Louis, op. cit., 8–9.
8. M. Thatcher, op. cit., 33.
9. Robert Blake: *The Decline of Power 1915–1964* (1985), 262.
10. Arthur Marwick: *Britain in our Century* (1984), 116.
11. Anthony Howard: *RAB: The Life of R. A. Butler* (1987), 137.
12. Richard Croucher: *Engineers at War, 1939–1945* (1982), 252.
13. Penny Summerfield: *Women Workers in the Second World War* (1984), 55. See also chapter in Martin Pugh: *Women and the Women's Movement in Britain 1914–1959* (1992).
14. M. Pugh, op. cit., 30.
15. Leila Rupp: *Mobilizing Women for War: German and American Propaganda, 1939–1945* (Princeton, 1978), 78.
16. John Terraine: *The Right of the Line: The Royal Air Force in the European War 1939–45* (1988), 701. Dame Felicity Peake: *Pure Chance* (Shrewsbury, 1993) gives an account of life in the WAAF.
17. P. Summerfield, op. cit., 196.
18. L. Rupp, op. cit., 185–6.
19. J. Terraine, op. cit., 13, 143.
20. J. Terraine, op. cit., 259.
21. J. Terraine, op. cit., 263, 265.
22. J. Terraine, op. cit., 459.
23. Martin Middlebrook: *The Battle of Hamburg* (1984), 328.
24. M. Middlebrook, op. cit., 324.
25. J. Terraine, op. cit., 229.
26. Liddell Hart: *History of the Second World War* (1973), 569.

27. Martin Gilbert: *Second World War* (1990), 641.
28. W. R. Louis, op. cit., 281.
29. A. J. P. Taylor: '1932–45' in David Butler (ed.): *Coalitions in British Politics* (1978), 92–3.
30. A. J. P. Taylor, op. cit., 93.
31. Angus Calder: *The People's War Britain 1939–45* (1969), 573. In his *Churchill on the Home Front* (1993), Paul Addison argues (p. 382) that Churchill's appointment of reformers like Butler and Hore-Belisha indicated his commitment to reform.
32. John Colville: *The Fringes of Power: Downing Street Diaries*, Vol. 2: 1941–April 1955 (1987), 259. Attlee told Colville, 'in his most optimistic dreams he had reckoned that there might . . . be a Conservative majority of only some forty seats'. According to Theo Aronson: *The Royal Family at War* (1993), 214, the King expected no party to have a working majority.
33. R. B. McCallum and Alison Readman: *The British General Election of 1945* (1947), 43. Of the 1.75 million service votes used, 1 million were cast directly and the rest by proxies.
34. J. Colville, op. cit., 254. Colville, a Conservative diplomat on secondment to Churchill, was with the Prime Minister when he made the broadcast. It met with 'widespread criticism and did not really go down well'.
35. M. Gilbert, op. cit., 712.
36. M. Gilbert, op. cit., 712.
37. M. Gilbert, op. cit., 715.

Notes to Chapter 5: Britain under Attlee, 1945–51

1. Robert J. Wybrow: *Britain Speaks Out, 1937–87: A Social History as Seen Through the Gallup Data* (1989), 20.
2. See Betty D. Vernon: *Ellen Wilkinson* (1982) for a biography of this interesting figure.
3. Douglas Jay: *Change and Fortune: A Political Record* (1980), 138.
4. Kenneth O. Morgan: *Labour in Power, 1945–51* (Oxford, 1984), 96, says Labour put the main emphasis on efficiency not social justice.
5. General Sir William Jackson: *Withdrawal from Empire: A Military View* (1986), 42.
6. General Sir W. Jackson, op. cit., 50.
7. Robin Edmonds: *Setting the Mould: The United States and Britain, 1945–1950* (New York, 1986), 124.
8. For Crossman and Zionism, see Tam Dalyell: *Dick Crossman: A Portrait* (1989). Towards the end of his life Crossman told the author that support for Zionism was his greatest achievement.
9. Michael Sissons and Philip French (eds): *The Age of Austerity, 1945–51* (1963), 77.

10. Sami Hadawi: *Bitter Harvest: Palestine 1914–67* (New York, 1967), 88.
11. For Bevan, see John Campbell: *Nye Bevan and the Mirage of British Socialism* (1987).
12. J. J. Lee: *Ireland 1912–1985: Politics and Society* (Cambridge, 1989), 321.
13. Walter LaFeber (ed.): *The Origins of the Cold War, 1941–1947* (New York, 1971), 138.
14. Michael Balfour: *The Adversaries: America, Russia and the Open World, 1941–62* (1981), 83–5.
15. J. Campbell, op. cit., 229.
16. R. Edmonds, op. cit., 86. For an interesting short account of 'Anglo–US defence co-operation, 1945–51', see Alex Canchev, in Richard J. Aldrich (ed.): *British Intelligence, Strategy and the Cold War, 1945–51* (1993).
17. Alec Cairncross: *The British Economy since 1945* (Oxford, 1992), 49.
18. K. B. Smellie: *The British Way of Life* (1955), 105.
19. A. Cairncross, op. cit., 60.
20. A. Cairncross, op. cit., 57.
21. K. B. Smellie, op. cit., 57.
22. Peter Self and H. Storing: *The State and the Farmer* (1962), 72.
23. A. Cairncross, op. cit., 68.
24. K. B. Smellie, op. cit., 35, quotes *The Economist*, 19th July 1952.
25. Robert Murphy: *Realism and Tinsel: Cinema and Society, 1938–49* (1989) gives an interesting account of the British films of the time.
26. Christy Campbell: *The World War II Fact Book, 1939–45* (1985), 329.
27. Sarah Bradford: *King George VI* (n.d.), 402–3.
28. Correlli Barnett: *The Audit of War* (1987) discusses the issue at length.
29. Colin Homes: *John Bull's Island: Immigration and British Society, 1871–1971* (1988), 214.
30. See Philip Bean and Joy Melville: *Lost Children of the Empire* (1990) for the details.
31. D. Jay, op. cit., 162.
32. C. Campbell, op. cit., 204–5.
33. J. D. Hoffman: *The Conservative Party in Opposition, 1945–51* (1964), 137.
34. Anthony Howard: *RAB: The Life of R. A. Butler* (1987), 156–9.
35. *The Times Guide to the House of Commons 1950* (1950), 17.
36. *The Times Guide to the House of Commons 1950*, op. cit., 21.
37. For the Communist Party during this period see, David Childs: 'The Cold War and the "British Road", 1946–53', *Journal of Contemporary History*, vol. 23 (1988).

Notes to Chapter 6: From Churchill to Macmillan, 1951–60

1. Hans-Peter Schwarz: *Adenauer Der Aufstieg,* 1876–1952 (Stuttgart, 1986), 895.
2. Piers Brendon: *Our Own Dear Queen* (1986), 154.
3. Alan Clark: *The Tories: Conservatives and the Nation State 1922–1997* (1998), 293.
4. A. Clark, op. cit., 290.
5. John Singleton: *Lancashire on the Scrapheap: The Cotton Industry, 1945–1970* (Oxford, 1991) traces the fall of this once great industry, concluding that it could not have been saved.
6. Robert J. Wybrow: *Britain Speaks Out, 1937–87: A Social History as Seen Through the Gallup Data* (1989), 44.
7. Obituary of Albert Pierrepoint in the *Guardian,* 13th July 1992.
8. George E. Kirk: *A Short History of the Middle East* (1961), 172.
9. Robert Blake: *The Decline of Power, 1915–1964* (1985), 364.
10. R. Blake, op. cit., 371.
11. Stephen E. Ambrose and Douglas G. Brinkley: *Rise to Globalism American Foreign Policy since 1938* (New York, 1997), 157.
12. Richard Lamb: *The Failure of the Eden Government* (1987), 268.
13. R. Lamb, op. cit., 371.
14. Michael Dockrill: *British Defence since 1945* (1988), 63.
15. General Sir William Jackson: *Withdrawal from Empire* (1986), 148.
16. R. Lamb, op. cit., 259.
17. R. Lamb, op. cit., 74–5.
18. General Sir W. Jackson, op. cit., 103.
19. General Sir W. Jackson, op. cit., 112.
20. General Sir W. Jackson, op. cit., 114.
21. Philip Bean and Joy Melville: *Lost Children of the Empire* (1990), 1.
22. P. Bean and J. Melville, op. cit., 78.
23. P. Bean and J. Melville, op. cit., 170.
24. John Campbell: *Nye Bevan and the Mirage of British Socialism* (1987), 302.
25. D. E. Butler: *The British General Election of 1959* (1960), 59.
26. D. E. Butler, op. cit., 83.

Notes to Chapter 7: Conservatives on the Run, 1961–4

1. Ministry of Education: *Statistics of Education, Part 1: 1961* and *Report of the Scottish Education Department, 1961.*
2. As given in Labour Party: *Twelve Wasted Years* (1963), 210.
3. D. E. Butler: *The British General Election of 1959* (1960), 179.
4. Richard Lamb: *The Failure of the Eden Government* (1987), 20.
5. R. Lamb, op. cit., 22.
6. James Callaghan: *Time and Chance* (1987), 150.
7. Trevor Royle: *The Best Years of Their Lives* (1986), 248.

8.   Roy Sherwood: *Superpower Britain* (Willingham, 1989), 55.
9.   R. Sherwood, op. cit., 57.
10. Arthur Koestler (ed.): *Suicide of a Nation?* (1963), 14.
11. John P. Duggan: *A History of the Irish Army* (Dublin, 1991), Appendix 5, 315–18.
12. Philip John Stead: *The Police of Britain* (New York, 1985), 97.
13. The background to the Profumo affair is discussed in David Thurslow: *The Hate Factor* (1992). Chapman Pincher: *Their Trade is Treachery* (1982) deals with all the spy cases mentioned. Sheila Kerr has some interesting comments on Burgess and Maclean in 'British Cold War Defectors: the Versatile Durable Toys of Propagandists', in Richard J. Aldrich (ed.): *British Intelligence, Strategy and the Cold War, 1945–51* (1993).
14. Alan Clark: *The Tories* (1998), 328–9.
15. A. Clark, op. cit., 335.
16. D. E. Butler and Anthony King: *The British General Election of 1964* (1965), 296.

Notes to Chapter 8: Harold Wilson at the Helen, 1964–70

1.   Marcia Williams: *Inside Number 10* (1975), 20. Ben Pimlott: *Harold Wilson* (1992) must be regarded as the definitive biography of Wilson.
2.   M. Williams, op. cit., 21.
3.   Richard Crossman: *The Diaries of a Cabinet Minister, vol. 1: Minister of Housing, 1964–66* (1975), 29.
4.   James Callaghan: *Time and Chance* (1987), 163.
5.   Lord Wigg: *George Wigg* (1972), 309. Wigg implies that these factors influenced the decision. He felt it had been a mistake.
6.   J. Callaghan, op. cit., 173.
7.   J. Callaghan, op. cit., 171.
8.   J. Callaghan, op. cit., 153; and Harold Wilson: *The Labour Government, 1964–1970: A Personal Record* (Harmondsworth, 1971), 3–4. George Brown: *In My Way* (Harmondsworth, 1971) gives his version. Having met both Wilson and Brown on several occasions by that time, the author can well believe the taxi account, but Peter Hennessy: *Whitehall* (1990), 182–3 seems to show otherwise.
9.   J. Callaghan, op. cit., 165.
10. P. Hennessy, op. cit., 183.
11. J. Callaghan, op. cit., 166.
12. Peter Paterson: *Tired and Emotional: The Life of Lord George-Brown* (1993), 181.
13. William Horsley and Roger Buckley: *Nippon New Superpower: Japan since 1945* (1990), 39.
14. M. Williams, op. cit., 28.
15. General Sir William Jackson: *Withdrawal from Empire* (1986), 228.

16. H. Wilson, op. cit., 181.
17. Denis Healey: *Time of My Life* (1989), 331.
18. Jeffrey Pickering: *Britain's Withdrawal from East of Suez: The Politics of Retrenchment* (Basingstoke/New York, 1998), 144–5.
19. J. Pickering, op. cit., 148.
20. H. Wilson, op. cit., 187.
21. General Sir W. Jackson, op. cit., 207.
22. General Sir W. Jackson, op. cit., 210.
23. Clark, *The Tories* (1948), 336.
24. Butler and King, *The British General Election of 1966* (1966), 72.
25. Lord Wigg, op. cit., 311.
26. Butler and King, *The British General Election of 1966* (1966), 102.
27. Ibid., 202.
28. Margaret Stewart: *Frank Cousins: A Study* (1968), 136. Later, the author found that Cousins did not wish to discuss his Cabinet experiences.
29. Ruth Winstone (ed.), *The Benn Diaries* (1995).
30. Willy Brandt: *My Life in Politics* (New York, 1992), 420.
31. Caroline Rathbone and Michael Stephenson: *Guide to Political Quotes* (1985), 106.
32. Frank Stacey: *British Government, 1966–1975: The Years of Reform* (Oxford, 1975), 182.
33. J. J. Lee: *Ireland 1912–1985: Politics and Society* (Cambridge, 1989), 420. Patrick Buckland: *A History of Northern Ireland* (Dublin, 1981) gives details of lack of Catholic advancement. Sabine Wichert: *Northern Ireland since 1945* (1991) is a useful survey of this troubled area.
34. John A. Murphy: *Ireland in the Twentieth Century* (Dublin 1975), 164; see comment of J. J. Lee, op. cit., 422.
35. J. J. Lee, op. cit., 424–5; the author interviewed O'Neill in 1962 and found him very pleasant but very upper-class British.
36. Douglas E. Schoen: *Enoch Powell and the Powellites* (1977), 32.
37. D. E. Schoen, op. cit., 34.
38. J. Callaghan, op. cit., 265.
39. J. Callaghan, op. cit., 264.
40. H. Wilson, op. cit., 504.
41. J. Callaghan, op. cit., 265.
42. Colin Holmes: *John Bull's Island: Immigration and British Society 1871–1971* (1988), 268.
43. David Butler and Michael Pinto-Duschinsky: *The British General Election of 1970* (1971), 341.
44. D. Butler and M. Pinto-Duschinsky, op. cit., 336.
45. D. Butler and M. Pinto-Duschinsky, op. cit., 320.
46. Roy Jenkins: *A Life at the Centre* (1991), 301.
47. Clark, op. cit., 338.
48. John Campbell: *Edward Heath* (1993), 282.

Notes to Chapter 9: Trouble and Strife, 1970–4

1.   Alan Clark: *The Tories* (1998), 339.
2.   Ian Gilmour: *Whatever Happened to the Tories: The Conservatives since 1945* 1997, 248.
3.   I. Gilmour, op. cit., 249.
4.   I. Gilmour, op. cit., 261.
5.   Roy Jenkins: *A Life at the Centre* (1991), 329.
6.   James Callaghan: *Time and Chance* (1988), 272.
7.   J. Callaghan, op. cit., 274.
8.   J. Callaghan, op. cit., 275.
9.   Bentley Gilbert: *Britain since 1918* (1974), 209.
10. John Campbell: 'Edward Heath', in *Contemporary Record* (Summer 1988), 28.
11. Peter Walker: *Staying Power* (1991), 96.
12. Tim Pat Coogan: *Disillusioned Decades: Ireland 1966–87* (Dublin, 1987), 57.
13. Terence Brown: *Ireland: A Social and Cultural History, 1922–1985* (1985), 283–92, discusses this in full.
14. J. J. Lee: *Ireland 1912–1985: Politics and Society* (Cambridge, 1989), 471.
15. J. J. Lee, op. cit., 473.
16. John A. Murphy: *Ireland in the Twentieth Century* (Dublin, 1975), 166.
17. I. Gilmour, op. cit., 270.
18. Colin Holmes: *John Bull's Island: Immigration and British Society, 1871–1971* (1988), 267. Douglas E. Schoen: *Enoch Powell and the Powellites* (1977), 70.
19. Zig Layton-Henry (ed.): *Conservative Party Politics* (1980), 66.
20. Chris Cook: *A Short History of the Liberal Party 1900–92* (1993), Appendix II.
21. David McKie and Chris Cook: *The Guardian/Quartet Election Guide* (1974), 77.
22. 'The Trade Unions and the Fall of the Heath Government', *Contemporary Record* (Spring 1988), 42. I. Gilmour, op. cit., 282.
23. Robert J. Wybrow: *Britain Speaks Out, 1937–87: A Social History as Seen Through the Gallup Data* (1989), 105.
24. David Butler and Dennis Kavanagh: *The British General Election of February 1974* (1974), 73–4.
25. D. Butler and D. Kavanagh, op. cit., 336.
26. 'The Wasting of Assets', the Hudson Report, quoted in David Coates and John Hillard (eds): *The Economic Decline of Modern Britain: The Debate between Left and Right* (Brighton, 1986).

Notes to Chapter 10: Trouble and Strife, 1974–9

1. David Butler and Dennis Kavanagh: *The British General Election of October 1974* (1975), 18.
2. D. Butler and D. Kavanagh, op. cit., 102.
3. Roy Jenkins: *A Life at the Centre* (1991), 397.
4. Michael Dintenfass: *The Decline of Industrial Britain 1870–1980* (1992), 47.
5. M. Dintenfass, op. cit., 37.
6. Conservative Party: *Campaign Guide 1977* (1977), 581.
7. Ian Gilmour: *Whatever Happened to the Tories? The Conservatives since 1945* (1997), 298.
8. Quoted by Geoffrey Howe: *Conflict of Loyalty* (1994), 89.
9. Ruth Winstone (ed.): *The Benn Diaries* (1995), 302.
10. R. Jenkins, op. cit., 407.
11. R. Jenkins, op. cit., 410.
12. Dr George Grower: *Kinnock* (1994), 30.
13. James Callaghan: *Time and Chance* (1987), 461.
14. Philip Ziegler: *Wilson: The Authorised Life of Lord Wilson of Rievaulx* (1995), 31.
15. Robert J. Wybrow: *Britain Speaks Out, 1937–87: A Social History as Seen Through the Gallup Data* (1989), 99.
16. Jonathan Dimbleby: *The Prince of Wales: A Biography* (1994), 133–4.
17. Alan Hamilton: *The Real Charles: The Man Behind the Myth* (1989), 178.
18. J. Callaghan, op. cit., 392.
19. R. Jenkins, op. cit., 434.
20. Joe Haines: *The Power of Politics* (1977), 55.
21. J. Haines, op. cit., 8.
22. Peter Wright: *Spy Catcher* (New York, 1987), 369.
23. David Leigh: *The Wilson Plot* (1988), 251.
24. Chapman Pincher: *Their Trade is Treachery* (1981), 254.
25. Kenneth O. Morgan: *The People's Peace: British History, 1945–1990* (Oxford, 1992), 381.
26. Ben Pimlott: *The Queen: A Biography of Elizabeth II* (1996), 431.
27. D. Butler and D. Kavanagh, op. cit., 328.
28. D. Butler and D. Kavanagh, op. cit., 98.
29. Geoffrey Alderman: *The Jewish Community in British Politics* (Oxford, 1983), 134.
30. G. Alderman, op. cit., 135.
31. G. Alderman, op. cit., 146.
32. G. Alderman, op. cit., 148.
33. David McKie *et al.*: *The Guardian/Quartet Election Guide* (1978), 124.
34. J. Callaghan, op. cit., 478.
35. J. Callaghan, op. cit., 518.
36. J. Callaghan, op. cit., 537.
37. R. Winstone, op. cit., 408.
38. J. Callaghan, op. cit., 558.

39. R. J. Wybrow, op. cit., 155.
40. R. J. Wybrow, op. cit., 154.
41. David Butler and Dennis Kavanagh: *The British General Election of 1979* (1980), 36.
42. R. J. Wybrow, op. cit., 160.
43. R. J. Wybrow, op. cit., 118.
44. R. Winstone op. cit., 468.
45. Margaret Thatcher: *The Path To Power* (New York, 1995), 449.
46. D. Butler and D. Kavanagh, op. cit., (1980), 306.
47. D. Butler and D. Kavanagh, op. cit., (1980), 420.
48. This is a view put by the then Liberal leader, Sir David Steel, in his *Against Goliath: David Steel's Story* (1989), 147–8. See also I. Gilmour, op. cit., 388.

Notes to Chapter 11: The Thatcher Era, 1979–87

1. Brendan Evans, *Thatcherism and British Politics, 1975–1999* (1999), 213.
2. Geoffrey Smith: *Reagan and Thatcher* (1990) gives a brief but good account of the early development of 'Thatcherism'.
3. James Prior: *A Balance of Power* (1986), 119. Thatcher also makes a tribute to the help of her husband Denis, an accountant and businessman, in sizing up the financial side of politics. See Margaret Thatcher: *The Downing Street Years* (1993), 22.
4. Ian Gilmour: *Whatever Happened to the Tories? The Conservatives since 1945* (1997), 308.
5. Geoffrey Howe: *Conflict of Loyalty* (1994), 125.
6. G. Howe, op. cit., 126.
7. G. Howe, op. cit., 129.
8. Samuel Brittan's chapter, 'The Economy', in *Financial Times: The Thatcher Years: The Policies and the Prospects* (1987), 15.
9. I. Gilmour, op. cit., 311.
10. M. Thatcher, op. cit., 122.
11. G. Howe, op. cit., 135.
12. I. Gilmour, op. cit., 312.
13. Norman Tebbit: *Upwardly Mobile: An Autobiography* (1988), 187.
14. Robert J. Wybrow: *Britain Speaks Out, 1937–87: A Social History as Seen Through the Gallup Data* (1989), 126.
15. R. J. Wybrow, op. cit., 159.
16. Denis Healey: *The Time of My Life* (1989), 469.
17. D. Healey, op. cit., 482–3.
18. Dr George Drower: *Kinnock* (1994), 54.
19. Roy Jenkins: *A Life at the Centre* (1991), 469.
20. Dr Chris Cook (ed.): *Pears Cyclopaedia 100th Edition* (1991), A31.
21. Conservative Research Department (CRD): *Campaign Guide 1983*, 87.
22. G. Howe, op. cit., 245.

23. CRD, op. cit., 432.
24. I. Gilmour, op. cit., 317; M. Thatcher, op. cit., 175.
25. Lord Carrington: *Reflect on Things Past* (1988), 357.
26. Lord Carrington, op. cit., 363.
27. I. Gilmour, op. cit., 317.
28. M. Thatcher, op. cit., 217. For intelligence, Stephen E. Ambrose and Douglas G. Brinkley: *Rise to Globalism: American Foreign Policy since 1939* (New York, 1997), 315.
29. G. Howe, op. cit., 245; N. Tebbit: op. cit., 194.
30. Kenneth Baker: *The Turbulent Years: My Life in Politics* (1993), 68–9, attributes these words to Norman Lamont.
31. Max Hastings and Simon Jenkins: *The Battle for the Falklands* (1983), 174–6. Lawrence Freedman and Virginia Gamba-Storehouse: *Signals of War: The Falklands Conflict of 1982* (1990) gave an authoritative account, Gamba-Storehouse with the benefit of Argentine experience.
32. M. Hastings and S. Jenkins, op. cit., 357–8.
33. M. Thatcher, op. cit., 181, especially regarding the Argentine leader. She recalls (174) that a Soviet general later commented that the British victory had a bearing on East–West relations.
34. Ruth Winstone (ed.):*The Benn Diaries* (1995), 535–6.
35. R. Winstone, op. cit., 531.
36. Lord Carrington, op. cit., 290–91.
37. General Sir William Jackson: *Withdrawal from Empire* (1986), 255.
38. I. Gilmour, op. cit., 321.
39. D. Healey, op. cit., 500.
40. Cecil Parkinson: *Right at the Centre* (1992), 229.
41. G. Drower, op. cit., 64–5.
42. G. Drower, op. cit., 61.
43. G. Drower, op. cit., 61.
44. C. Parkinson, op. cit., 222.
45. I. Gilmour, op. cit., 322.
46. G. Drower, op. cit., 85–6 for both results.
47. C. Parkinson, op. cit., 43.
48. Drower, op. cit., quotes from colleagues and adversaries.
49. Arthur Marwick: *A History of the Modern British Isles 1914–1999* (Oxford, 2000), 298.
50. M. Thatcher, op. cit., 272. She believed that the level of unemployment was related to the level of trade union power. Prior, she believed, 'was the badge of our reasonableness,' 28.
51. CRD, op. cit., 101–2.
52. N. Tebbit, op. cit., 153.
53. I. Gilmour, op. cit., 316.
54. Mervyn Jones: *Michael Foot* (1994), 523.
55. D. Healey, op. cit., 504.
56. M. Jones, op. cit., 524.
57. *Financial Times*, op. cit., 18.
58. *Financial Times*, op. cit., 47.

59. G. Howe, op. cit., 254.
60. Peter Riddell: *The Thatcher Era and its Legacy* (1991), 114–15.
61. M. Thatcher, op. cit., 604.
62. M. Thatcher, op. cit., 603.
63. G. Howe, op. cit., 144–5.
64. Michael Dockrill: *British Defence since 1945* (1988), 122.
65. M. Dockrill, op. cit., 112.
66. Philip Gould: *The Unfinished Revolution: How the Modernisers Saved the Labour Party* (1998), 76.
67. P. Gould, op. cit., 79.
68. P. Gould, op. cit., 79–80.
69. *The Times Guide to the House of Commons, June 1987* (1987), 286.

Notes to Chapter 12: Thatcher in Decline, 1987–90

1. Roy Jenkins: *A Life at the Centre* (1991), 593.
2. R. Jenkins, op. cit., 597.
3. Margaret Thatcher: *The Downing Street Years* (1993), 651.
4. M. Thatcher, op. cit., 651.
5. Alan Clarke: *Diaries* (1993), 289.
6. Ian Gilmour: *Whatever Happened to the Tories? The Conservatives since 1945* (1997), 343.
7. I. Gilmour, op. cit., 338.
8. Kenneth Frampton: *Modern Architecture: A Critical History* (1985), chapter 2.
9. Lionel Esher: *A Broken Wave: The Rebuilding of Britain, 1940–1980* (Harmondsworth, 1983) analyses the modern architecture of these towns.
10. Alan Clark: *The Tories: Conservatives and the Nation State 1922–1997* (1998), 291.
11. A. Clark (1998), op. cit., 291.
12. L. Esher, op. cit., 288.
13. HRH The Prince of Wales: *A Vision of Britain* (1989).
14. James Callaghan: *Time and Chance* (1987), 411.
15. Stuart Maclure: *Education Re-formed* (1988), 56.
16. S. Maclure, op. cit., 88–9.
17. R. Jenkins, op. cit., 460.
18. Lord Carrington: *Reflect on Things Past* (1988), 311.
19. Lord Carrington, op. cit., 313.
20. Lord Carrington, op. cit., 316.
21. Lord Carrington, op. cit., 319.
22. Stanley Henig: *The Uniting of Europe: From Discord to Concord* (1997), 61.
23. R. Jenkins, op. cit., 477.
24. R. Jenkins, op. cit., 484.
25. Geoffrey Howe: *Conflict of Loyalty* (1994), 405.

26. G. Howe, op. cit., 404.
27. G. Howe, op. cit., 572. See identical words in Nigel Lawson: *The View From No. 11 Memoirs of a Tory Radical* (1993), 922.
28. N. Lawson, op. cit., 580.
29. M. Thatcher, op. cit., 792–4.
30. M. Thatcher, op. cit., 757.
31. N. Lawson, op. cit., 843; A. Clark (1998), op. cit., 395 and 405.
32. A. Clark (1998), op. cit., 401; Kenneth Baker: *The Turbulent Years* (1993), 320.
33. A. Clark, *The Tories* (1993), 401.
34. A. Clark (1998), op. cit., 281.
35. A. Clark (1998), op. cit., 289.
36. John Major: *The Autobiography* (1999), 185.
37. M. Thatcher, op. cit., 852. According to Malcolm Balen: *Kenneth Clarke* (1994), 206, Clarke made it clear he would resign if she continued.
38. M. Thatcher, op. cit., 835.
39. M. Balen, op. cit., 202.
40. James Prior: *A Balance of Power* (1986), 114.
41. J. Major, op. cit., calls one chapter 'An Empress Falls'.
42. I. Gilmour, op. cit., 3.

Notes to Chapter 13: Major's Avalanche of Problems

1. John Major: *The Autobiography* (1999), 189.
2. J. Major, op. cit., 185 and 198.
3. Robert Shepherd: *The Power Brokers: The Tory Party and its Leaders* (1991), 200.
4. Dr George Drower: *Kinnock* (1994), 268.
5. J. Major, op. cit., 269.
6. R. Shepherd, op. cit., 200–1.
7. Patrick Sheehy: 'Case of the Hostile Cops', *Guardian*, 26th July 1993.
8. The quotes are from the *Independent on Sunday* Supplement, 1st October 1992, giving the full text.
9. J. Major, op. cit., 266.
10. *The Times Guide to the House of Commons, April 1992* (1992), 290. Anthony King *et al.* (eds): *Britain at the Polls, 1992* (Chatham, NJ, 1993) contains thoughtful contributions on the election.
11. *The Times Guide*, op. cit., 279.
12. *The Times Guide*, op. cit., 254.
13. *The Times Guide*, op. cit., 279.
14. *Independent on Sunday*, 18th October 1992, gives a figure of 250,000. Ian Gilmour: *Whatever Happened to the Tories: The Conservatives since 1945* (1997), 354, records the figure of 700,000.
15. *The Times Guide*, op. cit., 315.
16. I. Gilmour, op. cit., 356.

17. Philip Gould: *The Unfinished Revolution: How The Modernisers Saved the Labour Party* (1998), 152.
18. J. Major, op. cit., 290.
19. P. Gould, op. cit., 148.
20. Edwina Currie (ed.): *What Women Want* (1990) is a comprehensive look at women in society at the time.
21. *Independent*, 25th July 1993. The facts on maternity were given in the *Guardian*, 29th September 1993, 7.
22. *Independent*, 21st September 1992, 3.
23. E. Currie, op. cit., 45–6.
24. Raymond Snoddy: *The Good, the Bad and the Unacceptable: The Hard News about the British Press* (1993), 117.
25. Snoddy, op. cit., 124.
26. Steve Peak and Paul Fisher: *The Media Guide 2000* (2000), 28.
27. *Evening Standard*, 27th January 1993.
28. Conservative Research Department: *Campaign Guide 1992* (1992), 219.
29. *Daily Telegraph*, 27th January 1993.
30. Norman Lamont: *In Office* (1999), 249.
31. J. Major, op. cit., 334.
32. J. Major, op. cit., 334.
33. J. Major, op. cit., 536.
34. J. Major, op. cit., 536.
35. J. Major, op. cit., 545.
36. J. Major, op. cit., 552.
37. J. Major, op. cit., 566.
38. J. Major, op. cit., 556.
39. J. Major, op. cit., 557.
40. J. Major, op. cit., 566.
41. J. Major, op. cit., 568.
42. J. Major, op. cit., 570.
43. J. Major, op. cit., 554.
44. J. Major, op. cit., 342.
45. J. Major, op. cit., 619.
46. J. Major, op. cit., 645.
47. J. Major, op. cit., 645.
48. Malcolm Balen: *Kenneth Clarke* (1994), 215.
49. I. Gilmour, op. cit., 357.
50. Hugo Young *et al.*: *The Election: A Voters' Guide* (1997), 151.
51. J. Major, op. cit., 454.
52. J. Major, op. cit., 484.
53. J. Major, op. cit., 485.
54. J. Major, op. cit., 488.
55. J. Major, op. cit., 491.
56. J. Major, op. cit., 431.
57. A. Clark, *The Tories*, 436.
58. N. Lamont, op. cit., 484; J. Major, op. cit., 690.
59. Norman Lamont: *In Office* (1999), 495.

60. J. Major, op. cit., 692.
61. I. Gilmour, op. cit., 379–380; J. Major, op. cit., 707.
62. J. Major, op. cit., 712.
63. J. Major, op. cit., 713.
64. N. Lamont, op. cit., 486.
65. N. Lamont, op. cit., 485.
66. I. Gilmour, op. cit., 381.
67. I. Gilmour, op. cit., 380.
68. A. Clark, *The Tories*, 438.
69. *The Vacher Dod Guide to the New House of Commons 1997* (1997), xiii.
70. P. Gould, op. cit., 361.
71. P. Gould, op cit., 362.
72. *Vacher Dod*, op. cit., xiii.
73. I. Gilmour, op cit., 381.
74. J. Major, op. cit., 726.

Notes to Chapter 14: New Labour in Office

1. *Daily Mail*, 9th November 1999.
2. *Independent*, 30th December 1999.
3. *Daily Telegraph*, 16th February 2000.
4. *Times*, 8th September 2000.
5. *Independent*, 8th December 1999.
6. *Times Education Supplement*, 1st December 2000.
7. *Times Education Supplement*, 1st December 2000.
8. *Times*, 19th April 2000.
9. *Daily Mail*, 6th January 2000.
10. *Independent on Sunday*, 6th August 2000.
11. The global challenge, *The University of Nottingham Annual Report 1999–2000*, 7.
12. *Manchester Evening News*, 12th November 1999.
13. *Independent*, 6th January 2000.
14. *Times Higher Education Supplement*, 14th January 1999.
15. *Times Higher Education Supplement*, 14th January 1999.
16. Andrew Rawnsley: *Servants of the People* (2000), 202, for details.
17. The details that follow are taken from House of Lords *Register of Lords' Interests, Category 3 Discretionary* as at 6th December 2000.
18. *The Asian*, 2nd–9th February 2000.
19. *Independent*, 22nd December 1999.
20. *The Asian*, 2nd–9th February 2000.
21. *Police Review*, 4th February 2000.
22. National Criminal Intelligence Service (http://www.ncis.co.uk/PRESS/24_00. Html), 24/00, 28th June 2000.
23. *Sunday Telegraph*, 3rd October 1999.
24. *Sunday Telegraph*, 25th July 1999.
25. Figures compiled by Police Complaints Authority.

26. National Criminal Intelligence Service (http://www.ncis.co.uk/tiu.html) 8th December 2000.
27. *Observer*, 23rd January 2000.
28. National Criminal Intelligence Service (http://www.ncis.co.uk/PRESS/30_00.html), 30/00, 6th November 2000.
29. Hugo Young *et al.*: *The Election: A Voters' Guide* (1997), 289–91.
30. *Independent*, 13th January 2000.
31. *Guardian*, 20th December 2000.
32. *Independent*, 18th February 2000.
33. John Major: *The Autobiography* (1999), 456.
34. Irish Embassy, Washington, DC.
35. *Irish Post*, 13th May 2000.
36. *Irish Post*, 13th May 2000.
37. *Irish Post*, 13th May 2000.
38. Tony Gray: *Ireland This Century* (1994), 184.
39. *Irish Post*, 9th December 2000.
40. *Irish Post*, 9th December 2000.
41. *Daily Telegraph*, 26th August 1999.
42. *Independent*, 18th November 2000.
43. *Times*, 31st January 2000.
44. *Observer*, 13th February 2000.
45. House of Commons Defence Committee: *Lessons of Kosovo* (vol. 2), 23rd October 2000, 204.
46. House of Commons Defence Committee (vol. 2), op. cit., 233.
47. House of Commons Defence Committee: *Lessons of Kosovo* (vol. 1), 23rd October 2000, cxl.
48. House of Commons Defence Committee (vol. 1), op. cit., cxxxvii–cxxxviii.
49. House of Commons Defence Committee (vol. 1), op. cit., cxiii.
50. House of Commons Defence Committee (vol. 1), op. cit., cxxiii.
51. *Sunday Times*, 2nd January 2000.
52. *Times*, 23rd December 1999.
53. *Guardian*, 24th December 1999.
54. Peter Brierley (ed.): *UK Christian Handbook Religious Trends 2000/2001 No 2* Table 2.15.
55. P. Brierley, op. cit., Table 10.8.
56. *Observer*, 16th January 2000.
57. *Observer*, 3rd September 2000.
58. Penny Junor: *Charles: Victim Or Villain?* (1998), 27.
59. *The Observer*, 3rd September 2000.
60. John Patten: *The Things to Come: The Tories in the 21st Century* (1995), 195.
61. *Social Trends*, 30, Table 2.15, 43.
62. National Asthma Campaign, February 2000.
63. *Daily Telegraph*, 6th January 2000, quoting Eurostat.
64. The Howard League for Penal Reform, Fact Sheet 32.
65. *Social Trends*, 30, Table 5.22, 95.
66. *Guardian*, 20th October 2000.

67. *Das Parlament*, 15th December 2000.
68. Dudley Fishburn (ed.): *The Economist, The World in 2001* (2000), 29.
69. *Times*, 27th June 2000.
70. *Sunday Times*, 18th June 2000.

Select Bibliography

(The place of publication is London unless otherwise stated.)

Official Publications and Reference Publications

Chartered Institute of Public Finance and Accountancy, *Police Statistics 1998–1999 Actuals* (1999).
Cook, Dr Chris (ed.), *Pears Cyclopaedia 100th Edition* (1991). *E P News*
Fishburn, Dudley, *The Economist: The World In 1999* (1998).
Fishburn, Dudley, *The Economist: The World In 2001* (2000).
Hansard (Parliamentary Debates)
HMSO, *Police Complaints Authority: The First Ten Years* (1995).
HMSO, *1991 Census Ethnic Group and Country of Birth Great Britain* (vol. 1) (1993).
House of Commons Defence Committee *Lessons of Kosovo* (2 volumes), ordered 23rd October 2000.
House of Lords, *Report of the Select Committee on Overseas Trade* (1985).
NATO Review
Office of National Statistics, *International Migration: Migrants Entering or Leaving the UK and England and Wales,* 1997 (1999).
Reade, Stefan (ed.), *Inland Revenue Statistics 1999* (1999).
Social Trends
The Times Guide to the House of Commons (published after each election).
The Vacher Dod Guide to the New House of Commons 1997 (1997).

Newspapers and Magazines

The Asian
Contemporary Record
Contemporary Review
Das Parlament
The Economist
History Today
Inside Labour The New Labour Magazine
International Affairs
Irish Political Studies

Irish Post
Jewish Chronicle
Journal of Contemporary History
Labour Research
Media Culture and Society
New Statesman
Parliamentary Affairs
The Political Quarterly
Political Studies
Talking Politics
Teaching History
The Voice

Biographies and Memoirs

Anderson, Bruce, *John Major: The Making of a Prime Minister* (1991).
Ashdown, Paddy, *The Ashdown Diaries Vol. 1 1988–1997* (2000).
Ashley, Jack, *Acts of Defiance* (1992).
Baker, Kenneth, *The Turbulent Years: My Life in Politics* (1993).
Baridge, Trevor, *Clement Attlee: A Political Biography* (1985).
Benn, Tony, *Out of the Wilderness: Diaries, 1963–67* (1987).
——, *Office without Power: Diaries, 1968–72* (1988).
Bevins, J. R., *The Greasy Pole* (1965).
Blaxland, Gregory, *J. H. Thomas: A Life for Unity* (1964).
Brandt, Willy, *My Life In Politics* (New York, 1992).
Brittan, Leon, *A Diet of Brussels: The Changing Face of Europe* (2000).
Brown, George, *In My Way* (Harmondsworth, 1971).
Lord Butler, *The Art of the Possible* (1971).
Callaghan, James, *Time and Chance* (1987).
Campbell, John, *Nye Bevan and the Mirage of British Socialism* (1987).
——, *Edward Heath* (1993).
Carlton, David, *Anthony Eden: A Biography* (1981).
Carpenter, Humphrey, *Robert Runcie The Reluctant Archbishop* (1996).
Lord Carrington, *Reflect on Things Past; The Memories of Lord Corrington* (1988).
Carvel, John, *Turn Again Livingstone* (1999).
Carver, Michael, *Out of Step: The Memoirs of Field Marshal Lord Carver* (1989).
Castle, Barbara, *The Castle Diaries 1964–70* (1974).
——, *The Castle Diaries 1974–76* (1980).
Charmley, John, *Chamberlain and the Lost Peace* (1989).
——, *Churchill: The End of Glory* (1993).
Chisholm, Anne, and Davie, Michael, *Beaverbrook: A Life* (1992).
Clark, Alan, *Diaries* (1993).
Colville, John, *The Fringes of Power: Downing Street Diaries, Vol. 2: 1941–April 1955* (1987).

Cosgrave, Patrick, *Thatcher: The First Term* (1985).

Crosland, Susan, *Tony Crosland* (1982).

Cross, Colin, *Philip Snowden* (1966).

Crossman, Richard, *The Diaries of a Cabinet Minister, vol. 1: Minister of Housing, 1964–66* (1975).

Dalton, Hugh, *Memoirs, 1945–60: High Tide and After* (1962).

Dalyell, Tam, *Dick Crossman: A Portrait* (1989).

Dilks, David, *Neville Chamberlain, vol. 1: 1869–1929* (1984).

Donoughue, Bernard, and Jones G. W., *Herbert Morrison: Portrait of a Politician* (1973).

Drower, Dr George, *Kinnock* (1994).

Eden, Sir Anthony, *Full Circle* (1960).

Ellis, Nesta Wynne, *John Major* (1991).

Fisher, Nigel, *Ian Macleod* (1973).

Foot, Michael, *Aneurin Bevan, 1945–1960* (1973).

Fowler, Norman, *Ministers Decide: A Memoir of the Thatcher Years* (1991).

Gilbert, Martin, *Winston Spencer Churchill* (1976).

Goodman, Geoffrey, *The Awkward Warrior* (1979).

Gormley, Joe, *Battered Cherub* (1982).

Griffiths, James, *Pages from Memory* (1969).

Haines, Joe, *The Power of Politics* (1977).

Halliwell, Leslie, *Seats in All Parts* (1986).

Hamilton, Alan, *The Real Charles: The Man Behind the Myth* (1989).

Hamilton, Willie, *Blood on the Walls* (1992).

Harris, Kenneth, *Attlee* (1982).

——, *Mrs Thatcher* (1988).

Harris, Robert, *The Making of Neil Kinnock* (1984).

Hattersley, Roy, *A Yorkshire Boyhood* (Oxford, 1983).

Healey, Denis, *The Time of My Life* (1989).

Heath, Edward, *The Course of My Life,* (1998).

Heffer, Simon, *Like the Roman: The Life of Enoch Powell* (1998).

Herzog, Chaim, *Living History: A Memoir* (1997).

Heseltine, Michael, *Life In the Jungle: My Autobiography* (2000).

Higham, Charles, *Wallis: Secret Lives of the Duchess of Windsor* (1988).

Lord Hill, *Both Sides of the Hill* (1964).

Hoggart, Simon, and Leigh, David, *Michael Foot: A Portrait* (1981).

Hopkinson, Tom, *Of This Our Time* (1982).

Ingham, Bernard, *Kill The Messenger* (1991).

James, Robert Rhodes, *Anthony Eden* (1986).

Jay, Douglas, *Change and Fortune: A Political Record* (1980).

Jenkins, Roy, *A Life at the Centre* (1991).

——, *Mr Attlee: An Interim Biography* (1948).

——, *Baldwin* (1987).

——, *The Chancellors* (1998).

Jones, Jack, *Union Man* (1986).

Jones, Tom, *A Diary with Letters 1932–1950* (1954).

Junor, Penny, *Charles: Victim or Villain?* (1998).

Lord Kilmuir, *Political Adventure: The Memoirs of the Earl of Kilmuir* (1964).

King, Cecil, *The Cecil King Diary, 1965–1970* (1972).
Kirkpatrick, Ivone, *The Inner Circle* (1959).
Lamont, Norman, *In Office* (1999).
Lawson, Nigel, *The View from No. 11: Memoirs of a Tory Radical* (1993).
Lee, Jennie, *This Great Journey* (1963).
——, *My Life with Nye* (1980).
Lyttelton, Oliver, *The Memoirs of Lord Chandos* (1962).
Macmillan, Harold, *Memoirs, vol. iii: Tides of Fortune, 1945–1955* (1969).
——, *Memoirs, vol. iv: Riding the Storm, 1956–1959* (1972).
——, *Memoirs, vol. v: Pointing the Way, 1959–1961* (1972).
——, *Memoirs, vol. vi: At the End of the Day, 1961–63* (1973).
Major, John, *The Autobiography* (1999).
Marquand, David, *Ramsay MacDonald* (1977).
Martin, Kingsley, *Editor: A Volume of Autobiography* (1968).
Maudling, Reginald, *Memoirs* (1978).
McAlpine, Alistair, *Once a Jolly Bagman: Memoirs* (1997).
McSmith, Andy, *John Smith: Playing the Long Game* (1993).
Mitchell, Senator George, *Making Peace* (1999).
Lord Moran, *Winston Churchill: The Struggle for Survival, 1940–1965* (1966).
Morrison, Herbert, *Autobiography* (1960).
Mosley, Oswald, *My Life* (1970).
Nicolson, Nigel (ed.), *Harold Nicolson: Diaries and Letters, 1930–39* (1966).
Owen, David, *Time to Declare* (1991).
Parkinson, Cecil, *Right at the Centre* (1992).
Paterson, Peter, *Tired and Emotional: The Life of Lord George-Brown* (1993).
Patten, Chris, *East And West* (1998).
Pimlott, Ben, *Hugh Dalton* (1985).
—— (ed.), *The Political Diary of Hugh Dalton, 1918–40, 1945–60* (1986).
Ponting, Clive, *Churchill* (1994).
Prior, James, *A Balance of Power* (1986).
Roberts, Andrew, 'The Holy Fox', The Life Of Lord Halifax* (1991).
Roberts, Frank, *Dealing with Dictators: The Destruction and Revival of Europe, 1939–70* (1991).
Rose, Norman, *Churchill: An Unruly Life* (New York, 1994).
Routledge, Paul, *Scargill: The Unauthorised Biography* (1996).
——, *Gordon Brown: The Biography* (1998).
——, *Mandy, The Unauthorised Biography of Peter Mandelson* (1999).
Schoen, Douglas E., *Enoch Powell and the Powellites* (1977).
Selwyn, Francis, *Hitler's Englishman: The Crime of Lord Haw-Haw* (1987).
Sharman, Helen and Priest, Christopher, *Seize the Moment: The Autobiography of Britain's First Astronaut* (1993).
Shinwell, Emmanuel, *I've Lived Through It All* (1973).
Short, Edward, *Whip to Wilson* (1989).
Silver, Eric, *Vic Feather, T.U.C.* (1973).
Sinclair, David, *Two Georges: The Making of the Modern Monarchy* (1988).
Skidelsky, Robert, *Oswald Mosley* (1990).
——, *Keynes* (2000).

Steel, David, *Against Goliath: David Steel's Story* (1989).
Stewart, Margaret, *Frank Cousins: A Study* (1968).
Taylor, A. J. P., *Lord Beaverbrook* (1972).
——, *A Personal History* (1983).
Tebbit, Norman, *Upwardly Mobile: An Autobiography* (1988).
Thatcher, Margaret, *The Downing Street Years* (1993).
——, *The Path to Power* (New York, 1995).
Vernon, Betty D., *Ellen Wilkinson* (1982).
Walker, Peter, *Staying Power* (1991).
Weinbren, Daniel, *Generating Socialism. Recollections of Life in the Labour Party* (1997).
Wheeler-Bennett, J. W., *King George VI* (1958).
Whitelaw, William, *The Whitelaw Memoirs* (1989).
Lord Wigg, *George Wigg* (1972).
Williams, Francis, *A Prime Minister Remembers* (1961).
——, *Nothing So Strange: An Autobiography* (1970).
Williams, Marcia, *Inside Number 10* (1975).
Williams, Philip, *Hugh Gaitskell* (1979).
—— (ed.), *The Diary of Hugh Gaitskell, 1945–56* (1983).
Wilson, Harold, *The Labour Government, 1964–70: A Personal Record* (Harmondsworth, 1971).
——, *Memoirs 1916–1964: The Making of a Prime Minister* (1986).
——, *Final Term: The Labour Government, 1974–1976* (1979).
Wright, Peter, *Spy Catcher* (New York, 1987).
Wyatt, W., *Into the Dangerous World* (1952).
Young, Hugo, *One of Us* (1989).
Zeigler, Philip, *Wilson: The Authorised Life of Lord Wilson of Rievaulx* (1993).

Britain and the World Pre-1945

Addison, Paul, *The Road to 1945* (1975).
——, *Churchill on the Home Front* (1993).
Adelman, Paul, *The Decline of the Liberal Party 1910–1931* (1995).
Ashworth, William, *An Economic History of England, 1870–1939* (1972).
Balfour, Michael, *Withstanding Hitler* (1988).
Black, Jeremy, *Modern British History Since 1900* (2000).
Branson, Noreen, *Britain in the Nineteen-Twenties* (1975).
——, *History of the Communist Party of Great Britain, 1927–41* (1985).
Calder, Angus, *The People's War: Britain 1939–45* (1969).
Calder, Angus and Sheridan, Dorothy, *Speak for Yourself: A Mass Observation Anthology, 1937–49* (1984).
Campbell, Christy, *The World War II Fact Book, 1939–45* (1985).
Carsten, F. L., *Britain and the Weimar Republic* (1984).
Chester, Lewis, *et al.*, *The Zinoviev Letter* (1967).
Childs, David, and Wharton, Janet, (eds), *Children in War* (Nottingham, 1990).

Cowling Maurice, *The Impact of Hitler* (1975).
Croucher, Richard, *Engineers at War, 1939–1945* (1982).
Cruickshank, Charles, *The German Occupation of the Channel Islands* (1975).
Dewar, H., *Communist Politics in Britain: The CPGB from its Origins to the Second World War* (1976).
Dewey, Peter, *War And Progress Britain 1914–1945* (1997).
Dower, John, *War Without Mercy: Race and Power in the Pacific War* (1986).
Ereira, Alan, *The Invergordon Mutiny* (1981).
Gilbert, Martin, *Second World War* (1990).
Gilbert, Martin and Gott, Richard, *The Appeasers* (1963).
Gupta, P. S., *Imperialism and the British Labour Movement* (1975).
Harman, Nicholas, *Dunkirk* (New York, 1990).
Hinsley, F. H. *et al.*, *British Intelligence in the Second World War* (1979).
Hirschfeld, Gerhard (ed.), *Exile in Great Britain* (Leamington Spa, 1984).
Hobsbawm, E. J., *Industry and Empire* (Harmondsworth, 1969).
Jones, Helen, *Women in British Public Life 1914–1950* (2000).
LaFeber, Walter (ed.), *The Origins of the Cold War, 1941–1947* (New York, 1971).
Lewis, Julian, *Changing Direction, British Military Planning for Post-War Strategic Defence, 1942–47* (1988).
Liddell Hart, B. H., *History of the Second World War* (1973).
Louis, William Roger, *Imperialism at Bay: the United States and the Decolonization of the British Empire 1941–1945* (New York, 1978).
Lukacs, John, *The Duel: Hitler vs Churchill, 10 May–31 July 1940* (1990).
Middlebrook, Martin, *The Battle of Hamburg* (1984).
Middlemas, Keith (ed.), *Thomas Jones, Whitehall Diary, vol. 2: 1926–1930* (1969).
——, *The Strategy of Appeasement* (Chicago, 1972).
——, *Politics in Industrial Society: The Experience of the British System since 1911* (1979).
Morris, Margaret, *The General Strike* (Harmondsworth, 1976).
Mowat, C. L., *Britain between the Wars, 1918–1940* (1955).
Peden, G. C., *British Rearmament and the Treasury, 1932–1939* (Edinburgh, 1979).
Ponting, Clive, *1940: Myth and Reality* (1990).
Pope, Rex, *War and Society in Britain 1899–1948* (1991).
Priestley, J. B., *English Journey* (1934).
Pugh, Martin, *Women and the Women's Movement in Britain, 1914–1959* (1992).
Read, Anthony, and Fisher, David, *The Deadly Embrace: Hitler, Stalin and the Nazi–Soviet Pact, 1949–1941* (1988).
Rupp, Leila, *Mobilizing Women for War: German and American Propaganda, 1939–1945* (Princeton, 1978).
Shepherd, Robert, *A Class Divided: Appeasement and the Road to Munich, 1938* (1988).

Shirer, William, *The Rise and Fall of the Third Reich* (1964).
Stevenson, John, *The Penguin Social History of Britain: British Society 1914–45* (1984).
Stevenson, John, and Cook, Chris, *Britain in the Depression Society and Politics 1929–39* (1994).
Summerfield, Penny, *Women Workers in the Second World War* (1984).
Taylor, A. J. P., *English History, 1914–1945* (Oxford, 1965).
——, *The Second World War: An Illustrated History* (1976).
Terraine, John, *The Right of the Line: The Royal Air Force in the European War, 1939–45* (1988).
Thompson, M. L., *The Cambridge Social History of Britain, 1750–1950: vol. 1: Regions and Communities; vol. 2: People and their Environment; vol. 3: Social Agencies and Institutions* (Cambridge, 1990).
Thorpe, Andrew, *The British General Election of 1931* (Oxford, 1991).
——, *Britain in the 1930s* (Oxford, 1992).
Thurlow, Richard, *Fascism in Britain 1918–1985* (1987).
Warren C. E. T. and Benson, James, *The Admiralty Regrets . . .* (1958).
Watt, Donald Cameron, *How War Came* (2001).
Wilson, Trevor, *The Downfall of the Liberal Party, 1914–1935* (1966).

Britain since 1945

Aldermann, Geoffrey, *The Jewish Community in British Politics* (Oxford, 1983).
Aldrich, Richard J. (ed.), *British Intelligence: Strategy and the Cold War, 1945–51* (1993).
Ball, Stuart, *The Conservative Party since 1945* (1998).
Barnett, Correlli, *The Audit of War: The Illusion and Reality of Britain as a Great Nation* (1987).
Baston, Lewis, *Sleaze: The State of Britain* (2000).
Bean, Philip and Melville, Joy, *Lost Children of the Empire* (1990).
Beckerman, Wilfred (ed.), *The Labour Government's Economic Record, 1964–1970* (1972).
Blake, Robert, *The Decline of Power, 1915–1964* (1985).
——, *A History of the Conservative Party from Peel to Major* (1997).
Bradley, Ian, *Breaking the Mould? The Birth and Prospects of the Social Democratic Party* (Oxford, 1981).
Brendon, Piers, *Our Own Dear Queen* (1986).
Brittan, Samuel, *The Treasury under the Tories, 1951–63* (Harmmondsworth, 1964).
Butler, David, *The British General Election of 1959* (1960).
Butler, D. E., and Kavanagh, Dennis, *The British General Election of February 1974* (1974).
——, *The British General Election of October 1974* (1975).
——, *The British General Election of 1979* (1980).
——, *The British General Election of 1997* (1998).

Butler, D. E., and King, Anthony, *The British General Election of 1964* (1965).
——, *The British General Election of 1966* (1966).
Butler, D. E., and Pinto-Duschinsky, Michael, *The British General Election of 1970* (1971).
Cairncross, Alec, *The British Economy since 1945* (Oxford, 1992).
Clark, Alan, *The Tories: Conservatives and the Nation State, 1922–1997* (1998).
Coates, David, and Hillard, John (eds), *The Economic Decline of Modern Britain: The Debate between Left and Right* (Brighton, 1986).
Cockerell, Michael, *Live from Number 10* (1988).
Cohen, Nick, *Cruel Britannia* (1999).
Coleman, Terry, *Thatcher's Britain* (1988).
Collins, Bruce, and Robbins, Keith (eds), *British Culture and Economic Decline* (New York, 1990).
Cook, Chris, *A Short History of the Liberal Party 1900–92* (1993).
Cook, Chris, and Stevenson, John, *The Longman Companion to Britain since 1945* (2000).
Crew, Ivor *et al.* (eds), *Political Communications: Why Labour Won the General Election of 1997* (1997).
Crosland, Anthony, *The Future of Socialism* (1956).
Crystal, David, *English as a Global Language* (Cambridge, 1997).
Currie, Edwina (ed.), *What Women Want* (1990).
Deldon, Anthony, and Collings, Daniel, *Britain Under Thatcher* (1999).
Dell, Edmund, *A Strange Eventful History: Democratic Socialism in Britain* (2000).
Dintenfass, Michael, *The Decline of Industrial Britain, 1870–1980* (1992).
Dockrill, Michael, *British Defence since 1945* (1988).
Eatwell, Roger, *The 1945–51 Labour Governments* (1979).
Edmonds, Robin, *Setting the Mould: The United States and Britain 1945–1950* (New York, 1986).
Esher, Lionel, *A Broken Wave: The Rebuilding of Britain, 1940–1980* (Harmondsworth, 1983).
Fairclough, Norman, *New Labour, New Language* (2000).
Fielding, Steven, *The Labour Party since 1951* (1997).
Frampton, Kenneth, *Modern Architecture: A Critical History* (1985).
Freedman, Lawrence, and Gamba-Storehouse, Virginia, *Signals of War: The Falklands Conflict of 1982* (1990).
Geddes, Andrew, and Tonge, Jonathan (eds), *Labour's Landslide* (Manchester, 1997).
Gilmour, Ian, *Whatever Happened to the Tories: The Conservatives since 1945* (1997).
Gould, Philip, *The Unfinished Revolution: How the Modernisers Saved the Labour Party* (1998).
Gower, Margaret, *Independence and Deterrence: Britain and Atomic Energy 1945–52* (1974).
Gowland, David and Turner, Arthur, *Reluctant Europeans Britain and European Integration 1945–1998* (1999).

Gwyn, William B., and Rose, Richard (eds), *Britain, Progress and Decline* (1980).
Hadawi, Sami, *Bitter Harvest: Palestine 1914–67* (New York, 1967).
Hall, Stuart, and Jacques, Martin, *The Politics of Thatcherism* (1983).
Halliwell, Leslie, *Seats in All Parts* (1986).
Halsey, A. H., *Change in British Society* (Oxford, 1978).
Hansard Society, *Parliamentary Reform 1933–1960* (1961).
Harrison, Tom, *Britain Revisited* (1961).
Harvey-Jones, John, *Trouble Shooter 2* (1992).
Haseler, Stephen, *The Gaitskellites* (1969).
Hastings, Max, and Jenkins, Simon, *The Battle for the Falklands* (1983).
Hennessy, Peter, *Whitehall* (1990).
——, *Never Again: Britain 1945–51* (1992).
Heseltine, Michael, *The Challenge of Europe: Can Britain Win?* (1989).
Hoffman, J.D., *The Conservative Party in Opposition, 1945–51* (1964).
Hollingsworth, Mark, *MPs for Hire: The Secret World of Political Lobbying* (1991).
Holmes, Colin, *John Bull's Island: Immigration and British Society, 1871–1971* (1988).
Hooper, Alan, *The Military and the Media* (Aldershot, 1988).
Horsley, William, and Buckley, Roger, *Nippon New Superpower: Japan since 1945* (1990).
HRH The Prince of Wales, *A Vision of Britain* (1989).
Ignatieff, Michael, *Virtual War: Kosovo and Beyond* (2000).
Jackson, General Sir William, GBE KCB MC, *Withdrawal from Empire: A Military View* (1986).
Joyce, Peter, *Realignment of the Left?* (Basingstoke, 1999).
Judah, Tim, *Kosovo: War and Revenge* (2000).
Kavanagh, Dennis, *Thatcherism and British Politics* (Oxford, 1987).
——, *The Reordering of British Politics Politics After Thatcher* (Oxford, 1997).
Kavanagh, Dennis, and Seldon, Anthony, *The Powers Behind The Prime Minister* (1999).
Keegan, William, *Mrs Thatcher's Economic Experiment* (1984).
Kennedy, Paul, *The Realities Behind Diplomacy* (1981).
King, Anthony, *et al.*, *Britain at the Polls* (Chatham, NJ, 1993).
Kirk, George E., *A Short History of the Middle East* (1961).
Kitzinger, Uwe, *The 1975 Referendum* (1976).
Koestler, Arthur (ed.), *Suicide of a Nation?* (1963).
Labour Party, *Twelve Wasted Years* (1963).
Lamb, Richard, *The Failure of the Eden Government* (1987).
Layton-Henry, Zig (ed.), *Conservative Party Politics* (1980).
Lee, Stephen J., *Aspects of British Political History 1914–1995* (1996).
Leigh, David, *The Wilson Plot* (1988).
Lindsay, T. F., and Harrington, Michael, *The Conservative Party, 1918–1979* (1979).
Lipsey, David, *The Secret Treasury: How Britain's Economy is Really Run* (2000).

Louis, William Roger, and Owen, Roger (eds), *Suez 1956: The Crisis and its Consequences* (Oxford, 1989).

Lowe, Rodney, *The Welfare State in Britain since 1945* (1993).

Mackinnon, Donald *et al.*, *Education, The UK Facts and Figures* (1996).

Maclure, Stuart, *Education Re-formed* (1988).

Marquand, David, *The Progressive Dilemma: From Lloyd George to Kinnock* (1991).

Marr, Andrew, *The Day Britain Died* (2000).

Marsh, Catherine, and Arber, Sara (eds), *Families and Households* (1992).

Marwick, Arthur, *Class Image and Reality in Britain, France and the USA since 1930* (1981).

——, *Britain in our Century* (1984).

——, *British Society since 1945* (1992).

——, *A History of the Modern British Isles 1914–1999* (Oxford, 2000).

Maschler, Tom (ed.), *Declaration* (1957).

McCallum, R. B., and Readman, Alison, *The British General Election of 1945* (1947).

McKenzie, R. T., *British Political Parties* (1963).

McKie, David, and Cook, Chris, *The Guardian/Quartet Election Guide* (1974).

McKie, David *et al.*, *The Guardian/Quartet Election Guide* (1978).

Melvern, Linda, *The End of the Street* (1986).

Middlemas, Keith, *Politics in Industrial Society: The Experience of the British System since 1911* (1979).

Morgan, Kenneth O., *Labour in Power, 1945–51* (Oxford, 1984).

——, *Labour People: Leaders and Lieutenants, Hardie to Kinnock* (Oxford, 1987).

——, *The People's Peace: British History, 1945–1990* (Oxford, 1992).

Morris, J. A., *Writers and Politics in Modern Britain* (1977).

Murphy, Robert, Realism and Tinsel: *Cinema and Society 1939–49* (1989).

Nairn, Tom, *After Britain New Labour And The Return Of Scotland* (2000).

Nicholas, H. G., *The British General Election of 1950* (1951).

——, *The United States and Britain* (Chicago and London, 1979).

Parkin, Frank, *Middle Class Radicals* (Manchester, 1968).

Patten, John, *The Things to Come: The Tories In The 21st Century* (1995).

Peden, G. C., *British Economic Policy: Lloyd George to Margaret Thatcher* (Deddington, 1985).

Pelling, Henry, *A History of British Trade Unions* (1963).

——, *A Short History of the Labour Party* (1992).

——, *Churchill's Peacetime Ministry, 1951–55* (1997).

Pincher, Chapman, *Their Trade is Treachery* (1981).

Pollard, Sidney, *The Development of the British Economy, 1914–1980* (1983).

Ponting, Clive, *Breach of Promise: Labour in Power, 1964–70* (1988).

Pope, Rex, *The British Economy since 1914: A Study in Decline?* (1998).

Pugh, Martin, *Women and the Women's Movement in Britain, 1914–59* (1992).

Pym, Hugh, and Kochan, Nick, *Gordon Brown, The First Year In Power* (1998).

Rathbone, Caroline, and Stephenson, Michael, *Guide to Political Quotes* (1985).

Rawnsley, Andrew, *Servants of the People: The Inside Story of New Labour* (2000).

Richmond, W. Kenneth, *Education in Britain since 1944* (1978).

Riddell, Peter, *The Thatcher Era and its Legacy* (1991).

Royle, Trevor, *The Best Years of Their Lives* (1986).

Said, Edward W., *Culture and Imperialism* (1993).

Self, Peter, and Storing, H., *The State and the Farmer* (1962).

Shanks, Michael, *The Stagnant Society* (Harmondsworth, 1963).

Shepherd, Robert, *The Power Brokers: The Tory Party and its Leaders* (1991).

Sherwood, Roy, *Superpower Britain* (Willingham, 1989).

Singleton, John, *Lancashire on the Scrapheap: The Cotton Industry, 1945–1970* (Oxford, 1991).

Sissons, Michael, and French, Philip (eds), *Age of Austerity, 1945–51* (1963).

Sked, Alan, and Cook, Chris, *Post-War Britain: A Political History* (Harmondsworth, 1978).

Smellie, K. B., *The British Way of Life* (1955).

Smith, Geoffrey, *Reagan and Thatcher* (1990).

Smith, Keith, *The British Economic Crisis* (Harmondsworth, 1986).

Snoddy, Raymond, *The Good, the Bad and the Unacceptable: The Hard News about the British Press* (1993).

Stacey, Frank, *British Government 1966–1975: The Years of Reform* (Oxford, 1975).

Stead, Philip John, *The Police of Britain* (New York, 1985).

Stevenson, John, *Third Party Politics since 1945* (Oxford, 1993).

Thomas, W. A., *The Finance of British Industry, 1918–1976* (1978).

Thurlow, Richard, *Fascism in Britain: A History 1918–1985* (1987).

Tunstall, Jeremy, *The Media in Britain* (1983).

Walker, Alexander, *Hollywood England, the British Film Industry in the Sixties* (1974).

——, *National Heroes, British Cinema in the Seventies and Eighties* (1985).

Wass, Sir Douglas, *Government and the Governed* (1984).

Wilson, Harold, *The Governance of Britain* (1977).

Worcester, Robert, and Mortimore, Roger, *Explaining Labour's Landslide* (1999).

Wybrow, Robert J., *Britain Speaks Out, 1937–87: A Social History as Seen Through the Gallup Data* (1989).

Young, John W., *Britain and European Unity, 1945–1992* (1993).

Articles

Cowley, Philip, 'The Marginalisation of Parliament?', *Talking Politics*, Volume 12, No. 2, Winter 2000.

Davis, Aeron, 'Public relations, news production and changing patterns of source access in the British national media,' *Media Culture Society*, Volume 22, January 2000.
Jones, Alistair, 'UK Relations with the EU, and did *you* notice the elections?', *Talking Politics*, Volume 12, No. 2, Winter 2000.
Rallings, Colin, and Thrasher, Michael, 'Assessing the significance of the elections of 1999', *Talking Politics*, Volume 12, No. 2, Winter 2000.

Internet Material

http://news.bbc.co.uk

Books on Ireland

Adams, Gerry, *Before The Dawn: An Autobiography* (New York, 1996).
Arnold, Bruce, *Haughey: His Kife and Unlucky Deeds* (1993).
Bell, J. Bowyer, *The Irish Troubles: A Generation of Violence, 1967–1992*, (Dublin, 1993).
Bielenberg, Andrew, *The Irish Diaspora* (2000).
Boyce, D. G., *The Irish Question and British Politics 1868–1986* (1988).
Brown, Terence, *Ireland: A Social and Cultural History, 1922–1985* (1985).
Bruce, Steve, *God Save Ulster* (Oxford, 1989).
Buckland, Patrick, *A History of Northern Ireland* (Dublin, 1981).
Chubb, Basil, *The Government and Politics of Ireland* (1992).
Coakly, John, and Gallacher, Michael, (eds), *Politics in the Republic of Ireland* (1999).
Collins, Neil, and McCann, Frank, *Irish Politics Today* (Manchester and New York, 1989)
Coogan, Tim Pat, *The I.R.A.* (1980).
——, *Disillusioned Decades: Ireland 1966 -87* (Dublin, 1987).
Devlin, Bernadette, *The Price of My Soul* (1969).
Duggan, John P., *A History of the Irish Army* (Dublin, 1991).
Dwyer, T. Ryle, *De Valera: The Man and the Myths* (Dublin, 1991).
European Communities, 'Ireland', in *Portrait of the Regions* (Brussels, 1993).
Farrell, Michael, *The Orange State* (1980).
Finlay, Fergus, *Mary Robinson, President with a Purpose* (Dublin, 1990).
FitzGerald, Garret, *An Autobiography* (1991).
Gallacher, Michael, *Political Parties in the Republic of Ireland* (Dublin, 1985).
Hogant, Gerard, and Walker, Clive, *Political Violence and the Law in Ireland* (Manchester and New York, 1989).
Holland, Jack, *The American Connection: U.S. Guns, Money and Influence in Northern Ireland* (New York, 1989).

Hopkinson, Michael, *Green Against Green: The Irish Civil War* (Dublin, 1988).

Hutton, Sean, and Stewart, Paul (eds), *Ireland's Histories: Aspects of State, Society and Ideology* (1991).

Inglis, T., *Moral Monopoly: The Catholic Church in Modern Irish Society* (Dublin, 1987).

Joyce, Joe, and Murtagh, Peter, *The Boss: Charles J. Haughey in Government* (Dublin, 1983).

Kennedy-Pipe, Caroline, *The Origins of the Present Troubles in Northern Ireland* (1997).

Lee, J. J., *Ireland 1912–1985: Politics and Society* (Cambridge, 1989).

Earl of Longford and O'Neill, Thomas P., *Eamon De Valera* (1970).

MacManus, Francis (ed.), *The Years of the Great Test, 1926–39* (York, 1967).

Manning, Maurice, *The Blueshirts* (Dublin, 1987).

McAllister, Ian, *The Northern Ireland Social Democratic and Labour Party* (1977).

Miller, David, *Rethinking Northern Ireland* (1998).

Moloney, Ed, and Pollak, Andy, *Paisley* (Dublin, 1986).

Murphy, John A., *Ireland in the Twentieth Century* (Dublin, 1975).

Murray, C. H., *The Civil Service Observed* (Dublin, 1990).

Nowlan, Kevin B., and Williams, T. Desmond (eds), *Ireland in the War Years and After, 1939–51* (Dublin, 1969).

O'Brien, Conor Cruise, *States of Ireland* (1972).

O'Malley, P., *The Uncivil Wards: Ireland Today* (Belfast, 1983).

Pakenham, Frank, *Peace by Ordeal: The Negotiation of the Anglo–Irish Treaty 1921* (1991).

Ross, J. F. S., *The Irish Political System* (1959).

Taylor, Rex, *Michael Collins* (1970).

Townsend, Charles, *The British Campaign in Ireland, 1919–1921* (London, 1975).

White, J., *Minority Report: The Anatomy of the Irish Protestant* (Dublin, 1975).

Whyte, J., *Church and State in Modern Ireland, 1923–79* (Dublin, 1980).

Wichert, Sabine, *Northern Ireland since 1945* (1991).

Younger, Carton, *Ireland's Civil War* (1968).

Other books by David Childs

(the most recent edition is given in brackets)
The Fall Of The GDR, Germany's Road To Unity (2001).
Britain Since 1945: A Political History (2000).
The Two Red Flags, European Social Democracy and Soviet Communism since 1945 (2000).
The Stasi:The East German Intelligence and Security Service (with Richard Popplewell, 1999).

Germany in the 20th Century (1991).
Germany on the Road to Unity (1990).
Children in War (ed., 1989).
East Germany in Comparative Perspective (ed. 1989).
The GDR Moscow's German Ally (1988).
East Germany to the 1990s: Can it Resist Glasnost? (1987).
Honecker's Germany (ed., 1985).
West Germany Politics and Society (with Jeffrey Johnson, 1982).
The Changing Face of Western Communism (ed., 1980).
Germany since 1918 (1980).
Marx and the Marxists, an Outline of Practice and Theory (1973).
East Germany (1969).
From Schumacher to Brandt: the Story of German Socialism since 1945 (1966).

Name Index

396

Subject Index

405